1985

Rules for Predicate L[ogic]

Key Symbols	One-Way Rules					Two-Way Rules		Simple System
(x) $[x]$	$\dfrac{A(x)}{An}$ Universal to Name (UN)	$\dfrac{An}{A[x]^*}$ Name to Particular (NP)	$\dfrac{A(x)}{A[x]}$ Universal to Particular (UP)			$\dfrac{A(x)}{A(y)}$ Universal to Universal (UU)		
$=$ $(\forall x)$ $(\exists x)$	$\dfrac{\begin{array}{c}a=b\\b=c\end{array}}{a=c}$ Transivity for Identity (Trans Id)	$\dfrac{\begin{array}{c}a=b\\Za\end{array}}{Zb}$ Identity (Id)	$\dfrac{\begin{array}{c}Za\\\sim Zb\end{array}}{\sim(a=b)}$ Negation of Identity (Neg Id)	$\dfrac{a=b}{b=a}$ Commutation for Identity (Com Id)		$\dfrac{(\forall w)(Zw)}{Z(w)}$ Universal Instantiation and Generalization (UIG)	$\dfrac{(\exists w)(Zw)}{Z[w]^*}$ Existential Instantiation and Generalization (EIG)	

* Restriction: [x] is any existential quasi-name which has not been used earlier in the argument. For other restrictions, see Chapters Six and Seven.

LOGIC
ARGUMENT, REFUTATION, AND PROOF

LOGIC
ARGUMENT, REFUTATION, AND PROOF

Richard L. Purtill

Western Washington University

Harper & Row, Publishers

New York   Hagerstown   Philadelphia   San Francisco   London

Sponsoring Editors: Ann Ludwig and Sharmon Hilfinger
Special Projects Editor: Susan Schader
Project Editor: Molly Scully
Production Manager: Marian Hartsough
Designer and Cover Artist: Janet Bollow
Illustrators: Syntax International and Educational Media Services at
   Western Washington University
Compositor: Syntax International
Printer and Binder: Halliday Lithograph

Logic: Argument, Refutation, and Proof

Library of Congress Cataloging in Publication Data

Purtill, Richard L   1931–
    Logic: argument, refutation, and proof.

    Bibliography: p.
    Includes index.
    1. Reasoning. 2. Refutation (Logic) 3. Evidence.
4. Logic—Problems, exercises, etc.   I. Title.
BC177.P87   160   78-26207
ISBN 0-06-386900-4

This, my third logic book,
is dedicated to
my three sons

Mark
Timothy
and
Steven

CONTENTS

PREFACE

This book is an attempt to make the introduction to logic more interesting and more practical for both students and teachers. Using the experience gained in over 15 years of teaching and by the writing of two previous logic books, I have tried to identify the topics in an introduction to logic that give students special trouble and to remove the sources of trouble insofar as possible. For example, in statement logic students are often bored by the laborious technique of testing arguments by truth tables, puzzled by the paradoxes of material implication, and at a loss as to how to proceed in doing proofs. A common complaint is that there are so many rules that there is no way of knowing which one to use. To avoid these problems I begin the study of statement logic with a simple and somewhat restricted system that avoids the necessity for truth tables, postpones the problems of material implication, and makes it possible to do some fairly complex and interesting proofs with only a handful of rules.

When I go on to a complete development of statement logic, I motivate the use of truth tables, explain how the truth-functional approach leads to the paradoxes of material implication, and show how a greater number of rules can make proofs simpler. The student will have gained some confidence by doing proofs in the simple system, and I have given some quite detailed rules of thumb for doing more complex proofs.

Similarly, in introducing predicate logic I begin with a simple system that postpones some of the problems students have with quantifiers and with instantiation and generalization, while giving them a foundation they can build on in the next chapter, which gives a full treatment of first-order predicate logic with identity and some glimpses of second-order predicate logic.

I have tried to arouse and maintain student interest by using a great variety of exercises, including as many exercises as possible taken from philosophy, literature, and science. The question students often ask, "What are these techniques good for?" is answered by seeing how the techniques apply to the material in these exercises. Of course, I have used some artificial exercises as drill before launching the student on more realistic examples. In general, I have found that a series of connected exercises on a single subject makes more impact than exercises that jump from one subject to another, so I have used as many groups of related exercises as possible. Similarly, in giving examples while introducing a topic I have found it better to stick to a relatively small stock of related examples rather than varying the examples and risking the student's being distracted by the details of the examples instead of attending to the new techniques.

In the chapters that do not pose the same sort of difficulties for students as those on deductive logic, I have tried to be as clear and as relevant to student interests as I could. Chapter One introduces logic as the study of argument and points out that logic can not only keep us from being taken in by bad arguments but can also help us to increase our *available* information by seeing what follows from what we know. Logical puzzles are used as an illustration of this second advantage of studying logic.

Chapter Two carries on the theme of not being deceived by bad arguments by examining informal fallacies and weak arguments. The discussion parallels that in my practical logic book, *Logical Thinking*, but those who used the earlier book will find the material further developed and related to the more advanced topics of this book. Chapters

Three and Four give the simple and complete systems of statement logic. Chapter Five discusses traditional Aristotelian logic, and Chapters Six and Seven the simple and complete systems of predicate logic.

Chapters Eight and Nine are a discussion of inductive logic: Chapter Eight introduces the elements of probability theory, and Chapter Nine examines the basis of inductive logic. I have tried to keep to the topic of inductive reasoning without getting too deeply into philosophy of science, but in the examples and exercises I have tried to show how inductive reasoning works in actual scientific cases.

Chapter Ten gives, as briefly and clearly as possible, an indication of some exciting new developments in logic, where possible relating these to philosophical applications. This chapter is partly an effort to make this introductory logic book more interesting to the teacher and the student than the conventional texts. Another effort in this direction is the attempt to break out of some of the conventions that have become encrusted around the introductory logic course in the last 50 years or so. In deductive logic almost all the problems sets are proofs of a given conclusion from given premises. In real-life uses of logic we may find ourselves proving the denial of a possible conclusion—refuting it—or having to find what conclusion follows from some information we have. In my examples and exercises I have tried to imitate this feature of real life arguments, so that besides proofs this book features refutations and arguments about which we are uncertain whether they will be proof or refutations. This carries over naturally into a discussion of disconfirmation as well as confirmation in inductive logic.

Since everyone teaches an introductory logic course in his or her own way, I have tried to make the chapters as independent of each other as possible, so that different teachers may make their own selection of topics and treat them in the order they prefer. Parts of Chapter One that define basic terms should probably be treated first, but other parts of that chapter could be postponed or omitted. Chapter Two on fallacies and weak arguments is almost completely independent of other chapters, as is Chapter Five on traditional syllogistic logic. Either could be taught earlier or later than its position in the book indicates, or omitted if desired.

Chapters Three and Four on statement logic are intended to be taught in sequence, as are Chapters Six and Seven on predicate logic. However, I have made Chapters Four and Seven independent of Chapters Three and Six, so that those who do not want to use the somewhat innovative techniques of Chapters Three and Six may go directly to the more conventional development of statement logic in Chapter Four and predicate logic in Chapter Seven. Some parts of Chapter Eight on probability theory require as much knowledge of statement logic as is contained in Chapter Four, and ideally Chapter Eight would be covered before Chapter Nine on inductive logic—but it need not be. Chapter Ten on the frontiers of logic presupposes parts of Chapters Four and Seven.

I have not tried to eliminate all cross references between chapters that can be treated independently, but I have eliminated dependence of one chapter on another wherever feasible, even at the cost of some repetition. A practically oriented course might cover Chapters One, Two, Three, and Five or Six together with Chapter Nine, while a more technical course might cover Chapters One, Four, Seven, Eight, Nine, and Ten. A purely deductive course could cover parts of Chapter One and Chapters Three, Four, Six, Seven, and perhaps Chapter Eight. Various other combinations are possible, and independent chapters could be covered in a different order.

One word of encouragement and one cautionary note: I would urge some students and also some teachers not to be discouraged by the numerical aspects of Chapters Eight and Nine. If you can multiply one fraction by another and divide the result by a third fraction, then you have all the mathematical skill necessary to handle these two chapters. The analogies of probability theory with statement logic are interesting and illuminating, and a probabilistic approach to inductive logic is very rewarding.

The word of caution has to do with the many real-life arguments contained in this book. We are concerned with the logical structure of arguments, and to study this, arguments must be taken out of context and given a somewhat artificial isolation. There is a good deal more to be said about many of the arguments presented in this book, and knowledge of logic is an aid to, but not a substitute for, knowledge of the subject matters involved.

I have tried to take a fresh approach to the problems of teaching logic but I have changed nothing simply for the sake of innovation. The differences from conventional ways of treating topics are all, I hope, improvements; and when accepted techniques did not seem in need of improvement I have left them unchanged. My hope is that teachers who have used currently popular texts will find this one new enough to be interesting but not so new as to give them a feeling of insecurity.

Despite the many excellent teachers of logic I have had, I have probably learned much of what I know about logic from experimenting with it and enjoying it. If my approach leads teachers and students to experiment with logic and above all to enjoy it, it will be more than justified.

Acknowledgments

The cancellation techniques used in Chapters Three and Six are my own developments of the important and innovative work of Professor Fred Sommers of Brandeis University. I owe a good deal to my own teachers, especially Professor Henry K. Mehlberg and Professor Rudolf Carhap. My thanks to the students who have used some of the material in this book in experimental form and to the Bureau for Faculty Research at Western Washington University for help in preparing the manuscript, especially Bobbi Brewer and Robbi Burns for typing the manuscript. Thanks also to Mary Sutterman, the Philosophy Department secretary, for the typing. Thanks to the Educational Media Services at Western Washington University and to Kent Shoemaker for drawing or redrawing some of the mazes and other illustrations in this book. Special thanks to Ann Ludwig and Molly Scully of Harper & Row.

For permissions to use material from copyrighted sources, my thanks and acknowledgments are due to:

Cambridge University Press for permission to use the Ventris grid on page 23. It is from *The Decipherment of Linear B* by John Chadwick (Cambridge University Press, New York, 1970).

"The Dread Tomato Addiction" by Mark Clifton, on page 38, is copyrighted 1958 by Street and Smith Publications (now Conde Nast Publications) and is reprinted by arrangement with Forest J. Ackerman, 2495 Glendower Avenue, Hollywood, CA 90027.

The illustration of Linear B writing reproduced on page 110 is reprinted from *Mycenaeans and Mineans* by Leonard R. Palmer (Faber and Faber, London, 1963) by permission of Faber and Faber.

Richard L. Purtill

CHAPTER ONE

Logic and the Structure
of Arguments

CAN YOU SOLVE THIS PUZZLE?

In a certain country there are two tribes, the Abs and the Bas. The Abs always tell the truth, the Bas always lie. One day an explorer is lost and encounters two tribesmen. He is not sure whether they are Abs or Bas. His conversation might go as follows:

Explorer (to first tribesman):
Excuse me, are you an Ab or a Ba?
First tribesman: I am an Ab.
Explorer (to second tribesman): I'm not sure I understood him; what did he say?

Second tribesman: He said he was an Ab.
Explorer: Is he telling the truth?
Second tribesman: No, he is a lying Ba.
Explorer (to second tribesman): Thank you for telling me that; now can you tell me the way to the Valley of Rocks, where my camp is?

The explorer is quite sure that the second tribesman is one of the reliable Abs. Why?

What is logic and why should we study it?

Logic is the science that studies and evaluates kinds of arguments. By *argument* is meant not just a quarrel or a disagreement, but rather the attempt to give reasons or evidence for accepting a statement as true or rejecting it as false. Logic exists because human beings are neither completely reasonable nor completely unreasonable. If we were completely reasonable, we would probably not disagree about the truth of statements; we would look at the available facts and either come to the same conclusions or agree that the evidence was insufficient to come to any conclusion. If we were completely unreasonable, we wouldn't bother with reasons or evidence but would try to persuade each other by threats, bribes, or emotional appeals. As it is, we are often sufficiently unreasonable enough to disagree with others who have the same facts available to them as we do, but sufficiently reasonable to try to settle our disagreements by seeing what the evidence actually shows.

After we have studied argumentation and have begun to systematize its principles, we tend to isolate arguments from the social contexts in which they occur. For the *logician*—the person who makes a study of logic—an argument is simply a group of statements (occasionally only one statement) called the *premises* (or *premise*, if there is only one) offered as evidence for or against, as reason to accept the truth or the falsity of, some other statement (occasionally more than one statement) that is the *conclusion* (or are the *conclusions*) of the argument. But in real life,

arguments usually come into existence when two or more people disagree about the truth of some statement. One side tries to give an argument to show that the statement is true, and the other side often either
challenges the argument or tries to give a counterargument. This is the
process of *dialectic*, of giving the pro and con arguments on each side of
an issue. Logic developed out of dialectic and when it gets too far from
real-life arguments it tends to become dry, abstract, and impractical.

Proofs and Refutations

In real-life arguments sometimes we have evidence that can serve as the
premises of an argument but do not see at first what conclusion follows
from those premises. Sometimes we have premises and an alleged conclusion and try to show that given those premises that conclusion follows.
If we succeed we have given a *proof,* because a proof is a demonstration
that if certain premises are true a certain conclusion must be true. When
we can give a proof we are entitled to say that the premises *imply* the
conclusion, or that the conclusion *follows from* the premises.

However, sometimes we may discover that the conclusion in question
does not follow from the premises, that the conclusion could be false
even if the premises are true. This does not necessarily mean that the
conclusion is false—it might accidentally happen to be true—but if the
conclusion *can* be false when the premises are true then the conclusion
does not follow from those premises. Also the premises might turn out
to be false, and in that case even if the conclusion follows from the
premises we cannot be sure whether the conclusion is true.

There is one more possibility to consider. Sometimes in setting out
to examine the relation of a conclusion to given premises, we discover
that if those premises are true then the conclusion *must* be false. This
constitutes a *refutation* of the proposed conclusion, and we can say that
the *negation* of the conclusion follows from the premises or that the
premises imply the *negation* of the conclusion.

Validity and Invalidity

We can now explain the positive notion of a *valid* argument and contrast it with the idea of an *invalid* argument. If an argument is invalid,
then even if the premises are true we cannot be sure whether the conclusion

Table 1-1

If the argument is *invalid* and the premises are *true*, the conclusion *may be true or false*.

If the argument is *invalid* and the premises are *false*, the conclusion *may be true or false*.

If the argument is a *valid proof* and the premises are *true*, the conclusion *must be true*.

If the argument is a *valid proof* and the premises are *false*, the conclusion *may be true or false*.

If the argument is a *valid refutation* and the premises are *true*, the conclusion *must be false*.

If the argument is a *valid refutation* and the premises are *false*, the conclusion *may be true or false*.

---

is true or false. In contrast to this, there are two kinds of valid arguments: *proofs* and *refutations*. If we have a valid proof we know that if the premises are true the conclusion must be true, whereas if we have a valid refutation we know that if the premises are true the conclusion must be false. However, even in a valid argument, if the premises are false we cannot be sure whether the conclusion is true or false. Table 1-1 gives all the possible combinations.

Logicians very often find it convenient to regard refutations as a special kind of proof and ignore the fact that what is proved is in fact the negation of what was originally proposed as a conclusion. This has some advantages in the way of simplicity and generality; we would only have to consider two kinds of arguments, valid proofs and invalid proofs. An argument where the premises implied the negation of the conclusion would have to be regarded as invalid, since the premises do not imply *that* conclusion, or else the argument would have to be changed so that the conclusion was the negation of the original conclusion and then the argument would be a valid proof of the revised conclusion. But both choices ignore the fact that in the original, unchanged argument the premises had an important relation to the conclusion: If the premises were true the conclusion must be false.

Real-Life Arguments

Confining logic to the study of valid and invalid proofs also ignores some of the complexity and some of the interest of real-life arguments, where often a conclusion is in dispute, one side trying to prove it, the other side trying to refute it. Imagine a case where Jane and Mark, who know each other slightly, find themselves in the same introductory logic class. As they talk before class begins the following dialogue occurs:

MARK: Well, maybe in this class I'll get a better grade than you do for a change. After all, men are better at logic than women.

JANE: Oh, really? What makes you think *that*?

MARK: Oh, come on now; men have made all the important contributions to logic, surely that shows that men are better at logic.

In this bit of dialogue Mark has asserted a statement, "Men are better at logic than women." Jane could have ignored this statement or agreed with it, but in fact she challenged it. In the face of this challenge Mark produces an argument in an attempt to prove his statement, which now becomes the conclusion of an argument. The argument could be stated as follows:

PREMISE: If all the important contributions to logic have been made by men, then men are better at logic than women.

PREMISE: All the important discoveries in logic have been made by men.

CONCLUSION: Men are better at logic than women.

Jane might accept this argument or she might challenge one or the other of the two premises. For example, she might try to refute the statement "All the important contributions to logic have been made by men."

JANE: I asked our logic teacher about that when I signed up for the class. He said that several women had made important discoveries in logic; I remember he mentioned a woman named Ruth Barcan Marcus, and another named Susan Haack. Surely you'll take his word for it?

The argument Jane gives can be written as follows:

PREMISE: If the logic teacher can be trusted, then Ruth Marcus and Susan Haack have made important contributions to logic.

PREMISE: If Ruth Marcus and Susan Haack have made important contributions to logic, then not all the important contributions to logic have been made by men.

PREMISE: The logic teacher can be trusted.

CONCLUSION: Not all the important contributions to logic have been made by men.

Instead of or in addition to this argument, Jane might try to refute the other premise of Mark's argument:

JANE: Women haven't had a fair chance to study logic. If women don't have a fair chance to study a subject, their not making important contributions to it while men do doesn't show they aren't as good at it as men.

The argument would be:

PREMISE: If women haven't had a fair chance to study a subject, then it is not true that if they don't make important contributions to it while men do then they are not as good at it as men.

PREMISE: Women haven't had a fair chance to study logic.

CONCLUSION: It is not true that if men have made important contributions to logic and women have not, then women are not as good at logic as men.

Or finally, Jane could have attacked the conclusion of the original argument directly:

JANE: The teacher of this class told me that on the average women do better in his logic classes than men. Surely that shows that you're wrong about men being better at logic than women.

We could restate this argument as follows:

PREMISE: If men were better at logic than women, then women would not do better on the average than men in this teacher's classes.

PREMISE: Women do better on the average than men in this teacher's classes.

CONCLUSION: Men are not better at logic than women.

It is important to remember that even if Jane's first two arguments were completely successful, all she would have done is shown that not all of the premises of Mark's argument were true, and therefore, even if his argument were a valid proof the conclusion he came to *might* be false. But if Jane's last argument is successful, it shows that the negation of Mark's conclusion is true. That would mean that there must have been something wrong with his argument. Either it was not a valid proof or else one or the other of its premises would have had to be false, because if it *was* a valid proof *and* the premises were both true, the conclusion must be true. So if Jane's argument is sound, Mark's is not. However, if Mark's argument is sound, either Jane's argument is not valid or else one or more of *her* premises is false.

Sound Arguments

What do we mean by a *sound* argument? A sound *proof* is a valid proof with true premises; it succeeds in *establishing* a proposed conclusion, that is, in showing that conclusion to be true. A sound *refutation* on the other hand is a valid refutation with true premises; it succeeds in *condemning* a proposed conclusion, that is, in showing that conclusion to be false. Success in argument, as in most other things, consists in achieving the goal you set out to achieve: proving a conclusion, refuting a conclusion, or if no conclusion is given seeing whether any conclusion follows from a set of premises.

Let us now go back to our original definition of logic and clarify some other points. We called logic a science; by this we meant that logic is a discipline in which there are agreed-upon procedures for settling questions, such as the validity or invalidity of a proof. While there are some disagreements over some points of logical theory, all competent practitioners of logic agree on the *practice* of logic: what kinds of arguments are valid or invalid, the difference between different kinds of argument, and so on. In this, logic is unlike almost every other part of philosophy, since philosophers are known for challenging the most basic assumptions and disagreeing on the most fundamental points.

The reason that logic was largely developed by philosophers and is still studied mostly by philosophers is that, at least in the Western tradition of philosophy which goes back to Socrates, philosophers attempt to solve their problems about what sorts of things exist, what things have value, and so on, by *argument*. Since logic is the tool used by philosophers to reach conclusions, philosophers have always been interested in understanding and improving this tool. But logical argument is not confined to philosophy; as we shall see, it occurs in many fields.

We also defined logic as the study of *kinds* of arguments. When the logician studies a particular argument, he or she is interested not just in that argument but also in all the other arguments that have the same basic pattern. The logician hopes eventually to find a limited number of basic patterns of argument under which we can classify large numbers of particular arguments. One reason we want to do this is that we discover that some patterns of argument are valid proofs or refutations, and we then know that any argument of that pattern is trustworthy; if the premises are true we can determine the truth (if we have a valid proof) or falsity (if we have a valid refutation) of a proposed conclusion. Correspondingly, if we find that some patterns of argument are invalid, then we know that any argument of that pattern is untrustworthy; even if the premises are true, we cannot be sure whether the conclusion is true or not.

We also said in our definition of logic that logic *evaluates* arguments; we can now see that the basic kind of evaluation of arguments in logic is the distinction between valid and invalid. Valid arguments are favorably evaluated because valid arguments are trustworthy; invalid arguments are unfavorably evaluated because invalid arguments are untrustworthy.

Table 1-2

VALID: *In logic* "valid" is applied only to arguments. A valid proof is one where if the premises are true the conclusion must be true. A valid refutation is one where if the premises are true the conclusion must be false. *Outside logic* "valid" can apply to statements or even experiences as well as to arguments and usually means "true," "well supported," or "authentic," for example, "His experience was valid for him" (i.e., seemed authentic to him).

INVALID: *In logic* "invalid" is applied only to arguments. An invalid proof or refutation is one where even if the premises are true the conclusion may be either true or false. *Outside logic* "invalid" is applied to statements as well as arguments and can mean "false," "unsupported," or "inauthentic," for example, "His statement was invalid" (i.e., he lied).

IMPLY: *In logic* one statement "implies" another if there is a valid proof in which the implying statement is the premise and the implied statement the conclusion. *Outside logic* persons are often said to imply as well as statements and "imply" may mean no more than "hint" or "suggest," for example, "She implied (*or* what she said implied) I was being dishonest" (i.e., she hinted it).

REFUTATION: *In logic* one statement "refutes" another if there is a valid argument in which the refuting statement is the premise and the refuted statement is the conclusion which must be false if the premise is true. *Outside logic* "refute" can merely mean "deny," "disagree," or "object to," for example, "I refuted his accusation" (i.e., I denied it).

But phrases like "a good argument" or "a bad argument" can be ambiguous. A "good" argument can be merely a valid argument (we sometimes say, "That's a good argument but you've got your facts wrong"). Or a good argument can be a sound argument: a valid argument with true premises. Similarly, a "bad" argument might describe a valid argument based on false premises or it might describe an invalid argument. We gain clarity by replacing the vague terms "good" and "bad" with relation to arguments by precisely defined terms such as "valid," "invalid," "sound."

It is a good idea to be aware of nonlogical uses of logical terms such as "valid," "refute," etc. In ordinary conversation these uses may cause no confusion, but imported into logical contexts they may cause a good deal of confusion. Table 1-2 gives the logician's definition of some key logical terms and the popular, nonlogical uses of these terms that are incorrect within logic.

Reconstructing Arguments

In examining arguments in everyday contexts, the first thing to do is to make sure what conclusion is being argued and what premises are being offered to establish or refute the conclusion. Real-life arguments are not arranged neatly like textbook examples. The conclusion may come first, last, or in the middle of the argument. There may or may not be words like "thus," "therefore," or "and so," which often indicate a conclusion, or words like "since" or "because," which often indicate a premise or premises. The conclusion may be left unexpressed or some premise may be left out, especially if it seems obvious. To understand the argument it often helps to reconstruct it in such a way that all the premises are clearly expressed and the conclusion is placed at the end of the argument, as we did with Mark's and Jane's arguments. There are no completely mechanical rules for doing this; we often have to make use of our intelligence and knowledge of our language to decide just what the person giving an argument is trying to prove or disprove.

Exercise 1-1

In each of the following quotations from Alice in Wonderland *find, if you can, an argument. State in your own words the premises and the conclusions. In each case state whether the conclusion follows from the premises and* *why you think so. (Items marked with an asterisk (*) are answered in Appendix A.)*

1.   She had never forgotten that, if you drink much from a bottle marked "poison," it is almost certain to disagree with you, sooner or later. However, this bottle was *not* marked "poison," so Alice ventured to taste it.

*2.   Soon her eyes fell on a little glass box that was lying under the table: she opened it, and found in it a very small cake, on which the words "EAT ME" were beautifully marked in currants. "Well, I'll eat it," said Alice, "and if it makes me grow larger, I can reach the key; and if it makes me grow smaller, I can creep under the door: so either way I'll get into the garden, and I don't care which happens!"

3.   Alice took up the fan and gloves, and, as the hall was very hot, she kept fanning herself all the time she went on talking. "Dear, dear! How queer everything is today! And yesterday things went on just as usual. I wonder if I've changed in the night? Let me think: *was* I the same when I got up this morning? I almost think I can remember feeling a little different. But if I'm not the same, the question is 'Who in the world am I?' Ah, *that's* the great puzzle!" And she began thinking over all the children she knew that were of the same age as herself, to see if she could have been changed for any of them.

"I'm sure I'm not Ada," she said, "for her hair goes in such long ringlets, and mine doesn't go in ringlets at all; and I'm sure I can't be Mabel, for I know all sorts of things, and she, oh, she knows such a very little! Besides, *she's* she, and *I'm* I, and—oh dear, how puzzling it all is!"

4. "But I'm not a serpent, I tell you!" said Alice. "I'm a—I'm a—"

"Well! What are you?" said the Pigeon. "I can see you're trying to invent something!"

"I—I'm a little girl," said Alice, rather doubtfully, as she remembered the number of changes she had gone through, that day.

"A likely story indeed!" said the Pigeon, in a tone of the deepest contempt. "I've seen a good many little girls in my time, but never *one* with such a neck as that! No, no! You're a serpent; and there's no denying it. I suppose you'll be telling me next that you never tasted an egg!"

"I *have* tasted eggs, certainly," said Alice, who was a very truthful child; "but little girls eat eggs quite as much as serpents do, you know."

"I don't believe it," said the Pigeon; "but if they do, why, then they're a kind of serpent: that's all I can say."

5. "There's no sort of use in knocking," said the Footman, "and that for two reasons. First, because I'm on the same side of the door as you are: secondly, because they're making such a noise inside, no one could possibly hear you."

6. "But I don't want to go among mad people," Alice remarked.

"Oh, you ca'n't help that, said the Cat: "we're all mad here. I'm mad. You're mad."

7. "Then you should say what you mean," the March Hare went on.

"I do," Alice hastily replied; "at least—at least I mean what I say—that's the same thing, you know."

"Not the same thing a bit!" said the Hatter. "Why, you might just as well say that 'I see what I eat is the same thing as I eat what I see'!"

"You might just as well say," added the March Hare, "that 'I like what I get' is the same thing as 'I get what I like'!"

*8. "Rule Forty-two. *All persons more than a mile high to leave the court.*"

Everybody looked at Alice.

"I'm not a mile high," said Alice.

"You are," said the King.

"Nearly two miles high," added the Queen.

"Well, I sha'n't go, at any rate," said Alice, "besides, that's not a regular rule: you invented it just now."

"It's the oldest rule in the book," said the King.

"Then it ought to be Number One," said Alice.

9.   "Please, your Majesty," said the Knave, "I didn't write it, and they can't prove that I did: there's no name signed at the end."

"If you didn't sign it," said the King, "that only makes the matter worse. You *must* have meant some mischief, or else you'd have signed your name like an honest man."

10.   "If there's no meaning in it," said the King, "that saves a world of trouble, you know, as we needn't try to find any. And yet I don't know," he went on, spreading out the verses on his knee, and looking at them with one eye; "I seem to see some meaning in them, after all. '—said I could not swim—' you can't swim, can you?" he added, turning to the Knave.

The Knave shook his head sadly. "Do I look like it?" he said. (Which he certainly did *not*, being made entirely of cardboard.)

Logic and Language

Another complexity of examining arguments in real life is the complexity of language itself. We have spoken of an argument as consisting of *statements*. And it is easy to think of statements as what we say when we utter ordinary indicative sentences—sentences which have neither question marks nor exclamation marks at the end. We tend to think of utterances of indicative sentences as being true or false and as doing something we vaguely call "describing" or "stating facts." But the real situation is much more complex. Grammatically, sentences that end in question marks are classified as "interrogative," sentences that end in exclamation marks as "imperative" or "exclamatory," while other sentences are classified as "indicative." But grammatical markers like "?" and "!" are very limited. Some sentences without exclamation marks express wishes or hopes, rather than "stating facts"; some sentences with exclamation marks are merely emphatic statements of fact.

Furthermore, grammatical form can be misleading as to how a sentence is being used. By saying "I suppose the door is closed," I can merely state a fact about myself. But by uttering the same sentence with a different intonation, I may make it into a question or a request. Sometimes, but not always, we indicate this in writing by placing a question mark or an exclamation mark after the sentence, and perhaps emphasizing words by italics: "I suppose the door *is* closed?", "I *suppose* the door is closed!" A sentence with a question mark at the end may, in fact, be a *rhetorical* question, one that makes a statement by asking a question that calls for a "yes" answer. "Didn't *I* close the door?" may be a genuine question or it may be a way of saying "I did close the door."

Of course, there is usually a connection between grammatical form and the use of the sentence. Most interrogative sentences are questions and vice versa. But where grammatical form is misleading as to use (as when a statement is put as a rhetorical question or a command as a statement), this can complicate our reconstruction of an argument. For example, in Jane's first argument one premise was a rhetorical question, "Surely you can take his (the logic teacher's) word for it?" This actually amounted to the statement "The logic teacher can be trusted."

Philosophers who have studied language distinguish three aspects of any utterance of a sentence: what the sentence says, what the sentence is being used to do, and what the sentence actually accomplishes. Sometimes this is different from what is intended by the speaker. Thus Jane might say to a friend, "Mark is a male chauvinist pig." She would be using this sentence to make a judgment about Mark, to evaluate him unfavorably. The intended effect of her remark might be to warn her friend against becoming friendly with Mark, but the actual effect might be to interest Jane's friend in getting to know Mark, perhaps with a view to reforming him.

Philosophers have sometimes held simplistic views of the uses of language. For instance, a group of philosophers called Logical Positivists divided statements into two classes. The first was the class of "empirically meaningful" statements—those that could ultimately be shown to be true or false by sense experience or by the meaning of words. All other statements the Positivists called "emotive" statements—those that merely expressed emotions or attitudes. For the Positivists, ethical statements, religious statements, judgments about art or music, and the like, were all classified as emotive. The Positivists held that only empirically meaningful statements (such as descriptions of sense experience, or scientific statements) could be true or false.

Whether this theory points out a philosophically important distinction between two major classes of statements is a matter for philosophical argument. But as a theory of language it ignores many things about our use of language. We ordinarily talk of value judgments as being true or false; Jane's friend might reply to Jane's unfavorable judgment about Mark by saying "That's not true!" Value judgments as well as descriptions that can be checked by sense experience are *descriptive* in a wide sense, as opposed to, for example, questions, which are *interrogative*. There is another class of uses of language called the *prescriptive* use, which includes commands and requests. *Optative* uses of language express wishes or desires, *expressive* uses of language express emotions or feelings, while *performative* uses of language can change status or relationships, as when we make a promise, name a baby or a ship, or make a bet.

These various uses of language may be mixed in a given locution. Thus if Jane says, "I know that Mark is out of town," she not only gives information but, to some extent, also gives her assurance that the information is true, by using the words "I know." If Jane tells her friend, "If you go out with Mark I'll never speak to you again," she not only gives information but also attempts to influence her friend's behavior.

For our study of logic, the main purpose of this brief discussion of uses of language is to remind us that grammatical form can sometimes be an unreliable guide to the way a sentence is being used, and that for the purpose of examining arguments we must separate the descriptive uses of language from other uses. Some work has been done on the logic of questions and the logic of commands, but this is still in a very early

Table 1-3

Grammatical Types	Example
Declarative sentence	You won.
Interrogative sentence	Did you win?
Imperative sentence	Win!
	Please win!
Optative sentence	I hope you win!

Uses of Language	Purpose
Descriptive	inform
Interrogative	gain information
Prescriptive: Command	influence action
Request	influence action
Optative: Wish	influence action or express feeling
Desire	influence action or express feeling
Expressive	express feelings
Performative	change status

Disagreement of Grammar and Use	Example
Declarative questions = questions	The door is *shut*(?)
Rhetorical questions = declarations	(I asked you to shut the door; and)
	is the door shut? (no)
Prescriptive declarations	Shut that door or I'll shoot.

and tentative state; for the purposes of this book we will confine ourselves to the logical relations between descriptive statements (taking *descriptive* in the wider sense in which it includes value judgments). But as a reminder of some of the complexities of language, Table 1-3 lists some of the different grammatical forms and different uses of language.

Exercise 1-2

In the following Foreword to a Student Handbook of the early 1930s:

1. Identify all the different grammatical forms to be found in the passage (interrogative, indicative, etc.).
2. Identify the different uses of language (description, prescription, etc.) found in the passage.
3. Point out any cases where grammatical form is different from use (e.g., rhetorical questions).
*4. What were the purposes of writing this passage? Were these purposes adequately served by the passage?
5. How would this foreword have to be rewritten for a contemporary student audience?

FOREWORD

Hello, Freshmen! We greet you with this Student Handbook. We welcome you to Bellingham Normal and our aim is to introduce you to the school. We know you're going to enjoy it here once you become one of us. So let's get acquainted.

The paramount purpose of this school is to train school teachers, but more than that, the purpose is to build men and women. It is a school with a definite but comprehensive objective. That objective is to develop intelligent, well-rounded persons into capable and successful educators.

May your own purpose in this school be as broad as the purpose of the school itself. Will you enter with us into the college life and activities and realize that degrees, scholarship, social life, and esthetic orientation, are each only a part of the education you are entitled to?

In coming to Bellingham Normal you have chosen to attend a school recognized nationally as an outstanding educational institution. The Associated Students have had this handbook prepared to acquaint you with the school, with the administration, the faculty and the student activities.

May we make some suggestions for new students? Get acquainted as soon as possible; make friends; become interested in some activity, club life, athletics, journalism, etc.; always combine work and recreation in your daily program; keep informed as to what is going on in the school; read the Northwest Viking; patronize its advertisers; and always, BOOST FOR THE NORMAL SCHOOL.

Sincerely,
THE EDITORS

Exercise 1-3

The following signs each involve at least two uses of language. Identify the primary use that seems to be intended, and give any secondary uses you can find.

1.

2.

3.

4.
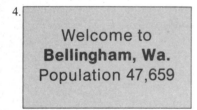

5.

Deduction and Induction

So far we have been speaking as if the only kinds of arguments considered by logic are arguments that are failures unless they are valid—unless the premises imply the conclusion or imply the negation of the conclusion, so that if the premises are true the conclusion must be true (in a proof), or if the premises are true the conclusion must be false (in a refutation). These kinds of arguments are called *deductive* arguments. However, many logicians think that logic should also deal with arguments that are not valid but in which the premises give *some* support to the conclusion or its negation. Such arguments are frequently called *inductive* arguments. It is said that even though inductive arguments are not valid in the sense in which deductive arguments are, some inductive arguments are, nevertheless, better than others and logicians should find ways of classifying and evaluating inductive arguments. However, there is no general agreement as to how this should be done, and most logicians would agree that the classification and evaluation of inductive arguments is much more difficult and uncertain than that of deductive arguments.

It is, however, possible to arrive at a workable way of treating many, if not all, inductive arguments. We start off by replacing the vague idea of premises giving *some* support to a conclusion by the more precise idea of premises giving a certain *probability* to that conclusion. This may be a probability we can express as a number (10% or $\frac{1}{2}$), or we may merely be able to say that the probability of the conclusion if the premises are true is "high" or "low." If the probability of a conclusion is very high if certain premises are true, we have something like a proof; whereas if the probability of a conclusion is very low if certain premises are true, we have something like a refutation.

The next step is to treat the conclusions of inductive arguments as really being statements of probability whether they explicitly mention probability or not. Take a very simple inductive argument:

Almost all U.S. citizens speak English.
Concha Garcia is a U.S. citizen.
Therefore . . .

If we make the conclusion

Concha Garcia speaks English.

we have a deductively invalid argument. Some U.S. citizens, for example, are babies and don't speak any language. Concha Garcia may be one of these babies. Or as her Spanish surname and nickname suggest, she may be from a Spanish-American family: in some parts of the United States children in such families speak Spanish at home and don't learn English until they go to school. However, the great majority of Spanish Americans who are U.S. citizens do speak English, so if we make our conclusion

The probability that Concha Garcia speaks English is high.

then the conclusion becomes much more defensible.

In fact, quite a lot is known about probability and its relation to arguments in science and everyday life, and by treating inductive arguments as arguments with probabilistic conclusions we can apply the theory of probability to the classification and evaluation of inductive arguments. We will find it possible to treat many inductive arguments as arguments in which a statement of probability follows from certain premises, so that many if not all inductive arguments are not deductively invalid but rather deductively valid arguments whose conclusions are statements of probability. Some nondeductive arguments in everyday life cannot be usefully analyzed in this way, but a good many arguments in science and in everyday life can.

To decide whether a given argument is deductive or inductive, we may have to ask ourselves whether the person giving the argument is trying to establish a conclusion as true or condemn it as false, or whether he or she is merely trying to show that the statement has a high or low probability. Some arguments fail as deductive arguments—they do not establish their conclusions as true or condemn them as false; but these same arguments may succeed as inductive arguments—they may establish or condemn the statement that a conclusion has a certain probability. So sometimes in evaluating an argument we have to say, "If this argument is intended as a deductive argument it is invalid, but if it is intended as an inductive argument it establishes that the conclusion has a certain probability."

Exercise 1-4

The Bronze Age Minoan palace at Knossos in Crete was destroyed about 1400 B.C. When it was excavated in the nineteenth century, clay tablets were found with two forms of writing: an early form called Linear A and a later form called Linear B. Somewhat later, the palace at Pylos on the Greek mainland, which was destroyed 200 years later, was excavated, and tablets with Linear B writing were discovered. In light of these discoveries, the following arguments were put forward.*

A.   In a remote Greek palace like Pylos, two centuries after the destruction of Knossos, it is almost certain that Greek would be used for record keeping. If the Linear B tablets at Knossos, two centuries earlier, look exactly the same, the Knossos Linear B tablets are also in Greek.

---

* Suggested by the arguments of Sterling Down in *A Land Called Crete*, Smith College Studies in History XLV, (Northampton, Mass.: Smith College, 1968), pp. 109–147.

B.   Linear B is much like Linear A. Linear A had served the Minoans at Knossos well for some time. If the Minoans had begun to find Linear A inadequate, they could have modified it. But Linear B is not just a modification of Linear A; at least half its symbols are not found in Linear A. This would occur only if Linear B was created to write a new language. If it was created for a new language, that language must have been Greek. Thus Linear B was invented to write Greek, and so the Linear B tablets at Knossos are in Greek.

C.   Both the Linear A tablets and the Linear B tablets are essentially records and inventories. But the Linear B tablets at Knossos list chariots and armor, while the Linear A tablets do not. The Greeks were warlike, but the Minoans were peaceful. Thus the presence of war material on the Linear B tablets supports the idea that the Knossos tablets were written in Greek—for warlike Greeks, not for peaceful Minoans.

D.   The system of measures used with Linear B is different from that used with Linear A. A change of measures is likely to make farmers think they are being cheated. The Minoans were good administrators and would not disturb the farmers by changing the measures. But if Greeks invaded and occupied Knossos at the time Linear B replaces Linear A, they would use their own measures. Thus the change in measures along with the change in writing supports the idea that Greeks invaded and occupied Knossos and that the Knossos Linear B tablets are in Greek.

E.   At the same period that Linear B replaces Linear A, there is a change in style of pottery at Knossos and in the subject matter of pottery decorations and other art work. The style becomes more formal and the subject matter more militaristic. The Greeks were more formal and militaristic than the Minoans. Thus it is probable that Greeks invaded and occupied Knossos at this time.

Do the following:

1.   State the premises and conclusions of each argument in your own words.

2.   If any additional premises seem to be needed to establish the conclusion, suggest what these might be.

*3.   Classify each argument as inductive or deductive and give your reasoning.

4.   Give your opinion as to whether the arguments establish their conclusions and support your opinion.

5.   If there seem to be possible counterarguments that would refute any of the conclusions, state them in your own words.

Logical Puzzles

So far we have seen that the importance of studying arguments is that once we can recognize and evaluate kinds of arguments we know which arguments are trustworthy and which are untrustworthy. But argument can also serve another purpose; it enables us to increase our *available* information by showing us what follows from information we already have. Often we have enough information to solve a problem, but have not "put two and two together to make four." Logical puzzles and "brain teasers" bring this point out because in a well-constructed puzzle you have all the information you need for a solution, and what you need to do is follow out all the implications of that information to find the solution. For example, consider the puzzle about the explorer and the two tribes given at the beginning of this chapter.

The solution is as follows: Since Abs always tell the truth, an Ab will say he is an Ab, but Bas, who always lie, will also claim to be Abs. Thus the first tribesman's answer gave the explorer no indication what the first tribesman was. But by pretending not to understand, the explorer now had a way of checking the status of the second tribesman. Since Bas *always* lie, if the second tribesman were a Ba he would not have told the truth about what the first tribesman said. Since he did tell the truth, he must be an Ab. So the explorer can trust his information about the first tribesman and about the location of the valley. Given the information about the two tribes and the answers given, it follows that the second tribesman must be an Ab. But until we go through a process of reasoning, we can have all the relevant information and yet not see the answer. This is the whole point of a well-made puzzle—to give you the information necessary for a solution but make you work to find the solution.

Artificial puzzles like this are merely mental exercise, but many important problems can be solved by clear and careful reasoning. One of the most important discoveries in recent archeology was made, not by an archeologist, but by a young architect, Michael Ventris, who managed to decipher the mysterious writing called Linear B found on clay tablets unearthed at two Bronze Age sites in Greece: Knossos in Crete and Pylos on the Greek mainland. Most archeologists thought that the language in which these tablets were written was the still unknown language of Crete. After trying out various solutions, Ventris finally discovered that the tablets were written in an archaic form of Greek, using symbols that stood for syllables rather than for vowels and consonants. An important breakthrough came when he showed that a tablet found at Pylos had pictures of tripods (a sort of three-legged kettle) and symbols

LOGIC AND THE STRUCTURE OF ARGUMENTS

LOGIC AND THE STRUCTURE OF ARGUMENTS

that could be deciphered as "ti-ri-po" (the Greek word is *tripos*) along with other symbols that were known to be number symbols. Where several tripods were listed, he found symbols that could be deciphered as "ti-ri-po-do" (the Greek plural is *tripodes*). Ventris's solution to the puzzle of the writing on these tablets has led to important changes in our thinking on Bronze Age civilization in the area of Greece. By deciphering other tablets, which turned out to be records and inventories, archeologists have built up a fairly detailed picture of Bronze Age life in this area.

Actually, information already available to archeologists should have told them that the language of the Linear B tablets was Greek, and Ventris in his deciphering of the tablets made use of information discovered by previous archeologists and linguists who had tried to decipher the tablets. But Ventris was the first person to put the information together to get the right answer. Solutions to artificial puzzles and to real-life puzzles tend to look obvious once the puzzle has been solved, but the first person to put the information together to solve the puzzle has to draw the right conclusions from the information and put these conclusions together in the right way, which is by no means easy. One can see that the first native would have said he was an Ab whether he was an Ab or a Ba, but in order to solve the puzzle this has to be put together with the information that the second native told the truth about what the first native said.

No hard and fast rules can be given as to how to solve logical puzzles, but it often helps to lay out all the possibilities on some sort of grid or table and then use the information in the puzzle to eliminate some possibilities. Thus in the case of the Abs and the Bas, we might lay out the possible answers to each question as follows:

	(A) First native says he is an Ab	(B) First native says he is a Ba
(1) Second native says first said he was an Ab		
(2) Second native says first said he was a Ba		

We can eliminate both right-hand boxes by the argument that an Ab will tell the truth and say he is an Ab, while a Ba will lie and claim to be an

Ab. Thus the two right-hand boxes can be crossed out because they represent a case that cannot occur.

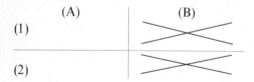

     (A)   (B)

(1)

(2)

We can see that if possibility A1 is realized, the second native will be telling the truth and so be an Ab; whereas if possibility A2 is realized, the second native will be lying and so be a Ba.

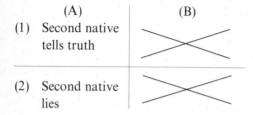

     (A)   (B)

(1) Second native
    tells truth

(2) Second native
    lies

Since in the problem, as we have it, the second native told the truth, he must be an Ab, and we can trust his word about the first native and about the location of the valley. Of course, he may not know, but if he doesn't he will truthfully say so; a Ba who didn't know would lie and mislead the explorer.

In deciphering Linear B, Michael Ventris used grids of possible values for the Linear B symbols and eliminated some possible values because they were inconsistent or assigned some values because they fit in with other information. For instance, in some records a pictograph of a sheep, a chariot, etc., was written and then the word for "sheep" or "chariot" was written along with a number. Because the problem of Linear B was not an artificial puzzle but a real problem, there are, of course, many differences between solving such a problem and solving a puzzle. For example, the value of some of the Linear B symbols is still unknown and may never be known, whereas in a good puzzle there are no loose ends. But the kind of thinking needed for problems like the decipherment of Linear B is very similar to the kind of thinking needed to crack codes and that needed to solve logical puzzles.*

* A fascinating account of how Ventris worked can be found in John Chadwick, *The Decipherment of Linear B* (Cambridge: Cambridge University Press, 1967).

LINEAR SCRIPT B SYLLABIC GRID
(2ND STATE)

WORK NOTE 15

DIAGNOSIS OF CONSONANT AND VOWEL EQUATIONS
IN THE INFLEXIONAL MATERIAL FROM PYLOS:

ATHENS, 28 SEPT 51

THESE 51 SIGNS MAKE UP 90% OF ALL SIGN-OCCURRENCES IN THE PYLOS SIGNGROUP INDEX. APPENDED FIGURES GIVE EACH SIGN'S OVERALL FREQUENCY PER MILLE IN THE PYLOS INDEX.	Impure ending, typical syllables before -ζ & -ᴇ in Case 2c & 3	'Pure' ending, typical nominatives of forms in Column 1	Includes possible 'accusatives'	Also, but less frequently, the nominatives of forms in Column 1	
	THESE SIGNS DON'T OCCUR BEFORE -ᴇ-	THESE SIGNS OCCUR LESS COMMONLY OR NOT AT ALL BEFORE -ᴇ-			
	MORE OFTEN FEMININE THAN MASCULINE?	·MORE OFTEN MASCULINE THAN FEMININE ?			MORE OFTEN FEMININE THAN MASCULINE ?
	NORMALLY FORM THE GENITIVE SINGULAR BY ADDING -ζ	NORMALLY FORM THE GENITIVE SINGULAR BY ADDING -ᴇ			
	vowel 1	vowel 2	vowel 3	vowel 4	vowel 5
pure vowels?	ᴇ 30.5				⊤ 37.2
a semi-vowel?				ⴹ 34.0	29.4
consonant 1	14.8	32.5	21.2	28.1	18.8
2	19.6	17.5			13.7
3		7.2		3.3	10.0
4	17.0	28.6			0.4
5	17.7	10.3		4.1	10.2
6	7.4	20.5		14.8	14.4
7	4.1	44.0			
8	6.1	6.1		13.5	15.2
9		33.1		32.3	2.4
10	22.2		38.2	3.5	2.2
11	31.2	33.8	34.4	8.3	0.7
12	17.0			37.7	24.0
13		9.4	14.2		
14	5.0				
15	12.6				

MICHAEL VENTRIS

Ventris' 'grid', 28 September 1951.

Logical Paradoxes

Some apparent logical puzzles are in fact *paradoxes*. A paradox is a problem with two incompatible answers, both of which seem to be equally justified. Thus, for example, consider this case:

```
The sentence written
    in this box
      is false.
```

Is the sentence in the box true or false? If it is true, then what it says is false. So if it is true, it is false. But if it is false, then what it says about itself is true; so if it is false, it is true. Both answers seem to be correct. But they are contradictory. So we seem to have been led by correct reasoning to a contradictory conclusion: The sentence seems to be both true and false!

A number of ways of avoiding this paradox have been given. For example, part of the trouble seems to be that the sentence refers to itself. Perhaps no sentence can meaningfully talk about itself. But how about:

```
The sentence in this
  box is in English.
```

That seems to talk about itself and to be straightforwardly true.

Others have said that the difficulty with the original sentence in the box is that it is not "about" anything. It has no subject matter. But, of course, in one sense it does have a subject matter: itself. Still, there does seem to be some force in this criticism. Consider the nonparadoxical "twin" sentence:

```
The sentence in this
  box is true.
```

What would it *mean* for the sentence in the box to be true? How would we discover its truth or falsity? How would we check it?

Paradoxes are useful precisely because to solve or understand them we have to think about very basic problems, in this case problems of truth or meaning. A paradox often shows that we have too easily assumed that a situation is simpler than it actually is. However, some apparent paradoxes are not true paradoxes. An early version of the paradox discussed above was the sentence "Epimenides the Cretan says all Cretans always lie." One side of the apparent paradox goes through: If Epimenides is telling the truth he, being a Cretan, is lying. But if he is lying, then it does not follow that he is telling the truth: If Epimenides lies about all Cretans lying, then Cretans may sometimes lie and sometimes tell the truth. Thus we have not a pradox but a puzzle: Epimenides must be lying—for if he is telling the truth, he is lying, and if he is lying, he is lying. The only true paradoxes are "two-sided" ones: two incompatible conclusions equally justified.

One point of mentioning paradoxes is to warn you that all logical puzzles may not be solvable. Some may be paradoxes. Some may simply be badly constructed and not give you sufficient information for a solution. This reminds us of the limitations of logic itself. Logic tells us what conclusions follow from given premises. Thus it enables us to avoid being deceived by bad arguments, helps us to recognize good arguments, and enables us to extract the maximum information from what we already know. But logic does not take the place of information or data gathered from experience, observation, and experiment; it only enables us to make the best use of the information we have. Logic can solve a problem only if our information is sufficient.

Mazes are a special kind of logical puzzle in concrete form. The history of mazes and their solutions are briefly discussed in Appendix B. Mazes have been used as decorations at the beginnings of chapters in this book, because they represent a puzzle or problem which can be dealt with by logical thinking. But since mazes represent a highly specialized kind of logical problem, they are discussed in an appendix rather than in the text.

Exercise 1-5

The following logical puzzles all have solutions. Give your answer to the problem and the reasons for your answer.

1. A terrorist took over a neighborhood health clinic, taking captive a junior nurse, a senior nurse, and a patient with bandages over her eyes. After several hours the terrorist said, "I can't keep all three of you here; I am going to let one of you go or shoot one of you. But I'll give you a chance: Shut your eyes for a minute, you two nurses. All right: I had two green surgical caps and three white ones. I've put one cap on each of your heads. I'm giving each of you a chance to guess the color of the cap on her own head. Guess right and you go free. Guess wrong and I'll shoot you." The junior nurse had the first turn but, after looking at the other two caps (which the wearers could not get even a glimpse of) and racking her brains, she refused to guess. The senior nurse was next. She was an intelligent woman and had kept her head very well but, after looking at the other two and trying to examine all the possibilities, she said, "I can't be sure; I won't guess either." But the patient told the terrorist, "I can't even see the color of their caps but I know the color of mine. If I not only give you the right answer but tell you how I know, will you release us all?" The terrorist scornfully agreed, but when the patient made good her claim, he did let them go. What was the patient's answer and how did she know?

2. In a certain college class, for every male in the class there is *some* person (male *or* female, that person himself *or* someone else) over 20. But at least one male in the class is under 20. Can you *prove* there must be at least one female in the class? If there were just one female, could you be sure of whether she was over 20?

3. A scholarship is offered under the following conditions:

A. Candidates must be high school graduates with an "A" average or non-high school graduates who are orphans.

B. Every candidate who is a high school graduate must be either not an "A" student or be an orphan.

C. Every candidate who is an orphan must be an "A" student and a high school graduate.

Show that under these conditions it is impossible for any candidate to qualify. Suggest one small change in the rules that will allow some candidates to qualify, and describe which candidates could qualify given this change.

4. When Adrian, Buford, and Carter eat out, each orders either ham or pork.

A. If Adrian orders ham, Buford orders pork.

B. Either Adrian or Carter orders ham, but not both.

C. Buford and Carter do not both order pork.

Who could have ordered ham yesterday, pork today?

*5.   In a small Spanish town a barber advertises, "I shave everyone who doesn't shave himself and I shave no one who shaves himself." Can this claim be true? Under what conditions?

Exercise 1-6

The following puzzles have no generally agreed upon solutions. State what the difficulty is in giving a solution, and if you can think of a plausible solution give one.

1.   A man says that he is lying. Is what he says true or false?*

2.   A certain manor was divided by a river upon which was a bridge. The lord of the manor had erected a gallows at one end of the bridge and had enacted a law that whoever would cross the bridge must first swear whither he were going and on what business; if he swore truly, he should be allowed to pass freely; but if he swore falsely and did then cross the bridge, he should be hanged forthwith upon the gallows. One man . . . swore "I go to be hanged on yonder gallows," and thereupon crossed the bridge.

The vexed question whether the man shall be hanged is brought to Sancho Panza as governor of Barataria.†

*3.   Protagoras agreed to teach Euathlus rhetoric, on condition that Euathlus would pay him a certain sum of money when he won his first court case. But after completing the course, Euathlus did not engage in any lawsuits. Growing impatient, Protagoras sued Euathlus for payment of his fee. He argued: "If I win this case, Euathlus will be bound to pay me, for the court will have so decided; if I lose it, Euathlus will still be bound to pay, by our agreement, for he will have won his first case. So whatever happens, Euathlus will be bound to pay; the court should therefore find in my favor." But Euathlus, having learnt his lessons well, replied: "If Protagoras wins this case, I shall not be bound to pay, for I need not pay until I win a case; but if Protagoras loses, this court will itself have decided that I need not pay; the court should therefore find for me."

What should the court have done?

4.   Mr. X, who thinks Mr. Y a complete idiot, walks along a corridor with Mr. Y just before six on a certain evening, and they separate into

* Cicero, *Prior Academics*, II, 96.

† Cervantes, *Don Quixote*, Part 2, Chapter 51.

two adjacent rooms. Mr. X thinks that Mr. Y has gone into Room 7 and himself into Room 8, but owing to some piece of absent-mindedness Mr. Y has in fact entered Room 6 and Mr. X Room 7. Alone in Room 7 just before six, Mr. X thinks of Mr. Y in Room 7 and of Mr. Y's idiocy, and at precisely six o'clock reflects that nothing that is thought by anyone in Room 7 at six o'clock is actually the case.

Can Mr. X think this? Why or why not?

5.   MINIAC: WORLD'S SMALLEST ELECTRONIC BRAIN

In this age of computers, it seems a pity that sincere but impecunious scholars should be deprived of their benefits. Herewith are presented do-it-yourself plans for constructing a computer that will answer questions not resolvable by any other present machine.

Among its many advantages, MINIAC is (a) small enough to be carried in one's watch pocket; (b) inexpensive; (c) infallible; (d) easy to build; and (e) child's play to operate.

To build MINIAC:

(1)   Obtain a penny. (The substitution of a ha'penny will not materially affect MINIAC's operation.)

(2)   Typewrite the words YES and NO on two pieces of paper and glue one to each side of the penny.

To operate MINIAC:

(1)   Hold MINIAC on the thumb and forefinger (either hand, either side up) and ask it question A (e.g., "Will it rain tomorrow?").

(2)   Flip MINIAC and allow it to come to rest.

(3)   Note the answer, either YES or NO.

Now MINIAC has given us either a true answer or a false answer. To determine which:

(4)   Hold MINIAC as in operating instruction (1). Ask it question B: "Will your present answer have the same truth-value as your previous answer?" and flip.

(5)   Note MINIAC's response to this question, either YES or NO.

Suppose MINIAC's answer to question B is YES. This is either a true answer or a false answer. If true, then it is true that the answer to question

A has the same truth-value as the answer to question B, hence the answer to question A was a true answer. If false, then it is false that the answer to question A has the same truth-value as the answer to question B (which is false), hence the answer to question A was a true answer. In either case, if MINIAC answers YES to question B, its answer to question A was a true answer.

If MINIAC answers question B with NO, a similar line of reasoning shows that its answer to question A was a false answer.

The electronic character of MINIAC is obvious from the fact that there are two free electrons in the outer shell of the copper atom.*

Will MINIAC really work as described? Why or why not?

Logical Truths

Some truths can be discovered purely by logical reasoning. But none of these truths tells us anything about particular matters of fact. Statements like "A figure is either a triangle or not a triangle" or "No triangle has four sides" are true because *triangle* is a clear-cut concept and because words like *or* and *not* have the meaning they do. When we get to vaguer statements such as "Either it is raining or it is not raining" or "No bachelor is married," there are possible borderline cases that give us pause, though most logicians would regard those two statements as "logically true"—true because the words in them have the meanings they do.

Philosophers argue over whether there are any true statements that can be discovered by reason alone that are not just about the way we use words and symbols. But even those who think that there are such truths believe that they are very general truths about the nature of things and not particular facts about individual things.

Thus we can regard logic and experience as partners: experience gives us the data, logic enables us to make the most of the data. There are similar "partnerships" between areas of mathematics and parts of science, but the logical principles we will be discussing are common to all areas of life; they apply to everyday experience as well as to science. Thus the person familiar with logic has a tool that can be used for many purposes, a key that will open many doors.

* Thomas Storer, "MINIAC: World's Smallest Electronic Brain," *Analysis*, 22 (1961–62), 151–152.

Chapter Summary

We began by defining an *argument* as a group of statements one or more
of which (the *premise* or *premises*) is offered as evidence for or against
as reason to accept the truth or the falsity of some other statement or
statements (the *conclusion* or *conclusions*). We noted that in real life arguments usually occur in the context of *dialectic*, giving pro and con arguments on each side of an issue. We introduced the notions of *valid*
and *invalid*, *proof* and *refutation*. A *valid proof* is one in which the conclusion must be true if the premises are true; a *valid refutation* is one in
which the conclusion must be false if the premises are true. An *invalid*
argument is one in which even if the premises are true the conclusion
may be either true or false. We defined a *sound* argument as a valid
argument with true premises; a sound proof *establishes* its conclusion
as true, while a sound refutation *condemns* its conclusion as false. We
noted that logicians are interested in *kinds* of arguments and evaluate
valid arguments favorably because they are trustworthy, invalid arguments unfavorably because they are untrustworthy. We looked briefly
at some ways of reconstructing arguments and made a quick survey of
different grammatical forms and uses of language as they relate to logical
argument.

We considered the difference between *deductive* and *inductive* arguments and suggested that at least a great many inductive arguments can
be regarded as having conclusions that are explicitly or implicitly statements of probability. Looking at inductive arguments in this way, we
can regard the probability statements as following from the conclusions
and avoid the problems of regarding inductive arguments as invalid
arguments.

Finally, we looked briefly at logical puzzles, logical paradoxes, and
logical truths. We concluded by pointing out that logic and experience
are partners: experience provides the data and logic enables us to make
the most of it.

The question with which we opened this chapter was "What is logic
and why should we study it?" We answered the question as to what logic
is by defining it as the study of argument and by examining what argument
is and what kinds of arguments there are. The question as to why we
should study logic we answered by pointing out that logic can help us
to avoid being deceived by bad arguments and enable us to increase
our available information by finding what is implied by information we
already have.

Practical Applications

Begin an "Argument File": a notebook of arguments you encounter in your reading, viewing, and listening. Make a rough classification of these arguments into deductive and inductive and make a preliminary evaluation of them as good or bad arguments. You can also keep an eye out for real-life puzzles and problems that can be solved by logical thinking. There are many books of artificial logic puzzles; you may want to work some of these as mental exercise.

Exercise 1-7

In 1977 the Cambridge, Massachusetts, City Council debated using its zoning powers to prevent Harvard University from building a laboratory for experimentation with recombinant DNA because it was thought that this might pose new and unusual health hazards. The following selections from the testimony given by scientists and other concerned citizens contain some arguments. Identify the premises and conclusions of any arguments you can find in the testimony quoted and discuss briefly the strength of the argument given. (Where no other conclusion is given, understand the conclusion of 1 to 4 to be "The proposed laboratory is safe and should be built," and the conclusion of 5 to 10 to be "The proposed laboratory is not safe and should not be built.")

1.   "During the past two years millions of bacterial cells carrying pieces of foreign DNA from other bacteria, from yeast, fruit flies, and frogs, have been constructed in many laboratories in this country. So far as we know none of these cells containing foreign DNA has proved itself hazardous. Not only has no known dangerous organism ever been produced but I believe it to be the opinion of the overwhelming majority of microbiologists that there is in fact no significant risk involved in experiments authorized to be done by the federal guidelines."

*2.   "A vast array of microbiological studies has taught us that creation of a pathogenic bacterium requires the simultaneous presence of a large number of factors not present in our laboratory strains. It is extraordinarily unlikely that the addition of a small piece of foreign DNA could impart to these strains the ability to survive in intestinal tracts, cause disease and be transmissible to other animals, humans or plants."

3.   "We cannot say that there is absolutely no risk involved in these experiments. But then Mr. Mayor, I ask you to consider. That statement,

no risk, can be made about few human activities. The degree of risk involved in carefully regulated recombinant DNA experiments is almost certainly in my estimation less than that involved in maintaining a household pet and is certainly less than that involved in maintaining a room of mice, rats, hamsters, monkeys or certain other animals all of which are known to be carriers of serious human pathogens."

4.   "The vast majority of informed opinion believe that these experiments per se are not dangerous, but because of general considerations of welfare, because of the remotest possibility that something might be dangerous. these very elaborate laboratories are being invested in, providing an extra measure of protection. Though I believe you can never say in any biological experiment, well almost every biological experiment, that there is zero risk. I believe these experiments done under extraordinary conditions will probably have less risk than many of the experiments that now go on in every university and every hospital and every research institute in the country."

5.   "The transfer of genes from higher to lower organisms occurs rarely if ever in nature. We therefore have no way of evaluating the safety of this new kind of technology that is in fact manufacturing new organisms."

6.   "It was said that there was no danger of escape. I'd like to go down on record as saying that this is a false statement. In fact it is absolutely certain that they will escape since in the highest containment facility that ever existed in the United States where every single person associated with it was highly trained, there were 423 cases of laboratory acquired infections."

7.   "Now I don't know how scientists can know that none of these organisms are dangerous because I know that Harvard does not, nor does MIT, have a program in which every person who works in a laboratory is regularly medically screened to make sure that they haven't picked up a lab acquired infection. How do you know when someone comes in and says, "Gee, I was out the last few days, I didn't feel good, I had a bug, I had the flu," that it wasn't something picked up from the lab. With organisms you don't know anything about, you won't be able to identify their symptoms. It might take 20 years before it gets into a bacteria which causes trouble. I don't possibly see how you can say that 1) there is no danger of escape when you know there will be escape and 2) there is nothing to worry about."

*8.   Now I also don't see how a committee of people who believe that the stuff isn't dangerous could possibly protect my health. If you have a committee of people charged with protecting us from the danger and these people are willing to get up in public and say that there is absolutely no danger, there is absolutely nothing to worry about, the facilities are super safe, the bugs won't make you sick, well, that is the last person that I am willing to trust in terms of my health and my danger."

9. "You are against all the DNA recombinant research?"

"Yes, I am a biologist. The millions and millions and millions of years of evolution from my point of view, is about not exchanging, you know elephants and frogs, don't ever exchange, it's like two computer tapes, it's like cutting them up and mixing them back together again. That's not the way organisms work. They all have to have a very special set of instructions and they can't handle having any old set of instructions plugged in without a kind of muck up. It's tampering, as far as I am concerned, at the most profound biological level."

10. "Did I understand you to say that you are against this research in any form, in any place, anywhere in the world?"

"Well, it seems to me that it is essentially irreversible. It's not like an oil spill that you can wipe up. Once the organisms in the genes get out you can't change it. Well, that seems to me qualitatively different than things that if you make an error, you can go back on it. Since I fear that the proliferation of it would lead to things, it is an irreversible step. In other words, once you embark on it, if you are wrong about the hazards, essentially it's too late. I would say, stop it."

Exercise 1-8

The following passage is from the Stoic philosopher Epictetus (50?–120? A.D.). Do the following:

1. Identify grammatical forms and uses of language as in Exercise 1-2.

*2. Find as many different arguments as you can in this passage.

3. Give the premises and conclusions of each argument.

4. For each argument discuss briefly whether the conclusion follows from the premises.

5. Restate each argument in your own words, filling in any understood premises.

It is not understood by most persons that the proper use of inferences and hypotheses and interrogations, and logical forms generally, has any relation to the duties of life. In every subject of action, the question is, how a wise and good person may come honestly and consistently out of it. We must admit, therefore, either that wise persons will not engage in difficult problems; or that, if they do, they will not think it worth the care to deal with them thoroughly. If we allow neither of these alternatives, it is necessary to confess that some examination ought to be made of those points on which the solution of these problems chiefly depends. For what is reasoning? To establish true positions; to reject false ones; and to suspend the judgment in doubtful cases. Is it enough, then, to have merely learned this? Say it is enough. Is it enough, then, for one who would not commit any mistake in the use of money, merely to have heard, that we are to receive good money, and to reject counterfeit?—This is not enough.—What must be added besides? That skill which tries and distinguishes what money is good, what counterfeit.—Therefore, in reasoning too, the definition just given is not enough; but it is necessary that we should be able to prove and distinguish between the true, and the false, and the doubtful. This is clear.

And what further is done in reasoning?—To admit the consequences of what you have properly granted. Well? and is it enough merely to know this necessity?—It is not; but we must learn how such a thing is the consequence of such another; and when one thing follows from one premise, and when from many premises. Is it not also necessary, that one who would behave skillfully in reasoning should both prove what is asserted and be able to comprehend the proofs of others; and not be deceived by such as merely give the appearance of proving? So arises the use and practice of logic; and it appears to be indispensable.

But it may possibly happen, that from the premises which we have honestly granted, there arises some consequence, which, though false, is nevertheless a valid inference. What then ought I to do? To admit a falsehood?—Impossible.—To deny my concessions?—But will this be allowed?—Or assert that the consequence does not validly follow from the premises?—But I cannot do that.—What then is to be done in the case?—Is it not this? As having once borrowed money is not enough to make a person a debtor, unless he still continues to owe money, and has not paid it; so having granted the premises is not enough to make it necessary to grant the inference, unless we continue our concessions. If the premises continue to the end, such as they were when the concessions were made, it is absolutely necessary to continue the concessions, and to admit what follows from them. But if the premises do not continue such as they were when the concession was made, it is absolutely necessary to revoke the concession, and refuse to accept the inference. For this inference is no consequence of ours, nor belongs to us, when we have revoked the concession of the premises. We ought then thoroughly to consider our premises, and their different aspects, on which any one, by laying hold, either on the question itself, or on the answer, or on the inference or elsewhere, may embarrass the unthinking who did not foresee the result. So that in this way we may not be led into any silly or confused position.

The same thing is to be observed in hypotheses and hypothetical arguments. For it is sometimes necessary to require some hypothesis to be granted, as a kind of step to the rest of the argument. Is every given hypothesis then to be granted, or not every one; and if not every one, which? And is he who has granted an hypothesis, forever to abide by it? Or is he sometimes to revoke it, and admit only consequences, but not to admit contradictions?—Yes, but a person may say, on your admitting a possible hypothesis I will lead you to an impossibility. With such ones as this, shall the wise person never discuss, but avoid all argument and conversation with them?—And yet who beside the wise person is capable of treating an argument, or who beside is good at reasoning, and incapable of being deceived and imposed on by bad arguments?—Or will we indeed discuss, but without regarding whether we behave rashly and heedlessly in the argument?—Yet how then can we be wise? And without some such exercise and preparation, can we hold our own? If that could be shown, then indeed all these forms of reasoning would be superfluous and absurd, and unconnected with our idea of the virtuous person.

Why then are we still lazy, and slothful, and sluggish, seeking excuses for avoiding labor? We must be watchful to render our reasoning accurate!— "But suppose after all, I should make a mistake in these points? It is not as if I had killed my father."—O foolish man! in this case you had no father to kill; but the only fault that you could commit in this instance, you have committed. This very thing I myself said to Rufus, my teacher, when he reproved me for not finding the weak point in some syllogism. Why, said I, have I burned down the capitol then? Fool! answered he, was the thing here involved the capitol! Or are there no other faults, but burning down the capitol, or killing your father! And is it no fault to treat rashly, and vainly, and heedlessly the things which pass before our eyes; not to comprehend a reason, nor a demonstration, nor a logical trick; nor, in short, to see what is strong in reasoning and what is weak? Is there nothing wrong in this?

CHAPTER TWO

Fallacies and
Weak Arguments

What is wrong with this argument?

THE DREAD TOMATO ADDICTION

Mark Clifton

Ninety-two point four percent of juvenile delinquents have eaten tomatoes.

Eighty-seven point one percent of the adult criminals in penitentiaries throughout the United States have eaten tomatoes.

Informers reliably inform that of all known American Communists, ninety-two point three percent have eaten tomatoes.

Eighty-four percent of all people killed in automobile accidents during the year 1954 had eaten tomatoes.

Those who object to singling out specific groups for statistical proofs require measurements within a total. Of those people born before the year 1800, regardless of race, color, creed or caste, and known to have eaten tomatoes, there has been one hundred percent mortality!

In spite of their dread addiction, a few tomato eaters born between 1800 and 1850 still manage to survive, but the clinical picture is poor—their bones are brittle, their movements feeble, their skin seamed and wrinkled, their eyesight failing, hair falling, and frequently they have lost all their teeth.

Those born between 1850 and 1900 number somewhat more survivors, but the overt signs of the addiction's dread effects differ not in kind but only in degree of deterioration. Prognostication is not hopeful.

Exhaustive experiment shows that when tomatoes are withheld from an addict, invariably his cravings will cause him to turn to substitutes—such as oranges, or steak and potatoes. If both tomatoes and all substitutes are persistently withheld—death invariably results within a short time!

The skeptic of aprocryphal statistics, or the stubborn nonconformist who will not accept the clearly proved conclusions of others may conduct his own experiment.

Obtain two dozen tomatoes— they may actually be purchased within a block of some high schools, or discovered growing in a respected neighbor's back yard!— crush them to a pulp in exactly the state they would have if introduced into the stomach, pour the vile juice and pulp into a bowl, and place a goldfish therein. Within minutes the goldfish will be dead!

Those who argue that what affects a goldfish might not apply to a human being may, at their own choice, wish to conduct a direct experiment by fully immersing a live human head* into the mixture for a full five minutes.

* It is suggested that best results will be obtained by using an experimental subject who is thoroughly familiar with and frequently uses the logic methods demonstrated herein, such as the average politician or the advertising copywriter. From *Astounding Fiction*, February, 1954.

What are some common ways in which we can be misled or deceived by arguments?

The two most common ways in which arguments can lead us astray are accepting fallacies as good arguments and putting too much trust in weak arguments.

A *fallacy* is an argument that is sufficiently plausible to be deceptive but from the premise or premises of which no conclusion follows, or not the alleged conclusion, or in which the conclusion follows only because some illegitimate assumption has been made. You sometimes see *fallacy* used as meaning simply "a false or misleading *statement*," but as logicians use the term a fallacy is always a deceptive *argument*.

Logicians as early as Aristotle began the practice of collecting common fallacies and naming them so they could be more easily identified. The difficulty with this practice was that the fallacies were often merely listed and described, with no effort at any system or organization. Furthermore, some of the fallacies on the traditional list overlapped with others and some of them were not really arguments, or only marginally arguments. For instance, on many lists of fallacies you will find listed the Appeal to Force (Latin *argumentum ad baculum*, literally, "argument from the club"). But rarely if ever did anyone put forward as an *argument* something like "Believe this statement because I am stronger than you, and will harm you if you don't." That is often enough used as a *threat*, or more subtly as an effort to persuade or influence someone to accept some statement or at least not to dispute it, but seldom as a *reason* to believe a statement.

Other traditional fallacies are more likely to be taken as actual arguments, for instance, the Fallacy of Unqualified Generalization, which goes from the information that *some* members of a class have a certain characteristic to the generalization that *all* the members of the class have it. For instance, if you have known a number of Irish people who love to talk, you may jump to the generalization "All Irish are talkative."

Remember that attaching a name to a fallacious argument is less important than being able to describe what is wrong with it. People are not likely to be impressed if you merely label an argument as a Fallacy of Unqualified Generalization. But if you can demonstrate that the argument shows only that *some* members of a group have a certain characteristic, not that every member of the group does, people can see what is wrong with the argument.

What I will do in this chapter is to give some broad classifications of fallacies and put many of the traditionally listed fallacies under these classifications. Other arguments sometimes listed as fallacies I will consider under the heading of *weak arguments*. By a weak argument I will mean an argument that can in some cases give us good reason to accept a certain conclusion, but which has dangers or difficulties that are too often ignored. Thus, for example, it is not a fallacy to appeal to authority; we appeal to authority every time we consult an encyclopedia or a textbook. But appeals to authority are dangerous, because they are often used in case where the question is not one that can be settled by authority or at least by the authority cited.

Kinds of Fallacies

Since fallacies are arguments, we can speak of their premises and their conclusions. The major subdivision of fallacies I make is into Not the Point fallacies, where the premises do not imply anything related to the conclusion, Beside the Point fallacies, where the premises do not imply the conclusion that is claimed but do imply something which has some relation to the conclusion, and Beyond the Point fallacies, where the premises imply the conclusion but only because some illegitimate assumption has been made.

When I speak in this context of premises not implying a conclusion, I mean that they do not imply either the conclusion itself or a statement that the conclusion has a certain degree of probability. In most arguments traditionally classified as fallacies, the premises do not make the conclusion even somewhat probable; if they do, we can regard these as weak inductive arguments rather than fallacies.

Some fallacies are very much tied up with attempts to get us to *do* something rather than with attempts to get us to *believe* something. Manufacturers do not just want us to believe that their products are the best—they want us to buy these products.

Without going too deeply into the question of the logic of commands, advice, etc., we can see that many arguments having to do with actions that we are advised or requested to perform have something like the following form:

You have a favorable attitude to Y.
X is the best means to Y.

Do X!

For example:

You want to get to Europe quickly.

Flying to Europe is the best way to get to Europe quickly.

Fly to Europe!

If we symbolize "You have a favorable attitude toward Y" as $Y+$ and "X is the best means to Y" as $X \Rightarrow Y$ and "Do X" as $X!$ we can write the pattern of argument as

$$Y+$$
$$\frac{X \Rightarrow Y}{X!}$$

To do full justice to such arguments, we would have to consider such cases as those where desires conflict, where there is more than one means to an end, etc. But for our purposes of seeing how fallacies fit into cases where someone is trying to persuade us to do something, we can see that the fallacy is often an attempt to establish either the first or the second premise in our argument pattern, to convince us that some state of affairs is desirable, or that some action is the best means to a desired end.

For instance, a good deal of the advertising of cigarettes at the present time emphasizes how low in "tar" a particular brand is. Since "tar" is a major factor in the link between smoking and lung cancer, we might say that such advertising implicitly contains some such argument as

You want to smoke and yet minimize the danger of lung cancer.

Smoking our low-tar cigarette is the best means to smoke and yet minimize the danger of lung cancer.

Smoke our low-tar cigarette!

The various devices used in the advertising, such as charts, comparisons with other cigarettes, etc., may be taken as *arguments*, often bad ones, for the statement "Smoking our low-tar cigarette is the best means to smoke and yet minimize the danger of lung cancer."

Added Premises

As an argument for the statement "Smoking our low-tar cigarette is the best way to smoke and yet minimize the danger of lung cancer," you might, for example, find the argument

Our brand is the lowest in tar.

Therefore, smoking our brand is the best way to smoke and yet minimize
the danger of lung cancer.

Obviously, as it stands the argument is incomplete; for the conclusion
to follow we would have to add some such premise as

If our brand is lowest in tar, then smoking our brand is the best way to
smoke and yet minimize the danger of lung cancer.

This would give us an argument in which the conclusion followed
from the premises, but the added premise might very well be an unjustified
assumption. Some smokers, it seems, find low-tar cigarettes less satisfying
and therefore smoke more cigarettes, often canceling out any advantage
from the lower tar per cigarette. We could, of course, modify the premise
to take account of this; for example:

If our brand is lowest in tar *and* you smoke the same number as you do
of your present brand, then our brand is the best way to smoke and
yet minimize the danger of lung cancer.

But if we modify the "supplied" premise in this way, then to make
the whole argument a good one we will need to add the premise "You
will smoke the same number as you do of your present brand." This may
well not be true, for the reasons suggested or for other reasons.
This example brings out the point that we can always make a fallacy
into a *valid* argument (one in which the conclusion follows from the premises) by supplying further premises, which we will refer to as *Added Premises*. But the Added Premises are often extremely implausible, and thus
the strengthened fallacy does not establish its conclusion. Indeed, one
way of seeing what is wrong with a given fallacy is to supply the most
plausible Added Premise we can find that would make it a valid argument,
and see whether the added premise is true or even very probable. This is
a technique we will use as we go through some of the common fallacies.

The Fallacy of Association

The most common fallacy, especially in advertising, is a Not the Point
fallacy that is called the Fallacy of Association. This fallacy can be thought
of as having the pattern

You have a favorable attitude toward Y.

X is associated with Y.

Have a favorable attitude toward X!

For example:

You have a favorable attitude toward having a good time.

Our soft drink is associated with having a good time.

Have a favorable attitude toward our soft drink!

If we let $X @ Y$ stand for "X is associated with Y," then we can symbolize this as

$Y+$

$X @ Y$

$X + !$

where $Y+$, as before, means "You have a favorable attitude toward Y" and $X + $! means "*Have* a favorable attitude toward X!"

The difficulty of this pattern of argument is not just that particular premises, such as "Our soft drink is associated with having a good time," are questionable. Rather, the pattern *itself* is highly questionable, even if we give a very strong interpretation to "X is associated with Y."

Probably the strongest way that X would normally be associated with Y would be for X to be a necessary condition of Y; that is to say, if X did not occur or obtain, Y could not occur or obtain. Consider the argument

You have a favorable attitude toward having a good time.

If you do not use our soft drink, you will not have a good time.

Therefore, have a favorable attitude toward our soft drink!

This argument sounds much more convincing than the earlier one: If the premises were true (a big "if" in the case of the second premise), we would be more inclined to accept the conclusion than if we only had some unspecified association in the second premise.

But even this stronger version of the argument is still a fallacy: Something may be a necessary condition of something we have a favorable attitude toward, but still not be regarded unfavorably. Consider

You have a favorable attitude toward nurses and doctors.

If there were no diseases or injury, there would be no nurses or doctors.

Have a favorable attitude toward disease and injury!

The first two premises are quite plausible, but it is not unreasonable to reject the conclusion. And in general, no matter how strong the association between two things, our favorable attitude to one does not necessarily carry over to the other. If the association is weak, there is even less temptation to carry over attitudes.

The same applies to Negative Association:

You have an unfavorable attitude toward Y.

X is associated with Y.

Have an unfavorable attitude toward X!

If we let $Y-$ symbolize "You have an unfavorable attitude toward Y," we can symbolize this as

$Y-$

$X @ Y$

$X-!$

But it is open to objections very similar to those made to the positive version.

Nevertheless, an astounding amount of advertising consists of an attempt to get us to make an association between a product and something toward which we have a favorable attitude. Some cigarettes associate themselves with "he-man" images, while another brand attempts to associate itself with the cause of women's liberation. Presumably, the advertisers hope that favorable attitudes toward "he-men" or women's liberation will rub off on their products.

Other Not the Point Fallacies

Specific forms of the fallacies of Positive or Negative Association are the Fallacy of Appeal to Popular Prejudice (Latin *ad populum*), Fallacy of Personal Attack (*ad hominem*), Fallacy of Ridicule, and Fallacy of Opposition. Each of these has specific features. An Appeal to Popular Prejudice depends on establishing an association between an idea, product, etc., and some group, movement, person, etc., that is currently regarded with extreme favor or extreme disfavor by the public at large. Thus during the Cold War period, politicians often tried to associate their opponents, or the views of their opponents, with Communism, which was feared and disliked by many Americans. At other times, politicians, advertisers, and others attempting to persuade or influence will attempt to "hop on the bandwagon" of some currently popular cause, such as ecology, energy, or conservation, in an attempt to associate themselves with what is popular.

The Fallacy of Personal Attack is an instance of negative association applied to an individual; an idea or statement is rejected because it is associated with a person who is regarded unfavorably. Often the individual is attacked in an effort to bring the ideas or statements of that individual into disrepute. Thus, for example, if a mayor makes statements damaging to some special interest group, that group instead of replying to what the mayor *said* may attack his competence or honesty.

The Fallacy of Ridicule attacks a statement, idea, individual, institution, etc., by trying to make the object of attack seem not worth taking seriously. When Jimmy Carter was first a candidate for President, he was often dismissed by ridicule of his accent, appearance, origins, etc. The Fallacy of Ridicule attempts to make it seem that its object is not worth taking seriously, and sometimes this can backfire, as it largely did in the case of Carter. But politicians have been seriously damaged by ridicule, and very likely Gerald Ford was at least somewhat damaged by ridicule of his supposed clumsiness, alleged stupidity, and so on.

The Fallacy of Opposition is the fallacy of rushing to the opposite extreme from your opponent—disagreeing with some individual or group on *every* issue because you disagree with them on some issues. Thus conservatives often attack income tax as "Communist" because it is advocated in the Communist Manifesto. But if you attacked everything that is in the Manifesto simply because you disagree with Communism, you would find yourself opposing such recommendations as the end of child labor and the payment of fair wages.

Something common to all Not the Point fallacies is their extreme implausibility if taken seriously as arguments, and the difficulty of finding any remotely convincing Added Premise to make them into valid arguments. Consider the argument

This cigarette is being smoked by a tough-looking cowboy with a tattoo on his hand.
_____
This is a good cigarette.

The argument is obviously ridiculous. We could add the premise

If a cigarette is smoked by a tough-looking cowboy with a tatoo on his hand, it is a good cigarette.

But this premise is extremely implausible.

If you very much dislike and distrust someone, call him Sam Sneaky, you may be tempted by the argument

Sam Sneaky says he was in Chicago.
_____
Therefore Sam Sneaky was not in Chicago.

But the only premise that would make this a valid argument would be something like

If Sam Sneaky says something, then that thing is false.

But this is extremely implausible. Even if Sam Sneaky was a very dishonest and unreliable person, he would still make all sorts of true statements. Someone who *always* lied would be completely ineffective and would be detected in a moment. We might substitute the premise

If Sam Sneaky says something, that thing is very probably a lie.

But even this is too strong. Even a stupid liar mixes a considerable amount of truth with his lies.

Beside the Point Fallacies

The second group of fallacies that we will consider are the Beside the Point fallacies, where some conclusion follows from the premises offered, but not the conclusion is claimed to follow. Just as Association was the broadest category of Not the Point fallacies and many of the other Not the Point fallacies could be regarded as special forms of Association, so the broadest category of Beside the Point fallacies is the Fallacy of Irrelevant Conclusion. An example of this fallacy would be the following: A cigarette that is not as low in tar as some brands, but lower in tar than some others, might put out an advertisement giving evidence that it was lower in tar than some brands, either mentioning these brands by name or giving a description that applied to them but not to other cigarettes, for example, "the ten best selling extra-length cigarettes." The evidence offered might very well show that the brand being advertised was lower in tar than the ten best selling extra-length cigarettes, but the conclusion the advertisement tries to convey is that the advertised cigarette is especially low in tar, or lower in tar than *most* or *all* other cigarettes. However, the evidence offered does not support this conclusion, but rather the other conclusion that the advertised brand is lower in tar than the other specified brands. Thus the conclusion is "irrelevant" in the sense that you have evidence for another conclusion than the seeming conclusion. (Usually, the real conclusion has some relation to the seeming conclusion and is thus not irrelevant in a strict sense.)

The Fallacy of Unqualified Generalization is a special form of Fallacies of Irrelevant Conclusion, where the real conclusion supported by the premises is that *some* of a group has a characteristic, whereas the supposed conclusion is that all of the group has that characteristic. In the case just discussed, if the advertised cigarette claimed or suggested it was lower in tar than *all* other cigarettes, this would be a Fallacy of Unqualified Generalization.

As we will see when we discuss induction, there are good inductive arguments that reason from "some" to "all," but we have defined the Fallacy of Unqualified Generalization in such a way that it occurs only when the premises support only the conclusion that *some* members of a group have the characteristic in question. Thus a good inductive argument from "some" to "all" will not be a Fallacy of Unqualified Generalization.

Another fallacy with some connection to inductive reasoning is the Fallacy of After, Therefore Because (Latin *post hoc ergo propter hoc*). Given two events, A and B, we may wonder if A is the cause of B. If A occurs and is followed by B, this gives us some reason to suspect that A may cause B, especially if we see A followed by B in more than one case. For instance, if someone gets a rash every time he eats strawberries, that person may conclude that the strawberries are the cause of the rash.

However, cases of A followed by B do not prove that A causes B and do not even give a high probability that A is the cause of B. A and B may occur together by coincidence, because both are effects of some third cause, etc. Thus clock A may strike and be followed by clock B striking, not because the clocks are connected but because they were set to the same time and A is a trifle fast. The rash may be caused not by the strawberries, but by a weed that releases pollen about the time strawberries are in season. Thus even a good deal of evidence that A is followed by B does not show a *causal* correlation between the two.

The major arguments in "The Dread Tomato Addiction," which appears at the beginning of this chapter, are After, Therefore Because fallacies. Because after eating tomatoes people become criminals, have auto accidents, etc., does not mean that eating tomatoes *caused* any of these things. The death of tomato eaters born before 1850 and the "symptoms" of those born between 1850 and 1900 are, of course, due to time and old age. The "experiment" suggested at the end of the article is a parody of a device used by some temperance lecturers: immersing a goldfish in alcohol to show the dangers of drinking. In both the tomato and the alcohol case this is a Beside the Point fallacy: Many things that are safe to eat or drink in the usual quantities would kill us if taken in excess, and we could drown or be smothered by being immersed in something (e.g., milk or flour) that is quite safe to eat or drink.

A frequent use of the Fallacy of After, Therefore Because is in politics, where politicians frequently state that such and such good effects followed their election or their support of a particular bill. They hope, of course, to give you the impression that their election or their efforts were the cause of the good effects. But this is rarely realistic: Government today is sufficiently complex so that the efforts of one individual are seldom enough to achieve anything important. At best, a politician's election or his or her efforts on behalf of some program contribute to the good effects.

Causes

In discussing causes an important distinction is made between what we will call *enabling* causes and *effecting* causes (the old terminology of "necessary" and "sufficient" causes is confusing for many students today). An enabling cause is a cause without which an event will not occur, but which is not in itself sufficient for the occurrence of that event. Thus oxygen is an enabling cause of fire: Without oxygen you cannot have fire, but the presence of oxygen alone will not cause fire.

An *effecting* cause is a cause that is sufficient to make an event occur, but which is not necessarily the only way to make it occur: The event may occur in some other way. Thus both drowning and decapitation are effecting causes of death, but one can die without being drowned and without being decapitated.

If A is an effecting cause of B, A will always be followed by B, but you cannot reverse this and conclude that if A is always followed by B, then A must be an effecting cause of B. Also, you cannot argue from A being an enabling cause of B to A being an effecting cause of B or vice versa. If a given member of Congress votes for a measure, he or she may take credit for the passage of that measure. Say it passed by a bare majority, 51 votes to 49. Each of the 51 who voted for the measure might claim that his or her vote was an enabling cause of the measure passing, since if any had voted against the measure it would not have passed. All of the votes jointly could be regarded as the effecting cause of the measure passing, and each might justly lay claim to *part* of the credit on these grounds. But politicians are rarely so modest; they tend to say, "I voted, the measure passed," suggesting, if not explicitly claiming, a larger causal role.

Another argument that goes some way, but not far enough, toward proving its alleged conclusion is the Fallacy of Arguing from Ignorance. This fallacy has two versions. The first claims that a proposition is true because it has not been disproved, whereas the second claims that a proposition is false because it has not been proved. Both arguments jump to conclusions. If a statement has had a reasonable chance of being disproved and has not been disproved, this indicates it *may* be true, but it may show little more than that. Similarly, if the statement in question has had a reasonable chance to be proved and has not been proved, it *may* be false. But in both cases the statement may just be hard to prove or disprove.

Arguments from ignorance are often found in disputes about the Abominable Snowman, Bigfoot, the Loch Ness Monster, and other such creatures. That they have not been conclusively shown to exist leads some people to assume they do not exist; but that they have not yet been conclusively proved not to exist leads others to believe that they do exist.

The final Beside the Point fallacy, the Fallacy of Circumstances, is the argument that because something is true in certain restricted circumstances, it is true in general. Thus one might argue that because a certain group of athletes frequently breaks world records, all athletes frequently break world records, where the athletes in the certain group are top Olympic competitors. Or someone urging educational reforms may argue that because they have worked in some schools they will work generally, where the schools in which the reforms have worked are highly unusual in some respects—having, for example, a highly selected student body or being in some special part of the country.

You will have noticed that many of the fallacies described overlap in some respects, that some bad arguments could probably be classified under more than one of these headings. This is understandable, because the traditional listing of fallacies came from a variety of sources and has not been organized very systematically. It is best to regard names of particular fallacies as convenient reminders of ways we can go wrong in argument, rather than as a completely satisfactory classification of all the possible fallacies.

However, the common feature of the fallacies listed under Beside the Point fallacies should also be clear: All of them in some way jump to conclusions, taking evidence that is at best adequate to establish a weaker conclusion as sufficient to establish a stronger one. If we try supplying Added Premises to make these fallacies into valid arguments, the Added Premises would be extremely implausible. For example, an Added Premise for an Argument from Ignorance would have to be "What is not disproved is true"; an Added Premise for a Fallacy of Circumstances would have to be "What is true in special circumstances is true in general." Similarly, implausible Added Premises would have to be supplied for other types of Beside the Point fallacies.

Beyond the Point Fallacies

The final broad classification of fallacies, the Beyond the Point fallacies, assume what they should be proving. The most obvious kind of Beyond the Point Fallacy is the Fallacy of Arguing in a Circle, where the conclusion itself is in some way smuggled into the premises. Thus someone who hated Sam Sneaky might argue, "Sam is obviously a crook. Look at his associates, only a crook would associate with men like that. And we can be sure that they are crooks because only crooks would associate with a crook like Sam." The argument goes in a circle in the sense that when we work through the premises we find premises that depend on another premise, which turns out to be the conclusion itself. Anything can be "proved" in this fashion, and though the argument will be formally valid, since a statement implies itself (*if* it is true, *then* it is true), it will obviously not be an effective way of establishing the conclusion.

It is worth noting that circular arguments often occur when people are highly committed or very much involved emotionally in an issue. The point to be proved seems so obvious to them that they do not realize that their argument goes in a circle.

Philosophers have found that in the most basic issues of philosophy— free will versus determinism, for example, or the existence or nonexistence of God—it is extremely difficult to give arguments that do not assume what they should be proving just because fundamental convictions are involved.

The Fallacy of Assumed Premise, however, though it may also arise from some premise seeming obvious to the arguer, is more likely to be used by dishonest arguers. The fallacy consists of treating some controversial key point in an argument as if it were obviously true or agreed on by the premises. Salespeople are sometimes told to use the tactic of never asking "will you buy it or not," but rather asking questions that assume that a prospect will buy the item, such as inquiring whether the customer will pay cash or charge the item. The Fallacy of Assumed Premise is the same technique applied to argument.

The advertising for certain whiskeys and other products, for example, uses the tactic of simply assuming that the brand advertised is the best, the one everyone wants, and then goes on to assure us that we are ready for this ultimate status symbol, or can really afford it despite the high price. Often such advertising makes the additional assumption that we are successful or well to do: "Now you can reap the fruits of success, now you can buy our product." This is, of course, highly flattering.

In a given case the assumption may be justified; the product may be the best, the person seeing the advertisement may be successful or wealthy. But in most cases the value of the product, which is what the advertisement should be trying to convince you of, is simply assumed. Carried to extremes, this fallacy merges into the Big Lie technique. Propagandists have claimed that even the biggest lie, confidently repeated over and over, will convince many people. Indeed, the bigger the lie, they claim, the more successful the technique, for people unconsciously assume that someone would not dare to say something so outrageous if it were not true.

The techniques of deductive and inductive logic we will be examining later in this book are the best antidote to fallacious reasoning. Once we see how to put arguments in a precise way and test them for validity, we will be unlikely to be misled by arguments whose premises are irrelevant to their conclusions, arguments whose premises support a different conclusion than that alleged, or arguments that assume what they should be trying to prove. But this brief rundown on common fallacies will serve somewhat the same purpose as the "Wanted" posters in post offices: We can recognize some troublemakers in the realm of argument and be wary if we encounter something resembling them. The practical usefulness of being aware of the common kinds of fallacies should be fairly obvious. We are surrounded by people who try to get our money or our votes or try to influence our behavior in various ways. They sometimes try to achieve their purposes by argument, and many of their arguments are fallacies. When we recognize them as fallacies we will not be influenced by them, but can make up our minds on the basis of the best information and arguments available.

Exercise 2-1

The following are real commercials with the name of the product "bleeped" out. Identify the fallacy committed by the commercial in question. If it is a Fallacy of Association, identify the favorably regarded thing with which the product is associated.

1. *Bleep* is lower in tar than all leading long cigarettes. Smoke *Bleep*!
*2. You asked for it, you got it! Buy a new *Bleep* car or truck today!
3. *Bleep* is the first great perfume born in America. Give her *Bleep* for Christmas!
4. If you know several people who deserve *Bleep* whiskey for Christmas, they are very fortunate. So are you. Give them *Bleep* for Christmas!
5. *Bleep*! Only one milligram of tar. Smoke *Bleep*!
6. *Bleep* started as the number one airline in the Pacific, and we still are. Fly *Bleep*!
7. The fabulous *Bleep*! A fragrance so fresh, so natural, we named it just for you. Use *Bleep* perfume.
8. Give the holiday gift everybody wants, *Bleep* whiskey!
9. Now's the time for *Bleep*, the low-tar, light-menthol cigarette.

*10. The ultra touch of leather seats in first class and coach. *Bleep* gets you there in luxury. Fly *Bleep*!

11. You've come a long way, baby! *Bleep* cigarettes, slimmer than the fat cigarettes men smoke. Smoke *Bleep*!

12. *Bleep* voted best low-tar cigarette. Smoke *Bleep*!

13. *Bleep* hair dye; makeup for your hair. Go ahead and make yourself beautiful with *Bleep*!

14. There are rooms too elegant for ordinary carpets. These are the rooms for which you will want to buy *Bleep* carpets.

15. The lady has taste. She smokes *Bleep* cigarettes.

16. Children should be seen and not blurred. Take pictures of your children with *Bleep* film.

17. *Bleep* is an airline run by professionals. Fly *Bleep*!

18. *Bleep* cigarettes: the taste that took ten years to make. Smoke *Bleep*!

19. Your new pen should have as much class as your new suit. Buy a *Bleep* pen!

20. Why is this cigarette selling with no advertising and why is it so hard to come by? Try *Bleep* cigarettes and see for yourself!

Exercise 2-2

Go through the advertisements in a current issue of Time, Newsweek, *or similar mass-circulation magazine, then answer the following questions.*

1. How many of the ads involved Fallacies of Association? With what favorably regarded things, persons, events, etc., were products associated? What does this show about American values (at least as seen by advertisers)?

2. Find one fallacy in an ad that is not a Fallacy of Association and discuss it in detail. What are the premises and the alleged conclusion? What fallacy is committed?

3. What ad, if any, impressed you as giving good reasons to buy the product in question? What were these reasons and why did they impress you?

*4. What products are most frequently advertised? Do these products have anything in common?

5. What common products or commodity did you *not* find advertisements for? Why do you think that this product is not advertised in this magazine? Where might you find it advertised?

Watch television for about an hour at two different times of the day; keep track of any fallacies you detect.

6. In commercials involving Fallacies of Association, with what favorably regarded things, persons, and so forth were products associated? Were there differences in kinds of associations used in the two time periods?

7. What persuasive devices were used in television commercials that would be impossible or difficult to use in a magazine ad? Are different fallacies committed in the two media?

8. In commercials that involve appeals to popular prejudices, what persons, things, and so forth do the advertisers seem to assume will be regarded favorably or unfavorably?

9. Discuss a commercial where comic elements are involved. Was a Fallacy of Ridicule committed? Why or why not?

10. Has a television commercial ever convinced you to buy a product? If one did, was it because you were given good reasons to buy the product or was it because you were fooled by fallacious arguments?

In ancient times mazes were associated with the legend of the Minotaur, a fabulous bull-headed man-monster who lurked at the center of a maze, or labyrinth, waiting for victims. The Minotaur's maze was usually pictured as having only one path leading inexorably to the center. This version with the Latin words "Labyrinth, here lies the Minotaur" was found scrawled on the wall of a house in Pompeii. It has been suggested the house was that of a moneylender. A maze such as this, a trap rather than a puzzle, resembles a fallacy, which is a trick rather than an argument.

Weak Arguments: Authority

The next group of arguments we will consider is that of *weak* arguments, not fallacies. If we put the proper amount of reliance on them and pay attention to their limitations, they can be very useful. But if we use them incautiously, they can be as dangerous as fallacies.

The first weak argument we will look at is the Argument from Authority. The general pattern of this argument is

A is a recognized expert on subject *X*.

Y is a statement about subject *X* of a kind that is generally agreed can be settled by expert testimony.

A says *Y* is true.

It is highly probable that *Y* is true.

If all the conditions listed as premises are satisfied, arguments of this pattern are unlikely to get us into trouble, but it is still possible for the premises to be true and the conclusion false. Experts are human; they sometimes lie or try to mislead others, and even if they are completely honest they can have blind spots, prejudices, or biases in their fields of expertise. In such a case the testimony of an expert does not make a statement highly probable.

Far more often, however, something is wrong with one of the premises when arguments from authority go wrong. The alleged expert is not an expert, or not an expert in the right field. An "expert" cited may have formerly been an authority in the field but may no longer be so recognized. The expert may be misquoted, or quoted out of context.

Again, if experts agree, what they agree on in their field is likely to be true, but experts do not always agree. Often handwriting experts or psychiatrists are called in both for the defense and for the prosecution in a criminal trial, and the nonexpert jurors have to decide which expert to believe.

We could try to take care of bias on the part of experts, disagreement of experts, etc., by building into the premises of the argument pattern requirements that the expert be honest and unbiased, that there be no disagreement among experts, and so on. But it is unlikely that we could stop every possible loophole, and it is better to keep the pattern simple and be aware of things that can go wrong even when all the conditions are satisfied. This is what is meant by calling arguments from authority *weak* arguments; there is probably no set of conditions that would ensure absolutely that the conclusion would follow from the premises, even though the conclusion is put in terms of probability.

Nevertheless, if we are cautious in our use of arguments from authority they can be of considerable use. To try to establish everything for ourselves, instead of making use of the experience and expertise of others, would make life impossibly difficult. We consult encyclopedias or almanacs for facts, dictionaries for the meaning of words, learn from textbooks and teachers, and so on. In a complex civilization like ours, we could not even begin to check for ourselves all that is vital for us to know.

What we can do is treat arguments from authority with due caution, being aware of sources of possible error. Where a matter is vital—most people would put political and religious beliefs in this category—we must consider expert testimony but make up our own minds, especially where experts differ or might be biased.

One way to remember the questions that must be satisfactorily answered before we can put much weight on an argument from authority is to use the interrogative pronouns *who, what, when, where* and *why* as reminders:

1.   *Who* is the authority in question? Is he or she well known and respected as an expert in a given field, or is he or she in a position to give eyewitness testimony or testimony from personal experience? The "faceless expert" technique "Doctors say . . . " or "Science has discovered . . . " is still used in some advertisements.

2.   *What* is the person in a position to give authoritative testimony about? Is the area of expertise or experience the one relevant to *this* claim? For instance, Linus Pauling, a Nobel Laureate in Chemistry, recommends massive doses of Vitamin C for curing colds. Does his chemical expertise carry over into questions of how to treat illness?

3.   *When* was the expertise acquired or the experience gained that makes this person an expert? On a historical question the evidence of an eyewitness may carry great weight, even though the testimony is very old. But about a scientific theory we probably want the most recent expertise, since science changes so rapidly.

4.   *Where* was the experience gained or the expertise acquired? If there is any geographical dimension at all to a question, we may want on the

spot testimony or expertise acquired in the relevant area. Someone who has gained great experience at farming in a tropical area may be unfamiliar with problems of farming in colder climates. A social worker with great experience of the problems of urban youth may be quite unaware of some problems that arise with young people in rural areas.

5.   *Why* is the testimony being given? Does the person we are taking as an authority have any financial stake in or personal bias about the question at issue? The fact that handwriting experts or psychiatrists can often be found to testify for the defense as well as for the prosecution in many criminal trials makes us somewhat wary of simply taking the word of the experts as to whether certain handwriting is that of a given person or whether a defendant is competent to stand trial.

A good example of arguments involving authority is the dispute between traditionalists and modernists over the authority of the New Testament. Here questions of Who, What, When, and Where are intermingled, and Why questions follow not far behind. The traditional argument for the authority of the New Testament was that Matthew and John had been immediate disciples of Christ and had observed his words and deeds at closehand, while Mark and Luke had collected firsthand accounts from the original disciples. Thus if these accounts were not true, the writers of the Gospels must have been either insane or liars, which seemed implausible in view of the character of their writings and of their lives. Therefore, even though they reported astounding events and teachings that were sometimes hard to understand, they had the authority of firsthand witnesses.

The modernist position was due to the "Higher Criticism" of the New Testament, beginning around the middle of the last century, which rejected most of the bases of the traditionalists' argument. The Higher Critics argued that the Gospels were not written by Matthew, Mark, Luke, and John, but were compilations of doctrine and history made a century or so after the events they record. Thus, for example, the compiler of the "Gospel According to Matthew" was not, according to modernists, the Apostle Matthew and could not be claimed to have either the authority of an eyewitness or the sanctity of an apostle. In a period of time as long as that postulated, legendary elements would have time to creep into the account of Christ's deeds, and theological controversies in the early church would color the account of Christ's teaching.

Many contemporary New Testament scholars are midway between the two positions described, but some extreme modernists remain and traditionalist scholars have made a vigorous counterattack on the modernist claims. Archeological evidence, discovery of fragments of early manuscripts, etc., have pushed the probable date of the Gospels back nearer the traditional dates, and traditionalists argue that the new evidence does not give adequate time for the interpolations and developments postulated by the modernists.

Of course, many important questions of proof and probability remain even if we decide questions about the authorship of the New Testament accounts, but this is a good example of an issue that is vitally important to many people and which turns, at least to some extent, on whether certain documents can be taken to be authoritative: *who* wrote them, *what* acquaintance the writers had with the things to which they testified, *when* and *where* the documents were written, and *why* the writers wrote what they did.

Analogy

A second kind of weak argument we will briefly consider is the Argument from Analogy. The basic pattern of an argument from analogy can be stated as follows:

A has property p.
B is like A in respect to r, s, t . . . which are relevant to possession of property p.

B very probably has property p.

Many diagnoses are basically analogy arguments. A doctor sees a child with a high fever and sore throat and decides that the child has a bacterial infection that will respond to antibiotics. He gives the child antibiotics and the symptoms soon disappear. When he sees another child with the same symptoms, he infers that the second child has the same illness and will very probably respond to the same treatment. Or an auto mechanic finds that a car that is very noisy when first started, but not after the engine warms up, has a cracked manifold that would be expensive to repair and does not significantly affect the safety or operation of the car. The next time he encounters a similar problem he is likely to infer that very probably the car in question has a cracked manifold that can safely be left unrepaired. In the medical case the symptoms were of the kind that experience has shown to be linked with certain bacterial infections, and experience has also shown that anti-biotics are effective against many such infections. Two children may be similar or dissimilar in all sorts of irrelevant ways: IQ, family income, middle name, etc., but if they have very similar symptoms they are likely to have the same ailment. Similarly, the mechanic ignores irrelevant features—number of windows in the car, material of seat covers, etc.—and pays attention to the kind of noise, how soon it disappears after the car is started, and the like, because experience has shown him that similar problems usually have similar causes.

If an analogy argument is put in terms of probability, not of certainty, and if the features in which the cases resemble each other are relevant to the characteristics being predicted, argument from analogy can be quite helpful. Even if the child's symptoms or the car's noisiness are the results of quite different causes than those supposed, it is reasonable to check out the probable cause suggested by the analogy argument before going on to other possibilities. The assumption that similar effects have similar causes can be mistaken in particular cases, but the world would be much harder to deal with if we could not rely on analogies from past experience.

Overreliance on analogy arguments can consist of drawing a con-clusion more certain than any analogy argument warrants, or can consist of putting too much weight on a particular analogy. In either case we go beyond our evidence and draw conclusions on which we cannot rely.

An interesting example of an argument from analogy in science was the attempt by archeologists to reconstruct the effects of the eruption about 1500 B.C. of a volcano on the island of Thera near Crete in the Aegean Sea by analogy with the eruption of a volcano on the island of Krakatoa near Java in 1883 A.D. There are a number of important and relevant similarities between the two eruptions which can be listed as follows:

1. The two volcanoes have been behaving similarly as far back as we can trace their activity.
2. Both volcanoes lie at the junction of major fault lines.
3. Originally, both were large volcanic cones. Both had violent eruptions that led to the collapse of the central core and massive ejections of a material called tephra, which is an ash or pumice created by volcanoes. The eruptions left a sort of low-walled basin called a caldera, which filled with sea water. After this, new eruptions built up smaller cones.

4. After a period of dormancy, each had a new and even more violent eruption preceded by earthquakes. In the period after this, minor volcanic activity built up new islands.

5. Great quantities of dust and masses of a very light, spongy rock called pumice were ejected, some of which eventually sank to the ocean bottom where it could be recovered by oceanographic techniques.

All of this information is well established by the geological record: the record of successive layers of lava, pumice protected by the ocean from being broken down and washed or blown away by rain and wind, and so on. These similarities in the histories of the two volcanoes were used as the basis for arguments from analogy like the following:

1. The Krakatoa eruption resulted in major tsunamis (huge sea waves caused by earthquakes or volcanic eruption) which caused extensive damage on the coast of the large nearby islands of Java and Sumatra. Therefore, probably the Thera eruption caused extensive damage on the coast of Crete, the large island near Thera.

2. The fallout volcanic ash from Krakatoa caused long-lasting damage to crops and other vegetation on nearby islands. Therefore, the fallout of ash from Thera probably caused long-lasting damage to crops and other vegetation on Crete.

3. The blast effects of the Krakatoa eruption caused damage to buildings of nineteenth-century construction up to 160 kilometers from Krakatoa. Therefore, probably structures on Crete, which were of more primitive materials and were even nearer Thera than 160 kilometers, were even more severely damaged.

There is no direct evidence for any of the conclusions of the three analogy arguments above. Archeological evidence for tsunamis is suggestive but scanty; there are no surviving records of crops, etc., for the relevant period; and the buildings that would have been damaged have been in ruins for so long that assessment of the cause of damage at a particular period is very uncertain. But the analogies are sufficiently impressive that many competent archeologists and vulcanologists are convinced that the eruption of Thera accounts for the fall of the very high Bronze Age civilization of Crete. The Minoan culture, as it is called, was at least sufficiently weakened that Crete could be invaded and conquered by its more warlike neighbors from mainland Greece.

The fact that an analogy argument can give us impressive evidence as to what happened to a culture at the very dawn of European civilization, over 3000 years ago, is a powerful tribute to the power of analogical argument when properly used. But this is rather a special case, since volcanoes behave in ways that are beginning to be fairly well understood, and vulcanological forces are so strong that few if any other factors can interfere with them or change their effect. In more ordinary analogical arguments there may be a strong resemblance between two cases, but factors present in one case and not the other may cause very different outcomes. Even in the Krakatoa-Thera case, there are some such factors, as the greater depth of the sea around Thera. But in this case these factors would act to intensify rather than weaken the effects discussed, such as tsunamis. (Shallow water has a braking action on tsunamis.)

Ad Hoc Hypotheses

The final weak argument pattern to be considered is the method of Ad Hoc Hypotheses. The general pattern of such arguments can be put this way:

> Observation or experiment has given us data D.
> Hypothesis H will completely account for data D.
> _____
> Hypothesis H is very probably true.

This is an especially dangerous type of argument when data D are relatively simple and could be accounted for in any number of ways. The first hypothesis we hit on may explain the data but still be false, because one or several alternative hypotheses are true.

When there are a number of plausible hypotheses, the reasonable thing to do is not to seize on the first hypothesis that comes to mind that will explain the data. Rather we should try to state various hypotheses that explain the data at hand and then find some way of testing these hypotheses to find out which comes off best. Forming and testing hypotheses and accepting the one best confirmed by the data is essentially the method of science, and we will discuss it in detail in later chapters. Merely devising a hypothesis that accounts for the data currently known— the method of Ad Hoc Hypotheses—is dangerous because it leaves off the testing and comparison stages.

Still, if the data are extremely complex, it may happen that only one hypothesis can be devised that explains the data, and the fact that the hypothesis accounts for all of a set of relatively complex data does give us reason to accept that hypothesis. Many high-level scientific theories, for example Darwin's theory of evolution, are not easily tested. Darwin's theory has to do with very gradual changes over long periods of time, which are not directly observable or reproduceable in the laboratory. What gives most biologists considerable confidence in the modern version of Darwin's theory is that it gives an organized and understandable account of a great mass of complex data having to do with the fossil record, the structure of present-day living things, and so on.

But even the most plausible hypothesis is always open to challenge if another hypothesis can be found that explains the same data just as well. When such a rival hypothesis is put forward it does not prove that the first hypothesis is false, but having two possible explanations of the same data tends to weaken our confidence in both. Similarly, if there is only one witness to a given event, we tend to accept the account given by that witness, unless there is some good reason to doubt the witness. But if there are two witnesses and they give different accounts, we hesitate to accept *either* without further investigation. In fiction, if not in real life, we find cases where one of a pair of twins is suspected of a crime and if it cannot be shown which twin was the criminal they both have to be let go.

A danger of ad hoc hypotheses is that they tend to extinguish curiosity; by giving a plausible but possibly false explanation of a given set of data we think we have accounted for the data and stop looking for other and possibly better explanations. This is why ingenuity in devising alternative explanations is useful in science.

A good illustration of some of the pitfalls of ad hoc hypotheses is the recent controversy over "life after life." Considerable anecdotal evidence has been collected by researchers that many people who have been revived by modern medical technology after being pronounced "clinically dead" report very similar experiences. These include a rapid (or perhaps somehow timeless) overview of their whole lives and often the experience of looking at their own bodies from a viewpoint outside those bodies. Other experiences reported include a feeling of traveling down a sort of tunnel, being met by dead friends and relatives, and in some cases meeting a radiant being who inspires feelings of awe but also a feeling of comfort. Many people report having been reluctant to be brought back to ordinary life.

Probably the majority of doctors would dismiss these reports as hallucinations due to oxygen starvation of the brain; during "clinical death" heart action and respiration stop. These doctors would ascribe the similarity of the experience reported to cultural conditioning: Even those who are not religious believers are aware of and have been influenced to some extent by religious ideas of life after death.

Nevertheless, many of those who have done research into such reports are convinced that they have found empirical evidence of life after death. They point out factors that are hard to explain as hallucination. For instance, some people revived after clinical death have apparently reported accurately on the activities of those working to revive them, including activities they could not have observed even if their bodies had been functioning normally, whereas, in fact, their eyes were closed, they were often anesthetized, and so on.

Since human hopes and fears are so powerfully engaged in cases like this, it is to be expected that people might jump to conclusions on these matters. But what is very striking is the extent to which those who hear such reports second hand are inclined to form their opinions on the basis of their previous opinions and how prone they are to content themselves with ad hoc hypotheses. Those inclined to accept survival after death often accept such accounts without very adequate investigation as being of real experiences and tend to facile explanations of difficulties. However, those who had rejected the idea of survival after death before hearing such reports tend to dismiss them out of hand, often with no explanation or very inadequate explanation of the alleged facts.

There are cautious and skeptical investigators who have looked at the evidence and take one side or another of this question or suspend judgment. But the typical reaction among people who hear of these reports for the first time is a striking instance of how inclined we are to judge new evidence on the basis of our preconceived ideas, and how we dismiss evidence after forming often very inadequate ad hoc hypotheses to explain it. If you doubt this, try raising this question or some similarly challenging question among your own friends and acquaintances.

Chapter Summary

The subject of this chapter has been common ways of going wrong in argument. Some arguments are *fallacies:* arguments that are deceptive but whose premises don't really prove their conclusion. The general classification of fallacies into Not the Point, Beside the Point, and Beyond the Point fallacies was more important than the subclassification of individual fallacies, but names of particular fallacies are useful reminders of some common tricks and mistakes in argument. The fallacies were classified as follows:

NOT THE POINT FALLACIES
    Association
    Popular Prejudice (*ad populum*)
    Personal Attack (*ad hominem*)
    Ridicule
    Opposition

BESIDE THE POINT FALLACIES
    Irrelevant Conclusion
    Unqualified Generalization
    After, Therefore Because
    Arguing from Ignorance
    Circumstances

BEYOND THE POINT FALLACIES
    Arguing in a Circle
    Assumed Premise

The three types of weak arguments discussed were:

    Argument from Authority
    Argument from Analogy
    Ad Hoc Hypotheses

Each of the weak arguments, if used cautiously, can give some probability, even high probability, to a given conclusion. But overreliance on any of them will lead to error.

The method of studying ways of going wrong in argument has its limitations. Bad arguments are all around us, and some familiarity with the commoner kinds of bad or weak arguments is a useful sort of preventive medicine. But preventive medicine alone will not make us healthy; we need good food and exercise. Similarly, an appreciation of good arguments, to which we now turn, is necessary for our mental well-being.

Practical Applications

Add a section on fallacies to your Argument File. Try to find a good example of each type of fallacy. Do the same for weak arguments. Look out for instances where too much reliance might be placed on weak arguments and, from the other point of view, where a weak argument seems to give good reasons to accept a conclusion. Be especially on the lookout for fallacies and weak arguments in areas where you have to make decisions, or in subjects that are especially important to you.

Exercise 2-3

1. Find an example of an argument from authority in a newspaper, magazine, etc. Discuss it in terms of Who, What, When, Where, Why, and give your conclusion as to how strong the argument is.
2. Find an example of an argument from analogy. How many relevant similarities and dissimilarities can you find between the two cases? How strong is the analogy argument?
3. Find an example of an ad hoc hypothesis in a real-life context. What alternative explanations can you think of for the phenomenon that the ad hoc hypothesis is supposed to explain? How could the ad hoc hypothesis be tested?
4. Name an authority you are prepared to accept on a specific subject. Give an argument that this authority can be trusted on this subject.
5. Cite an argument from analogy or an ad hoc hypothesis that you believe is successful and that avoids the pitfalls discussed in this chapter. Give an argument to support your confidence in the analogy or the hypothesis.

Exercise 2-4

The article below is taken from a popular magazine of 1874. The author accuses Darwin of commiting some fallacies and perhaps is guilty of some fallacies or overreliance on weak arguments himself. After reading the article:

1. Identify at least one fallacy and any weak arguments *mentioned* by the author of this article.
2. Identify at least one fallacy and at least one weak argument *used* by the author of this article.
*3. Discuss whether Darwin or his supporters are actually guilty of the alleged fallacies or weak arguments.
4. Discuss some counterinstances to claims made by the writer.
5. Insofar as you can, describe the prejudices or points of view that the writer presumes his audience will share with him.

Was Mr. Darwin Correct, Or Are Men Really Like Their Dogs?

There have been so many accounts of the origin of the human race, and the study of animalism enters so largely into the philosophy of expression, that some presentation of the recent state of science is due to the educational world, and especially to that portion of the people who are interested in the study of man's nature.

How came man on earth?

All science agrees with the Bible, for that book states results and not processes. Even the Darwinian theory, startling as it is, does not conflict with the Mosaic account. The latter cites the great fact that man is made of the dust of the earth; but science admits this well-known fact.

Is the Darwinian theory true?

When it first appeared, it attracted the attention of the thinking world, because Mr. Darwin was a scholar, and the facts he cited were known to be true. But, while facts may be true, the conclusions drawn from them may be unwarranted. For instance, gray-haired men and women have wrinkled faces; but it would be an unwarrantable conclusion to say that gray hairs cause wrinkles. Darwin's facts are admittedly correct; but, when he associates one fact with another as the cause of the other, the incorrectness begins, if there is any.

Louis Agassiz, the greatest scientist of his day, examined Darwin's claims very carefully, and finally decided that it could not be true that man was descended from the ape and its earlier animal ancestry. Within six months the greatest of German biologists, and the most learned anthropologist now living, have declared that the Darwin theory of the origin of man could not be true. In spite of the opinions of these, the two leading investigators of the century, the theory of Darwinism is being taught in the universities of America. There is such a thing as a little knowledge leading to a great error, and this is an example.

There are certain reasons why the claims of Darwin cannot be accepted; and these reasons will ultimately lead to its rejection by the coming age of scientists.

Our first objection is that two associate facts do not necessarily prove that one is the cause of the other. An infant is bald and toothless; an old man is bald and toothless. Infancy is not the cause of age, nor age of infancy; nor is baldness the cause of toothlessness. Two common circumstances may have a single cause, and a common origin. Darwin produced many similarities between men and beasts; and his followers have added to the testimony; but the proof went no further than to show associate facts, not cause and effect.

Let us imagine the face of a beefy man, such as would be expected to engage in brutal sports. In the strength and carriage of his head, and the solid build of his neck, he resembles the beef-brute, or bull. These facts are associates merely. They have a common cause—the natural tendency of creation. The Shaftesbury Philosophy teaches us that all species in the animal and vegetable kingdoms are daily supplied from the common atoms, the intelligent indivisible particles which originate all forms of matter. The use of life is the cause of their arrangement into form and being. Thus originates every species of creation.

That this theory is a fact, and that it will account for every fact stated by Darwin, we shall endeavor to prove in subsequent issues of this Magazine. In the first place we find that the use of life is constantly affecting man and his companions alike. The same man, imagined earlier, who looks so strong and beefy, might become a moral brute, and the chances are that his dog would be like him. The sleek and well-fed animal that attends a sleek and well-fed man, is sure to run down the physical scale with his master. The uses of life change one completely. "A dog is like his master" is a truism.

The philosophy referred to also states that there are good and evil agencies in atoms, in germ life, in weeds and plants, in animals and in man; and that the uses of life draw them forth. To show this let us look at any bartender and the dog he keeps about him. Once asked what human face came nearest to the typical devil, a philosopher replied, "For a man, a bartender; for a woman, a gossip who pretends not to believe in gossiping." A bartender is the crime-stained destroyer of homes; and the dog is like his master. Whether fat or lean, the bartender always has this certain look.

In mental deficiency the same law holds true. Take the willfully ignorant farmer, the city curbstone loafer, the backwoodsman who prefers liquor to books, or any man or woman who "does not believe in education," and you will see the stamp of ignorance on the face of the master, and of his dog.

Exercise 2-5

In 1977 the Cambridge, Massachusetts, City Council debated using its zoning powers to prevent Harvard University from building a laboratory for experimentation with recombinant DNA because it was thought that this might pose new and dangerous health hazards (as noted in Exercise 1-7). The following selections from the testimony given by scientists and other concerned citizens contain some fallacies and weak arguments. Identify any fallacies or weak arguments you can find in the testimony quoted and discuss briefly the strength of the argument given.

1. "I'm getting the feedback that this experiment is really not that hazardous. Then why is this such a controversy, why are the scientists even split on this one. I have had several calls from scientists, from people who are affiliated with Harvard and MIT. They have never ever called me before on even nuclear experimentation that is being done within the walls of MIT. Why are scientists calling us, the city council, putting it in our laps to deal with this, when all of these other experiments are going on that we have no knowledge of. This makes me wary, very much, because you are just telling me that, well, the chances of the public being hurt is extraordinarily low."

*2.   "You said that we're building an expensive and quite highly contained laboratory and therefore the experiments must be dangerous. But the implication of that is that had we not bothered to build the facility, had

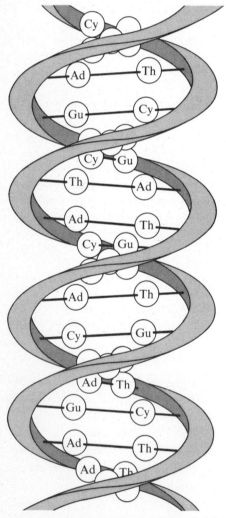

A fragment of the double-stranded helical DNA molecule.

the scientists not bothered about regulations and guidelines, you'd assume they were safe."

3. "I'm still wondering why this has been dropped in our laps. There must be a great division that now the political world which is known to make crazy decisions now has to settle an issue in the scientific world. It must be something terribly wrong going on that nobody knows what kind of guidelines should be adhered to."

4. "Dr. Singer, your organization is obviously quite interested in the development of this research."

"Yes, I think that the organization takes the view that the opportunities that are afforded by these new techniques have extraordinary promise in terms of meeting the missions and goals that have been given to the National Institutes of Health by the Congress."

"So not only is your organization responsible for promulgating this type of research, it's responsible for regulating it."

"Under the present circumstances the NIH is the only institution which has taken on serious consideration of this problem."

5. "Dr. Singer, do you believe that there should be civilian control over the military?"

"That's a very difficult question for me to answer, personally, since I have commented on behalf of the National Institutes of Health, and it's a question which is surprising to me because it is something unexpected and not right on the topic."

"Well, you see, I think it is right on the topic because I think that is, in fact, the fundamental issue here. I really don't give a damn about a P3 laboratory at Harvard University because I can't visit that laboratory and discover if it's P1, P2, P4, or whatever. I don't have the expertise to analyze or investigate any type of laboratory facility at Harvard University, but it strikes me as very to the point that there is an important principle in this country that the people who have a vested self-interest in certain types of activity shouldn't be the ones who are charged with not only promulgating but regulating it."

6. "I find it strange that Dr. Tashni on the one hand asserts that the reason that we want to do this research is that we don't know enough about the organization of DNA in higher organisms and yet he has and his colleagues have enough knowledge to establish that the risk is minimal."

7. "Can I say in answer to that, look, if one took that attitude, one would do no experiments. Before we knew about how genes were organized in lower organisms we would make the statement, 'We do not know how genes are organized in the lower organisms, we do not believe there is a significant risk in doing these experiments.' They are two quite different questions and there is no reason you should assume that the risk is related to what we know about the organization. Had we taken the view that we had to know in advance about that organization, we could not have done that experiment, that series of experiments, or, in fact, any experiment in the history of medical microbiology."

8. "The transfer of genes from higher to lower organisms occurs rarely, if ever, in nature. We therefore have no way of evaluating the safety of this new kind of technology that is in fact manufacturing new organisms." "The point is that we don't know and that the people who want to go ahead with the work don't know, because this kind of work has not been done before. The best course, therefore, is to be extremely cautious until we know more."

9. "Some people, and you have heard it here tonight, have begun to say that since all research involves delving into the unknown why single this work out as more dangerous. The answer is simply this. The ordinary research that most of us do is unpredictable in the same way that I cannot predict what will happen any time I go into the kitchen to bake a cake, but I'm pretty darn sure it's not dangerous. The recombinant DNA research is different because we are bringing together living elements that have not been together before and we therefore have no way of predicting what will happen."

*10. "Now, with respect to that statement about there has been no documented case of a recombinant organism causing disease. May I give an analogy? I'm sure it is true that there is no evidence that these organisms cause danger. The vinyl chloride industry for years said that there was no evidence that vinyl chloride caused danger. The asbestos industry said for years that there was no evidence that asbestos caused any danger. Look at all of these workers, they haven't dropped dead yet. The argument that because we haven't seen the negative results means that we shouldn't worry about it is absurd and is simply a way of pulling the fog over the eyes."

Exercise 2-6

The following quotations from Immanuel Kant's Observations on the Beautiful and Sublime *express sexual and racial prejudices characteristic of Kant's period and society. But at least some of them also involve fallacies*

*or weak arguments. In each case identify the fallacy or weak argument
and comment briefly on what is questionable in the argument.*

1.   Laborious learning or painful pondering, even if a woman should
greatly succeed in it, destroy the merits that are proper to her sex, and
because of their rarity they can make of her an object of cold admiration;
but at the same time they will weaken the charms with which she exercises
her great power over the other sex. A woman who has a head full of Greek,
like Mme Dacier, or carries on fundamental controversies about me-
chanics, like the Marquise de Chatelet, might as well even have a beard;
for perhaps that would express more obviously the mien of profundity
for which she strives.

2.   A woman is embarassed little that she does not possess certain high
insights, that she is timid, and not fit for serious employments, and so
forth; she is beautiful and captivates, and that is enough. On the other
hand, she demands all these qualities in a man, and the sublimity of her
soul shows itself only in that she knows to treasure these noble qualities
so far as they are found in him. How else indeed would it be possible that
so many grotesque male faces, whatever merits they may possess, could
gain such well-bred and fine wives!

3.   The fault on which the French national character borders nearest is
the trifling, or with a more polite expression, the frivolous. Weighty
matters are treated as sport, and trivialities serve for the most earnest
business. In old age the Frenchman still sings sportive songs, and is, as
much as he can be, still gallant towards the ladies. In these remarks I
have great authorities from this nation itself on my side, and I retreat
behind a Montesquieu or a D'Alembert, in order to be safe against any
anxious indignation.

*4.   The Negroes of Africa have by nature no feeling that rises above the
trifling. Mr. Hume challenges anyone to cite a single example in which
a Negro has shown talents, and asserts that among the hundreds of thousands of blacks who are transported elsewhere from their countries,
although many of them have even been set free, still not a single one was
ever found who presented anything great in art or science or any other
praiseworthy quality, even though among the whites some continually
rise aloft from the lowest rabble, and through superior gifts earn respect
in the world.

5.   In the lands of the black, what better can one expect than what is
found prevailing, namely the feminine sex in the deepest slavery? A de-
spairing man is always a strict master over anyone weaker, just as with
us that man is always a tyrant in the kitchen who outside his own house

hardly dares to look anyone in the face. Of course, Father Labat reports that a Negro carpenter, whom he reproached for haughty treatment toward his wives, answered: "You whites are indeed fools, for first you make great concessions to your wives, and afterward you complain when they drive you mad." And it might be that there were something in this which perhaps deserved to be considered; but in short, this fellow was quite black from head to foot, a clear proof that what he said was stupid.

CHAPTER THREE

Statement Logic: The Simple System

THE ARCHEOLOGIST'S ARGUMENT

An archeologist gives the following argument to explain the fact that while writing was known in Greece between about 1700 B.C. and 1200 B.C., it was then forgotten and this whole area became illiterate until the rediscovery of writing about 700 B.C.

The loss of literacy could be explained by the killing of all the people who knew how to read and write or by the failure of older persons who were literate to teach writing to younger persons. If older literate people failed to teach younger people to write then this must either be because of some religious reason or because writing was useless. If writing was used for poetic purposes it would not have become useless. If writing was used only for keeping palace accounts then if the palaces were destroyed then writing would become useless. All of the people who knew how to read and write could not have been killed. There were no religious reasons for not teaching writing to younger people. The palaces were destroyed; and writing was used only for keeping palace accounts. Thus, we can explain the loss of literacy.

What is the explanation and how does it follow from the information given?

What are the basic arguments involving statements?

There are, in fact, about a dozen simple arguments involving statements that are not broken down into subject and predicate. However, all of these arguments can be reduced to only two even more basic arguments. In order to see how this works, we will need to show how simple statements can be combined into more complex statements. A simple statement is one that has only one predicate term and one or more subject terms, for instance, "Spock is a Vulcan" or "Spock is more logical than McCoy." We will begin with two basic things we can do to simple statements: negation and disjunction. To negate a simple statement is just to indicate in some way that it is not true. There are a great variety of ways of negating a simple statement. For example, the simple statement "Spock is a Vulcan" can be negated in any of the following ways:

Spock is not a Vulcan.
It is not true that Spock is a Vulcan.
It is false that Spock is a Vulcan.

Although there are stylistic and perhaps even subtle logical differences between these different ways of negating the statement, we will simplify the situation by regarding them all as equivalent. If Spock *is* a Vulcan, all of the denials that he is are false. In general, if a statement is true its negation is false, and if a statement is false its negation is true.

It will be convenient to abbreviate simple statements by using single capital letters, usually an initial letter of a key word in the statement. Thus we might abbreviate "Spock is a Vulcan" by using the letter *V*. To keep track of what letters we are using as abbreviations for statements in a given argument, we will usually write a "dictionary" showing what letter stands for what statement. Some authors use an equal sign between letter and statement:

V = Spock is a Vulcan

but I prefer to have a special symbol not used for other purposes to indicate that a letter stands for a given statement. So I will use a crosshatch symbol # and will let

V   #   Spock is a Vulcan

be our way of saying that the letter *V* stands for the statement "Spock is a Vulcan." To indicate the denial of a statement, we will write a squiggle or "tilde," the symbol ∼, in front of the letter that stands for the statement. So ∼*V* is our way of writing "Spock is not a Vulcan" if our dictionary indicates that *V* stands for "Spock is a Vulcan."

Disjunction and Cancellation

Denial can apply to one or more statements, as we will see, but *either . . . or* statements, called *disjunctions*, must consist of at least two statements. (The two statements could be the same, but we will consider this complication later.) If we add to our dictionary

E   #   Spock is emotional

we can consider the possibility of saying "Either Spock is a Vulcan or Spock is emotional," using the abbreviating letters *V* and *E* and a new symbol that stands for the *either . . . or* relationship. The new symbol is a wedge or ∨ written between two letters, so that with the dictionary we have so far, $V \lor E$ would stand for "Either Spock is a Vulcan or Spock is emotional." The *either* is often dropped, but any *or* statement is a disjunction and is symbolized with $\lor$.

However, sometimes when we say *either . . . or* we mean "one or the other but not both" and sometimes we mean "one or the other and maybe both." The first is called an *exclusive disjunction* and the second is called an *inclusive disjunction.* An example of an exclusive disjunction would be "Either pay your registration fee at the cashier's office or mail in a check to the Registrar." Obviously, you are being told to do one or the other but not both. But if a first-year student is advised, "Either take courses that are especially interesting to you or take courses that satisfy college requirements," the person giving the advice would not normally intend to advise the student not to take courses that *both* especially interested him *and* satisfied college requirements. Because this ambiguity in *either . . . or* statements can be confusing, we will make it a rule that our disjunction symbol $\lor$ will always be interpreted as inclusive disjunction: perhaps one or perhaps the other, and perhaps both.

In some cases even though the $\lor$ symbol leaves open the "maybe both" possibility, something about the statements joined by $\lor$ may rule out this possibility. If "Vulcan" and "emotional" are interpreted in such a way that someone cannot be both, then $V \lor E$ does not leave open the possibility "maybe V and E." But this is because of the meaning of V and E, not because of the meaning of $\lor$. Similarly, if we write $V \lor \sim V$ or $E \lor \sim E$ the "maybe both" option is ruled out because, as we interpret negation, a statement and its negation cannot both be true. But again this is because of the relation of V to $\sim V$ and E to $\sim E$, not because of anything about the $\lor$ symbol.

Given this very simple machinery, we can now describe our two basic argument patterns. Suppose I know that Spock is either a Vulcan or emotional, and then discover that he is definitely not emotional. It must be true, then, that he is a Vulcan, since we knew he was one or the other and he is not emotional. The pattern made by arguments like this can be put in a perfectly general way. For any two statements A and B we can say that B follows from $A \lor B$ and $\sim A$. It will often be useful to write this like an arithmetical sum with a line between premises and conclusion:

$A \lor B$

$\sim A$

B

This argument is traditionally called Disjunctive Syllogism (*syllogism* is from a Greek word meaning an argument with two premises and one conclusion). It is a form of reasoning we use whenever we are aware that there are only two alternatives in a given situation and then get further information that reduces the possibilities to one. For example, if I am sure that my car keys are in the car or else have them in my pocket, then if I feel in my pocket and don't find the keys, I am sure that the keys must be in the car. If I checked the car and *didn't* find the keys, then some of the premises I started out with must be false. Either the keys are in my pocket after all, or else there is some possibility other than "in the car," "in my pocket." But if it were true that those *are* the only two possibilities *and* that the keys are not in my pocket, then it must be true that the keys are in the car. This is just the situation we discussed in Chapter One: The argument from $A \vee B$ and $\sim A$ to B is a valid one. So if the premises are true, the conclusion must be true, while if the conclusion is false, one or the other of the premises must be false.

Nor does it really matter whether the two alternatives are positive or negative. It is an equally good argument to reason, "Either my car keys aren't lost or I dropped them between the car and the house. I didn't drop them between the car and the house, so they aren't lost." This has the form

$$\sim A \vee B$$
$$\underline{\sim B \qquad\quad}$$
$$\sim A$$

Again we had two alternatives, one of which was negative: We eliminated the second alternative, leaving the first negative one. But I could also have positive information that eliminates the negative alternative, for example, "Either my car keys aren't lost or I dropped them between the car and the house. They are lost, so I must have dropped them between the car and the house." This argument has the form

$$\sim A \vee B$$
$$\underline{A \qquad\quad\;\;}$$
$$B$$

and is the same basic pattern as the other two: Of two possibilities one is eliminated, leaving the other.

It may help to see the underlying sameness of these arguments if we use a mathematical analogy. Consider a mathematical calculation of the form

$$\begin{array}{r} N + M \\ -N \\ \hline M \end{array}$$

For example:

$$\begin{array}{r} 2 + 3 \\ -2 \\ \hline 3 \end{array}$$

In the arithmetical case we could think of the plus and minus numbers as canceling out, leaving the other number:

$$\begin{array}{r} \cancel{N} + M \\ -\cancel{N} \\ \hline M \end{array}$$

It may be helpful to think of the A and $\sim A$ in our argument pattern as "canceling out" in a way analogous to the way numbers cancel out, leaving the other part of the disjunction:

$$\begin{array}{r} \cancel{A} \vee B \\ \sim\!\cancel{A} \\ \hline B \end{array}$$

This analogy proves to be very useful, and so we will refer to this pattern of argument as Simple Cancellation (SC). There are a number of variations on this pattern, all of which can be tied together by the idea of a statement and its denial "canceling each other out." Some of the variations are:

$A \vee B$	$\sim A \vee B$	$A \vee \sim B$	$\sim A \vee \sim B$	
$\sim B$	A	B	A	etc.
A	B	A	$\sim B$	

So far, we have not considered disjunctions with more than two components. (The component statements of a disjunction are called *disjuncts*.) But there is no reason not to have more than two disjuncts. If

L # Spock is logical

C # Spock is a competent officer

We could write

$V \lor E \lor L$ (Spock is a Vulcan or Spock is emotional or Spock is logical)

$V \lor E \lor \sim L$ (Spock is a Vulcan or Spock is emotional or Spock is not logical)

$V \lor E \lor L \lor C$ (Spock is a Vulcan or Spock is emotional or Spock is logical or Spock is a competent officer) etc.

But the addition of further statements does not really alter the argument.

$A \lor B \lor C$	$A \lor B \lor C \lor D$
$\sim A$	$\sim A$ etc.
$B \lor C$	$B \lor C \lor D$

are all examples of Simple Cancellation.

Cancel and Collect

What happens when we have two disjunctions as premises of an argument? If the two disjunctions have a statement in common such that the statement appears not negated in one disjunction and negated in the other, then we can eliminate the disjunct that appears negated in one disjunction but not in the other. For instance, if I have the information, "The keys are either in my pocket or lost. The keys are either not lost or are between the car and the house." The common statement in these two disjunctions is "the keys are lost," which is not negated in the first disjunction and is negated in the second. We can thus cancel this statement out and conclude, "The keys are either in my pocket or they are between the car and the house." This pattern is a little less obvious than Simple Cancellation. But we can see that it is also a valid pattern. If the premises are true, it will never lead us to a false conclusion. So, if we have a pattern like

$A \lor B$

$\sim B \lor C$

then we can conclude

$A \lor C$

We will call this rule Cancel and Collect (CC) and it too has many variations:

$A \lor B$	$A \lor {\sim}B$	${\sim}A \lor {\sim}B$	${\sim}A \lor B$
${\sim}B \lor C$	$B \lor C$	$B \lor C$	${\sim}B \lor C$
$A \lor C$	$A \lor C$	${\sim}A \lor C$	${\sim}A \lor C$

This pattern too will work with more than two disjuncts per line:

$A \lor B \lor {\sim}C$	$A \lor B \lor C \lor D$	
$C \lor D \lor E$	${\sim}D \lor E$	etc.
$A \lor B \lor D \lor E$	$A \lor B \lor C \lor E$	

All of these are analogous to many simple calculations in arithmetic; for example:

$2 + 3$	$2 + 3 + 4$		
$-3 + 4$	$-4 + 5 + 6$	$2 + 3 + 4 + 5$	
$2 + 4$	$2 + 3 + 5 + 6$	$-5 + 6$	etc.
		$2 + 3 + 4 + 6$	

Verbal arguments that follow this pattern are not hard to find; for example "Spock is either a Vulcan or emotional. Either he is not emotional or he is not logical. So Spock is either a Vulcan or not logical." In symbols:

$V \lor E$

${\sim}E \lor {\sim}L$

$V \lor {\sim}L$

Another way of connecting simple statements to make more complex statements is by joining them with *and* or *both . . . and*. Thus we can say, "Spock is a Vulcan and Spock is logical" or "Spock is both a Vulcan and logical." However, in order to keep our system as simple as possible, we will not introduce a symbol for *and* in this chapter. When we wish to symbolize something like "Spock is a Vulcan and Spock is logical," we will write these two statements on separate lines; for example, not

V and L

but rather

V

L

This is fine so long as we have only a simple *conjunction* (as *and* statements are called). But what if we have a conjunction combined with a disjunction, as in "Either Spock is a Vulcan and a competent officer or Spock is logical and a competent officer"?

In every case there will be some way, though often a very complicated one, of writing a statement containing *and* and *or* on several lines so that no *and* occurs; for example, (V and C) or (L and C) can be written

$V \lor L$

C

For the moment, we will rewrite statements to avoid the use of *and;* in the next chapter we will expand our system to include *and* as a connective.

Another way of joining simple statements to make a more complex statement is with *if . . . then*. This is called a *conditioned* statement. For example: "If Spock is a Vulcan, then Spock is logical." The words *if . . . then* in English can have all sorts of interpretations: "If A then B" can mean that B follows logically from A, that A is the cause of B, and a great many other things. But all of the uses of *if . . . then* have one thing in common: They all deny that A can be true while B is false. The weakest and broadest way of expressing this idea is to say that *either A is false or B is true.*

This captures part of the meaning of each of the various uses of *if . . . then*. Suppose "If A then B" means that B follows from A in the sense explained in Chapter One that if A is true B must be true. Then either we must reject A or we must accept B. Suppose on the other hand that A is an effecting cause of B. Then either A fails to occur or B occurs. And so on with each of the various senses of "If A then B," all of them have as part of their meaning that either A is false or B is true. Logicians have found that a great many arguments can be adequately dealt with by taking this "common core" meaning of *if . . . then* as if it adequately expressed the meaning of *if . . . then* as it occurs in various arguments. So for the time being, whenever we have a statement of the form "If A then B," we will write it as

$\sim A \vee B$

Arguments with *If . . . Then*

There are some immediate advantages to this way of writing conditional statements. The first advantage is that several basic argument patterns involving conditional statements become special cases of the two rules we have already set down. For instance, consider the argument

If Spock is a Vulcan, then Spock is logical.

Spock is a Vulcan.

Spock is logical.

This argument and any argument of this general pattern are fairly obviously good arguments. If we write the argument using the suggested way of writing conditional statements and the dictionary already given, it becomes

$\sim V \vee L$
$\underline{\quad V \quad}$
$\quad L$

and it can be seen to be a variation of Simple Cancellation. We get a similar result with another type of conditional argument:

If Spock is emotional, he is like McCoy.

Spock is not like McCoy.

Spock is not emotional.

If we let

$M \quad \# \quad$ Spock is like McCoy

then we can write the argument

$\sim E \lor M$
$\underline{\sim M}$
$\sim E$

and again we can see that it is a variation of Simple Cancellation.

Another type of argument with conditional statements involves two conditional statements as premises in a pattern like this:

If Spock is a Vulcan, he is logical.

If Spock is logical, he is a competent officer.

If Spock is a Vulcan, he is a competent officer.

This can be written

$\sim V \lor L$
$\underline{\sim L \lor C}$
$\sim V \lor C$

and can be seen to be a variation of Cancel and Collect.

Another kind of argument involving conditionals has the following pattern:

If Spock is emotional, he is like McCoy.

If Spock is logical, he is a Vulcan.

Either Spock is emotional or he is logical.

Either Spock is like McCoy or he is a Vulcan.

Written out in symbolic form, the argument becomes

$\sim E \lor M$
$\sim L \lor V$
$\underline{E \lor L}$
$M \lor V$

This is a variation of Cancel and Collect. We can see that one Cancel and Collect step could be applied to the first and third premise

$\sim E \lor M$
$\underline{E \lor L}$
$M \lor L$

and then this conclusion used with the second premise to get the final conclusion

$$\frac{\begin{array}{c} \sim L \lor V \\ M \lor L \end{array}}{M \lor V}$$

The same can be said about another pattern of argument:

If Spock is emotional, he is like McCoy.

If Spock is logical, he is a Vulcan.

Either Spock is not like McCoy or he is not a Vulcan.

Either Spock is not emotional or Spock is not logical.

This can be written

$$\frac{\begin{array}{c} \sim E \lor M \\ \sim L \lor V \\ \sim M \lor \sim V \end{array}}{\sim E \lor \sim L}$$

and is another complex example of Cancel and Collect.

Equivalence Rules

In addition to Simple Cancellation and Cancel and Collect, it will be useful to have two other rules at this point. The first rule tells us that two $\sim$s cancel each other out: "It is not true that Spock is not a Vulcan" comes to the same thing as "Spock is a Vulcan." Since for any statement, A, $\sim \sim A$ means the same as A, we can write the pattern as

$$\frac{A}{\sim \sim A}$$ which we will call Double Negation (DN for short)

This is our first *equivalence* rule: The double line means that you can go in either direction from A to $\sim \sim A$ or from $\sim \sim A$ to A. By using this rule repeatedly we can reduce any even number of $\sim$s before a statement to zero, for example, $\sim \sim \sim \sim \sim \sim A$ is the same as A, and any odd number of

$\sim$s in front of a statement to one, for example, $\sim \sim \sim \sim \sim \sim \sim A$ is the same as $\sim A$.

Another equivalence or two-way rule is one that tells us that with any statement of the form $A \vee B$ the order to the disjuncts does not matter. We can write the pattern

$$\frac{A \vee B}{B \vee A}$$

which we will call Commutation (Com.), and repeated application of the rule will enable us to shuffle any disjunction into any order we like; for example: $A \vee B \vee C \vee D$ is the same as $B \vee A \vee D \vee C, D \vee A \vee C \vee B$, etc.

It will sometimes be useful, in giving a proof or refutation, to use a given line more than once, or reduce a line that occurs more than once to only one line. To enable us to do this we will add the two equivalences that we will call *Repetition* (Rep.):

$\dfrac{A}{A \vee A}$	$\dfrac{A}{\begin{array}{c} A \\ A \end{array}}$

That is, a line may be rewritten as a disjunction with itself, or conversely a disjunction of a statement with itself may be written as one statement. Similarly, a line may be repeated or two identical lines reduced to one.

The five rules discussed so far—Simple Cancellation, Cancel and Collect, Double Negation, Commutation, and Repetition—will enable us to deal with a great number of arguments, probably over 90 percent of all real-life arguments involving statements only as unanalyzed wholes. But it will also be useful to be familiar with some variations in the way *if . . . then* statements occur in English, and some ways of handling complex *if . . . then* statements.

All of these are ways of making equivalent conditional statements:

If A then B
If A, B
B if A
A only if B

For example:

If Spock is a Vulcan, then he is logical.
If Spock is a Vulcan, he is logical.
Spock is logical if he is a Vulcan.
Spock is a Vulcan only if he is logical.

The last statement sounds most unlike the others, but trying out examples will help you to see that "A only if B" comes to the same thing as "If A then B."

Two complex forms of *if . . . then* statements are "If A then B and C" and "If A and B then C"; for example: "If Spock is a Vulcan, he is logical and a competent officer" and "If Spock is a Vulcan and logical, then he is a competent officer." Statements of the first form

If A then B and C

are equivalent to two statements

If A then B
If A then C

So "If A then B and C" would be written

$\sim A \vee B$
$\sim A \vee C$

and the statement of this form, "If Spock is a Vulcan, he is logical and a competent officer," would be written

$\sim V \vee L$
$\sim V \vee C$

The other pattern

If A and B then C

is equivalent to

If A then if B then C

and can be symbolized

$\sim A \lor \sim B \lor C$

The statement, "If Spock is a Vulcan and logical, he is a competent officer," can be written

$\sim V \lor \sim L \lor C$

If we combine *or* with *if . . . then* we get two kinds of possibilities, one quite simple and one rather complex. If the *or* comes *after* the *then*, as in "If *A* then *B* or *C*," the translation is simple:

$\sim A \lor B \lor C$

However, if the *or* comes *before* the *then*, as in "If *A* or *B* then *C*," we have to realize that this comes to the same thing as "If *A* then *C and* if *B* then *C*" and translate as

$\sim A \lor C$
$\sim B \lor C$

in two statements rather than one.

In the next chapter we will have special symbols for *if . . . then* and for *and*, and we can write out these equivalences more formally. For the moment, however, they are merely directions for translating from English to symbols.

Exercise 3-1

See if these arguments cancel out to the indicated conclusion, or find a conclusion if there is only a ?. If the premises do not cancel out to the indicated conclusion, or if no conclusion can be drawn where there is only a ?, write NC. Does any argument refute the alleged conclusion?

1. $\left.\begin{array}{l} \sim P \lor \sim E \\ P \end{array}\right\}$ E?

*2. $\left.\begin{array}{l} B \lor \sim F \\ F \end{array}\right\}$ B?

3. $\left.\begin{array}{l} \sim W \lor C \\ \sim C \lor U \\ U \end{array}\right\}$?

4. $\left.\begin{array}{l} W \lor B \\ \sim W \end{array}\right\}$?

5. $\sim Q \vee \sim A \left.\right\}$?
    $\sim Q$

6. $\sim P \vee G \left.\right\}$ $\sim P$?
    $\sim P \vee \sim G$

7. $\sim L \vee P \left.\right\}$?
    $\sim P \vee L$

*8. $\sim P \vee J \left.\right\}$ $\sim \sim G \vee \sim P$?
    $\sim J \vee G$

9. $\sim H \vee I$
    $\sim H \vee B$
    $\sim I \vee \sim B \vee N \left.\right\}$ $\sim H$?
    $\sim I \vee \sim B \vee D$
    $\sim N$

10. $\sim S \vee P$
    $\sim S \vee O \left.\right\}$ $\sim O$?
    $\sim S$

Exercise 3-2

Translate these arguments into symbols and see if they cancel out to the indicated conclusion. If no conclusion is indicated, find and prove a conclusion. If the indicated conclusion is not provable or if no conclusion can be drawn where no conclusion is given, write NC. Use the dictionary:

K # Kirk is aboard the *Enterprise*.

S # Spock is aboard the *Enterprise*.

C # Spock is in command.

E # Spock is second in command.

T # Scotty is second in command.

1. If Spock is not in command, Kirk is aboard the *Enterprise*. Kirk isn't aboard the *Enterprise*, so Spock is in command.

*2. Either Kirk is aboard the *Enterprise* or Spock is in command. Spock is in command if Spock is aboard the *Enterprise*. Kirk is not aboard the *Enterprise*, therefore, Spock is not aboard the *Enterprise*.

3. Kirk is not aboard the *Enterprise* or Spock is in command. If Spock is not aboard the *Enterprise*, then Spock is not in command. If Kirk is aboard the *Enterprise*, Spock is not aboard the *Enterprise*. Therefore . . .

4. If Kirk is not aboard the Enterprise, Spock is in command. Spock is in command if and only if Spock is the second in command. Either Spock is second in command or Scotty is. Scotty is not second in command. Therefore . . .

5. Either Scotty is second in command or Spock is. If Spock is second in command, then if Kirk is not aboard Spock is in command. If Scotty is second in command, then if Kirk is not aboard Spock is not in command. Kirk is not aboard. Therefore . . .

Exercise 3-3

Symbolize these arguments with ∼ and ∨ and see if they cancel out to the conclusion indicated, or find a conclusion if none is given.

1. If the bottle is marked "poison," it is not safe to drink. It is not marked "poison," so it is safe to drink.

*2. If Alice grows larger she will get into the garden, and if she grows smaller she will get into the garden. She will grow larger or smaller if she eats the cake. Therefore . . .

3. If Alice were Ada her hair would go in long ringlets, and if she were Mabel she would know very little. But Alice's hair doesn't go in ringlets and she knows all sorts of things. Therefore, Alice is not Ada, and Alice is not Mabel.

4. If Alice eats eggs, she is a kind of serpent so far as the pigeon is concerned. Little girls eat eggs and Alice is a little girl. Therefore . . .

5. If there were any use in knocking, then either the Footman could answer the door or someone else could hear Alice. But the Footman can't answer the door if he is on the same side of it as Alice, and he is. Therefore . . .

6. If Alice is not to go among mad people, someone must be sane. But if the Cheshire Cat is right, no one is sane. So Alice can't help going among mad people.

7. If saying what you mean were the same as meaning what you say, then seeing what you eat would be the same as eating what you see. But eating what you see is different from seeing what you eat. Therefore . . .

*8. If Rule Forty-two is the oldest in the book, then if Alice is a mile high she must leave the court. But if Rule Forty-two were the oldest in the book it would be Number One. So, Alice need not leave the court.

9. If the Knave wrote the note, then if he didn't sign it, he meant some mischief. He didn't sign the note. Therefore . . .

10. If the Knave is made of cardboard, he can't swim. If he can't swim, he fits the verses. The knave is made of cardboard, but he doesn't fit the verses. Therefore, he can swim.

LOGIC

A Sample Argument

Consider now a fairly complex argument, which occurs in Plato's dialogue *Meno*. Socrates and his young friend Meno are considering the question of whether virtue—that is, moral goodness—is something that can be taught. Socrates argues that if a thing can be taught there ought to be identifiable people who teach it. Are there any likely candidates for teachers of virtue? Two possibilities are considered: a group of teachers called the Sophists who claimed to be able to teach anything for a price, and the noblest citizens of Athens who would surely try to teach virtue to their own children. But both the Sophists' students and the noblest Athenians' children show by their actions that they have failed to learn virtue. So Socrates and young Meno agree that neither group can teach virtue; they conclude, therefore, that virtue cannot be taught.

We can set out the argument as follows:

If *virtue* can be taught, there will be *teachers* of virtue.
If there are *teachers* of virtue, either the *Sophists* are teachers of virtue
       or the *noblest* Athenians will be teachers of virtue.
The *Sophists* are not teachers of virtue.
The *noblest* Athenians are not teachers of virtue.
Therefore virtue cannot be taught.

Let us symbolize the argument, using the letters italicized above as abbreviations for the simple statements in which the letters occur. The argument will be

1. $\sim V \vee T$
2. $\sim T \vee S \vee N$ $\sim V$
3. $\sim S$
4. $\sim N$

(We number lines to make it easier to refer to them.) We could simply cross out terms

1. $\sim V \vee \cancel{T}$
2. $\sim \cancel{T} \vee \cancel{S} \vee \cancel{N}$
3. $\sim \cancel{S}$
4. $\sim \cancel{N}$

leaving only $\sim V$: this amounts to a proof that $\sim V$ follows from these premises. Or we could set out the proof more formally, writing down each step and justifying it:

1. $\sim V \vee T$
2. $\sim T \vee S \vee N$
3. $\sim S$
4. $\sim N$
5. $\sim T \vee S$ 4, 2 SC
6. $\sim T$ 5, 3 SC
7. $\sim V$ 1, 6 SC

where by writing the numbers of the lines used and the abbreviation of the rules used we provide a complete justification for each step. The proof ends when we arrive at $\sim V$, which we were trying to prove. This is not the only possible way of proving this conclusion from these premises; we could also write the proof as

1. $\sim V \vee T$
2. $\sim T \vee S \vee N$
3. $\sim S$
4. $\sim N$
5. $\sim V \vee S \vee N$ 1, 2 CC
6. $\sim V \vee N$ 5, 3 SC
7. $\sim V$ 6, 4 SC

This would correspond to canceling from the top down instead of from the bottom up:

1. $\sim V \vee T^1$
2. $\sim T \vee S^2 \vee N^3$ rather than
3. $\sim S$
4. $\sim N$

1. $\sim V \vee T^3$
2. $\sim T \vee S^2 \vee N^1$
3. $\sim S$
4. $\sim N$

However, real arguments do not always work out so neatly. In the complete argument in the *Meno*, Socrates brings in learners as well as teachers: His full argument has as its first premise, "If virtue can be taught there will be *teachers and learners* of virtue." From our earlier discussion we can see that this would have to be symbolized as

1. $\sim V \vee T$
2. $\sim V \vee L$

He then adds a premise, "If there are learners of virtue, there will be teachers of virtue," which we can write

3. $\sim L \vee T$

The full argument then becomes

1. $\sim V \vee T$
2. $\sim V \vee L$
3. $\sim L \vee T$
4. $\sim T \vee S \vee N$
5. $\sim S$
6. $\sim N$

In canceling we can simply ignore the two new premises 2 and 3 and cancel as before, or we can cancel differently:

1. $\sim V \vee T$ **1.** $\sim V \vee T$
2. $\sim V \vee L$ **2.** $\sim V \vee L$
3. $\sim L \vee T$ or   **3.** $\sim L \vee T$
4. $\sim T \vee S \vee N$ **4.** $\sim T \vee S \vee N$
5. $\sim S$ **5.** $\sim S$
6. $\sim N$ **6.** $\sim N$

In either case we will have $\sim V$ plus some "left-over" premises. But the extra premises do no harm.

Rules of Proof and Refutation

We can give a general Rule of Proof governing cancellation arguments, as follows:

Rule of Proof: A statement is proved by given premises if after cancellation operations have been carried out on the premises, the statement is the only remaining line *or* one of the remaining lines. (Being *part* of a remaining line is not enough; the conclusion must be the same as one whole remaining line.)

As used here, "cancellation operations" means the application of SC or CC, and a "line" means either one of the original lines of the premises or a line formed from two or more original lines by Cancel and Collect.

Paralleling the Rule of Proof we could give a Rule of Refutation:

Rule of Refutation: A statement is refuted by given premises if after the cancellation operations have been carried out on the premises, the denial of the statement is the only remaining line *or* one of the remaining lines. (Being *part* of a remaining line is not enough.)

To mark the parallels between proof and refutation, we will write both proofs and refutations by writing the statement in question to the right of the premises, followed by a question mark. Then if the last line of the argument is the same as the questioned statement, we have given a proof; if it is the denial of the questioned statement, we have given a refutation. Thus our argument from Plato, above, is a proof of $\sim V$ and a refutation of V:

1.	$\sim V \vee T$			**1.**	$\sim V \vee T$	
2.	$\sim T \vee S \vee N$	$\sim V?$		**2.**	$\sim T \vee S \vee N$	$V?$
3.	$\sim S$			**3.**	$\sim S$	
4.	$\sim N$			**4.**	$\sim N$	
5.	$\sim T \vee S$	2, 4 SC		**5.**	$\sim T \vee S$	2, 4 SC
6.	$\sim T$	5, 3 SC		**6.**	$\sim T$	5, 3 SC
7.	$\sim V$	6, 1 SC		**7.**	$\sim V$	6, 1 SC

If neither the statement in question *nor* its denial follows from the premises by cancellation, we have neither proved *nor* refuted the statement in question. Thus if we raise the question, "Are there learners of virtue?," $L?$, the argument we have just written down neither proves nor disproves L. We will say that a set of premises that neither confirms nor disconfirms a given statement *leaves open* that statement. It should be clear that for any set of premises and any statement, these premises either prove *or* refute *or* leave open that statement.

There are some cases that rarely come up in practice but that ought to be mentioned for the sake of completeness. First, any statement must be regarded as proving itself and refuting its negation; that is:

$$L \;\}\; L? \qquad\qquad\qquad L \;\}\; \sim L?$$

can be regarded as a proof and a refutation respectively. This sounds strange, but all we are saying is that *if* a statement is true it follows that it is true, and *if* a statement is true it follows that it is not false. This brings out the point that proof and refutation, as we are using them, are relative terms: A statement is proved or refuted *by* or *relative to* certain premises. As we said in Chapter One, a statement is *established* if it is proved from true premises, and a statement is *condemned* if it is refuted by true premises. Instead of "true premises" we will sometimes simply say "the facts," so that a statement is established if it is proved by the facts and condemned if it is refuted by the facts. A statement that is neither established nor refuted by *any* set of premises known to be true will be said to be undecided by the facts.

A useful equivalence that does not involve a new rule concerns the equivalence of "If *A* then *B*" and "If not *B* then not *A*." The first would be written $\sim A \vee B$, and the second would be written $\sim \sim B \vee \sim A$. (The *if . . . then* gives us the first $\sim$ and the $\vee$, the other two $\sim$s translate the *not* in *not-B* and *not-A*.) But since by DN $\sim \sim B$ is the same as *B*, and by Com. $B \vee \sim A$ is the same as $\sim A \vee B$, we can see that in our symbolism "If *A* then *B*" is essentially written the same as "If not *B* then not *A*." If we try out various English *if . . . then* sentences, such as "If Spock is a Vulcan, he is logical," "If Spock is not logical, he is not a Vulcan," we see that this feature of our symbolism reflects an equivalence in meaning in English; in general, for any statement "If *A* then *B*" means the same as "If not-*B* then not-*A*." The same use of DN and/or Com. will also enable us to see the equivalence of other *if . . . then* statements; for example: "If Spock is a Vulcan, he is not emotional" and "If Spock is emotional, he is not a Vulcan," which are $\sim V \vee \sim E$ and $\sim E \vee \sim V$ respectively.

In the case where an *and* conclusion is to be proved or refuted, we have some further complications. Consider the argument:

1. $\sim L \vee T$
2. $\sim T \vee S \vee N$ $\sim T$?
3. $\sim S$ $\sim L$?
4. $\sim N$

(Note that we wrote $\sim T$ and $\sim L$ as separate lines.)

Mere cancellation would "use up" the $\sim T$; it would not be left as one of the lines left after cancellation. To avoid this we proceed as follows:

5. $\sim T \vee S$ 2, 4 SC
6. $\sim T$ 5, 3 SC
7. $\sim T$ 6 Rep.
8. $\sim L$ 1, 6 SC

We interpret this as follows: Line 6 was "used up" in canceling *T* from line 1, but line 7, its repetition, was not used and can be regarded as one of the lines left after cancellation. It should be made clear that only a complete line can be repeated in this fashion, *not part of a line*. However, Repetition will always enable us to get complex conclusions that consist of one or more of the original premises plus whatever conclusions follow from those premises. To avoid mistakes, regard a line as "used up" and so *not* left over after cancellation operations if its number is cited with SC or CC in justifying a step. Thus we cannot regard 6 as part of the conclusion proved, but we can so regard 7.

In refuting an *and* conclusion it is enough to refute one conjunct. Thus to give a refutation:

1.	$\sim L \vee T$	
2.	$\sim T \vee S \vee N$	*T*?
3.	$\sim S$	*L*?
4.	$\sim N$	
5.	$\sim T \vee S$	2, 4 SC
6.	$\sim T$	3, 5 SC

I can, if I wish, stop at line 6; since $\sim T$ is proved *T* is refuted, and if *T* is refuted *L and T* is refuted. (That is, if one is disproved they cannot *both* be proved.)

Proofs with *if . . . then* or *either . . . or* conclusions cause no special problems; in our symbolism either will be a disjunction and we will usually get a disjunctive conclusion by one or more CC steps, or perhaps by SC on a more complex disjunction. Examples of such proofs would be:

1.	$\sim L \vee T$	
2.	$\sim T \vee S \vee N$	$\sim V \vee S \vee N$?
3.	$\sim V \vee L$	
4.	$\sim V \vee T$	1, 3 CC
5.	$\sim V \vee S \vee N$	2, 4 CC

or

1.	$\sim L \vee T$	
2.	$\sim T \vee S \vee N$	$\sim L \vee N$?
3.	$\sim S$	
4.	$\sim T \vee N$	2, 3 SC
5.	$\sim L \vee N$	1, 4 CC

To *refute* a disjunction we must refute *both* disjuncts, since a disjunction claims only that one or the other or both of its disjuncts is true. Thus consider the refutation:

$$
\left.
\begin{array}{ll}
\textbf{1.} & \sim L \vee T \\
\textbf{2.} & \sim T \vee S \vee N \\
\textbf{3.} & \sim S \\
\textbf{4.} & \sim N
\end{array}
\right\} \quad L \vee T?
$$

5.	$\sim T \vee S$	2, 4 SC
6.	$\sim T$	3, 5 SC
7.	$\sim T$	6 Rep.
8.	$\sim L$	1, 6 SC

It must be a proof of both $\sim L$ *and* $\sim T$ in order to refute $L \vee T$.

We can add a clause to our Rule of Refutation to this effect or make it an independent subrule:

Rule of Refutation for Conjunctions and Disjunctions: To refute a conjunction at least one conjunct must be refuted (i.e., its denial must be a remaining line after cancellation procedures); to refute a disjunction all disjuncts must be refuted (i.e., the denial of each must be a remaining line after cancellation procedures).

We will now consider two problems that will put a considerable strain on our simple system of statement logic: *if and only if* statements and contradictory premises. The problems are soluble but push us in the direction of a more complete system.

Bi-Conditionals

Sometimes we wish to say that two statements "stand or fall together"— that if one is true so is the other, and if one is false so is the other. In these cases we say "*A just in case B*" or sometimes "*A if and only if B.*" The second form brings out the fact that such statements are *bi-conditionals;* "*A* if and only if *B*" is equivalent to "If *A* then *B and* if *B* then *A.*" That is why we use the *if and only if* form. "*A* only if *B*" is the same as "If *A* then *B,*" and "*A* if *B*" is the same as "If *B* then *A*"; so by saying "*A* if and only if *B*" we concisely express both conditionals.

It is easy enough to write "A if and only if B"; we would write it as two lines:

$\sim A \vee B$

$\sim B \vee A$

Thus, "There are teachers of virtue just in case there are learners of virtue" would be

$\sim T \vee L$

$\sim L \vee T$

The difficulty when we are using a cancellation method is that it is natural to cancel an *if and only if* with itself, leaving a trivially true statement, "T is either true or false" $(T \vee \sim T)$:

1.	$\sim T \vee L$			1.	$\sim T \vee L$	
2.	$\sim L \vee T$	or		2.	$\sim L \vee T$	
3.	$\sim T \vee T$	1, 2 CC		3.	$\sim L \vee L$	1, 2 CC

But when an *if and only if* occurs as part of an argument, this "self-cancellation" is almost never what we really want to do with it; we usually, in fact, want to use one or both of the *if . . . then* statements alone or with other statements to get a conclusion. Thus one quite natural way of canceling will lead us astray unless we have a special way of dealing with *if and only if* statements.

The device we will use in this chapter is to write *if and only if* statements as *split lines* in this fashion:

1a. $\quad \sim A \vee B$

1b. $\quad \sim B \vee A$

and allow the use of either "half" of a split line just as if it were a whole line, except that we forbid cancellation of a split line with itself. Thus if we had the argument

There are *t*eachers of virtue if and only if there are *l*earners of virtue.

If there are *l*earners of virtue, the *c*hildren of the noblest Athenians will be learners of virtue.

The children of the noblest Athenians are not learners of virtue.
Therefore, there are not teachers of virtue.

1a.	$\sim T \vee L$	
1b.	$\sim L \vee T$	
2.	$\sim L \vee C$	$\sim T?$
3.	$\sim C$	
4.	$\sim L$	2, 3 SC
5.	$\sim T$	1a, 4 SC

Notice we have treated the "b" part of line 1 as simply a "leftover" line;
the only difference between a split line and a regular line is that split
lines will not cancel with each other. This is a workable, if slightly cumbersome solution to the problem of how to deal with *if and only if* statements.
    Notice, by the way, that we do not allow cancellation *within* a line;
"Spock is emotional, or he is not emotional, or he is logical"

$$E \vee \sim E \vee L$$

does not cancel out to L. Thus the "split-line" strategy makes an *if and
only if* like one line in some respects (no cancellation) and like two lines
in other respects. If we allowed internal cancellation, we could get invalid
arguments. Thus, for example, "Either there are teachers or there are
not teachers," $T \vee \sim T$, is trivially true, since either T or $\sim T$ must be
true. If we add some statement, say C, to $T \vee \sim T$, the result $T \vee \sim T \vee C$
is still trivially true since, whether C is true or false, one or the other of
T, $\sim T$ will be true. But if we allowed the $T \vee \sim T$ to cancel out, we
could get from the trivially true $T \vee \sim T \vee C$ to C alone. But C might
not be true, so we could get from something trivially true to something
false.

Contradictory Premises

A more complex problem is created when we have contradictory premises.
Take a simple argument:

1.	$\sim T \vee S$	
2.	$\sim S$	$\sim T?$
3.	S	

Premises 2 and 3 contradict each other; they can't both be true. We *could* cancel 1 and 2 to get $\sim T$ and simply regard line 3 as a "leftover." But this doesn't seem to do justice to the peculiarity of the premises. Since the premises are contradictory they could not be true, and this argument could not *establish* $\sim T$.

In modern logic it is customary to say that contradictory premises prove *anything*, on the following grounds. "*B* follows from *A*" is defined by saying that *B* follows from *A* if it is impossible for *A* to be true while *B* is false. But if *A*, the premise or premises, is or are self-contradictory, it is impossible for *A* to be true and thus impossible for *A* to be true *and* any other statement to be false (or true). Thus, in a sense, anything follows from a contradiction, since if *B* is any arbitrary statement and *A* is a contradiction, it is impossible for *A* to be true *and* *B* false.

This is a reasonable and useful way to regard the situation for many purposes, but it is not the only way. Our present set of rules, in fact, does not enable us to show that for any statement and for any set of contradictory premises the statement follows from the premises: There is no way of getting a proof of *L* from the argument

$$
\begin{array}{ll}
\textbf{1.} & S \\
\textbf{2.} & \sim S
\end{array} \Biggr\} \ L?
$$

in the simple system of this chapter. Instead of following the modern view, we could modify our definition of *following from* and say that *B* follows from *A* if *A* is possible and it is impossible for *A* to be true and *B* false. This is a more complex, but not necessarily a worse, definition of *following from* than our earlier one.

Actually, the rule needed to make it generally provable that anything follows from a contradiction is not particularly intuitive. It is the rule

$$
\frac{A}{A \vee B}
$$

which is called *Addition* (Add.). Defenders of this rule point out that if *A* is true, then obviously for any statement *B*, *either A* is true *or B* is, *or* they both are. So Addition will never lead us from true premises to a false conclusion. All the same, Addition is an odd and rather uncomfortable rule to have in a system of logic, and it has other consequences just as odd as itself.

The basic oddness of the Addition rule is that it enables us to introduce statements into the conclusion that do not even occur in the premises. Some odd consequences of the Addition rule are that if you have a true statement, call it A, you can add the negation of any arbitrary statement, say $\sim Z$, to A by Addition to get $A \vee \sim Z$. By Commutation this is equivalent to $\sim Z \vee A$, and this is our way of writing "If Z then B." So given Addition and our admittedly rather weak sense of *if . . . then*, we can say that given a true statement we can get a true conditional with an entirely irrelevant antecedent. For instance, it is true that Neil Armstrong was the first man on the moon, so given this procedure it is also true that if the moon is made of green cheese, then Neil Armstrong was the first man on the moon.

Similarly, if we have a false statement, call it B, then the negation of B, that is, $\sim B$, will be true. We can add any arbitrary statement, say Y, to $\sim B$ by Addition and get the true statement $\sim B \vee Y$, which we can read "If B then Y." Since, for example, it is false that Buzz Aldrin was the first man on the moon, then it would be true that *if* Buzz Aldrin were the first man on the moon, the moon is made of cheesecake.

The word used for our weak sense of *if . . . then* is "material implication," and these consequences of Addition are sometimes called the "paradoxes of material implication": a true statement is materially implied by any statement and a false statement materially implies any statement. To accept Addition and the definition of "If A then B" as $\sim A \vee B$ is to accept those paradoxes.

So, for the moment, we will follow the practice of *starring* any proof or refutation with contradictory premises, marking it off as a special and somewhat peculiar kind of case. We will do this by putting *SCP (for "self-contradictory premises") below the questioned statement as soon as we discover the self-contradiction; for example:

1. S L?
2. $\sim S$ *SCP

We will not always discover the self-contradiction immediately. Sometimes it will become apparent only after some cancellation; for example, the argument

1. $\sim V \vee S \vee N$
2. $\sim N$
3. $\sim S$ V?
4. $\sim V$

depending on where we start canceling, we can get V and $\sim V$, N and $\sim N$ or S and $\sim S$ as final lines.

A final complication that may occur in actual arguments is that a subject or predicate term that is apparently the same in two statements may actually be different in the two statements. Thus it may be true that (Mr.) Spock is from the planet Vulcan and true that (Dr.) Spock is from the planet Earth, but the two Spocks are not the same, and it would be unwise to conclude that someone is both from Vulcan and from Earth.

The Archeologist's Argument

The archeologist's argument at the beginning of this chapter is an example of a complex argument with which we can now deal. We can symbolize the premises as follows, using the convention of underlining the first letter of a key word in each sentence and using that letter to symbolize the statement.

The loss of literacy could be explained by the killing of all the people who knew who to read and write or by the failure of older persons who were literate to teach writing to younger persons.

$K \vee F$

If older literate people failed to teach younger people to write, then this must either be because of some religious or social reason or because writing was useless.

$\sim F \vee R \vee U$

If writing was used for poetic or religious purposes, it would not have become useless.

$\sim P \vee \sim U$

If writing was used only for keeping palace accounts, then if the palaces were destroyed, writing would become useless.

$\sim A \vee \sim D \vee U$

All the people who knew how to read and write could not have been killed.

$\sim K$

There were no religious reasons for not teaching writing to younger people.

$\sim R$

The palaces were destroyed.

D

Writing was used only for keeping palace records.

   A

We can summarize the premises as follows:

1. $K \vee F$
2. $\sim F \vee R \vee U$
3. $\sim P \vee \sim U$
4. $\sim A \vee \sim D \vee U$
5. $\sim K$
6. $\sim R$
7. D
8. A

And complete the argument as follows:

9.	$K \vee R \vee U$	1, 2 CC
10.	$K \vee R \vee \sim P$	9, 3 CC
11.	$R \vee \sim P$	10, 5 SC
12.	$\sim P$	11, 6 SC
13.	$\sim A \vee U$	4, 7 SC
14.	U	8, 13 SC

We can see that the only two statements that do not cancel out are no P and U. So the conclusion of the archeologists' argument could be expressed as, "Writing was not used for poetic or religious purposes, and it became useless."

Invalid Arguments

Some arguments in ordinary language closely resemble good arguments, but the conclusion does not follow from the premises. Thus

If A then B

A
_____

B

is a good argument and so is

If *A* then *B*
not-*B*
___
not-*A*

But arguments that sound very much like these good arguments are

If *A* then *B*   If *A* then *B*
B   not-*A*
___   ___
A   not-*B*

and neither of these is a good argument. However, if the arguments are correctly translated into our symbolism, the two good arguments are, as we have seen, variations of simple cancellation, but the two invalid arguments do not cancel to yield the alleged conclusion:

$\sim A \vee B$ $\sim A \vee B$ $\sim A \vee B$ $\sim A \vee B$
A B $\sim B$ $\sim A$
___   ___   ___   ___
B A $\sim A$ $\sim B$

Similarly, the following is a good argument:

If *A* then *B*
If *B* then *C*
___
If *A* then *C*

In fact it is a variation of Cancel and Collect:

$\sim A \vee B$
$\sim B \vee C$
___
$\sim A \vee C$

But seemingly similar bad arguments such as

If *A* then *B*
If *C* then *B*
___
If *A* then *C*

do not "cancel out."

$$\sim A \lor B$$
$$\sim C \lor B$$
$$\overline{\sim A \lor C}$$

Most deceptive bad arguments, in fact, are deceptive precisely because they resemble good arguments, and it is useful to be aware of the most frequent "look alike" bad arguments. But if we put the arguments correctly into our symbolic form, the right answers come out automatically; an invalid argument is one that does not cancel to give the conclusion or the negation of the conclusion.

It is worth noting that invalid arguments are ones that we would mark NC if they were offered as proofs or refutations; the fact that an argument is invalid does not mean that its conclusion is false, just that the conclusion does not follow from the premises. Again, remember that the fact that a conclusion *does* follow from a set of premises does not mean that the conclusion is true *unless* the premises are true. True premises establish a conclusion that follows from them, but if a conclusion follows from false premises it may or may not be true.

In this section all of our premises are either simple statements or disjunctions. Simple statements will just be true or false, but a disjunction can go wrong in somewhat more complex ways. Suppose there are three possibilities in a given situation: for example, Spock is on the *Enterprise or* on a planet *or* on board another starship. If I say, "Spock is on the *Enterprise* or on a planet" this is *partly* correct, but it does not cover all the possibilities. If I go on to argue, "Spock is not on a planet, therefore he is on the *Enterprise*" I may be wrong, because he may be neither place and on board another starship. Thus a disjunction may be right in what it includes, but wrong in what it excludes.

A disjunction can therefore be more deceptive than a simple statement. If I say, "Spock is not a Vulcan" I am obviously wrong, but if I say, "Spock is on the *Enterprise* or on a planet" I am *partly* right; those are two of the three possibilities. One special source of misunderstanding is the difference between *contradictories* and *contraries*. If I say, "Either Spock is a Vulcan or he is not" this, which we would symbolize as $V \lor \sim V$, covers all the possibilities; either V or $\sim V$ must be true. But if I say, "Spock is a Vulcan or an Earthman," although *both* cannot be true they *could* both be false; Spock might be a Klingon.

In a number of cases it is easy to confuse contraries with contradictories; because we are aware that both of two possibilities cannot be true, we slip into thinking that one or the other must be. But many more

statements are contrary than are contradictory; even apparent contradictories may leave some possibility overlooked. If I say, "either it is
raining or it isn't" these sound like contradictories, but there may be
borderline cases that we would hesitate to call either rain or not rain.
Certainly, if we have in mind the extreme cases of clear weather or pouring
rain there are many intermediate cases. It is always wise, then, when we
have apparent contradictories to make sure that they really cover all the
possibilities and that there is not some concealed third possibility.

Chapter Summary

In this chapter we introduced the idea of *simple statement* and of abbreviating simple statements by single capital letters. We discussed the
denial of a simple statement and gave a symbol for denial, $\sim$, placed in
front of the statement. We defined *disjunction*, distinguished between
inclusive and *exclusive* disjunction, and gave a symbol for disjunction,
$\vee$ placed between two statements. We then examined some simple arguments involving disjunction and negation: Simple Cancellation (SC) and
Cancel and Collect (CC). The basic patterns are:

$A \vee B$	Simple		$A \vee B$	Cancel and
$\sim A$	Cancellation		$\sim B \vee C$	Collect
B	(SC)		$A \vee C$	(CC)

We saw that a great variety of arguments are variations of SC, CC,
or a combination of the two. We then introduced some *equivalences* or
"two-way" rules which enable us to go back and forth between alternative
forms of a statement. The two equivalences introduced first were:

A	Double		$A \vee B$	Commutation
$\sim \sim A$	Negation		$B \vee A$	(Com.)
	(DN)			

followed by two forms of Repetition:

A	Repetition		A	Repetition
$A \vee A$	(Rep.)		A	(Rep.)
			A	

We then gave a *Proof Rule* and a *Refutation Rule*, showing how cancellation methods could be used for proof and refutation. We distinguished between proving a statement from certain premises and *establishing* a statement by proving it from true premises, and between refuting a statement from certain premises and *condemning* a statement by refuting it from true premises.

We considered simple and complex arguments involving *and, if . . . then*, and *if and only if*, but did not give separate symbols for these connecting words. We considered some special problems arising from *if and only if* and from contradictory premises.

We introduced conventions for writing proofs, refutations, and arguments that leave open a given statement. We discussed some problems that arise in connection with real-life arguments: ambiguity of terms, "look alike" bad arguments, disjunctions that cover only some of the possibilities, and confusions between contraries and contradictories.

With the techniques you have learned in this chapter, you should be able to symbolize almost any set of premises involving only simple statements and complex statements made up of simple statements, to prove or refute a questionable statement relative to those premises, or show that it is left open by those premises. If no conclusion is indicated, you should be able to find a conclusion or show that no conclusion follows from those premises. You should be able to test most arguments given in the section on statement logic in standard textbooks.

You may have difficulty with any very complex sets of premises that do not fit easily into our disjunctive form, especially arguments involving complex combinations of *or, and, if . . . then*, or *if and only if*. You will not be able to make some of the kinds of tests for good and bad arguments found in some introductory books of logic, but this will usually be because you have had no need of such tests since you can perform the same tasks by cancellation methods. So far, you will not be familiar with common symbols for *and, if . . . then*, or *if and only if*, or be able to read statements or arguments written using these symbols. These deficiencies will be repaired in the next chapter.

Practical Applications

Check your Argument File for arguments that can be handled by the techniques of this chapter. Look out for uses of the "logical words" such as *not, or, if . . . then, if and only if.* (Hint: Remember that an *if . . . then* statement *by itself* is not an argument, but often is a clue to the presence of an argument.) If you cannot handle an argument in the simple system, set it aside to see if the techniques of the next chapter can handle it.

Exercise 3-4

Symbolize the following arguments and prove or refute the indicated conclusion, if possible. If the conclusion can be neither proved nor refuted, write "Invalid."

1. If the Universe is expanding, then light from the stars will exhibit a shift to the red end of the spectrum. Light from the stars does exhibit such a red shift. Therefore, the Universe is expanding.

*2. If the Universe is expanding, then if there is more matter in the Universe than an amount we will call M, the Universe will eventually stop expanding and begin to contract. If there is less matter than M, the Universe will expand infinitely. The visible matter in the Universe amounts to less than M. Therefore, the Universe will expand infinitely.

3. If the amount of visible matter in the Universe, plus the amount of invisible matter in the Universe, is more than M, then the Universe will eventually contract. Invisible matter must be in the form of "black holes" or of indetectable particles. If the amount of invisible matter plus the amount of visible matter in the Universe is greater than M then the Universe will contract.

4. If the Universe contracts after expanding, there is probably a cycle of expansions and contractions. If there is a cycle of expansions and contractions, the Universe would have no beginning. The Universe is expanding, and if the amount of matter is greater than M, it will contract after expanding. Thus, if the mass of the Universe is greater than M, the Universe would have no beginning.

5. If background radiation in the Universe is too great to be accounted for by one expansion-contraction cycle, it must be due to repeated cycles. But if the amount of background radiation is too great to be accounted for by one cycle but is still finite, then it must be due to a finite number of repeated cycles. If it is due to a finite number of repeated cycles, then the Universe had a beginning. Thus, if the background radiation is too

great to be accounted for by one cycle but is still finite, then the Universe had a beginning.

Exercise 3-5

These arguments represent some of Michael Ventris's reasoning in his decipherment of Linear B (see Chapter One). Symbolize the arguments and see if they are valid proofs. If the argument is not valid as it stands, see if you can supply an obvious missing premise that will make the argument valid.

1. Linear B writing is either ideographic or syllabic or alphabetic. Ideographic systems have thousands of symbols, alphabetic systems have only about 20 or 30, while syllabic systems have between 40 and 100 symbols. Linear B is a system of writing with about 90 symbols. Therefore, Linear B is a syllabic system.

*2. If words are written in a syllabic system that has signs only for pure vowels and for consonants followed by vowels, then a pure vowel will occur rarely inside a word but fairly often at the beginning of words. Signs number 8, 38, and 61 in Linear B occur rarely inside words, but often at the beginning of words. Therefore, they are pure vowels.

3. If one symbol visually unlike another is sometimes written by mistake for the other, then it is likely that they have the same sound. Sign 38 is sometimes written by mistake for 28, and 3 is sometimes written by mistake for 11. Therefore, it is likely that 38 has the same sound as 28, and that 3 has the same sound as 11.

4. If the language of Linear B is like other languages in the area, differences of number and gender are marked by differences in the final vowel of a word. If Linear B is a syllabary system, then differences in final vowel will be written as different syllables (consisting of a consonant and vowel). But if differences in final vowel are written as different syllables and the same vowels mark gender and number differences in different words, then we can discover which syllables have the same vowel. Thus, supposing that the language of Linear B is like the other languages in the area and that the same vowels mark number and gender differences in different words, we can discover which syllables have the same vowel.

5. If descriptive words found with pictographs of women and lists of women's names have different final syllables than the same words found with pictographs of men and lists of men's names, then the final syllables of these words mark differences in gender. If these final syllables mark differences in gender, then they probably have the same vowel. So if descriptive words found with pictographs of women and lists of women's names do have different final syllables than the same words found with

Linear B writing. The tripod tablet from Pylos.

pictographs of men and lists of men's names, then the final syllables of these words probably have the same vowel.

Exercise 3-6

Symbolize these arguments from Plato's dialogue Meno, *giving your own "dictionary" of letters to symbolize each simple statement. Then prove or refute the conclusions given, or if there is no conclusion find the conclusion. If the argument is invalid or if you think a conclusion cannot be reached in an argument with no conclusion given, write Invalid or NC.*

1. If Meno's first definition of virtue is a good one, then it would be reasonable to define *bee* by naming the kinds of bees. But that would not be reasonable. So Meno's first definition of virtue is not a good one.

*2. If we define *bee* by saying what all kinds of bees have in common, we should define *virtue* by saying what all kinds of virtue have in common. We do define *bee* by saying what all kinds of bees have in common. Therefore . . .

3. Justice is either the whole of virtue or part of virtue. If justice is the whole of virtue, then if courage is a virtue courage is justice. Courage is not justice. Therefore . . .

4. If the power of acquiring good things is virtue, then either we would have to acquire these good things justly or we acquire them unjustly. If we would have to acquire these good things justly, then all virtue is justice. If we would not have to acquire these good things justly, then theft would be virtuous. But theft is not virtuous, and all virtue is not justice. Therefore . . .

5. A man cannot discover what he knows and he cannot discover what he does not know. For if he knows it he cannot discover it, and if he does not know it he does not know what to look for. If he does not know what to look for, he cannot discover it. He either knows it or does not know it.

6. If the slave boy knows geometrical truths, he either learned them in this life or in a previous existence. He does know geometrical truths and he did not learn them in this life. If the slave boy learned something in a previous life, then the soul preexists the body. Therefore . . .

*7. If virtue is wisdom, then it must be acquired. If virtue comes by nature, it is not acquired. Virtue does not come by nature. Therefore . . .

8. If true opinion is as good as knowledge for acting correctly, then if virtue is not knowledge it could be true opinion. Virtue is not knowledge,

but true opinion is as good as knowledge for acting rightly. If virtue could be true opinion, then it could be a gift of the gods. Therefore . . .

9. If virtue is the same as acquiring wealth, then either it consists of acquiring wealth justly or acquiring it unjustly. Virtue could not consist of acquiring wealth unjustly. Therefore, if virtue does not consist of acquiring wealth justly . . .

10. If virtue consisted of acquiring wealth justly, we would have to understand what *justly* meant before we understood what *virtue* means. But if justice is a kind of virtue, we could not understand what *justly* meant before understanding what virtue means. Since justice is a kind of virtue . . .

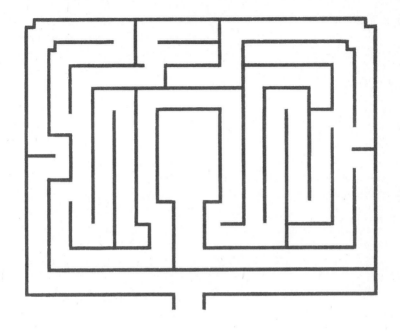

CHAPTER FOUR

Statement Logic: The Complete System

THE THEOLOGIAN'S ARGUMENT

A theologian* argues as follows:

Either eternal life is the fulfillment of our present hope, or it is not. If it is, then there can be nothing further to hope for. But a temporal existence without any further hope . . . could only appear as unending stagnation and boredom. If, on the other hand, it is not the fulfillment of present hope, then there must be something further for which we can hope, and eternal life could no longer be the destiny which man seeks.

If we supply the understood premise, "If eternal life could only appear as unending stagnation and boredom, it could not be the fulfillment of our present hope," can we validly derive the conclusion, "If eternal life is the fulfillment of our present hope, it is not a temporal existence"?

* Michael Simpson, S. J., *Death and Eternal Life* (Hales Corners, Wisconsin: Clergy Book Service, 1971).

How can we extend the basic principles of statement logic to deal with arguments that could not be handled in the simple system?

In the previous chapter we defined a *simple statement* as one with one predicate and one or more subjects, introduced the negation operator ~ that forms new statements from other statements, and the "either . . . or" connective ∨ that forms compound statements from simple or compound statements. In this chapter we will introduce several more connectives and give rules for their use, but we will also provide a new way of looking at statement logic and some new rules that accompany this new way of looking at it. Some of the difficulties we encountered in the simple system of statement logic suggest the new approach we will take to statement logic.

Consider, for example, the problem of contradictory premises. If we define deductive *following from* so that B follows from A just in case it is unreasonable to accept A but reject B, it is not clear what we are to say about arguments with contradictory premises. True enough, it is unreasonable to accept contradictory premises, so it follows that it is unreasonable to accept contradictory premises *and* reject a given conclusion. But it is also unreasonable to accept contradictory premises *and accept* a given conclusion, since the unreasonableness of accepting a contradiction carries over to accepting a contradiction *and* another statement.

One way of solving the problem of contradictory premises and some related problems is simply to define deductive *following from* in a new and somewhat more restricted way: B follows from A just in case it is impossible for A to be true and B false. This has the effect of deciding that any statement whatsoever follows from a contradiction since it is impossible that a contradiction be true and so impossible that a contradiction be true *and* any other statement be false. Defining deductive *following from* in terms of truth and falsity in this way pushes us in the direction of what is called a *truth-functional* statement logic, where everything is defined in terms of the truth or falsity of statements, rather than, for example, the meaning or the context of utterance of statements.

Truth Tables and Variables

We can see how this works by considering how we can define $\sim$ and $\vee$ in terms of truth and falsity. If a statement A is true its denial $\sim A$ is false, and if A is false $\sim A$ is true. We can now define $\sim$ in terms of this fact by giving the following *truth table*:

p	$\sim p$
T	F
F	T

We interpret this as follows: p is a "place-holder"—it marks a place into which we can insert any particular statement, simple or compound. The table tells us that if what we insert in the place of p is a true statement then the negation of that statement is false, and if what we insert in the place of p is a false statement the negation of that statement is true.

The letter p and other lower-case letters we will use presently are *variables* somewhat like the letters x, y, etc., in algebra. The variables in algebra are not numbers but rather mark places in which numerals can be inserted. Similarly, the variables we will use in statement logic are not themselves statements. By definition, statements must be definitely true or definitely false. We may not know which it is but a definite statement must be one or the other. But a variable simply works a place into which a statement can be inserted, perhaps a true statement, perhaps a false one. In an algebraic equation like $y^2 = y \times y$ it is pointless to ask whether y is larger than 13; it depends on what you fill in for y. So in a statement pattern written with variables, such as $p \vee \sim p$, it is pointless to ask whether p is true; it depends on which statement you substitute for p. But just as $y^2 = y \times y$ will be true for any number you substitute for y, $p \vee \sim p$ will be true for any statement you substitute for p.

To see this, let us define $\vee$ in terms of truth or falsity. We will need two variables p and q and a systematic way of writing down *combinations* of truth values. Thus we could substitute true statements for both p and q, a true statement for p and a false one for q, a false statement for p and a true one for q, or false statements for both p and q. We write down these combinations and then show the value of $p \vee q$ for each possible combination:

p q	$p \vee q$
T T	T
T F	T
F T	T
F F	F

This corresponds to our definition of $\vee$ as an *inclusive or:* a statement $A \vee B$ is true if A is true *or* if B is *or* if they both are, and only false if both A and B are false.

Whenever we write truth tables we will use this format, writing the possible values of the statements that can be substituted for the variables in "reference columns" to the left, and putting the corresponding values of the compound expression under the connective of that expression. Where there is more than one connective, we will put the value of the compound under the *main* connective, a term we will define presently.

The reference columns we will construct as follows: For n variables there will be 2^n lines. The rightmost column will consist of alternative T and F, the next column to the left pairs of T's and F's, and for each succeeding column to the left we will double the number of T's and F's in a group. Thus the reference columns for three and four variables respectively will be:

p	q	r		p	q	r	s
T	T	T		T	T	T	T
T	T	F		T	T	T	F
T	F	T		T	T	F	T
T	F	F		T	T	F	F
F	T	T		T	F	T	T
F	T	F		T	F	T	F
F	F	T		T	F	F	T
F	F	F		T	F	F	F
				F	T	T	T
				F	T	T	F
				F	T	F	T
				F	T	F	F
				F	F	T	T
				F	F	T	F
				F	F	F	T
				F	F	T	F

Tautologies

We can now see that the expression $p \lor \sim p$ must be true no matter what statements we substitute for p. We need only one reference column:

p	$p \lor \sim p$
T	
F	

and we can fill in the columns under p in the expression by copying the reference column:

p	$p \lor \sim p$	
T	T	T
F	F	F

The definition of $\sim$ tells us to reverse the T and F under the $\sim$:

p	$p \lor \sim p$	
T	T	F T
F	F	T F

and the definition of $\lor$ tells us how to fill in the column under the connective:

p	$p \lor \sim p$
T	T T F T
F	F T T F

So we can see that the expression $p \lor \sim p$ will give a value of true for *any* statements that are substituted for its variables. Patterns of variables with this property are called *tautologies*, and expressions formed from such patterns by putting specific statements in the gaps marked by the variables will be *logically true statements*—true by definition of the operators and connectives they contain.

Some tautologies and the logically true statements that result from substituting statements for the variables are so useful for dealing with arguments that we will name them and refer to them as *rules*. A rule of deductive logic is a logically true statement, or the tautology that is the pattern of such a statement, which we find useful to list and name to enable us to deal with arguments. Remember that a tautology, or any expression written with variables, is *not* a statement and is not true or false. An expression written with variables is a statement *pattern*, and a tautology is a statement pattern that always gives a true statement no matter what statements are substituted for the variables. Of course, we must always substitute the *same* statement for the same variable.

New Connectives

We will now define in terms of truth tables several new connectives. The first connective corresponds to the English *and*. A compound statement composed of two statements joined by our *and-like* connective · will be true if both component statements are true, and false if either component statement is false or if both are. In terms of a truth table this is:

p q	*p · q*
T T	T
T F	F
F T	F
F F	F

Our next connective will be one that resembles the English words *if . . . then*. As we saw in the last chapter, *if . . . then* can have many meanings, but the common core of all these meanings is given by saying that "If *A* then *B*" is false whenever *A* is true and *B* false. In Chapter Three we conveyed this by translating "If *A* then *B*" as $\sim A \vee B$. We will now introduce a specific connective $\supset$ defined as follows:

p q	*p ⊃ q*
T T	T
T F	F
F T	T
F F	T

This amounts to just the same as writing *if . . . then* as $\sim p \vee q$. In fact, that would give us the same column of T's and F's under the connective, as we can see:

p q	~p ∨ q
T T	F T T T
T F	F T F F
F T	T F T T
F F	T F T F

Note that when we *define* a connective using a truth table we simply put the appropriate column of T's and F's under the connective; however, where we have to figure out the value of an expression we fill in the columns under the variables by copying the appropriate reference columns, and then get the value of the whole expression by using the definitions of ∼ and the connectives. We always fill in the columns under ∼ applied to single variables before going on to the connectives.

The final connective we will define in this chapter is *if and only if*. As we saw in Chapter Three, "*A* if and only if *B*" is equivalent to "If *A* then *B* and if *B* then *A*." The symbol for *if and only if* will be ≡ and the truth table will be:

p q	p ≡ q
T T	T
T F	F
F T	F
F F	T

As you can see $A \equiv B$ will be true where A and B have the *same* value, whether both true or both false, but $A \equiv B$ will be false if A and B have different truth values. This gives us the same pattern as the combination of the two appropriate *if . . . then*'s.

p q	(p ⊃ q) · (q ⊃ p)
T T	T T T T T T T
T F	T F F F F T T
F T	F T T F T F F
F T	F T F T F T F

The grouping of the two conditionals by parentheses is a device necessary to avoid ambiguity when we have more than one connective like ⊃ or ≡, and also when we have two different connectives in the same statement. In Chapter Three we were able to avoid using parentheses because we

had only expressions with one kind of connective, and that connective
∨ was such that order and grouping did not matter: $A \vee B$ was the
same as $B \vee A$, and in $A \vee B \vee C$ it did not matter how we grouped
A, B, and C. But $A \supset B$ is not the same as $B \supset A$, and even though $A \equiv B$
is the same as $B \equiv A$, still $(A \equiv B) \equiv C$ is not the same as $A \equiv (B \equiv C)$.
So from now on we will use parentheses to indicate grouping in *all*
expressions with more than one connective, even when all the connectives
are ∨ or ·, where it is not strictly necessary.

Parentheses and the Main Connective

Grouping by means of parentheses is a way of avoiding possible ambiguities, as we saw. For instance, $(p \supset q) \cdot (q \supset p)$ is a quite different
pattern from $p \supset ((q \cdot q) \supset p)$, which would read "If p then if q and q
then p". In fact, grouped in this way the pattern becomes a tautology:

p q	$p \supset ((q \cdot q) \supset p))$
T T	T T TTT T T
T F	T T FFF T T
F T	F T TTT F F
F F	F T FFF T F

The way we figure out complex expressions such as this or the last
one is as follows: We take the connective inside the greatest number of
parentheses, in this case $q \cdot q$, and fill in the column using the appropriate
definition (in this case the definition of ·).

p q	$p \supset ((q \cdot q) \supset p)$
T T	T TTT T
T F	T FFF T
F T	F TTT F
F F	F FFF F

We then go to the connective inside the next greatest number of parentheses, in this case the second ⊃ :

p q	$p \supset ((q \cdot q) \supset p)$
T T	T TTT T T
T F	T FFF T T
F T	F TTT F F
F F	F FFF T F

We finish by filling in under the connective inside the least number of parentheses, giving us the table we gave first. When this formula is used, it does not matter whether or not we enclose the *whole* expression in parentheses, but there is no point in doing so, and we will leave off outside parentheses unless we want to deny a whole complex expression. When we do, we will write the $\sim$ outside parentheses enclosing the whole expression, for example, $\sim(p \supset ((q \cdot q) \supset p))$. In such a case the $\sim$ is the *main operator* of the negated expression; where the whole expression is not negated, there will be a connective inside the least number of parentheses and this will be the *main connective*.

   An alternate definition of a tautology can now be given: an expression that when worked out by truth table in the way described will have only T's under its main operator or connective. A *contradiction* is an expression that when worked out in this way will have only F's under its main operator or connective. For example, $p \cdot \sim p$ is a contradiction:

p	$p \cdot \sim p$
T	T F F T
F	F F T F

   A *contingent* expression is one that when worked out has both T's and F's under its main operator or connective, for example, $p \cdot p$:

p	$p \cdot p$
T	T T T
F	F F F

Testing Validity by Truth Table

We are now in a position to give a new technique for showing that an argument is valid or invalid. To test an argument write out the premises joined with $\cdot$ and join the conclusion to the premises by $\supset$. Then replace the statements with variables and test the resulting pattern by truth table. If the resulting expression is a tautology, the argument is valid. We will demonstrate this on the valid argument patterns of Chapter Three. Simple Cancellation is:

$A \vee B$
$\sim A$
B

Written out as described above, the resulting statement is:

$((A \lor B) \cdot \sim A) \supset B$

Replacing statements with variables we get:

$((p \lor q) \cdot \sim p) \supset q$

and show that this is a tautology:

$p \ q$	$((p \lor q) \cdot \sim p) \supset q$
T T	T T T F F T T T
T F	T T F F F T T F
F T	F T T T T F T T
F F	F F F F T F T F

The same process for Cancel and Collect goes from

$\sim A \lor B$
$\sim B \lor C$
$\overline{\sim A \lor C}$

to $((\sim A \lor B) \cdot (\sim B \lor C)) \supset \sim A \lor C$
to $((\sim p \lor q) \cdot (\sim q \lor r)) \supset (\sim p \lor r)$

which checks out as a tautology. In working out this or any expression with some connectives inside the same number of parentheses, it does not matter which we do first, but for convenience always do the leftmost connectives first if they are inside the same number of parentheses.

New Rules

We will now begin to give some new rules in addition to those introduced in Chapter Three. All of them can be shown to be valid argument patterns by the truth-table method just described, but we will not bother to work out the truth tables. The first two rules have to do with ·

Simplification	$A \cdot B$
	A
(Simp.)	B

Conjunction	A
	B
(Conj.)	$A \cdot B$

In other words, two statements joined with · can be written as separate lines, and two separate lines can be written as one line joined with ·. Combining these rules with Cancel and Collect gives us a handy new rule

Cancel and Join	$\sim A \vee B$
	$A \cdot C$
(CJ)	$B \cdot C$

This can be shown to be a valid argument by truth table, but we can think of it as a new form of cancellation

$$\sim \cancel{A} \vee B$$
$$\cancel{A} \cdot C$$
$$\overline{B \cdot C}$$

We did not introduce it with the other cancellation rules since it would have been hard to explain why the conclusion is a *conjunction* (a statement whose main connective is ·) rather than a *disjunction* (a statement whose main connective is ∨. But we can now see why this must be so by the series of moves

1.	$\sim A \vee B$	$\left.\vphantom{\begin{matrix}a\\b\end{matrix}}\right\}$ $B \cdot C?$	
2.	$A \cdot C$		
3.	A		2 Simp.
4.	C		2 Simp.
5.	B		1, 3 SC
6.	$B \cdot C$		5, 4 Conj.

Our next several rules deal with arguments using ⊃ :

Modus	$A \supset B$	Modus	$A \supset B$	Hypothetical	$A \supset B$
Ponens	A	Tollens	$\sim B$	Syllogism	$B \supset C$
(MP)	B	(MT)	$\sim A$		$A \supset C$

All of these are arguments we dealt with in the last chapter by translating "If A then B" as $\sim A \vee B$ and using SC or CC; but it is useful to have them in this form if we want to avoid translating all of our statements into statements containing only $\vee$ and $\sim$ and no other connectives. Two patterns involving $\supset$ and $\vee$ are:

Constructive	$A \vee B$		Destructive	$\sim A \vee \sim B$
Dilemma	$A \supset C$		Dilemma	$C \supset A$
	$B \supset D$			$D \supset B$
	$C \vee D$			$\sim C \vee \sim D$

These can also be done by cancellation if the $A \supset C$, etc., are replaced by $\sim A \vee C$, etc.

Two arguments that work out by truth table but *cannot* be done by cancellation methods are:

Contradiction	$A \cdot \sim A$		Addition	A
(Contr.)	B		(Add.)	$A \vee B$

It is impossible for either argument to have a true premise and a false conclusion: The premise of Contradiction cannot be true, and if the premise of Addition is true the conclusion must be by definition of $\vee$. But both arguments are somewhat counterintuitive. In both cases we can get a statement in the conclusion that does not even appear in the premises and has nothing at all to do with the premises. These rules also have odd consequences, as we saw in Chapter Three, but it is important to realize that they are perfectly valid arguments: They will never lead us from premises to a false conclusion.

Most contemporary logicians have no reservations, or very few reservations, about Addition and Contradiction, and since these rules are included in the standard systems of statement logic, we will include them in ours. In fact, Addition is the important extension of our system. Given Addition, Contradiction is unnecessary, as the following proof shows:

1. $A \cdot \sim A$} B?
2. A 1 Simp.
3. $\sim A$ 1 Simp.
4. $A \vee B$ 2 Add.
5. B 4, 3 SC

Some logicians have been sufficiently troubled about this kind of derivation, and the fact that conclusions can be proved that have nothing to do with the premises, that they have tried to find systems of "relevance logic" that do not allow these consequences. Oddly enough, some of them have tried to block derivations like the one above by dropping Disjunctive Syllogism (the rule we call Simple Cancellation) rather than Addition. Of course this is technically feasible: We could block the proof above by doing away with Simplification, for that matter. But Simple Cancellation and Simplification are so basic and so intuitive that blocking proofs from contradictory premise by dropping them seems much too radical a solution.

For the rest of the book we will use Addition and Contradiction where necessary, but will call attention to proofs that need to make use of these rules; we will find that surprisingly few proofs of real-life arguments need either of these rules. The most frequent use of Addition is to show that if a statement is false, the conjunction of that statement with any other statement is false. Contradiction is useful in doing certain kinds of proofs, as we will see in the last section of this chapter. It is also true that given Contradiction and the other rules, Addition could be proved unnecessary, but we would need some techniques to which we have not yet come.

With SC, CC, CJ, Simp., Conj., MP, MT, HS, CD, DD, Rep., and Add., we have a dozen one-way rules. We previously had several two-way rules, Double Negation, Commutation, and Repetition:

$$\text{DN} \quad \frac{A}{\sim\sim A} \qquad \text{Com.} \quad \frac{A \vee B}{B \vee A} \qquad \text{Rep.} \quad \frac{A}{A \vee A} \qquad \text{Rep.} \quad \frac{A}{\begin{array}{c} A \\ A \end{array}}$$

To these we will add an absolute minimum of other two-way rules. First we will add Commutation for $\cdot$ and $\equiv$, and we will rewrite the second form of Repetition:

$$\text{Com.} \quad \frac{A \cdot B}{B \cdot A} \qquad \text{Com.} \quad \frac{A \equiv B}{B \equiv A} \qquad \text{Rep.} \quad \frac{A}{A \cdot A}$$

(With Simplification we can get the previous version of Repetition from this one.)

We next introduce some translation rules for $\supset$, which is called *Material Implication*, and $\equiv$, which is called *Material Equivalence*:

Definition of Material Implication (DMI)	$$\frac{A \supset B}{\sim A \lor B}$$	Definition of Material Equivalence (DME)	$$\frac{A \equiv B}{(A \supset B) \cdot (B \supset A)}$$

We next give some transformations with $\sim$ and $\cdot$ and $\lor$, called De Morgan's Rules (De M):

$$\frac{\sim(A \lor B)}{\sim A \cdot \sim B}$$	De Morgan's Rules (De M)	$$\frac{\sim(A \cdot B)}{\sim A \lor \sim B}$$

Two rules involving negation and $\supset$ or $\equiv$ are:

Transposition (Transp.)	$$\frac{A \supset B}{\sim B \supset \sim A}$$	Complementarity (Comp.)	$$\frac{A \equiv B}{\sim A \equiv \sim B}$$

The next two rules enable us to regroup expressions, with several occurrence, of "$\cdot$" or "$\lor$".

Association (Assoc.)	$$\frac{(A \cdot B) \cdot C}{A \cdot (B \cdot C)}$$
	$$\frac{(A \lor B) \lor C}{A \lor (B \lor C)}$$

Remember that in Chapter Three we did not bother with parentheses for complex disjunctions: The Association rules tell us that where we use parentheses with strings of $\lor$ or $\cdot$ we can group disjuncts or conjuncts in any convenient pairs.

Finally a set of rules which enables us to transform complex expressions into equivalent forms which may be more useful in a given argument:

Exportation (Exp.)	$$\frac{A \supset (B \supset C)}{(A \cdot B) \supset C}$$

Distribution (Dist.)	$A \cdot (B \vee C)$
	$\overline{\overline{(A \cdot B) \vee (A \cdot C)}}$
	$A \vee (B \cdot C)$
	$\overline{\overline{(A \vee B) \cdot (A \vee C)}}$

Absorption (Absorb.)	$A \supset B$
	$\overline{\overline{A \supset (A \cdot B)}}$

Remember that all two-way rules can be applied to parts of lines, but one-way rules can only apply to whole lines.

Thus it would be a *misuse* of Simplification to argue

1. $(A \cdot B) \supset C$ ⎫
2. B ⎬   ?
3. $B \supset C$ 1 Simp. WRONG!
4. C 2, 3 MP

since $A \cdot B$ is not a line but only part of a line. However, it would be quite in order to apply a two-way rule such as Commutation to part of a line *or* to a whole line:

1. $(A \cdot B) \supset C$ ⎫
2. B ⎬   ?
3. $(B \cdot A) \supset C$ 1 Com.
4. $B \supset (A \supset C)$ 3 Exp.
5. $A \supset C$ 2, 4 MP

To sum up—we have 12 names for two-way rules: DN, Com., Rep., DMI, DME, De M, Transp., Comp., Assoc., Exp., Dist., and Absorb., but some of these stand for several variations; counting this way there are 18 rules. With the 12 one-way rules, this gives us 24 (or 30 depending on how we count) rules. This is rather a lot to remember, but any fewer rules would make many complex proofs extremely hard to do. For a great number of arguments it will be possible to translate lines into one or more lines with either no connective or only $\vee$ as a connective and then proceed by cancellation. However, it will usually be much more simple and direct to use our 24 new rules in proofs and refutations rather than translating to cancel.

Table 4-1

The following ways of speaking are especially difficult to translate:

FORM	*A* even if *B*
EQUIVALENT TO	If *B* then *A* and if not *B* then *A* or simply *A*.
SYMBOLIZATION	$(B \supset A) \cdot (\sim B \supset A)$ or *A*
EXAMPLE	Kirk will obey his orders even if his ship is endangered. i.e., If his ship is endangered Kirk will obey his orders, and if his ship is not endangered Kirk will obey his orders, *or* Kirk will obey his orders.
FORM	*A* unless *B*
EQUIVALENT TO	If not *B* then *A* and if *B* then not *A*.
SYMBOLIZATION	$(\sim B \supset A) \cdot (B \supset \sim A)$ or $(\sim B \equiv A)$
EXAMPLE	Kirk will command the *Enterprise* unless he is incapacitated. i.e., If Kirk is not incapacitated he will command the *Enterprise*, and if Kirk is incapacitated he will not command the *Enterprise*.
FORM	Neither *A* nor *B*
EQUIVALENT TO	It is not true that either *A* or *B or* Not *A* and not *B*.
SYMBOLIZATION	$\sim (A \vee B)$ *or* $\sim A \cdot \sim B$
EXAMPLE	Neither Spock nor Kirk is a doctor. i.e., It is not true that either Spock or Kirk is a doctor, *or* Spock is not a doctor and Kirk is not a doctor.

Exercise 4-1

Check these arguments for validity by truth table.

1. $P \supset \sim S$
    $\sim P$
    ___
    S

2. $L \supset G$
    $S \supset G$
    $L \vee S$
    ___
    G

3. $A \supset L$
    $M \supset U$
    $\sim L \cdot \sim U$
    ___
    $\sim A \cdot \sim M$

*4. $E \supset S$
    $L \supset E$
    L
    ___
    S

5. $K \supset (F \vee H)$
    $S \supset \sim F$
    S
    ___
    $\sim K$

6. $M \supset S$
    $R \supset \sim S$
    ___
    M

*7. $M \equiv E$
       $\sim M$
       ———
       $\sim E$

8. $O \supset (M \supset L)$
       $O \supset N$
       $\sim N$
       ————————
       $\sim L$

9. $W \supset (\sim S \supset M)$
       $\sim S$
       ————————————
       $W \supset M$

10. $C \supset \sim S$
       $\sim S \supset F$
       $C \cdot \sim F$
       ————————
       S

Exercise 4-2

Symbolize the following statements using the dictionary below and our new connectives. (Note: Translate "A even if B" as "If B then A and if not B then A".)

N # The new laboratories will be classified P1.
T # The new laboratories will be classified P2.
E # The new laboratories will be classified P3.
F # The new laboratories will be classified P4.
I # The new laboratories will be isolated in some way.
M # The new laboratories will be moderately contained.
H # The new laboratories will be highly contained.
O # Occasional microorganisms could escape.
S # Substantial quantities of microorganisms could escape.
V # Experiments with virulent pathogens are done in the new laboratories.
A # The new laboratories will be safe.
D # Recombinant DNA experiments will be done in the new laboratories.

1. The new laboratories will be classified P1, P2, P3, or P4.
2. If the new laboratories are classified as P1, they will not be isolated in any way, but they are designated as P4 if they will be highly contained.
3. If the new laboratories are classified as P3, they will be moderately contained and occasional microorganisms could escape but not substantial quantities.
*4. If experiments with virulent pathogens are done in the new laboratories, if even occasional quantities of microorganisms could escape the laboratories would not be safe.
5. If the new laboratories were classified as P1 or P2, then substantial quantities of microorganisms could escape and they could not be safe if experiments with virulent pathogens were done in them.

6. If recombinant DNA experiments are done in the new laboratories, then the new laboratories will not be safe. But if recombinant DNA experiments are done in the new laboratories, then experiments with virulent pathogens will be done.

*7. If it is the case that even if the new laboratories are classified as P4 occasional organisms will escape, then even if the new laboratories are highly contained they will not be safe if experiments with virulent pathogens are done there.

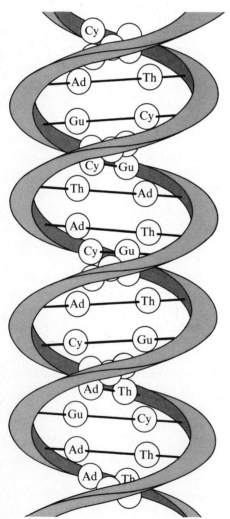

A fragment of the double-stranded helical DNA molecule.

8. If doing recombinant DNA experiments does lead to doing experiments with virulent organisms, then the new laboratories are not safe even if the laboratories are classified P4, supposing that occasional organisms will escape even if the new laboratories are highly contained.

9. If the new laboratories are safe if they are classified P4, then either it is not true that if recombinant DNA experiments are done at the new laboratories then experiments with virulent pathogens will be done, or else it is not true that even if the new laboratories are highly contained then at least some organisms will escape.

10. Provided that no experiments are done with virulent pathogens and the new laboratories moderately contained, then the new laboratories are safe even if they are not classified P4.

Exercise 4-3

Using your symbolic translation of statements 1–10 in Exercise 4-2:

*1. Show that statement 7 follows from statement 4.
2. Does statement 7 follow from statement 5?
3. Is statement 4 equivalent to or implied by statement 8?
4. Does statement 7 follow from any statements other than 4?
5. Is statement 10 refuted by statements 1 through 5?

Truth-Table Shortcut

It is possible to test any argument, however complex, for validity by the truth-table method described above. But for any argument of any appreciable degree of complexity, truth-table methods are extremely cumbersome and tedious. More useful is a truth-table shortcut method for showing that an argument is invalid.

To use this truth-table shortcut method to check the validity of an argument, we proceed as follows: Consider an argument such that we are not sure whether the conclusion can be proved or refuted by the premises; for example:

$$A \equiv \sim B$$
$$\sim B \equiv C \Big\} \quad A?$$
$$\sim C$$

To apply a truth-table shortcut to find whether the premises prove the conclusion, we assume that the conclusion is false and try to find a *consistent* assignment of truth values that make all the premises true. Assuming A false in the conclusion forces us to assume A false in premise 1; we show this by writing F over both A's:

$$
\left.
\begin{array}{l}
\text{F} \\
A \equiv \sim B \\
\sim B \equiv C \\
\sim C
\end{array}
\right\}
\quad
\begin{array}{l}
\text{F} \\
A
\end{array}
$$

If A is false, to make $A \equiv \sim B$ true $\sim B$ must have the same truth value, so B must be true in both occurrences to make $\sim B$ false:

$$
\left.
\begin{array}{l}
\text{F \quad F T} \\
A \equiv \sim B \\
\text{F T} \\
\sim B \equiv C \\
\sim C
\end{array}
\right\}
\quad
\begin{array}{l}
\text{F} \\
A
\end{array}
$$

To make $\sim B \equiv C$ true, we must make C false. But then $\sim C$ is true:

$$
\left.
\begin{array}{l}
\text{FT F T} \\
A \equiv \sim B \\
\text{F TT F} \\
\sim B \equiv C \\
\text{T F} \\
\sim C
\end{array}
\right\}
\quad
\begin{array}{l}
\text{F} \\
A?
\end{array}
$$

and all the premises are true while the conclusion is false. Thus the argument is invalid.

Consider a more complex case:

$$
\left.
\begin{array}{ll}
1. & A \equiv B \\
2. & B \supset (C \cdot D) \\
3. & D \supset E \\
4. & \sim F \supset \sim C \\
5. & \sim((E \cdot F) \cdot G) \\
6. & G
\end{array}
\right\}
\quad A?
$$

Again we start out by making both A's false.

      F   F
1. $A \equiv B\}$ $A?$
    $\vdots$

But if A is false, to make $A \equiv B$ true we must make B false:

     F T F
1. $A \equiv B$

If B is false in premise 1, it must be false in premise 2:

     F
2. $B \supset (C \cdot D)$

A conditional with a false antecedent will be true whether its consequent is true or false, so nothing so far forces us to give any particular values to C and D. It may be useful now to skip down to line 6; to make this line true, G must be true:

     T
6. G

But that forces us to make G true in line 5:

         T
5. $\sim((E \cdot F) \cdot G)$

This means that E or F or both must be false to make line 5 true. Try making them both false and we get:

     T F F F F T
5. $\sim((E \cdot F) \cdot G$

If E is false in line 5, it must be false in line 3, so D must be false to make line 3 true:

     F T F
3. $D \supset E$

If *F* is false in line 5, it must be false in line 4, and so *C* must be false to make line 4 true:

    T FT T F
4. $\sim F \supset \sim C$

To be consistent, *C* and *D* must be false in line 2; but that makes line 2 true:

    F T F F F
2. $B \supset (C \cdot D)$

Thus we *can* make all six premises true and the conclusion false:

    F T F
1. $A \equiv B$

    F T F F F
2. $B \supset (C \cdot D)$

    F T F
3. $D \supset E$ F

    T FT T F   A?
4. $\sim F \supset \sim C$

    T F F F F T
5. $\sim((E \cdot F) \cdot G)$

    T
6. *G*

Thus the premises do not prove the conclusion. Perhaps, however, they refute the conclusion. We check this by assuming the conclusion *true* and trying again to make all the premises true. *B* must now be true in line 1:

    T T T   T
1. $A \equiv B$ A?
    ⋮

Thus *C* and *D* must be true to make line 2 true:

    T T T T T
2. $B \supset (C \cdot D)$

and so *E* must be true to make line 3 true:

    T T T
3. *D* ⊃ *E*

and *F* must be true to make line 4 true:

    F T T F T
4. ~*F* ⊃ ~*C*

But now we face a dilemma. If we make G false to make line 5 true:

    T T T T   F F
5. ~((*E* · *F*) · ~*G*)

line 6 will be false:

    F
6. *G*

whereas if we make G true to make line 6 true, line 5 will be false:

    F T T T T T
5. ~((*E* · *F*) · *G*)

    T
6. *G*

Thus there is *no* way of making all the premises true if the conclusion is true and we know that the premise refutes the conclusion. Using our new rules we can give the refutation as follows:

1. *A* ≡ *B*
2. *B* ⊃ (*C* · *D*)
3. *D* ⊃ *E*   *A*?
4. ~*F* ⊃ ~*C*
5. ~((*E* · *F*) · ~*G*)
6. *G*
7. (*A* ⊃ *B*) · (*B* ⊃ *A*)   1 DME
8. *A* ⊃ *B*   7 Simp.
9. *B* ⊃ *A*   8 Simp.

10.	$A \supset (C \cdot D)$	8, 2 HS
11.	$\sim(E \cdot F) \vee \sim G$	5 De M
12.	$\sim(E \cdot F)$	6, 11 SC
13.	$\sim E \vee \sim F$	12 De M
14.	$C \supset F$	4 Transp.
15.	$\sim C \vee \sim D$	13, 14, 3 DD
16.	$\sim(C \cdot D)$	15, De M
17.	$\sim A$	16, 10 MT

This constitutes a refutation of the proposed conclusion: A?

Contrast with Cancellation

It is interesting to contrast this with a refutation in the simple system of the last chapter. In the simple system the premises would have to be written:

1a.	$\sim A \vee B$	
1b.	$\sim B \vee A$	
2.	$\sim B \vee C$	
3.	$\sim B \vee D$	
4.	$\sim D \vee E$	$\sim A$?
5.	$\sim \sim F \vee \sim C$	
6.	$\sim E \vee \sim F \vee \sim G$	
7.	G	

and the proof would go:

8.	$\sim E \vee \sim F$	6, 7 SC
9.	$\sim E \vee \sim C$	8, 5 CC
10.	$\sim D \vee \sim C$	9, 4 CC
11.	$\sim B \vee \sim C$	10, 3 CC
12.	$\sim B \vee \sim B$	11, 2 CC
13.	$\sim B$	12 Rep.
14.	$\sim A$	13, 1a SC

One might think that $\sim A$ could cancel A in $\sim B \vee A$, leaving only $\sim B$, but our rules forbid canceling a split line with itself, so this is not a possible cancellation. In the original refutation $\sim B$ does not appear as a line,

but it could easily be proved from the premises by adding one further
line to the refutation above:

18. $\sim B$ 17, 8 MT

The cancellation refutation is a little shorter and somewhat simpler
than the refutation given earlier. However, this depends on having the
premises in the right form for cancellation. If we had to transform the
premises as originally given to the appropriate form for canceling the refutation would be longer. The steps involved would be:

1. $\sim A \equiv B$
2. $B \supset (C \cdot D)$
3. $D \supset E$
4. $\sim F \supset \sim C$ $\qquad\}\ \sim A?$
5. $\sim((E \cdot F) \cdot G)$
6. G
7. $(A \supset B) \cdot (B \supset A)$ 1 DME
8. $A \supset B$ 7 Simp.
9. $B \supset A$ 7 Simp.
10. $\sim(E \cdot F) \vee \sim G$ 5 De M
11. $\sim A \vee B$ 8 DMI
12. $\sim B \vee A$ 9 DMT
13. $(\sim E \vee \sim G) \vee \sim G$ 10 De M

followed by the seven cancellation steps already given, and the refutation
would be one line longer than that using the rules of this chapter.

This brings out the point that simplicity and convenience are somewhat relative. To gain the ease and directness of the cancellation methods
we must do a little more work in putting premises into usable form. If
we put the premises in a form often closer to that of the original English
statements, we either have to use a more complex set of rules or else
do a series of transformations to enable us to cancel. No method is ideal
and each has something to teach us.

Doing Proofs

Probably the biggest problem students have with the complete system
of statement logic is not knowing how to make any headway in doing
proofs. There seem to be so many rules, and they do not know which

to use. This was part of the point in learning the simple system first, where we had only one operator, one connective, two one-way rules, and a few two-way rules. But the complete system of this chapter is not as complex as it may look at first. No hard and fast rules can be given for doing proofs, since proofs require creative ability which cannot be mechanized or reduced to a set of fixed procedures. But we can give some useful rules of thumb.

In the first place, notice that many of our one-way rules take two compound statements having one simple statement in common, eliminate the common term, and leave the remaining term(s). This is true of the six rules:

$$
\begin{array}{ccc}
\text{MP} \quad \dfrac{\begin{array}{c} A \supset B \\ A \end{array}}{B} &
\text{MT} \quad \dfrac{\begin{array}{c} A \supset B \\ \sim B \end{array}}{A} &
\text{SC} \quad \dfrac{\begin{array}{c} A \lor B \\ \sim A \end{array}}{B}
\end{array}
$$

$$
\begin{array}{ccc}
\text{HS} \quad \dfrac{\begin{array}{c} A \supset B \\ B \supset C \end{array}}{A \supset C} &
\text{CC} \quad \dfrac{\begin{array}{c} A \lor B \\ \sim B \lor C \end{array}}{A \lor C} &
\text{CJ} \quad \dfrac{\begin{array}{c} A \lor B \\ \sim B \cdot C \end{array}}{A \cdot C}
\end{array}
$$

The two dilemma rules have *three* compound statements, one of which has a component statement in common with each of the two others, and these two "common statements" are eliminated, leaving the "non-duplicated" statements:

$$
\text{CD} \quad \dfrac{\begin{array}{c} A \lor B \\ A \supset C \\ B \supset D \end{array}}{C \lor D}
\qquad
\text{DD} \quad \dfrac{\begin{array}{c} \sim A \lor \sim B \\ C \supset A \\ D \supset B \end{array}}{\sim C \lor \sim D}
$$

So our first rule of thumb can be:

1. Look for two premises with one or more component statements in common.

Once we have found two or more such premises, it is just a question of which rule to use to eliminate the "common statement." Very often the right rule is suggested by looking at the main connectives (if any) of the two statements. If one statement has a ⊃ and the other is the same as the component statement that is the antecedent or the negation of the consequent of the ⊃ statement, MP or MT will be appropriate; if one statement has a ∨ and the other is the same as one of the disjuncts, then SC is appropriate. Two ⊃'s indicate HS, two ∨'s suggest CC. If you find a statement with a ∨ having a common statement with a statement with a ⊃, you can check for another statement with a ⊃ that contains the other disjunct; if you find it, you may be able to use CD or DD. So our second rule of thumb is:

---

2. Try first the rules suggested by the main connective of the compound statements with common component statements.

However, the connectives ≡ and · give us problems with this rule. There are *no* one-way rules with ≡, and the only rules for · are just rules for manipulating statements, taking them apart or putting them together. So unless we have a complex argument in which an equivalence or conjunction are component statements, such as

$$(A \equiv B) \supset C \qquad\qquad (A \cdot B) \supset C$$
$$A \equiv B \qquad\qquad\text{or}\qquad\qquad A \cdot B$$
$$\overline{C} \qquad\qquad\qquad\qquad \overline{C}$$

we will usually want to reduce any ≡ to two ⊃'s by DME, and use Simplification on any statement whose main connective is · . So our third rule of thumb is:

---

3. Try using Definition of Material Equivalence on any equivalences and Simplification on any conjunctions in the argument.

If none of the rules of thumb given so far enables you to make much progress with the proof, there are probably some premises that need to be transformed into equivalent statements. For example, if you had

$$A \supset B$$
$$\sim B \vee C$$

you would want to use DMI on the first premise, then CC or DMI on the second premise, then HS:

1.	$A \supset B$			1.	$A \supset B$	
2.	$\sim B \vee C$			2.	$\sim B \vee C$	
3.	$\sim A \vee B$			3.	$B \supset C$	2 DMI
4.	$\sim A \vee C$	2, 3 CC		4.	$A \supset C$	1, 3 HS

As before with one-way rules, what two-way rules can be applied to get equivalent statements depends on what main connectives you have. So our fourth rule of thumb is:

---

4. If two premises with a common component statement do not yield a conclusion, try transforming one or both to equivalent forms and then try one-way rules again.

Let us pause at this point and look again at the 17-line refutation given earlier:

1. $A \equiv B$
2. $B \supset (C \cdot D)$
3. $D \supset E$
4. $\sim F \supset \sim C$ $A?$
5. $\sim((E \cdot F) \cdot G)$
6. G

The first thing we did was apply Rule 3, using DME or the first premise, and Simp. on the resulting conjunction:

7. $(A \supset B) \cdot (B \supset A)$ 1 DME
8. $A \supset B$ 7 Simp.
9. $B \supset A$ 7 Simp.

We could then use Rule 1 and notice that 8 and 2 had a common component B; then use Rule 2 to suggest using HS to eliminate B, giving us:

10. $A \supset (C \cdot B)$ 8, 2 HS

We now look for other premises with common statements and find only 5 and 6. But no rules apply to 5 and 6 in their present forms. So trying Rule 4 we transform 5 into the equivalent form:

11. $\sim(E \cdot F) \vee \sim G$ 5 De M

We can now use SC on 6 and 11:

12. $\sim(E \cdot F)$ 6, 11 SC

We see that 12 has terms in common with 3 and 4 which are conditionals, but we have no rule for two $\supset$'s and a statement like 12. So we use an equivalence again:

13. $\quad \sim E \lor \sim F \qquad\qquad$ 12 De M

We now have two $\supset$'s and a $\lor$ and can almost use a dilemma form of argument. But first we need to transform 4 into the equivalent:

14. $\quad C \supset F \qquad\qquad$ 4 Transp.

We can now use DD:

15. $\quad \sim C \lor \sim D \qquad\qquad$ 13, 14, 3 DD

The statements C and D are common to 15 and either 2 or 10. Since what we are trying to prove or refute is A, we are more interested in 10. No rule links 10 and 15 as they are, so again we use an equivalence:

16. $\quad \sim(C \cdot D) \qquad\qquad$ 15 De M

and now we can use MT:

17. $\quad \sim A \qquad\qquad$ 16, 10 MT

thus refuting A.

In more complex proofs we may occasionally need one more rule of thumb:

---

5. If a statement is needed that does not appear in any of the premises, try Addition or Contradiction.

Thus suppose the conclusion of the argument above had been $(A \cdot H)$?. The statement H does not even appear in any of the premises, but we could refute $A \cdot H$ by adding to our proof, as follows:

17. $\quad \sim A \qquad\qquad$ 10, 16 MT
18. $\quad \sim A \lor \sim H \qquad\qquad$ 17 Add.
19. $\quad \sim(A \cdot H) \qquad\qquad$ 18 De M

Note that in the simple system we could not have proved this by Addition. But we had the special rule that said that refuting one conjunct of a conjunction is enough to refute the conjunction.

In connection with Rule 5 we may note that Addition is most likely to be useful where we are trying to prove a disjunction or refute a conjunction. If we need to prove a conjunction or a simple statement or refute a disjunction or a simple statement that does not appear in the premises, Contradiction is most likely to be useful. Of course, for Contradiction we need contradictory premises. This will rarely occur ordinarily, but we will find special cases where it does come in handy.

Conditional and Reductive Proofs

Two special proof techniques that can sometimes make a proof easier are *Conditional proof* and *Reductio proof*. Conditional proof is most useful for proving conclusions of the general form $A \supset B$ or equivalent forms. What we do is to assume the *antecedent* of the conditional statement, adding it to the premises with a special "flag" to show that it is an assumption, not a "real" premise. We will use an asterisk $*$ for this purpose. Suppose in the proof we have been using for an example we had only the first five premises and the proposed conclusion was $G \supset \sim A$.

We could put G as an assumption with the notation Assumption for Conditional Proof (ACP) and proceed very much as before, except that every line that used the assumption would also have to be "flagged" with an asterisk. The proof would look like this:

1.	$A \equiv B$	
2.	$B \supset (C \cdot D)$	
3.	$D \supset E$	$G \supset \sim A?$
4.	$\sim F \supset \sim C$	
5.	$\sim((E \cdot F) \cdot G)$	
*6.	G	ACP
7.	$(A \supset B) \cdot (B \supset A)$	1 DME
8.	$A \supset B$	7 Simp.
9.	$B \supset A$	7 Simp.
10.	$A \supset (C \cdot D)$	8, 2 HS
11.	$\sim(E \cdot F) \vee \sim G$	5 De M

So far we have not used the assumption and have not had to flag any lines, but now we do:

*12. $\sim(E \cdot F)$ 6, 11 SC
*13. $\sim E \vee \sim F$ 12 De M

Line 12 is "starred" because it uses 6 directly, while 13 is starred because it uses 12 and thus depends on a line that depends on the assumption. However, line 14 is not starred; it does *not* depend on any starred line, but just on a premise:

14. $C \supset F$ 4 Transp.

But 15 cites 13, a starred line, and must be starred:

*15. $\sim C \vee \sim D$ 13, 14, 3 DD

So must the next two lines, which depend on starred lines:

*16. $\sim(C \cdot D)$ 15 De M
*17. $\sim A$ 16, 10 MT

This was the end of the refutation, but we cannot end any proof or refutation on a starred line, we must "close out" the proof by showing that the line we have reached is true only if the assumption is true. We do this by an *unstarred* line:

18. $G \supset \sim A$ 6–17 RCP

where RCP means Rule of Conditional Proof. What 18 says is just what the sequence of lines 6–18 shows, that *if* we add G to the premises $\sim A$ is true; that is, "If G then not A" or $G \supset \sim A$.

The formal statement of the Rule of Conditional Proof is as follows:

Rule of Conditional Proof (RCP)   At any point in an argument, any proposition A may be put down as a line of the argument with the justification Assumption for Conditional Proof (ACP), provided that an asterisk is placed to the left of the number of that line. (This will be called starring the line.) Each line that cites that line is similarly starred, and each line that cites a starred line is starred. Starred lines may also cite premises or previous lines obtained from the premises.

The assumption may be *dismissed* after any starred line as follows: If the assumption is a proposition *A* and the last starred line is a proposition *B*, we may write an *unstarred* line $A \supset B$, citing *all* starred lines so far (in the style: first starred line, dash, last starred line) and the justification, Rule of Conditional Proof (e.g., 5–12 RCP). No starred line may be the conclusion of an argument and no starred line may be cited after its assumption is dismissed.

If another assumption is made before the first one is dismissed, it and every line dependent on it must receive two stars and it must be dismissed before the first one is dismissed. In general, any assumption made within another assumption must receive one more star than the assumption within which it is (as must all lines dependent on the new assumption) and must be dismissed before that assumption.

The word *argument* here includes both proofs and refutations, but RCP is more likely to be useful in proofs than in refutations. A useful subcase of Conditional proof is the case where we assume the opposite of what we are trying to prove, derive a contradiction from this together with the premises, and conclude that the assumption we have made must be false and thus the opposite of the opposite of the conclusion—that is, the conclusion itself—must be true. This type of proof is called a Reductio proof. It could be, and in some systems is, a separate proof rule, but we can treat it as a variant of Conditional proof. To see how it works consider the argument

1. $A \equiv B$
2. $B \supset (C \cdot D)$
3. $D \supset E$
4. $\sim F \supset \sim C$ $\sim A$?
5. $\sim((E \cdot F) \cdot G)$
6. G

We begin by assuming the opposite of our conclusion:

*7. $\sim \sim A$ ACP
*8. A 7 DN

We then must break down the $\equiv$ as usual:

9.	$(A \supset B) \cdot (B \supset A)$	1 DME
10.	$A \supset B$	9 Simp.
11.	$B \supset A$	9 Simp.

But now the proof begins to look different:

***12.**	B	8, 10 MP
***13.**	$C \cdot D$	12, 2 MP
***14.**	C	13 Simp.
***15.**	D	13 Simp.
***16.**	E	15, 3 MP
17.	$C \supset F$	4 Transp.
***18.**	F	14, 17 MP
***19.**	$E \cdot F$	16, 18 Conj.
20.	$\sim(E \cdot F) \vee \sim G$	5 De M
***21.**	$\sim G$	19, 20 SC

This is the first time we have used SC with a compound disjunct, but the rule holds for such complex cases as this as well as the simpler cases we have used up to now. We can now get a contradiction

***22.**	$G \cdot \sim G$	6, 21 Conj.

and from the Contradiction we can derive our original conclusion by Contradiction

***23.**	$\sim A$	22 Contrad.

We then close out the Conditional proof

24.	$\sim\sim A \supset \sim A$	7–23 RCP

get rid of the double negation

25.	$A \supset \sim A$	24 DN

use DMI and Repetition

26.	$\sim A \lor \sim A$	25 DMI
27.	$\sim A$	

and get our desired conclusion. At the cost of always using Contradiction to get our original conclusion, then using DMI and Repetition on the conclusion of the conditional proof, we avoid having to give and remember an additional rule. In this case a Reductio proof was longer than a "direct" proof, but perhaps a little simpler; in many cases a Reductio proof is much shorter than a direct proof. But if Conditional or Reductio-Conditional proofs confuse you, you may console yourself with the knowledge that in principle one can always do a direct proof. You will appreciate Conditional and Reductio proofs more, however, after seeing how they save a good deal of time and complication in many complex proofs.

A Reductio proof can be used for refutation in the following way: Assume the conclusion you wish to refute and derive a contradiction. Use the contradiction to get the denial of the proposed conclusion by Contradiction. You will then have something of the form $A \supset \sim A$, which by DMI and Repetition will reduce to $\sim A$. We will not bother to go through the steps of such a "Reductio refutation" for the argument we have been using as an example, since it will be essentially the same as the proof of $\sim A$ we have just done. Of course, in general a refutation is equivalent to a proof of the denial of a conclusion.

By now, no doubt, you will be heartily tired of the particular example we have been using. However, a single, fairly complex, proof has been deliberately used throughout our discussion of truth-table shortcut, direct proof and refutation, and indirect proof and refutation so that your attention would be concentrated on the differences in the techniques and you would not be distracted by differences due to various examples.

To illustrate a case where an assumption occurs within another assumption, consider the following:

1.	$B \supset C\}$ $\quad (A \supset B) \supset (A \supset C)$	
*2.	$A \supset B$	ACP
**3.	A	ACP
**4.	B	2, 3 MP
**5.	C	1, 4 MP

*6.	$A \supset C$	3–5 RCP
7.	$(A \supset B) \supset (A \supset C)$	2–6 RCP

Note that 4 and 5 were double-starred because they depend on 3, the second assumption. When the second assumption was closed out we kept a single star because the first assumption had not been dismissed. When we closed out the first assumption we had no stars and line 7 could function as a conclusion without breaking the Rule of Conditional Proof. If we had tried to close out the first assumption before the second or had tried to end the proof on a starred line, we would have violated one or another clause of the Rule of Conditional Proof.

The theologian's argument at the beginning of this chapter can be done as a Conditional proof. We reconstruct the argument as follows:

1. Either eternal life is the *fulfillment* of our present hopes or it is not: $F \vee \sim F$
2. If it is, there can be nothing further to *hope* for: $F \supset \sim H$
3. A *temporal* existence without any further *hope* $\cdots$ could only appear as unending stagnation and *boredom*: $(T \cdot \sim H) \supset B$
4. (Understood) If it could only appear as unending stagnation and boredom, it could not be the fulfillment of our present hopes: $B \supset \sim F$
5. If it is not the fulfillment of present hopes, there must be something further for which one can hope: $\sim F \supset H$
6. If there is something further for which we can hope, eternal life could no longer be the destiny that man seeks: $H \supset \sim F$

The symbolic form of the premises can then be put together and the proof done as follows:

1. $F \vee \sim F$		
2. $F \supset \sim H$		
3. $(T \cdot \sim H) \supset B$	$F \supset \sim T$	
4. $B \supset \sim F$		
5. $\sim F \supset H$		
6. $H \supset \sim F \cdot$		
* **7.** $F \cdot T$	ACP	
* **8.** F	7 Simp.	
* **9.** T	7 Simp.	
*10. $\sim H$	8, 2 MP	

*11.	$T \cdot \sim H$	9, 10 Conj.
*12.	B	11, 3 MP
*13.	$\sim \sim F$	8 DN
*14.	$\sim B$	13, 4 MT
*15.	$B \cdot \sim B$	12, 14 Conj.
*16.	$\sim (F \cdot T)$	15 Contrad.
17.	$(F \cdot T) \supset \sim (F \cdot T)$	7–16 RCP
18.	$\sim (F \cdot T) \vee \sim (F \cdot T)$	17 DMI
19.	$\sim (F \cdot T)$	18 Rep.
20.	$\sim F \vee \sim T$	19 De M
21.	$F \supset \sim T$	20 DMI

It is interesting that though the argument seems at first to be a dilemma, there is in fact no use of CD or DD. Premises 1, 5, and 6 are not needed for the proof and are in fact superfluous. There may be a shorter way of proving the conclusion than this rather unintuitive Reductio proof.

The three relevant premises, we now see, are:

1.	$F \supset \sim H$	
2.	$(T \cdot \sim H) \supset B$	
3.	$B \supset \sim F$	

We transform these into suitable form for cancellation:

4.	$\sim (T \cdot \sim H) \vee B$	2 DMI
5.	$(\sim T \vee \sim \sim H) \vee B$	4 De M
6.	$(\sim T \vee H) \vee B$	5 DN
7.	$\sim F \vee \sim H$	1 DMI
8.	$\sim B \vee \sim F$	3 DMI

and use CC as follows:

9.	$(\sim T \vee H) \vee \sim F$	6, 8 CC
10.	$\sim T \vee (\sim F \vee \sim F)$	9, 7 CC
11.	$\sim T \vee \sim F$	10 Rep.

then get the conclusion in two steps:

12.	$\sim F \vee \sim T$	11 Com.
13.	$F \supset \sim T$	12 DMI

In this case the effort needed to use cancellation methods was worthwhile: It made the proof noticeably shorter.

Many arguments can be done without Addition or Reductio, and so can be done by cancellation methods. But in order to do them by cancellation, you may have to translate the premises into the proper form, using some of the two-way rules listed in this chapter. If you want to go to the trouble of doing so, that is up to you. But you will usually find it easier to use the extra rules in this chapter to save steps. Again, you *need* never use Conditional or Reductio proofs, but you will usually save yourself work by doing so.

Many arguments are hard to translate directly from English to the form that would make cancellation easy. You will have to do a fair amount of translation in your head or on scratch paper to do so, risking possible mistakes. Again, it is up to you. If you translate correctly using only $\sim$ and $\vee$, your translation will be equivalent to a correct translation using a richer vocabulary that includes $\cdot$, $\supset$, and $\equiv$. If your proof or refutation by cancellation is correctly done, it will be as good as a proof using fuller rules. The complete system of statement logic has considerable redundancy; but the redundancy is there to make things easier for you, not to make things more difficult. However, only where you really need Addition to get a conclusion are you *forced* to go beyond the simple system.

Chapter Summary

We began by considering a new approach to statement logic based on the idea that if B follows from A it is impossible for A to be true and B false. This led us to a *truth functional* account of statement logic, where we defined the connectives $\vee$ and $\sim$ by using *variables* and *truth tables*. We also saw that the validity of arguments can be checked by truth tables. We then introduced the following new one-way rules:

Simplification (Simp.)	$A \cdot B$ $\overline{}$ A B	Conjunction (Conj.)	A B $\overline{}$ $A \cdot B$
Cancel and Join (CJ)	$\sim A \vee B$ $A \cdot C$ $\overline{}$ $B \cdot C$	Modus Ponens (MP)	$A \supset B$ A $\overline{}$ B

Modus Tollens (MT)	$A \supset B$ $\sim B$ / $\sim A$	Hypothetical Syllogism (HS)	$A \supset B$ $B \supset C$ / $A \supset C$
Constructive Dilemma (CD)	$A \lor B$ $A \supset C$ $B \supset D$ / $C \lor D$	Destructive Dilemma (DD)	$\sim A \lor \sim B$ $C \supset A$ $D \supset B$ / $\sim C \lor \sim D$
Contradiction (Contr.)	$A \cdot \sim A$ / B	Addition	A / $A \lor B$

We also gave some new two-way rules:

Commutation (Com.)	$A \cdot B$ / $B \cdot A$	$A \equiv B$ / $B \equiv A$
Repetition (Rep.)	A / $A \cdot A$	
Definition of Material Implication (DMI)	$A \supset B$ / $\sim A \lor B$	Definition of Material Equivalence (DME) : $A \equiv B$ / $(A \supset B) \cdot (B \supset A)$
De Morgan's Rules (De M)	$\sim(A \lor B)$ / $\sim A \cdot \sim B$	$\sim(A \cdot B)$ / $\sim A \lor \sim B$
Transposition (Transp.)	$A \supset B$ / $\sim B \supset \sim A$	Complementarity (Comp.) : $A \equiv B$ / $\sim A \equiv \sim B$
Exportation (Exp.)	$A \supset (B \supset C)$ / $(A \cdot B) \supset C$	Absorption (Absorb.) : $A \supset B$ / $A \supset (A \cdot B)$
Distribution (Dist.)	$A \cdot (B \lor C)$ / $(A \cdot B) \lor (A \cdot C)$	$A \lor (B \cdot C)$ / $(A \lor B) \cdot (A \lor C)$
Association (Assoc.)	$(A \cdot B) \cdot C$ / $A \cdot (B \cdot C)$	$(A \lor B) \lor C$ / $A \lor (B \lor C)$

We discussed a *truth-table shortcut* for showing invalidity and then showed how our new rules could be used in proofs and refutations. We discussed the difficulties of doing proofs and refutations and gave five rules of thumb for finding proof strategies:

1. Look for two premises with one or more components in common.
2. Try first the rules suggested by the main connectives of the compound statements with common components.
3. Try using DME on any equivalences and Simp. on any conjunctions in the argument.
4. If two premises with a common component do not yield a conclusion, try transforming one or both to equivalent forms and then try one-way rules again.
5. If a statement is needed that does not appear in any of the premises, try Addition or Contradiction.

We then discussed techniques of *Conditional proof* and *Reductio proof*, which we treated as a special case of Conditional proof, and showed that these techniques could be used both in proofs and in refutations.

Rule of Conditional Proof (RCP)   At any point in an argument, any proposition A may be put down as a line of the argument with the justification Assumption for Conditional Proof (ACP), provided that an asterisk is placed to the left of the number of that line. (This will be called starring the line.) Each line that cites that line is similarly starred, and each line that cites a starred line is starred. Starred lines may cite also premises or previous lines obtained from the premises.

The assumption may be *dismissed* after any starred line as follows: If the assumption is a proposition A and the last starred line is a proposition B, we may write an *unstarred* line $A \supset B$, citing *all* starred lines so far (in the style: first starred line, dash, last starred line) and the justification, Rule of Conditional Proof (e.g., 5–12 RCP). No starred line may be the conclusion of an argument and no starred line may be cited after its assumption is dismissed.

If another assumption is made before the first one is dismissed, it and every line dependent on it must receive two stars and it must be dismissed before the first one is dismissed. In general, any assumption made within another assumption must receive one more star than the assumption within which it is (as must all lines dependent on the new assumption) and must be dismissed before that assumption.

To use a Conditional proof as a Reductio proof, assume the opposite of what you want to prove, derive a contradiction, and use Contradiction to get the denial of the assumption. Close out the Conditional proof and use DMI and Rep. to get an unstarred line that is the denial of the assumption.

Practical Applications

Check your Argument File for arguments you could not handle earlier but which you can handle by the methods of this chapter. Set aside arguments involving "every" and "some" until you get to later chapters. If there are other arguments you still cannot deal with, try to see what makes it impossible to deal with them in statement logic. (Hint: Arguments involving numerical calculation and arguments that depend on the internal structure of statements probably cannot be handled.)

Exercise 4-4

Some of these arguments are valid, some invalid. If you do not see how to do a proof or refutation of the conclusion, try a truth-table shortcut disproof to make sure the argument is a valid proof or refutation of the conclusion.

  Arguments that do not use Addition or Contradiction:

(1) **1.** $A \supset (B \supset \sim C)$
  2. $\sim(D \cdot C)$ $A \supset \sim C$?
  3. $D \vee B$

*(2) **1.** $A \equiv B$
  2. $\sim(B \cdot C)$
  3. $C \supset \sim(B \cdot A)$ $\sim A$?
  4. $\sim A \vee C$

(3) **1.** $\sim(\sim A \vee \sim B)$
  2. $(E \cdot D) \supset C$
  3. $(D \vee F) \cdot G$ C?
  4. $\sim E \equiv \sim B$
  5. $\sim(F \cdot G)$

(4) **1.** $I \supset J$
  2. $M \supset K$
  3. $\sim(J \cdot L) \vee M$ $I \supset (I \cdot \sim L)$?
  4. $\sim K \vee N$
  5. $\sim N \cdot O$

(5) 1. $\sim P \vee (P \supset Q)$
    2. $R \vee (S \cdot T)$
    3. $U \supset \sim(V \vee W)$ } $\sim Q$?
    4. $(\sim R \vee W) \cdot (\sim R \vee V)$
    5. $((S \cdot \sim U) \cdot T) \supset P$

Arguments that need Addition:

(6) $\sim A$} $\sim(A \cdot B)$?
(7) $\sim A$} $A \supset B$?
*(8) B} $A \supset B$?

(9) 1. $\sim(C \cdot \sim D)$
    2. $\sim F \supset E$
    3. $(\sim D \equiv F)$ } $\sim G \vee H$?
    4. $\sim E \vee G$

(10) 1. $\sim I \vee \sim J$
    2. $K \supset I$
    3. $(J \vee L) \supset \sim M$ } N?
    4. $\sim(I \cdot J) \supset M$
    5. $\sim(N \cdot \sim I)$

Exercise 4-5

In 1–5 do a Conditional proof of the conclusion. In 6–10 use a Reductio proof to refute the conclusion.

1. $(A \vee B) \cdot \sim(A \cdot B)$
    $C \supset B$ } $A \supset \sim C$

*2. $(A \cdot B) \supset C$
    B } $A \supset C$

3. $A \vee (B \supset C)$
    $\sim C$ } $\sim B \vee A$

4. A
    $(B \vee C) \cdot \sim(B \cdot C)$
    $B \supset D$ } $C \supset (E \cdot F)$
    $C \supset E$
    $\sim B \supset F$

5. $A \supset B$
    $B \supset (C \supset D)$
    A } $(F \equiv C) \supset (E \supset D)$
    $E \supset F$

6. $A \supset (B \cdot C)$
   $D \supset A$
   $B \supset \sim F$ $D \cdot (F \vee G)$
   $C \supset \sim G$

7. $A \supset B$
   $B \supset (C \supset \sim D)$ $(D \cdot G) \cdot \sim H$
   $\sim D \supset (E \cdot F)$

*8. $F \supset (M \cdot \sim U)$
   $C \supset (P \supset F)$ $P \cdot \sim M$
   C

9. $A \supset \sim B$
   $C \supset (D \cdot \sim E)$ $(F \equiv (C \vee D)) \cdot \sim (F \supset (B \supset \sim E))$

10. $(A \cdot B) \vee C$
    $B \supset (D \cdot E)$ $F \cdot \sim E$
    $(C \cdot F) \supset (G \cdot E)$

Exercise 4-6

The following arguments are suggested by arguments given by David Hume in his Dialogues on Natural Religion. *Symbolize the arguments. If a conclusion is given as a statement, check to see if the argument is a valid proof. If the conclusion is a question, see if it is a valid proof or refutation. If no conclusion is given, find the conclusion.*

1. If you are a sincere sceptic, you will not trust either your senses or your experience. If you do not trust your senses or your experience, you will not believe that your body has gravity or can be injured by a fall. If you do not believe that your body can be injured by a fall, you will leave the room by the window rather than the door. Therefore, if you leave by the door, you are not a sincere sceptic.

*2. If your sceptical arguments are effective, you would not rely on accepted rules of behavior. If your arguments are not effective, I do not need to answer them. So, if you rely on accepted rules of behavior, I do not need to answer your arguments.

3. If we have no experience of God, we have no idea of God. If we have no idea of God, we cannot say whether God is like human beings in any respect. We have no experience of God. Therefore . . .

4. If the existence of anything is demonstrable, its nonexistence implies a contradiction. If anything can be thought of as existing, it can also

be thought of as not existing. If it can be thought of as not existing, its nonexistence does not imply a contradiction. Can we say that the existence of anything is demonstrable?

5.   If there is a necessarily existing being, it may have qualities which, if known, would make its nonexistence contradictory. The Universe may have qualities which, if known, would make its nonexistence contradictory. Therefore, the Universe is a necessarily existing being.

6.   If every part of the Universe has a different cause, the Universe as a whole does not need a cause. If the Universe as whole does not need a cause, then God is not needed to explain the Universe. Therefore . . .

7.   Even if happiness outweighs unhappiness, unhappiness exists. If a perfectly good, all-powerful God existed, unhappiness would not exist. Can a perfectly good, all-powerful God exist?

*8.   Even if the existence of God is consistent with evil, if God exists, then evil is not what we would expect. If evil is what we would expect if God does not exist, then there can be no argument from the world as it is to the existence of God. Therefore . . .

9.   If there is a good God and an evil God, both good and evil would exist in the world. But if there were a good God and an evil God, the world would not be orderly and uniform. Both good and evil exist, but the world is orderly and uniform. So can a good God and an evil God both exist?

10.   The causes of the Universe are either perfectly good, perfectly evil, are both good and evil, or are neither good nor evil. If the causes of the Universe were perfectly good, there would be no evil. If they were perfectly evil, there would be no good. There is both good and evil. Therefore . . .

CHAPTER FIVE

Traditional Aristotelian Logic

Can you find the conclusion that follows from these premises? (Find the conclusion for which you need to use all of the premises.)

Bilbo is a Hobbit.
Every Hobbit is fond of comfort.
Everyone who is fond of comfort gets tired of adventures.

Everyone who gets tired of adventures thinks longingly of his home.
No one who thinks longingly of home is sorry to be home again.
Everyone who is not sorry to be home again appreciates his home.
Everyone who appreciates his home is contented at home.

What is the next step after statement logic?

There are two possible ways to continue our development of logic after studying statement logic. Both of them involve the distinction between *all* and *some*, a distinction that cannot be made in statement logic. We could simply add some techniques for making an *all/some* distinction to the techniques of statement logic and go on from there; this is the path we take in Chapters Six and Seven. But in this chapter we will take a different course: We will study an older kind of logical system that is less "mathematical" and closer to the patterns of reasoning in ordinary language.

This kind of logic was the first to be developed and has been, until fairly recently, the most used and most useful variety of logic. It was first systematized by Aristotle in the fourth century B.C., and is often called "Aristotelian," or "traditional," logic. Because a kind of argument called a Categorical Syllogism is basic to Aristotelian logic, we will usually refer to it as "syllogistic logic." From Aristotle's time to the nineteenth century it was the main, and sometimes the only, kind of logic studied. Despite the more sophisticated logical tools available today, syllogistic logic can often be the most convenient method of analyzing certain arguments.

We will begin with *standard form statements*, which are statements with a single subject and a single predicate that have one of the six following forms:

A Every _____ is _____ .   A′ * is _____ .
E No   _____ is _____ .   E′ * is not _____ .
I Some _____ is _____ .
O Some _____ is not _____ .

(*Some* is regarded as meaning "at least one" and includes *many, most,* etc., which we have no way of expressing in standard form statements).

---

* Where the subject term designates an individual.

The letters *A, E, I, O, A',* and *E'* are convenient short ways of referring to these statements. Thus instead of saying "a statement of the form 'Every ———— is ————'," we will say "an *A* statement." The *A* and *E* statements are *universal* statements. The *I* and *O* statements are *particular* statements, whereas the *A'* and *E'* statements are *singular* statements. The *A, A',* and I statements are *affirmative* statements, whereas the *E, E',* and *O* statements are *negative*. Thus the six statement forms can be described as follows:

A	Universal Affirmative
E	Universal Negative
I	Particular Affirmative
O	Particular Negative
A'	Singular Affirmative
E'	Singular Negative

In statement logic, statements were treated as unanalyzed units and our concern was with compound statements formed from these units, whereas in syllogistic logic, we pay attention to the internal structure of statements. Thus we will need letters to stand for actual subject terms and predicate terms such as "human", "living thing", etc., which can be fitted into the standard patterns to make standard form statements, and the special letters *n, S, P,* and *M* to stand for subject terms and predicate terms when we want to talk about statement *patterns*.

Writing Standard Form Statements

We will use the following conventions:

1. All small letters except *n* will stand for designations of individuals; for example:

p	#	Plato
a	#	the author of this book
f	#	the first man to land on the moon

2. All capital letters except *S, P,* and *M* will stand for expressions other than designations of individuals that can serve as subjects or predicates when inserted into standard forms; for example:

R	#	(a) rich person
A	#	(an) author
W	#	(a) woman

Indefinite articles can be supplied or dropped to make grammatical English sentences. It would be convenient in some ways to make an indefinite article part of the form; for example:

Every _____ is a _____.
Some _____ is not a _____.

However, since we will sometimes wish to use terms such as "rich" rather than "a rich person," "red" rather than "a red thing," etc., we will not make the indefinite article part of the standard form.

There is a *strict* and a *looser* version of our standard form statements. In the stricter version we will use predicate terms that could also appear in the subject position, if the accompanying indefinite article were dropped, for example, "(a) rich person," "(a) running man," "(a) white thing." In the looser version we will use predicate terms, such as verbs or adjectives, that could not appear in the subject position, for example, "rich," "running," "white." Examples of the two forms are:

Strict
Every author is a rich person.
Some author is a running man.
Some book is not a white thing.

Looser
Every author is rich.
Some author is running.
Some book is not white.

3. The letters S, P, M, and n will be variables marking gaps into which any subject or predicate term may be inserted—the small n marking gaps into which only designations of individuals may be inserted, the capitals gaps into which predicate terms may be inserted but names of individuals may *not* be inserted. Using these variables we can rewrite the standard statement forms as:

A   Every S is P   A'   n is P
E   No S is P   E'   n is not P
I   Some S is P
O   Some S is not P

Examples of standard form statements using the dictionaries given above as examples, would be:

Every A is R (Every author is rich [*or* a rich person])
No A is R (No author is rich [*or* a rich person])
Some W is not A (Some woman is not an author.)

Some *R* is *W* (Some rich person is a woman.)
p is not *W* (Plato is not a woman.)
a is not *R* (The author of this book is not rich.)

Notice that

Some *W* is not *f* (Some woman is not the first man on the moon.)
No *R* is *p* (No rich person is Plato.)
p is not *f* (Plato is not the first man on the moon.)

are *not* standard form statements, since we do not allow standard form statements in which the name of an individual (or the negation of the name of an individual) appears as the predicate term.

A widely accepted interpretation of the standard form statements, developed long after Aristotle, regards them as statements about classes or groups of things. Thus "Every *S* is *P*" is interpreted to mean the same as "Every member of the class of things each of which is an *S* is a member of the class of things each of which is a *P*"; "No *S* is *P*" to mean the same as "No member of the class of things each of which is an *S* is a member of the class of things each of which is a *P*"; "Some *S* is *P*" to mean the same as "Some member of the class of things each of which is an *S* is a member of the class of things each of which is a *P*"; "Some *S* is not *P*" to mean the same as "Some member of the class of things each of which is an *S* is not a member the class of things each of which is a *P*"; "*n* is *P*" to mean the same as "*n* is a member of the class of things each of which is a *P*," and "*n* is not *P*" as "*n* is not a member of the class of things each of which is a *P*."

Diagrams

The class interpretation of standard form statements enables us to give a diagrammatic presentation of them:

To express the notion that "Every *S* is *P*" we could draw an *S* circle completely inside a *P* circle:

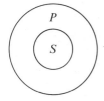

But instead we draw overlapping circles for S and P and indicate that the S class is completely included in the P circle by "crossing out" the part of the S circle outside the P circle by putting a zero in it to indicate that it is empty:

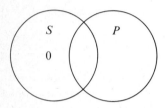

Thus the only part of the S circle left is the part inside the P circle.

Similarly, we could express "No S is P" by drawing two separate circles for S and P with no overlap:

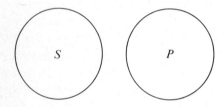

But instead we will draw overlapping circles and simply "cross out" the overlap by putting a zero in it:

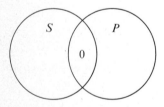

To say that "Some S is P" we could use numerous devices: partially dotted circles, circle segments, etc. But instead we use our same over-lapping circles and put a 1 inside the overlap to indicate that at least one thing is both S and P:

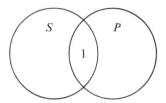

We use a similar device to draw a diagram for "Some S is not P."
In our overlapping circles we put a 1 in the S circle *outside* the P circle to
indicate that at least one thing is S but not P:

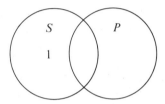

In diagraming statements about individuals, we use a heavy dot for
the individual n and need only one circle, for the P term. The individual n
is included in P in "n is P":

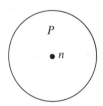

In "n is not P" the individual n is excluded from P:

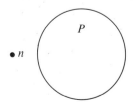

So we can diagram our six standard form statements as follows:

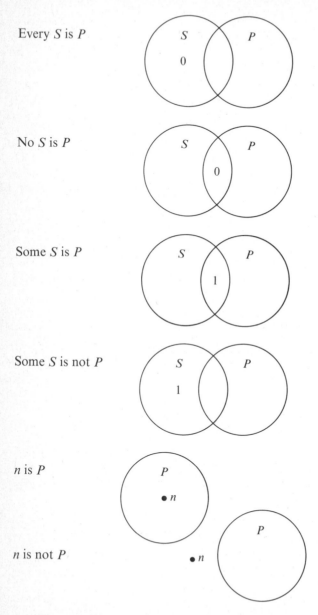

Every *S* is *P*

No *S* is *P*

Some *S* is *P*

Some *S* is not *P*

n is *P*

n is not *P*

These circles are called *Venn diagrams* and they have some very convenient features, as will see, but they do not represent all of the important facts about the standard form statements. One such fact is the *distribution* of terms in standard form statements.

Distribution

A term that says something about every member of a class is said to be *distributed;* one that says something about only some (less than all) members of a class is said to be *undistributed.* Consider the statement "Every author is a rich person" (which is unfortunately untrue). It says something about every author, but not about every rich person. In statements of this form the subject term is *distributed* while the predicate term is *undistributed.* However, the statement "No author is a rich person" (also untrue) says something about every author (that he is not rich) and about every rich person (that he is not an author). Thus both subject and predicate terms are distributed. The statement "Some author is rich" (which is true) says nothing about every author nor about every rich person; thus both its subject term and its predicate term are undistributed. The predicate term of "Some authors are not rich" is said to be distributed. This can be puzzling at first acquaintance. The justification for describing the predicated term of statements of the form "Some S is not P" as distributed is as follows: A term is said to be distributed in a statement if the statement tells us something about every thing of that sort or every member of that class. If the predicate term of a statement like "Some author is not a rich person" were *not* distributed, we would be saying in effect "Some authors are not *some* rich persons." But *this* would be true whether all authors were rich or none were, or some were and some weren't.

Suppose, for example, that all authors were rich. Still some author, say J. R. R. Tolkien, would not be *some* rich man, say Nelson Rockefeller. Similarly, in almost any situation, "Some author is not *some* rich person" would be true. It would be false only if there were one author and one rich person, who were the same person. But what we really want to say is that some author is different from *every* rich person. And this is what we are saying when we say that the predicate term of a statement like "Some authors are not rich persons" is distributed.

Finally, the subject term of a statement of the form "n is not P" and both the subject and predicate of a statement of the form "n is not P" are distributed, since an individual is either wholly within a class or wholly outside it, and thus we are saying that "every" (that is, the "only") n is included in the class P or else that "every" (that is, the "only") n is completely outside the class P, and thus that every member of the class P is different from n.

Some forms of diagrams for standard form statements make it easy to see at a glance which terms are distributed by using complete circles for distributed terms and partial circles for undistributed terms. The Venn diagrams do not have this convenient feature, but we can give the following relations between distributed terms in standard form statements and the Venn diagrams of these statements:

A term is distributed if and only if the Venn diagram representation of that term

1. Is a dot *or*
2. Is a circle that contains a zero *or*
3. Is a circle with a 1 or a dot *outside* it.

A term is *not* distributed if and only if the Venn diagram representative of that term is a circle and

1. The circle has a dot or a 1 *inside* it, *or*
2. The circle has nothing inside it and only a zero outside it.

These rules are not as complex as they look, and though it would be an exaggeration to say that you can tell at a glance which terms are distributed by looking at a Venn diagram, with practice it is fairly easy to tell by looking.

One convenient way to indicate that a term is distributed is to circle it. Thus we can summarize what we have said about distribution by circling the distributed terms in the standard forms:

A	Every Ⓢ is *P*
E	No Ⓢ is Ⓟ
I	Some *S* is *P*
O	Some *S* is not Ⓟ
A'	ⓝ is *P*
E'	ⓝ is not Ⓟ

If a statement in ordinary English can be translated into standard form at all, it can be translated by a series of steps, in which we ask questions like the following:

1. Is it about an individual?
2. Is it affirmative?
3. Is it universal?
4. What term is the subject and what is the predicate?

Try this process with a simple statement: "Babies are illogical."

1. About an individual?   No (not A' or E')
2. Positive?   Yes (not E, so A)
3. Universal?   Yes (not I or O)
4. What are the subject and predicate terms? Subject: "Babies"; Predicate: "illogical persons"
Final form: "Every baby is an illogical person." The diagram would be:

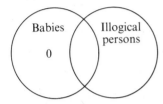

A word about the labeling of diagrams: Although the *terms* we are using are singular, for examples, "(a) baby," the class names on our diagrams will be in the plural. For the class of things each of which is a baby is more conveniently and concisely referred to as the class of babies, or simply as "babies." Thus when a statement like "Every baby is illogical" is given a class interpretation, it becomes "The class of babies is included in the class of illogical persons" or "Babies are included in illogical persons." Of course, it would be absurd to label a circle representing a class with a singular term, and there is no need to use circumlocutions such as "class of things each of which is a baby" rather than "babies," at least for labeling purposes.

To fit the statements into our standard form we had to:

1. Change the plural subject "babies" to the singular "(a) baby" which can appear before the "is" of the standard form.
2. Change the original predicate "_____are illogical" to a term "(an) illogical person" which can appear after the "is" of the standard form.

In some cases we may have to do more. For example: "Illogical is what babies are" seems to mean the same as "Babies are illogical," but "illogical" comes first, and "babies," the real subject, is "buried."

In this case I have to ask, "What am I talking *about*? Babies? Illogical Persons? What am I *saying* about the subject?" The answer is often somewhat arbitrary and will depend to a great extent on our purpose in analyzing the sentence.

In many cases insistence on singular forms leads to rather unnatural sentences, but in other cases consistent use of the plural leads to equally strained sentences. Any attempt to be precise and rigorous by using a few rigid forms where ordinary language has a multiplicity of expressions is bound to run into some difficulties. The forms we use have disadvantages, but they have fewer disadvantages for our purposes than any of the alternatives.

Immediate Inference

Once we have put a statement into standard form, we can more or less mechanically determine that certain other statements are true or false under the same conditions as our original statement. This enables us to give for syllogistic logic something like the table of equivalences we gave for statement logic. Traditionally, however, these "equivalences" have been regarded somewhat differently—as transformations that can be applied to standard form statements. There is no real difference in the two points of view; we can say either that "No S is P" is equivalent to "No P is S" or that "No S is P" can be transformed into "No P is S", and vice versa. When regarded as a permissible transformation, this process of switching the position of subject and predicate is called *conversion*, and the converted form is called the *converse*. Only E and I statements can be converted, as seen in the following table.

Table 5-1

Standard Form Statement		Converse
A	Every S is P	None
E	No S is P	No P is S
I	Some S is P	Some P is S
O	Some S is not P	None
A'	n is P	None
E'	n is not P	None

Of course, we *can* switch subject and predicate in an A, O, A', or E' statement, but by doing so we do not get a statement that is true and false under the same conditions as the original.

We can see why in two ways—by diagram and by considering distribution. The diagram of "Every S is P" is:

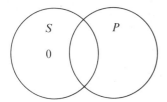

and only the subject term is distributed. If we attempted to get from "Every S is P" to "Every P is S," we would be arguing from the fact that the nonempty part of the S circle is in the P circle to the statement that the P circle was contained in the S circle. We would be going from a statement that said something about every S but not something about every P to a statement that said something about every P. An example makes it clear how absurd it would be to regard such a transformation as legitimate: We could argue from "Every woman is human" to "Every human is woman."

In an E statement, however, both subject and predicate are distributed, and the diagram: ·

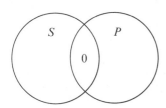

can equally be read as showing that the S circle is "outside of," that is, has no nonempty overlap with the P circle, or that the P circle is outside the S circle. An example would be the passage from "No mother is a male" to "No male is a mother."

Similarly, in an I statement both subject and predicate are *undistributed*, and the diagram:

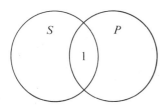

shows that at least one S is P and that at least one P is S. Thus "Some woman is a doctor" implies and is implied by "Some doctor is a woman."

Finally, in an O statement only the predicate is distributed. The diagram:

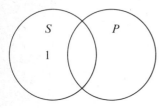

shows that at least one S is outside of the P circle, but that tells us nothing about whether any P is outside the S circle. So we cannot convert O statements. For example, it would be silly to try to argue from "Some female is not a mother" to "Some mother is not a female." A' and E' statements cannot be converted because this would involve putting individual names in the predicate position, which cannot occur in a standard form statement.

If we allow the introduction of negative terms such as *nonwoman*, *nonauthor*, etc., we describe two other sorts of "immediate inference." Negative terms will be formed by prefixing *non-* to a word or, in some cases, by inserting the phrase "a thing that is not" (e.g., to form the negative of "a person who likes coffee" we must write "a thing that is not a person who like coffee"). Negatives are so interpreted in Aristotelian logic that either a term or its negative applies in any given case. *Nonwoman* includes not only men and bears, but also inanimate objects, abstractions, etc. Similarly, a person who has never tasted coffee, a chair, and the square root of 144 all come under the description "a thing that is not a person who likes coffee." Negative terms are thus highly peculiar: They apply to everything *except* a small class of things.

Symbolically, we will represent negative terms in the following way. We will give the positive term in our dictionary; for example:

C #   (a) person who likes coffee

and put a bar over the letter to represent the negative term. This is called "negating" the term, and such a term is said to be "negated." Thus "$\bar{C}$" would be "a thing that is not a person who likes coffee."

Negative terms have the following effect on distribution: A negated term is *not* distributed if it is in a position where a nonnegated term would be distributed, and a negated term *is* distributed if it is in a position where a nonnegated term would not be distributed. Thus, for example, in "Every $\bar{S}$ is $\bar{P}$," S is *not* distributed and P *is* distributed.

With this rule in mind, we can show the validity of two new immediate inferences in which the subject and predicate are switched and both are negated. If we go from

Every S is P

to

Every $\bar{P}$ is $\bar{S}$

S remains distributed and P remains undistributed. Similarly, if we go from

Some S is not P

to

Some $\bar{P}$ is not $\bar{S}$

P remains distributed and S remains undistributed. However, if we could go from

No S is P

to

No $\bar{P}$ is $\bar{S}$

which is not a valid inference, S and P which were distributed would both become undistributed, and if we could go from

Some S is P

to

Some $\bar{P}$ is $\bar{S}$

which is not a valid inference, S and P which were undistributed would become distributed. The point is, that the negation and interchange of positions have the effect of keeping the "distribution quality" the same

for each term in a valid inference, but not in an invalid one. This is important because if a transformation makes a term distributed that was
formerly undistributed, we are concluding something about all of a class
when we have information about only part of it, which is unjustified. If
a distributed term becomes undistributed, we have a weaker statement,
which is not equivalent to the one with which we began. We can now give
the following table for these inferences, which are called *contraposition*.

Table 5-2

Standard Form Statement	Contrapositive
A Every *S* is *P*	Every $\bar{P}$ is $\bar{S}$
(e.g., Every Hobbit is fond of comfort.)	(e.g., Everyone not fond of comfort is not a Hobbit.)
E No *S* is *P*	None
I Some *S* is *P*	None
O Some *S* is not *P*	Some $\bar{P}$ is not $\bar{S}$
(e.g., Some Hobbit is not adventurous.)	(e.g., Some unadventurous person is not a non-Hobbit.)
A' *S* is *P*	None
E' *S* is not *P*	None

The reasons for not allowing contraposition for *A'* and *E'* statements
again involve the fact that individual names cannot appear in the predicate
position. Notice that terms that have contrapositives are those that lacked
converses, and vice versa.

There is another form of immediate inference, which can be applied
to all standard form statements. It is called *obversion*, and the formula
is somewhat complex. You must change a *universal* affirmative (*A*) to a
universal negative (*E*) and vice versa, or a particular affirmative to a
particular negative and vice versa, or an individual affirmative to an
individual negative and vice versa and negate the predicate. That is, the
formula can be expanded as follows:

If the original statement is:	Change it to:
A	*E*
E	*A*
I	*O*
O	*I*
A'	*E'*
E'	*A'*

and negate the predicate.

This formula gives us the following transformations.

Table 5-3

Standard Form Statement	Obverse
Every S is P (e.g., Every Hobbit is brave.)	No S is $\bar{P}$ (No Hobbit is not brave.)
No S is P (e.g., No Hobbit is brave.)	Every S is $\bar{P}$ (Every Hobbit is nonbrave.)
Some S is P (e.g., Some Hobbit is brave.)	Some S is not $\bar{P}$ (Some Hobbit is not nonbrave.)
Some S is not P (e.g., Some Hobbit is not brave.)	Some S is $\bar{P}$ (Some Hobbit is nonbrave.)
n is P (e.g., Bilbo is brave.)	n is not $\bar{P}$ (Bilbo is not nonbrave.)
n is not P (e.g., Bilbo is not brave.)	n is $\bar{P}$ (Bilbo is nonbrave.)

You can check each case and see that distribution is preserved. We can sum up our results so far in the following table.

Table 5-4

	Standard Form Statement	Converse	Contrapositive	Obverse
A	Every S is P	———	Every $\bar{P}$ is $\bar{S}$	No S is $\bar{P}$
E	No S is P	No P is S	———	Every S is $\bar{P}$
I	Some S is P	Some P is S	———	Some S is not $\bar{P}$
O	Some S is not P	———	Some $\bar{P}$ is not $\bar{S}$	Some S is $\bar{P}$
A'	n is P	———	———	n is not $\bar{P}$
E'	n is not P	———	———	n is $\bar{P}$

Every valid immediate inference "preserves" distribution, and every immediate inference is in fact an equivalence, so that one can go, for example, from a standard form statement to its obverse, or from the obverse to the original form.

The Square of Opposition

Another kind of immediate inference can be described as follows. For any standard form statements with the same subject and predicate, either the A statement or the O statement will be true, but not both, and similarly either the *E* statement or the *I* statement will be true, but not both. Accordingly, *A* and *O* statements with the same subject and predicate are *contradictories:* They have the same relation as a proposition and its negation in statement logic. This means that from the truth of one we can infer the falsity of the other, and from the falsity of one we can infer the truth of the other. One way of expressing this is the following diagram, called a *partial square of opposition.*

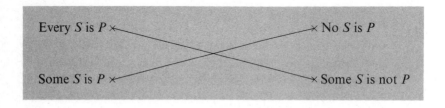

The universal statements are above, the particular below, the affirmative at the left, the negative at the right. The diagonal lines which cross to make an X and have X's at their ends suggest conflict or opposition. The contradictory of any statement can be found by following the diagonal line from that statement to the opposite corner of the square.

One useful feature of the Venn diagrams we used earlier is that they give us a visual reminder that *A* and *O* statements are contradictory and that *E* and *I* statements are contradictory. In the diagrams for "Every *S* is *P*" and "Some *S* is not *P*":

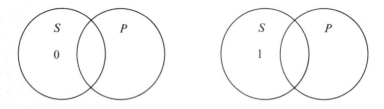

we can see that the *A* statement has a zero where the *O* has a one: The *A* statement asserts a class is empty which the *I* statement asserts has at least one member. Both things cannot be true, but one must be: The class is either empty or has at least one member. *E* and *I* statements are related in the same way. In the diagrams for "No *S* is *P*" and "Some *S* is *P*":

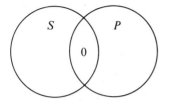
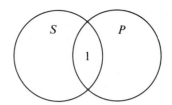

we can see that the *E* statement asserts the overlap class is empty while the *I* statement says that the same class has at least one member. The *A'* and *E'* are also contradictory, but statements about individuals are not usually discussed in connection with the square of opposition, since this would complicate the square a great deal without adding much useful information.

The next step is extremely crucial. *If* there exist things to which the subject term applies *and* things to which the predicate term applies, then if an *A* statement is true, the *I* statement with the same subject and predicate is also true, and if the *I* statement is false, then the *A* is also false. Also, if an *E* statement is true, then the *O* statement with the same subject and predicate is true, and if the *O* statement is false, so is the *E*.

But this condition is not always fulfilled, so the restriction is necessary. Consider, for example, the statement "No woman is a witch." Most people would feel this is true, since they believe no witches exist. But without our restriction we could infer from the truth of "No woman is a witch" the truth of "No witch is a woman" by conversion, then infer "Some witch is not a woman," which sounds as if we were saying that witches *did* exist!

Similar problems arise with *A* and *I*. Suppose I say, "Every trespasser on my land is a person who is going to be prosecuted." This may be true even if there have been no trespassers so far. But if I could infer, "Some trespasser on my land is a person who is going to be prosecuted" and, using conversion, I could get, "Some person who is going to be prosecuted is a trespasser on my land," either of these statements might falsely suggest that there had been trespassers already.

Therefore, we can allow the inference of *I* statements from *A* and of *O* from *E* (with the same subject and predicate, of course), only subject to the condition mentioned. (And it is not a matter of logic whether the condition is fulfilled.)

The relation between *A* and *I* and *E* and *O* is traditionally called *subalternation* and we put it on the "square of opposition" as follows.

The arrows remind us that the relation is directional, and the stars remind us that the relation is subject to a condition. When this condition is satisfied, we will say that subalternation holds.

Now if subalternation holds, so do two other relationships. First, if the subalternation condition is satisfied, *A* and *E* statements with the same subject and predicates cannot both be true, since if the *A* statement is true, its contradictory, the *O* statement with the same subject and predicate, will be false, and if the *O* is false so is the *E*. Similarly, if the *E* is true, then the *I* is false, and therefore the *A* is false too. Thus though *A* and *E* statements with the same subject and predicate can both be false (e.g., "Every woman is a mother," "No woman is a mother"), they cannot both be true. This relationship is called *contriety*, or *contrariety*, and *A* and *E* are *contraries*.

Secondly, *I* and *O* are *subcontraries*. An *I* and an *O* with the same subject and predicate may both be true ("Some woman is a mother," "Some woman is not a mother") but cannot both be false if subalternation holds. For if an *I* statement is false, its contrary, the *E* statement, is true, and thus the *O* statement which is the subaltern of the *E* is true.

Similarly, if we assume the *O* is false, then the *A* will be true and thus its subaltern, the *I*, will be true. So if *I* is false, *O* is true, and if *O* is false, *I* is true, and they can never both be false. This gives us finally the *complete square of opposition*.

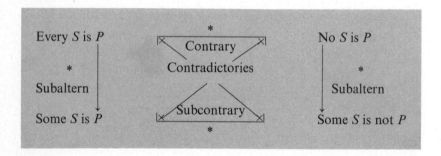

The stars remind us that all relations except contradiction hold only subject to a condition. The ⌐‾‾¬ symbol for contraries and the ⌊___⌋ symbol for subcontraries remind us of their position in the square.

Exercise 5-1

A. Put the following statements in strict standard form. B. Give the converse or contrapositive depending on which is equivalent to the original statement. C. Give the obverse. D. Identify as A, E, I, O, A' or E'. E. Say which terms are distributed.

  1. No fat creatures run well.
  2. None but the brave deserve the fair.
  3. No one looks poetical unless he is pale.
 *4. Some judges lose their tempers.
  5. What is difficult needs attention.
  6. All the laws passed last week relate to excise.
  7. Unexciting books make one drowsy.
  8. Some bald people wear wigs.
  9. Those who are fully occupied never talk about their grievances.
 10. No riddles interest me if they can be solved.

Categorical Syllogisms

Immediate inference gives us a certain insight into the structure of standard form statements, but it is not of much direct use. Syllogistic arguments, however, have been extensively used by many philosophers since Aristotle first developed syllogistic logic. Much of medieval philosophy, for example, becomes much more accessible if you have a good grasp of syllogistic logic. Even in modern philosophical writing, you will encounter arguments that are in syllogistic form, or can be put in this form.

A categorical syllogism is an argument consisting of three standard form statements, two of which are the premises of the argument and the other of which is the conclusion of the argument. By definition, a syllogism has three terms. Of these three terms, one called the *middle term* appears in both premises but not in the conclusion. Another of the three terms, called the *minor term*, appears in one premise and is the subject of the conclusion. The remaining term, called the *major term*, appears in one premise and is the predicate of the conclusion. The premise in which the major term appears is called the *major premise;* that in which the minor term appears is called the *minor premise.* By convention, syllogisms are written as follows:

major premise
minor premise
_____
conclusion

For example, consider the following syllogism:

Every Hobbit loves comfort.
Bilbo is a Hobbit.
_____
Bilbo loves comfort.

"Hobbit" is the middle term, "Bilbo" the minor term, "a lover cf comfort" the major term. The order of premises is major premise first, minor premise second. Since the middle term may be either subject or predicate in either major premise or minor premise, and major premise, minor premise, and conclusion can be A, E, I, O, A' or E' statements, there are $(6 \times 2 \times 6 \times 2 \times 6 =)$ 864 distinguishable syllogisms. Since for many purposes A' and E' statements may be treated like A and E statements, it is more usual to say that there are $(4 \times 2 \times 4 \times 2 \times 4 =)$ 256 separable syllogisms. Of this very large number, only a handful are valid argument forms. Of the invalid forms, some are very unconvincing and would probably deceive no one, while others are quite similar to valid arguments and frequently take people in. Of the valid arguments, some are more obviously good arguments than others. So if presented with an argument in syllogistic form, it is by no means easy to decide "intuitively" whether the argument is good or bad.

In this section we will present two techniques for deciding the validity of arguments in syllogistic form. The first technique consists of a set of rules. Every valid syllogism satisfies all of these rules, and every invalid syllogism breaks at least one of them. The rules can be quickly and easily applied and are a completely mechanical technique for separating valid from invalid syllogistic arguments. However, it is not always easy to see why a syllogism that breaks the rules is invalid. Therefore, we will give a second technique which is by no means so easily applied, but which gives a different way of seeing the reason for the validity or invalidity of a particular syllogistic argument. This second technique consists of a diagrammatic method that is an extension of the diagrams already used for immediate inference.

We will first state the rules, then apply them to show the validity or invalidity of sample arguments. Then at this stage we will introduce the diagrammatic techniques to illustrate and illuminate the decisions reached by the rules.

The first step in checking an alleged syllogistic argument for validity is to make sure it *is* a syllogism—that is, that it has two premises and a conclusion, that it has only three terms, and that no term occurs twice in the same statement. It may also be necessary to rearrange the order of statements so that the conclusion is at the end and, less important, that the major premise comes first and the minor premise comes second. If there are more than two premises, the argument may be a *sorites* or chain of syllogisms, which we will discuss later. If there is only one premise, the missing premise may be obvious or easy to supply. In this case the argument is called an *enthymeme* and such arguments are also discussed later. Mere lack of standard order does not affect the validity of a syllogism, though it may lead to confusion. However, if there are more than three terms we may have a fallacious argument that looks like a syllogism but is not. Such arguments can be extremely misleading, especially if they use a term in two different senses or use different terms that seem to be synonymous but are not. For example, consider the two seemingly syllogistic arguments:

Every rat has a tail.
Jack is a rat.
Jack has a tail.

and

Every professor has tenure.
Jack is a college teacher.
Jack has tenure.

In the first argument, "rat" is used first literally, then metaphorically. In the second argument, "professor" and "college teacher" might appear synonymous, but are not. We will call arguments with ambiguous terms of this kind *pseudosyllogisms* and will be on our guard against them.

Syllogistic Rules

If the syllogism is a genuine one, it is valid if and only if it satisfies all of the following conditions.

1. At most one premise is negative.
2. At most one premise is particular.
3. The conclusion is negative if and only if one premise is negative.
4. The conclusion is particular if and only if one premise is particular.
5. The middle term is distributed once.
6. If a term is distributed in the conclusion, it is distributed in a premise.

(Condition 2 is redundant but convenient, as is part of condition 4.)

The rules are arranged in such a way that those points that are easier to check come first. Looking only at the premises, we see if these satisfy conditions 1 and 2. Then we look at the conclusion, and check the premises to see if conditions 3 and 4 are met. Finally, we can draw distribution circles around terms. If the middle term is circled once, condition 5 is satisfied. If a term is circled in the conclusion, it must be circled in a premise to satisfy condition 6.

Remember, *all* you need to know in order to know what terms are distributed is their position (subject or predicate) and the type of statement in which they appear. For convenience the distribution table is reproduced here.

Every Ⓢ is P
No Ⓢ is Ⓟ
Some S is P
Some S is not Ⓟ
Ⓝ is Ⓟ
Ⓝ is not Ⓟ

(The circles indicate distributed terms.)

With the set of rules above, we can decide mechanically whether a syllogistic argument is valid or not. We also want to understand why the syllogism is a good or bad argument, and for this the diagrams are useful. To diagram a syllogistic argument, we use the same diagrams introduced in the last section.

Consider, for example, the following valid syllogism:

Every dragon is greedy for gold.
Some dragon is not wealthy.

Some creature greedy for gold is not wealthy.

It satisfies Rule 1: At most one premise is negative. It also satisfies Rule 2: At most one premise is particular. The conclusion is negative, but since one premise is negative, Rule 3 is satisfied. Similarly, the conclusion is particular, but since one premise is particular, Rule 4 is satisfied. The middle term is "dragon" and it is distributed once, since it is the first term of an *A* statement. Thus Rule 5 is satisfied. The term "wealthy" is distributed in the conclusion, but since it is also distributed in the second premise (since it is the predicate of an *O* statement), Rule 6 is also satisfied. Thus all the rules are satisfied and the syllogism is valid.

In contrast, consider the following invalid syllogism:

Every dragon is fond of gold.
Some banker is fond of gold.
_____
Some banker is a dragon.

Rules 2 and 4 do not apply, since there are no negative terms. Rules 1 and 3 are satisfied, since there is only one particular premise, and the conclusion is particular. Rule 6 does not apply, since no term is distributed in the conclusion. But Rule 5 is broken, since "(creature) fond of gold," the middle term, is not distributed in either premise.

Venn Diagrams for Syllogisms

Every real syllogism has three terms, so in using Venn diagrams for testing syllogisms, we must have a device for representing the relation between three terms. Where one of the terms is an individual name, we need two circles which will stand for the middle and major terms. We will also need a dot for the individual *n*. Consider an argument like the following:

No person pursued by Black Riders is safe.
Frodo is pursued by Black Riders.
_____
Frodo is not safe.

We diagram the major premise first:

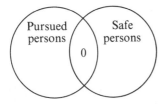

We then put in the dot for Frodo, according to the minor premise. It must go in the nonempty part of the "Pursued Persons" circle, *since neither a dot nor a "1" can go in the part of a circle which has an "0" in it* (this is crucial for our technique of diagraming syllogisms).

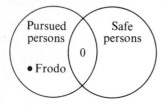

And we can "read off" the conclusion: Since Frodo is in the "pursued" circle and no nonempty part of the "pursued" circle overlaps with the "safe" circle, Frodo must be outside the "safe" circle. To give a geographical analogue, it is like saying that no part of the United States is in South America, that I am in the United States, and therefore I am not in South America.

Now consider an invalid argument, such as:

No person pursued by Black Riders is safe.
Odo is not pursued by Black Riders.
_____

Odo is not safe.

We draw the same diagram for the major premise, but when we come to place the dot for Odo, it could be either inside or outside the "safe" circle:

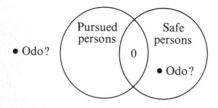

Either placement would satisfy the premises, and we are not forced to put the dot in a position such that we can "read off" the conclusion after having diagramed the premises.

This is the key to determining validity or invalidity at arguments by Venn diagrams: In a valid argument, diagraming the premises forces you to diagram the conclusion: whereas in an invalid argument, the conclusion is left open—given the diagram of the premises, the conclusion might or might not be true.

The syllogistic rules give us no direct help in deciding whether the premises of a given syllogism might *refute* the conclusion given, but Venn diagrams do: If the premises in fact refute the conclusion, diagraming the premises will force us to diagram the negation of the conclusion. Thus, in the argument:

No person pursued by Black Riders is safe.
Odo is safe.
_____
Odo is pursued by Black Riders.

the rules would merely tell you that the syllogism is invalid (affirmative conclusion with a negative premise—breaks Rule 3). But the Venn diagram:

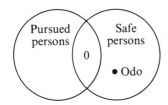

shows that Odo is *not* pursued by Black Riders—the negation of the conclusion.

When we have two universal premises or a universal and a particular premise, we need three circles in our Venn diagram which are drawn in an overlapping pattern:

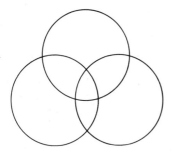

In such a syllogism we always diagram the major premise first, unless the major premise is particular and the minor is universal: In that case we diagram the universal premise first. In fact, one of the premises is universal in every valid syllogism, but we want to take care of cases where we are diagraming an invalid syllogism to show that it is invalid, so if both premises are particular, diagram the major first.

Consider the argument:

Every Ranger is an enemy of Sauron.
No Orc is an enemy of Sauron.
_____
No Orc is a Ranger.

We diagram the major premise first:

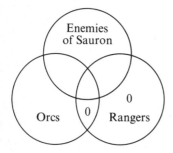

To diagram "Every Ranger is an enemy of Sauron," we emptied or crossed out the "Rangers" circle outside the "Enemies" circle. But this part of the "Rangers" circle was cut into two "cells" by the overlapping "Orcs" circle. So we put a zero in *both* cells, making it clear that *all* parts of the "Rangers" circle outside of the "Enemies" circle were empty. We now diagram "No Orc is an enemy of Sauron" by emptying both cells of the overlap between the "Orcs" circle and the "Enemies" circle:

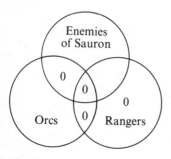

And we can see that by diagraming both premises we have automatically diagramed the conclusion: "No Orc is a Ranger." One premise emptied one cell of the overlap, the other premise emptied the other cell.

In contrast, consider the invalid argument:

Every Orc is a servant of Sauron.
No Orc is a Ranger.
_____

No Ranger is a servant of Sauron.

The major premise is diagramed first:

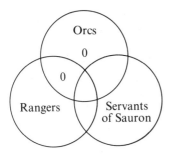

But when we diagram the minor premise:

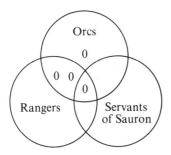

we empty the two cells of the "Orcs" circle overlapping the "Rangers" circle, which results in emptying for a second time a cell already emptied, but *not* in emptying both cells of the overlap between "Rangers" and "Servants of Sauron." Thus diagraming the premises does not result in a diagram of the conclusion.

A similar result occurs when we take valid and invalid syllogisms with one universal and one particular premise. Consider the argument:

Some Ranger is one of the Fellowship of the Ring.
Every Ranger is an enemy of Sauron.
_____
Some enemy of Sauron is one of the Fellowship of the Ring.

We diagram the universal premise first:

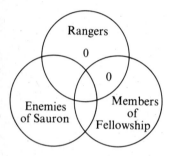

Remember that a 1 cannot go in a cell which has a zero in it, so when we come to diagram the minor premise there is only one nonemptied cell in which the 1 can go to represent "Some Ranger is one of the Fellowship of the Ring":

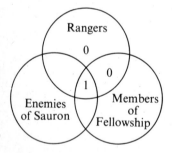

Thus the conclusion "Some enemy of Sauron is one of the Fellowship of the Ring" can be read off from the diagram of the premises.

In contrast, take the invalid argument:

Some Ranger is one of the Fellowship of the Ring.
Every relative of Aragorn's is a Ranger.
_____
Some relative of Aragorn's is a member of the Fellowship of the Ring.

Since the major premise is particular, we diagram the universal minor premise first:

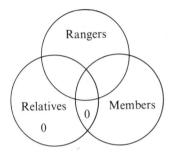

But when we come to diagram the major premise we find that the 1 could go in *either* of the two cells in the overlap between "Members" and "Relatives":

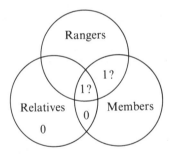

One cell or the other is occupied, or both are occupied. But we do not know which, so we do not know if anything is both a relative and a member.

Valid syllogisms all have two characteristics: first, no cell is emptied more than once. Second, in a syllogism with a particular conclusion a cell has been marked as empty by a universal premise, forcing the 1 into another cell so that the conclusion is diagramed by diagraming the premises. Since there are such a limited number of valid syllogisms, it is even possible to give a list of all the valid patterns of categorical syllogisms. We will find that any valid syllogism has one of the patterns shown in the following table.

Table 5-5

Pattern	Diagram

Two Universal Premises

Every M is P
Every S is M
—————
Every S is P

M
0
0
0
0
S   P

No M is P
Every S is M
—————
No S is P

M
0
0
0
0
S   P

Every P is M
No S is M
—————
No S is P

M
0
0
0
0
S   P

One Universal and One Individual Premise

Every M is P
n is M
—————
n is P

0   •
      n
M   P

No M is P
n is M
—————
n is not P

• n   0
M   P

• n

Every P is M
n is not M
—————
n is not P

0
M   P

Table 5-5 (*Continued*)

Pattern	Diagram

One Universal and
One Particular Premise

Every *M* is *P*
Some *S* is *M*
Some *S* is *P*

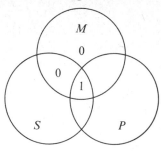

Every *P* is *M*
Some *S* is not *M*
Some *S* is not *P*

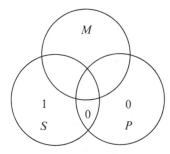

Every *M* is *S*
Some *M* is *P*
Some *S* is *P*

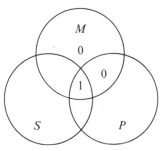

Every *M* is *S*
Some *M* is not *P*
Some *S* is not *P*

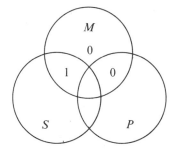

No *M* is *P*
Some *S* is *M*
Some *S* is not *P*

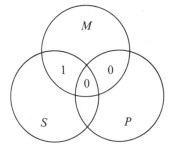

It would, in fact, be possible simply to learn these patterns and reject as invalid any argument that did not have one of the valid diagrams. Some patterns would look verbally different because of premises or conclusions that were valid converses, contrapositives, or obverses of those given. But the diagram would turn out to be marked in just the same way. Thus, for example, in the pattern

Every non-*P* is non-*M*
No *S* is non-*M*
———————————————
Every *S* is *P*

To mark the diagram for "Every non-*P* is non-*M*," we would empty the cells outside of *P* that are inside of *M*:

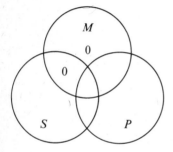

and to diagram "No *S* is non-*M*," we would empty the cells that are *S* and not *M*:

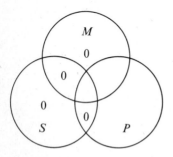

But this gives us just the same diagram as the first syllogism in Table 5-5.

In a case where the premises or conclusion are in a converted, contraposed, or obverted form, it is sometimes easier to get back to a form with no negated terms (if that is possible) by contraposing and obverting. But there is no need to do so if we keep in mind the following marking of the standard Venn diagram for syllogisms:

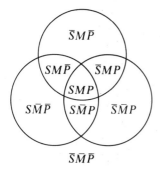

The overlap of all three circles is SMP, without any bars. The part of the diagram where S and P overlap outside of M, is $S\overline{M}P$, and so on. In general every area inside the S circle has S without a bar. Every area outside the S circle has $\overline{S}$ (with the bar) and so on for the other circles. The area outside all of the circles is of course $\overline{S}\,\overline{M}\,\overline{P}$.

We can see that to mark, for example, "No S is non-M," we want to empty any cell that has S and M without bars; to mark "Every non-M is non-S," we want to empty any cell that has $\overline{M}$ but $\overline{S}$, and so on.

The Venn diagram is, in fact, like a computer on paper; once we learn to "program" it by making the appropriate marks on it, we can "read out" the validity or invalidity of syllogistic arguments by looking to see whether in diagraming the premises we have been forced to diagram the conclusion. In fact, the Venn diagram can handle some nonsyllogistic arguments, but we have more convenient techniques for such arguments.

Exercise 5-2

A. Test each of these syllogisms for validity by the rules. If valid, write Valid. If not valid, give the rule or rules broken. B. Draw a Venn diagram for each syllogism. State which syllogisms are valid and which are not according to the Venn diagrams. (Results should agree with results of A above.)

1. Some unauthorized reports are false;
    All authorized reports are trustworthy.
        Some false reports are not trustworthy.

2. Some pillows are soft;
   No pokers are soft.
       Some pokers are not pillows.

3. Improbable stories are not easily believed;
   None of his stories is probable.
       None of his stories is easily believed.

*4. No thieves are honest;
   Some dishonest people are found out.
       Some thieves are found out.

5. No muffins are wholesome;
   All puffy food is unwholesome.
       All muffins are puffy.

6. No birds, except peacocks, are proud of their tails;
   Some birds that are proud of their tails cannot sing.
       Some peacocks cannot sing.

7. Warmth relieves pain;
   Nothing that does not relieve pain is useful in toothache.
       Warmth is useful in toothache.

8. No bankrupts are rich;
   Some merchants are not bankrupts.
       Some merchants are rich.

9. Bores are dreaded;
   No bore is ever begged to prolong his visit.
       No one who is dreaded is ever begged to prolong his visit.

10. All wise men walk on their feet;
    All unwise men walk on their hands.
        No man walks on both.

11. No wheelbarrows are comfortable;
    No uncomfortable vehicles are popular.
        No wheelbarrows are popular.

12. No frogs are poetical;
    Some ducks are unpoetical.
        Some ducks are not frogs.

13. No emperors are dentists;
    All dentists are dreaded by children.
        No emperors are dreaded by children.

14. Sugar is sweet;
    Salt is not sweet.
        Salt is not sugar.

15.   Every eagle can fly;
        Some pigs cannot fly.
            Some pigs are not eagles.

Soriteses

A more complex argument which is still basically syllogistic is the *sorites*, an argument that consists of a chain of syllogisms with the conclusion of one forming one of the premises of another syllogism, and so on until all of the premises have been used up. The argument at the beginning of this chapter is a sorites, and we could reconstruct the argument and find the conclusion as follows:
        The argument was:

Bilbo is a Hobbit.
Every Hobbit is fond of comfort.
Everyone who is fond of comfort gets tired of adventures.
Everyone who gets tired of adventures thinks longingly of his home.
No one who thinks longingly of home is sorry to be home again.
Everyone who is not sorry to be home again appreciates his home.
Everyone who appreciates his home is contented at home.

        The problem was to find a conclusion for which we needed all of these premises. Since the premises are in order and none is in an especially complicated form, we can proceed as follows:
        From the first two premises we draw the conclusion

Bilbo is fond of comfort.

From that and the third premise we draw the conclusion

Bilbo gets tired of adventures.

That with the fourth premise gives us

Bilbo thinks longingly of home.

This with the fifth premise yields

Bilbo is not sorry to be home again.

Together with the sixth premise this gives

Bilbo appreciates his home.

And that with the final premise gives us the conclusion of the whole sorites:

Bilbo is contented at home.

Soriteses in logic books are amusing puzzles, which require a certain amount of ingenuity to work out, especially if the premises are expressed informally. But essentially they can be solved by a mechanical process, even if the premises are given in scrambled form. One simply pairs off any premises that have a common term and then draws the conclusion that can be validly drawn from the paired premises. The resulting conclusion should have a term in common with one of the remaining premises. One then draws the conclusion from this pair, and so on until all the premises are exhausted. The resulting conclusion will be the conclusion of the whole sorites.

Take, for example, the following sorites, invented by Lewis Carroll.

P1   Babies are illogical.
P2   No one who can manage a crocodile is despised.
P3   Illogical persons are despised.

P2 and *P3* have the common term "despised." Interpreting them as universal statements, the first syllogism becomes:

P3   Every illogical person is a despised person.
P2   No crocodile-manager is a despised person.
_____
C1   No crocodile-manager is an illogical person.

C1 has the term "illogical (person)" in common with the original *P1* (which we again interpret as an *A* statement).

Thus, the second syllogism is:

C1   No crocodile-manager is a despised person.
P1   Every baby is a despised person.
_____
C2   No baby is a crocodile-manager.

We can discover what conclusion follows from the premise by application of the syllogism rules. *P2* and *P3* are universal, so the conclusion must be universal by Rule 6. *P2* is negative, so the conclusion must be negative by Rule 2. Since the order of subject and predicate does not matter in an *E* statement, either *C1* or its converse follows from *P1* and *P2*.

Suppose that instead of pairing *P2* and *P3*, we had paired *P1* and *P3*, which have the common term "illogical." Our chain would then have been:

P3	Every illogical person is despised.
P1	Every baby is an illogical person.
C1	Every baby is despised.
P2	No crocodile-manager is despised.
C2	No baby is a crocodile-manager.

This is an equally good sorites. Traditional logic books give certain rules about the order and arrangement of premises within a sorites. These are completely unimportant unless one wishes a particular artificial arrangement of premises. For example, if one insists that the major term of the final conclusion occur in the major premise of the first syllogism, and the minor term of the final conclusion occur in the minor premise of the final syllogism, one has what is called an Aristotelian sorites. Our second try at the "baby" sorites is Aristotelian. But no substantive purpose is served by such niceties and we shall ignore them in this book.

Two rules that cannot be so ignored are the following:

SR1   Only one of the original set of premises can be negative, as it appears in the final version of the sorites.

SR2   Only one of the original premise set can be particular or individual.

If either of these rules is broken, we get a syllogism somewhere in the chain with two negative premises or two particular premises or two individual premises or one particular and one individual premise; and no syllogism with these combinations is valid. The qualification in SR1 is intended to cover cases where an original premise is negative but by obversion or contraposition and double negation appears as positive when we formalize the argument.

Once one grasps the relatively simple principles involved, soriteses (this plural of *sorites* was coined by Carroll) are not very difficult to handle. Lewis Carroll invented dozens of moderately amusing soriteses for use in teaching logic. Since these are in the public domain, almost all logic books steal at least some of the easier ones for use as exercises, as we do in the next group of exercises.

Enthymemes

The other topic we will briefly examine in this section is that of enthymemes. An *enthymeme* is a syllogistic argument with either the major premise, the minor premise, or the conclusion omitted. A valid enthymeme is one for which the missing part can be supplied so that the result is a valid syllogism. An invalid enthymeme is one for which no standard form statement can be found that, when added to the enthymeme, will make it a valid syllogism. A Type 1 enthymeme is one that needs a major premise supplied; a Type 2 needs the minor premise supplied; and a Type 3 needs a conclusion supplied.

Strictly speaking, the original premise sets of soriteses have one Type 3 enthymeme, which when converted to a syllogism makes another premise into a Type 3 enthymeme, and so on. We sometimes speak of an *enthymatic sorites:* a sorites that has at least one premise missing which cannot be derived as a conclusion from other premises. Usually, the missing premise or premises must be few in number and fairly obvious, otherwise the line between an enthymatic sorites and a fallacious argument disappears (for given almost any random collection of standard form statements, we could with sufficient ingenuity link them into a sorites by adding enough additional premises).

If an enthymeme is valid, the missing part can be discovered mechanically by application of the rules. If it is a Type 3 enthymeme, we proceed as we did with soriteses. If it is a Type 1 or 2 enthymeme, we proceed as follows:

First, we identify the conclusion. It then follows that the term in the premise that does not appear in the conclusion is the middle term. The other term in the premise will be either the subject of the conclusion, in which case the major premise is missing, or the predicate of the conclusion, in which case the minor premise is missing. We now know which premise is missing and what terms it contains. Then, reasoning from the quality, quantity, and distribution of the conclusion and premise, we fill in the form of the missing premise.

For example, suppose we have the enthymeme:

Odo is a relative of Frodo.
_____
Odo is a relative of Bilbo.

Suppose that the context enables us to identify the second statement as the conclusion. Therefore, "relative of Frodo," which does not appear in the conclusion, must be the middle term. "Odo" is the subject of the conclusion, so we are missing the major premise. The major premise must contain the middle and major terms, "relative of Frodo" and "relative of Bilbo." Since the conclusion is individual affirmative, the missing premise must be universal affirmative. Since the middle is not distributed in the minor premise, it must be distributed in the missing major. Thus the missing premise is:

Every relative of Frodo is a relative of Bilbo.

Any enthymeme that is valid can be reconstructed by this method. If an enthymeme is invalid, the attempt to reconstruct it will lead to impossible or conflicting demands. For example, the enthymeme

Every relative of Frodo is a relative of Bilbo.
_____
Some Took is a relative of Bilbo.

is invalid if the second statement is the conclusion. The middle would have to be "relative of Frodo." Since the conclusion is particular affirmative, the missing minor premise must also be particular affirmative. Since "relative of Frodo" is not distributed in the major, it must be distributed in the minor; but this conflicts with the previous requirement, for if the missing minor is an *I* statement, the middle cannot be distributed in it, for neither the subject nor predicate of an *I* statement is distributed. So the enthymeme is invalid.

Chapter Summary

We started off with the *standard form statements*:

A	Every *S* is *P*	*O*	Some *S* is not *P*
E	No *S* is *P*	*A'*	*n* is *P*
I	Some *S* is *P*	*E'*	*n* is not *P*

We saw the manipulations possible with standard form statements: *conversion* of *E* and *I*, *contraposition* of *A* and *O*, and *obversion* of *A*, *E*, *I* and *O*:

	Original Statement	Converse	Contrapositive	Obverse
A	Every *S* is *P*	———	Every $\bar{P}$ is $\bar{S}$	No *S* is $\bar{P}$
E	No *S* is *P*	No *P* is *S*	———	Every *S* is $\bar{P}$
I	Some *S* is *P*	Some *P* is *S*	———	Some *S* is not $\bar{P}$
O	Some *S* is not *P*	———	Some $\bar{P}$ is not $\bar{S}$	Some *S* is $\bar{P}$

(Note: The bar over a letter indicates *non-*.)

We looked at various suggestions for a *square of opposition* and saw that only the relation of *contradictories* held without qualification.

We then examined two ways of checking syllogisms for validity. The first was by the rules:

1. At most one premise is negative.
2. At most one premise is particular.
3. The conclusion is negative if and only if one premise is negative.
4. The conclusion is particular if and only if a premise is particular.
5. The middle term is distributed once.
6. If a term is distributed in the conclusion, it is distributed in a premise.

(Condition 2 is redundant but convenient, as is part of condition 4.)

The second way involved the use of Venn diagrams, which had also been used to diagram statements earlier. Finally, we saw that syllogistic logic includes the logic of *enthymemes*, syllogisms with a premise or conclusion missing, and *sorites*, arguments consisting of chains of syllogisms.

Practical Applications

Check the arguments in your Argument File to see if any can be treated as syllogisms, enthymemes, or soriteses. Keep an eye out for syllogistic arguments now that you are aware of their characteristics. (Hint: Many arguments used by racially or sexually prejudiced people are enthymemes with highly questionable premises left unexpressed; for example: "She is a woman, so she is not good at logic" is a valid enthymeme, but the missing premise is the obviously false "No woman is good at logic." Because the premises are left unexpressed, it is easier to overlook them and harder to identify and challenge them.)

Exercise 5-3

A. Treat these pairs of sentences as premises and find a valid conclusion is possible. If no conclusion follows write NC. B. Go back through the pairs of statements treating the first of each of these pairs as a premise and the second as a conclusion. See if you can find a premise from which, along with the first statement, the second statement will validly follow. If no such premise is possible, write NP.

1. Busy folk are not always talking about their grievances;
   Discontented folk are always talking about their grievances.
2. None of my cousins is just;
   No judges are unjust.
3. All teetotalers like sugar;
   No nightingale drinks wine.
*4. No riddles interest me if they can be solved;
   All these riddles are insoluble.
5. All clear explanations are satisfactory;
   Some excuses are unsatisfactory.
6. All elderly ladies are talkative;
   All good-tempered ladies are talkative.
7. No kind deed is unlawful;
   What is lawful may be done without scruple.
*8. No babies are studious;
   No babies are good violinists.
9. All shillings are round;
   All these coins are round.
10. No honest men cheat;
    No dishonest men are trustworthy.
11. None of my boys is clever;
    None of my girls is greedy.
12. All jokes are meant to amuse;
    No Act of Parliament is a joke.
13. No eventful tour is ever forgotten;
    Uneventful tours are not worth writing a book about.

14. All my boys are disobedient;
   All my girls are discontented.

15. No unexpected pleasure annoys me;
   Your visit is an unexpected pleasure.

Exercise 5-4

In the soriteses by Lewis Carroll that follow, notice that Carroll is fond of using complicated forms that conceal the structure of the argument. In some cases all you can do is to take the two terms in the sentence and try them in each type of standard form statement, seeing which results in the statement closest to the meaning of the original. But to help you, here are a few typical "Carrollisms" with translations. Don't count on being able to apply these mechanically, however; context can alter meaning. Use your knowledge of English and your common sense, subject to these warnings:

"Nothing except A is B" usually means "Every B is A."
"No A fails to be B" usually means "Every A is B."
"Nothing is A unless it is B" usually means "Every A is B."
"Nothing is A if it is B" usually means "No A is B."

Also be careful of Carroll's habits of inverting subject and predicate by using subordinate clauses, and the way in which a term common to all the other terms (such as "man" if we are speaking of men, "picture" if we are speaking of pictures) is sometimes stressed, sometimes omitted. For each of the following soriteses find the conclusion that follows from all of the premises and reconstruct the chain of syllogisms that leads to that conclusion.

1. A. All hummingbirds are richly colored;
   B. No large birds live on honey;
   C. Birds that do not live on honey are dull in color.

2. A. All the old articles in this cupboard are cracked;
   B. No jug in this cupboard is new;
   C. Nothing in this cupboard that is cracked will hold water.

3. A. Showy talkers think too much of themselves;
   B. No really well-informed people are bad company:
   C. People who think too much of themselves are not good company.

*4. A. No boys under 12 are admitted to this school as boarders;
 B. All the industrious boys have red hair;
 C. None of the day boys learn Greek;
 D. None but those under 12 are idle.

5. A. The only articles of food that my doctor allows me are such as are not very rich;
 B. Nothing that agrees with me is unsuitable for supper;
 C. Wedding cake is always very rich;
 D. My doctor allows me all articles of food that are suitable for supper.

6. A. Things sold in the street are of no great value;
 B. Nothing but rubbish can be had for a song;
 C. Eggs of the Great Auk are very valuable;
 D. It is only what is sold in the street that is really rubbish.

7. A. There is no box of mine here that I dare open;
 B. My writing desk is made of rosewood;
 C. All my boxes are painted, except what are here.
 D. There is no box of mine that I dare not open, unless it is full of live scorpions;
 E. All my rosewood boxes are unpainted.

8. A. All writers who understand human nature are clever;
 B. No one is a true poet unless he can stir the hearts of men;
 C. Shakespeare wrote *Hamlet;*
 D. No writer who does not understand human nature can stir the hearts of men;
 E. None but a true poet could have written *Hamlet.*

9. A. I despise anything that cannot be used as a bridge;
 B. Everything that is worth writing an ode to would be a welcome gift to me;
 C. A rainbow will not bear the weight of a wheelbarrow;
 D. Whatever can be used as a bridge will bear the weight of a wheelbarrow;
 E. I would not take, as a gift, a thing that I despise.

10. A. The only animals in this house are cats;
 B. Every animal that loves to gaze at the moon is suitable for a pet;
 C. When I detest an animal, I avoid it;
 D. No animals are carnivorous, unless they prowl at night;
 E. No cat fails to kill mice;
 F. No animals ever take to me, except what are in this house;

G. Kangaroos are not suitable for pets;
H. None but carnivora kill mice;
I. I detest animals that do not take to me;
J. Animals that prowl at night always love to gaze at the moon.

Exercise 5-5

Put the following enthymemes and sorites from Duns Scotus's Ordinatio *into standard syllogistic form, supplying missing elements where necessary. Ignore phrases in parentheses.*

1. (The Philosopher argues that) the First Being has infinite power because it moves with an endless movement.

2. (One can argue equally well that) the First Being has infinite power since it can cause endless motion.

3. (Now it is clear that) since the First Being exists in virtue of itself, it has the ability to cause endless motion.

*4. The First Being has an infinite effect in its power, but whatever has an infinite effect in its power is infinite; therefore, etc.

5. Any being that possesses all causal power is infinite, but (Avicenna assumes) the First Being does possess all causal power; therefore, etc.

6. (Some argue that) the First Cause has infinite power, because any being that can bridge a gap between infinite extremes has infinite power. But a being that can create something from nothing can bridge a gap between infinite extremes (being and nothingness) and the First Cause can do this.

7. The First Being after God depends on Him totally and is made from no material; thus it is created from nothing.

8. The things that can be known are infinite in number, but they are all known by God. Therefore, the mind of God is infinite.

9. We can always love and seek something greater than any finite being. We cannot love or seek anything greater than God; therefore, etc.

10. An absolutely perfect being cannot be excelled in perfection. But any finite being can be excelled in perfection. God is an absolutely perfect being; therefore, etc.

CHAPTER SIX

Predicate Logic:
The Simple System

In the following example from Lewis Carroll's *Symbolic Logic,* find the conclusion that follows from these premises. (Find the conclusion for which you need to use all the premises.)

When I work a logic example without grumbling, you may be sure it is one that I can understand;

This sorites is not arranged in regular order like the examples I am used to;

No easy example ever makes my head ache;

I can't understand examples that are not arranged in regular order like those I am used to;

I never grumble at an example, unless it gives me a headache.

What are the most basic principles of reasoning that involve analyzing statements into their components?

The basic structure of statements in English is a *subject-predicate* structure; the subject "locates" a subject matter which the predicate then says something about. In our study of logic in Chapters One to Four we looked only at argument patterns that treated statements as unanalyzed wholes. In this chapter and the following one we will consider some of the arguments for which we need to dig more deeply into the structure of statements, separating subject and predicate and using separate symbols for each of them.

Thus in a simple statement like "Juktas is a mountain" we separate the subject, "Juktas," from the predicate, ". . . is a mountain." The subject by itself is a name that points out a subject but does not state anything true or false. If I said "Juktas," you might say "What about Juktas?" or something of the sort; you would certainly not label what I said true or false unless, for example, I was answering a question. If you asked, "What is the mountain visible from Knossos?" and if I replied "Juktas," my answer would be a short way of making the true statement "Juktas is the mountain visible from Knossos."

The predicate part of the statement "Juktas is a mountain," which consists of ". . . is a mountain," is not itself a statement either; it is an incomplete linguistic unit that needs a subject term in order to make a statement. If I "plug in" the name "Juktas," I get a true statement; if I "plug in" the name "Knossos," I get the false statement "Knossos is a mountain." In statement logic we would have abbreviated the whole statement with a single capital letter, but in subject-predicate logic we will have separate letters for subject and predicate. Logicians have the habit of using small letters for names of individuals and capital letters for predicates. We will follow this tradition, as well as the tradition of putting the name letter to the *right* of the predicate letter. So if

$$j \qquad \# \text{ Juktas}$$
$$M \ldots \quad \# \ldots \text{ is a mountain}$$

then Mj is short for "Juktas is a mountain"

We can also have relational predicates:

if $o \ \# \quad$ Olympus

and $H \ldots - \# \ldots$ is higher than $\ldots$ —

We can write the true statement

Hoj ("Olympus is higher than Juktas")

or the false statement

Hjo ("Juktas is higher than Olympus")

Placeholders and Quasi-Names

In order to help us keep straight the relation of the various blanks in complex predicates, we will follow the convention of using small letters that are not used very frequently, especially x, y, and z, as *placeholders* to indicate a gap where a name will go to make a statement out of a predicate. Thus we will write:

$Mx \quad \# \quad x$ is a mountain
$Hxy \quad \# \quad x$ is higher than y

and so on.

So far all we have done is to give a more complex way of writing simple statements. The next step, however, gets us into a new and important set of techniques. English uses a special set of words—*anything, everything, something, nothing,* and so on—to express *general* statements such as "It is not true that everything is a mountain," "Something is higher than Juktas," "Nothing is higher than Olympus." Such words are like names in some ways, unlike names in others: we will call them *quasi-names*. We will introduce some special symbols to enable us to make these kind of statements in our symbolic language and use such statements in symbolic arguments.

Note that in English we can use pronouns to refer back to words like *something* or *anything*; for example, we can say, "Something is higher than Juktas and *it* is a mountain" or "If anything is not a mountain, then *that thing* is not higher than Juktas." Sometimes it can be very hard in a complex English sentence to tie the right pronoun to the right antecedent. In our symbolic language we will avoid this problem by using an especially marked letter for *anything* or *something* and then *repeating* that letter where English would use pronouns like *he*, *she*, or *it*. To express the idea *anything* or *everything* we will use one of our placeholder letters x, y, z (and if we need them u, v and w) within parentheses, in the place where a proper name would ordinarily go. We will call these *universal quasi-names*. Thus to write, "If anything is higher than Juktas, then it is a mountain," we would write:

$$H(x)j \supset M(x)$$

where the second occurrence of (x) refers back to the first occurrence, as *it* in the English sentence refers back to *anything*. For *something* we will use a placeholder letter within square brackets. These we will call *existential quasi-names*. Thus we could write, "If something is higher than Juktas, then Juktas is not higher than that thing":

$$H[x]j \supset {\sim} Hj[x]$$

Of course, we can use the *anything* and *something* expressions alone and make the true statement "Something is a mountain":

$$M[x]$$

or the false statement "Everything is a mountain":

$$M(x)$$

When we use several existential quasi-names in an argument, we must take the precaution of using a new existential quasi-name for each new line. If we do not observe this precaution, we might have two lines referring to separate *somethings*, for example, "Something is a mountain" and "Something is not a mountain," and by using the same quasi-name give the false impression that this is the *same* something getting the contradiction

$$M[x] \cdot \sim M[x]$$

To make our notation as natural to read in English as possible, we will read our *something, everything, nothing* as *someone, everyone, no one* when the context makes it obvious we are talking about persons. Thus if

f	#	Frodo Baggins	Fx	#	x is fond of comfort
Hx	#	x is a Hobbit	Uxy	#	x is the uncle of y

we can write:

$F[x]$	Someone is fond of comfort.
Hf	Frodo is a Hobbit.
$H(x) \supset F(x)$	If anyone is a Hobbit, he or she is fond of comfort.
$U(x)f \supset H(x)$	If anyone is Frodo's uncle, then he is a Hobbit.

Translating into Symbolic Form

The words *not* or *it is not true that* can be confusing when used with *anyone, anything, someone,* and *something.* If I want to say, "Not everything is a valley" or "Not everyone is a Hobbit," I would write $\sim V[x]$ and $\sim H[x]$ respectively, because what I am saying is that *something* (at least one thing) is not a valley, and someone is not a Hobbit. But if I wanted to say "*Nothing* is a mountain" or "*No* one is a Hobbit," I would write $\sim M(x)$ and $\sim H(x)$ respectively.

In fact, English is full of tricky idioms here. In some cases *everyone* and *anyone* can be used indifferently, as in "Anyone who is a Hobbit is fond of comfort" and "Everyone who is a Hobbit is fond of comfort." If

Fx # x is fond of comfort

both would be written:

$$H(x) \supset F(x)$$

But "It is false that *everybody* is fond of comfort" would be:

$$\sim F[x]$$

(that is, "Somebody is not fond of comfort"), whereas "It is false that *anybody at all* is fond of comfort" would be:

$\sim F(x)$

(that is, "*Nobody* is fond of comfort").

You will soon get the hang of the various idioms involved and their translation from English to symbols as you see further examples and work exercises, but to help you here is a table of some common statements and their proper translations:

Table 6-1

---

1. If anybody is a Hobbit, he is fond of comfort.
    Everybody who is a Hobbit is fond of comfort.
    Every Hobbit is fond of comfort.
    All Hobbits are fond of comfort.
    Only those fond of comfort are Hobbits.

    $H(x) \supset F(x)$

2. If anybody is a Hobbit, he is not fond of comfort.
    Everybody who is a Hobbit is not fond of comfort.
    Nobody who is a Hobbit is fond of comfort.
    No Hobbit is fond of comfort.

    $H(x) \supset \sim F(x)$

3. Somebody is a Hobbit and fond of comfort.
    Some Hobbit is fond of comfort.
    Some Hobbits are fond of comfort.

    $H[x] \cdot F[x]$

4. Somebody who is a Hobbit is not fond of comfort.
    Some Hobbit is not fond of comfort.
    Some Hobbits are not fond of comfort.

    $H[x] \cdot \sim F[x]$

5. Frodo is a Hobbit.

    Hf

Table 6-1 (*Continued*)

6. Frodo is not a Hobbit.

    $\sim Hf$

    (Note: 1 and 2 are called *universal* statements, 3 and 4 are called *particular* statements, and 5 and 6 are called *individual* statements.)

7. Everyone is a Hobbit.
    Everybody is a Hobbit.
    All are Hobbits.

    $H(x)$

8. Somebody is a Hobbit.
    There are Hobbits.
    There is at least one Hobbit.

    $H[x]$

9. Somebody is not a Hobbit.
    Not everyone is a Hobbit.
    Everybody is not a Hobbit.

    $\sim H[x]$

10. Nobody is a Hobbit.
    No one is a Hobbit.
    There are no Hobbits.

    $\sim H(x)$

Rules for Changing Terms

For the time being, we will consider only statements that have just one of these namelike terms per statement. Thus we will postpone the problem of such statements as "If everybody is a Hobbit, somebody is fond of comfort" or "If everything were a mountain, nothing would be a valley." To use these quasi-names in arguments we will need some simple rules for "changing terms," that is, changing from one quasi-name to another or between quasi-names and proper names. The first rule we will call UN (Universal to Name).

UN If something is true of anything, it is true of any named individual. Symbolically:

$$\frac{A(x)}{An}$$

---

where A is any predicate or string of predicates and n is any proper name. This rule would justify, for instance, going from "If anybody is a Hobbit, that person is fond of comfort":

$H(x) \supset F(x)$

to "If Frodo is a Hobbit, he is fond of comfort":

$Hf \supset Ff$

So long as we replace every (x) with n (in this case every (x) with f), we are using this rule properly.

A second rule will be called NP (Name to Particular).

NP If something is true of a named individual, it is true of something. Symbolically:

$$\frac{An}{A[x]}$$

This would justify going from "Frodo is a Hobbit and fond of comfort" to "Someone is a Hobbit and fond of comfort":

$$\frac{Hf \cdot Ff}{H[x] \cdot F[x]}$$

Again we must be careful to replace every occurrence of the name with the same $[x]$. But if we use this rule on more than one name in an argument, *each* time we use it for a new name we must use a new existential quasi-name. Otherwise we could argue: "Frodo is a Hobbit, so someone is a

Hobbit; Gandalf is not a Hobbit, so someone is not a Hobbit. Therefore, someone is a Hobbit and not a Hobbit." Symbolically, if

g # Gandalf

1.	Hf	
2.	$\sim Hg$	
3.	$H[x]$	1 EG
4.	$\sim H[x]$	2 EG Forbidden
5.	$H[x] \cdot \sim H[x]$	3, 4 Conj.

A third rule we will call UP (Universal to Particular).

UP If something is true of everything, it is true of something. Symbolically:

$$\frac{A(x)}{A[x]}$$

For instance, this would justify going from "Every Hobbit is fond of comfort" to "If someone is a Hobbit, he is fond of comfort":

$$\frac{H(x) \supset F(x)}{H[x] \supset F[x]}$$

but not, of course, from "Every Hobbit is fond of comfort" to "Some Hobbit is fond of comfort" because that would go from $H(x) \supset F(x)$ to $H[x] \cdot F[x]$, and we cannot get from $\supset$ to $\cdot$ in this fashion.

    Some logicians would object to the rule UP because it involves the assumption that at least one thing exists and would not be true in a perfectly empty universe. Logic, they believe should be *absolutely* universal and should hold true even if nothing existed. But the assumption that at least one thing exists is a very modest one, and the rule UP is sufficiently useful for the sacrifice of a little generality to be worthwhile.

    Our final rule for the moment is an equivalence UU (Universal to Universal).

UU
$$\frac{A(x)}{A(y)}$$

---

where x and y are any two letters. We have not given an English statement here because this is basically a convenient rule for changing letters in universal quasi-names where necessary. Just as Commutation told us that it does not matter in which order we write $A \lor B$, so UU tells us that it does not matter whether we write $H(x) \supset F(x)$ or $H(y) \supset F(y)$ or $H(z) \supset F(z)$, and if we wish to change from one form to the other we may.

Syllogistic Logic

With this set of rules added to the rules of statement logic, we can now symbolize and test for validity a great number of arguments, including one whole area of traditional logic. We begin with simple statements of a certain standard kind. These standard form statements have one of the following six forms:

1. Every A is B
2. No A is B
3. Some A is B
4. Some A is not B
5. n is A (where n is the name
6. n is not A of an individual)

For example:

Every Hobbit is fond of comfort.
No Hobbit is fond of comfort.
Some Hobbit is fond of comfort.
Some Hobbit is not fond of comfort.
Frodo is a Hobbit.
Frodo is not a Hobbit.

From our point of view, each of the first four standard form statements contains two predicates, for example, "is a Hobbit," "is fond of comfort." But traditionally these statements were regarded as subject-predicate statements, the first "predicate" (as we see it) being the *subject term* and the second "predicate" (as we see it) being the *predicate term*. These terms were generally written in such a way that they could appear either first or second, either in the subject position or the predicate position. For example: "Every Hobbit likes food" would be written "Every Hobbit is a person who likes food" to make it easier to use the predicate term of that statement as the subject term of another, for example, "Every person who likes food likes to drink."

So long as we realize that when written in our way each of these "terms" really contains a predicate in our sense, it will do no harm to use the traditional terminology and speak of the subject term and predicate term in a standard form statement, or just of "terms."

This is the way we translate the standard form statements:

Every A is B	becomes	$\sim A(x) \vee B(x)$
No A is B	becomes	$\sim A(x) \vee \sim B(x)$
Some A is B	becomes	$A[x] \cdot B[x]$
Some A is not B	becomes	$A[x] \cdot \sim B[x]$
n is A	becomes	An
n is not A	becomes	$\sim An$

We are using the forms $\sim A(x) \vee B(x)$ and $\sim A(x) \vee \sim B(x)$ instead of $A(x) \supset B(x)$ and $A(x) \supset B(x)$ because syllogistic logic is simple enough to be done by cancellation methods together with some of the rules we have just given.

Equivalent Statements

Some simple manipulations of these standard form statements are possible. *No* and *some* statements are such that the order of subject and predicate is unimportant:

No A is B	is the same as	No B is A
Some A is B	is the same as	Some B is A

We can see why from the symbolic form:

$$\sim A(x) \vee \sim B(x) \quad \text{becomes} \quad \sim B(x) \vee \sim A(x)$$

by Commutation and

$$A[x] \cdot B[x] \qquad \text{becomes} \quad B[x] \cdot A[x]$$

by Commutation for *and* in our wider system. This reversal of subject and predicate in *no* and *some* statements is called *Conversion* and the equivalent statements are called the *converse* of each other.

A manipulation possible with *Every* and *some . . . not* statements consists of *reversing and negating* subject and predicate:

Every *A* is *B*   is equivalent to   Every non-*B* is non-*A*
Some *A* is not *B*   is equivalent to   Some non-*B* is not non-*A*

In symbolic form the equivalences hold by Commutation and Double Negation:

$$\sim\!A(x) \lor B(x) \quad \text{is equivalent to} \quad \sim\!\sim\!B(x) \lor \sim\!A(x)$$

(where the first $\sim$ is part of the way we translate *Every* statements)

$$A[x] \cdot \sim\!B[x] \quad \text{is equivalent to} \quad \sim\!B[x] \cdot \sim\!\sim\!A[x]$$

(where the first $\sim$ before the $A[x]$ is the *not* in *some . . . not*). These equivalences are called *Contraposition* and the equivalent statements are *contrapositives* of each other.

Finally, any of the first four standard form statements can be turned into an equivalent form by changing an *Every* to a *No* or vice versa, a *some* to a *some . . . not* or vice versa, and negating the predicate:

Every *A* is *B*   is equivalent to   No *A* is non-*B*
No *A* is *B*   is equivalent to   Every *A* is non-*B*
Some *A* is *B*   is equivalent to   Some *A* is not non-*B*
Some *A* is not *B*   is equivalent to   Some *A* is non-*B*

In the symbolic form each of these is just written the same way or is equivalent by Double Negation:

$$\sim\!A(x) \lor B(x) \qquad \text{is equivalent to} \quad \sim\!A(x) \lor \sim\!\sim\!B(x)$$
$$\sim\!A(x) \lor \sim\!B(x) \quad \text{is equivalent to} \quad \sim\!A(x) \lor \sim\!B(x)$$
$$A[x] \cdot B[x] \qquad\quad \text{is equivalent to} \quad A[x] \cdot \sim\!\sim\!B[x]$$
$$A[x] \cdot \sim\!B[x] \qquad \text{is equivalent to} \quad A[x] \cdot \sim\!B[x]$$

These equivalences are called *Obversion* and the equivalent forms are *obverses* of each other.

Actually, when we do traditional logic in symbolic form these equivalences are trivial, but it is worthwhile getting familiar with the equivalences in English because it will help us when we come to translate arguments into symbolic form.

Categorical Syllogisms

We are now ready to begin with syllogisms. To make a *categorical syllogism* you take two standard form statements that have one term in common, for example:

Every *A* is *B*
Every *B* is *C*

and draw a conclusion consisting of a standard form statement *not* containing the term common to the premises but containing the other two terms, one from each premise, for example:

Every *A* is *C*

Thus each syllogism has only three terms. The term that appears in both premises but not in the conclusion (*B* in the example) is called the *middle* term. Whatever term winds up as the subject term of the conclusion (*A* in the example) is called the *minor* term, and the premise it first appears in is the *minor premise*. Whatever term is the predicate of the conclusion (*C* in the example) is called the *major* term, and the premise it first appears in is the *major premise*.

So long as an argument consists of three standard form statements sharing three terms in the way described, it is a categorical syllogism. But hundreds of different argument patterns can be classified as categorical syllogisms and only about a dozen of these patterns are valid argument patterns.

Traditional logic had a number of ingenious ways of testing categorical syllogisms for validity, ranging from memorizing the valid patterns to using more or less complicated sets of rules. However, by combining our new rules with the simple system of statement logic from Chapter Three and a few of the rules from Chapter Four, we can give a simple, speedy, and effective test for any categorical syllogism.

There are three major types of valid categorical syllogisms. Some have two universal premises, some have one universal premise and one particular premise, and some have one universal premise and one individual premise. Those with two universal premises follow one of three patterns:

Every M is P	No M is P	Every P is M
Every S is M	Every S is M	No S is M
Every S is P	No S is P	No S is P

Translated into symbolism these are:

$\sim M(x) \vee P(x)$	$\sim M(x) \vee \sim P(x)$	$\sim P(x) \vee M(x)$
$\sim S(x) \vee M(x)$	$\sim S(x) \vee M(x)$	$\sim S(x) \vee \sim M(x)$
$\sim S(x) \vee P(x)$	$\sim S(x) \vee P(x)$	$\sim S(x) \vee \sim P$

and it can be seen that each is a case of the rule Cancel and Collect. In each case the two occurrences of the middle term cancel out leaving the minor and major terms in proper relationship:

$\sim M(x) \vee P(x)$	$\sim M(x) \vee \sim P(x)$	$\sim P(x) \vee M(x)$
$\sim S(x) \vee M(x)$	$\sim S(x) \vee M(x)$	$\sim S(x) \vee \sim M(x)$
$\sim S(x) \vee P(x)$	$\sim S(x) \vee \sim P(x)$	$\sim S(x) \vee P(x)$

Granted that such expressions as $M(x)$ and $\sim M(x)$ are not different with respect to cancellation from statements considered in Chapter Three; we have no need of any new rules to deal with these cases. Examples of syllogisms of this type would be:

Every Hobbit is fond of comfort.	$\sim H(x) \vee F(x)$
Every Took is a Hobbit.	$\sim T(x) \vee H(x)$
Every Took is fond of comfort.	$\sim T(x) \vee F(x)$

No Hobbit is a Wizard.	$H(x) \vee \sim W(x)$
Every Took is a Hobbit.	$T(x) \vee H(x)$
No Took is a Wizard.	$\sim T(x) \vee \sim W(x)$

Every Hobbit is fond of comfort.	$\sim H(x) \vee F(x)$
No Wizard is fond of comfort.	$\sim W(x) \vee F(x)$
No Wizard is a Hobbit.	$\sim W(x) \vee \sim H(x)$

Cases with one individual and one universal premise follow one of three patterns:

Every M is P	No M is P	Every P is M
n is M	n is M	n is not M
n is P	n is not P	n is not P

Symbolically:

$\sim M(x) \lor P(x)$	$\sim M(x) \lor \sim P(x)$	$\sim P(x) \lor M(x)$
Mn	Mn	$\sim Mn$
Pn	$\sim Pn$	$\sim Pn$

Each is valid by UP and Simple Cancellation:

1.	$\sim M(x) \lor P(x)$ ⎫		**1.**	$\sim M(x) \lor \sim P(x)$ ⎫	
2.	Mn ⎬ Pn?		**2.**	Mn ⎬ $\sim Pn$?	
3.	$\sim Mn \lor Pn$	1 UN	**3.**	$\sim Mn \lor \sim Pn$	1 UN
4.	Pn	2, 3 SC	**4.**	$\sim Pn$	2, 3 SC

1.	$\sim P(x) \lor M(x)$ ⎫	
2.	$\sim Mn$ ⎬ $\sim Pn$	
3.	$\sim Pn \lor Mn$	1 UN
4.	$\sim Pn$	2, 3 SC

Examples would be:

Every Hobbit is fond of comfort.	**1.**	$\sim H(x) \lor F(x)$ ⎫	
Frodo is a Hobbit.	**2.**	Hf ⎬ Ff?	
Frodo is fond of comfort.	**3.**	$\sim Hf \lor Ff$	1 UN
	4.	Ff	2, 3 SC

No Hobbit is a Wizard.	**1.**	$\sim H(x) \lor \sim W(x)$ ⎫	
Frodo is a Hobbit.	**2.**	Hf ⎬ $\sim Wf$?	
Frodo is not a Wizard.	**3.**	$\sim Hf \lor \sim Wf$	1 UN
	4.	$\sim Wf$	2, 3 SC

Every Hobbit is fond of comfort.	**1.**	$\sim H(x) \lor \sim F(x)$ ⎫	
Gandalf is not fond of comfort.	**2.**	$\sim Fg$ ⎬ $\sim Hg$?	
Gandalf is not a Hobbit.	**3.**	$\sim Hg \lor \sim Fg$	1 UN
	4.	$\sim Hg$	2, 3 SC

There are a number of patterns involving one universal and one particular premise:

Every M is P	No M is P	Every P is M
Some S is M	Some S is M	Some S is not M
Some S is P	Some S is not P	Some S is not P

Every M is S	Every M is S
Some M is P	Some M is not P
Some S is P	Some S is not P

Symbolically:

$$\frac{\begin{array}{ll} \sim M(x) \vee P(x) \\ S[x] \quad \cdot \quad M[x] \end{array}}{S[x] \quad \cdot \quad P[x]} \qquad \frac{\begin{array}{ll} \sim M(x) \vee \sim P(x) \\ S[x] \quad \cdot \quad M[x] \end{array}}{S[x] \quad \cdot \quad \sim P[x]} \qquad \frac{\begin{array}{ll} \sim P(x) \vee M(x) \\ S[x] \quad \cdot \quad \sim M[x] \end{array}}{S[x] \quad \cdot \quad \sim P[x]}$$

$$\frac{\begin{array}{ll} \sim M(x) \vee S(x) \\ M[x] \quad \cdot \quad P[x] \end{array}}{S[x] \quad \cdot \quad P[x]} \qquad \frac{\begin{array}{ll} \sim M(x) \vee S(x) \\ M[x] \quad \cdot \quad \sim P[x] \end{array}}{S[x] \quad \cdot \quad \sim P[x]}$$

Each involves a UP step and Cancel and Join. For example:

1. $\sim M(x) \vee P(x)$ ⎫
2. $S[x] \cdot M[x]$ ⎬ $S[x] \cdot P[x]$?
3. $\sim M[x] \vee P[x]$ ⎭   1 UP
4. $S[x] \cdot P[x]$ 2, 3 CJ

Since the general pattern of each of the others is the same, there is no point in going through the other four in detail. Notice that the rules NP and UU, which were given along with UP and UN, have not been necessary for any syllogistic argument. The eleven patterns given, along with minor variations, are all the valid syllogistic patterns.

You must not always expect to find these patterns in the exact pattern given; order of premises may be different, and in *some* and *no* statements, where order of subject and predicate is unimportant, you may find subject and predicate reversed. In some real-life syllogistic arguments you may even find contrapositives or obverses that need to be put back in their equivalent forms before you can recognize the pattern as one of those discussed. However, by doing syllogistic logic with our methods we can simply leave the premises in the form in which they occur, since the cancellation methods will work anyway.

Here are a few ingenious and complicated syllogisms by Lewis Carroll which can be dealt with directly by our methods, but which would have to be translated before they could be tested by traditional methods of pattern recognition or rules. Rather than give a dictionary, we will underline letters in key terms and use these to abbreviate the terms.

No *w*asp is *f*riendly.
No *u*nfriendly creature is *w*elcome.
Every wasp is unwelcome.

PREDICATE LOGIC: THE SIMPLE SYSTEM

In traditional syllogistic logic this would seem not to have three terms and so not be a syllogism at all, or else seem to break rules about syllogisms having two negative premises or about getting a positive conclusion from negative premises. The standard technique would have been to obvert both premises to get:

Every wasp is unfriendly.
Every unfriendly creature is unwelcome.
Every wasp is unwelcome.

But in our notation we can simply write:

$$\frac{\sim W(x) \vee \sim F(x)}{\sim \sim F(x) \vee \sim E(x)}$$
$$\sim W(x) \vee \sim E(x)$$

in which "unfriendly" has been translated as $\sim F(x)$ and "unwelcome" as $\sim E(x)$. The conclusion follows by Cancel and Collect without any need for manipulation of the premises.

Another example is:

No *eventful* journey is ever *forgotten*.
Uneventful journeys are not *worth* writing a book about.
Journeys worth writing a book about are never forgotten.

We can translate and solve directly:

$$\frac{\sim E(x) \vee \sim F(x)}{\sim \sim E(x) \vee \sim W(x)}$$
$$\sim W(x) \vee \sim F(x)$$

It may help to spell this one out in a proof:

1.	$\sim E(x) \vee \sim F(x)$	
2.	$\sim \sim E(x) \vee \sim W(x)$	$\sim W(x) \vee \sim F(x)$?
3.	$E(x) \vee \sim W(x)$	2 DN
4.	$\sim F(x) \vee \sim W(x)$	1, 3 CC
5.	$\sim W(x) \vee \sim F(x)$	4 Com.

Of course, the conclusion can be read as in the English or as "No journey worth writing about is forgotten" or as "Every journey worth writing about is unforgotten," and in several other equivalent ways.

Invalid Syllogisms

An invalid syllogism, like an invalid argument in statement logic, will not cancel out to yield the desired conclusion. Here are some invalid patterns:

Every P is M No M is P
Every S is M No S is M
——————   ——————
Every S is P No S is P

$\sim P(x) \vee M(x)$ $\sim M(x) \vee \sim P(x)$
$\sim S(x) \vee M(x)$ $\sim S(x) \vee \sim M(x)$
——————————   ——————————
$\sim S(x) \vee P(x)$ $\sim S(x) \vee \sim P(x)$

Every M is P Every M is S
No S is M Some P is not M
——————   ——————————
No S is P Some S is not P

$\sim M(x) \vee P(x)$ $\sim M(x) \vee S(x)$
$\sim S(x) \vee \sim M(x)$ $P[x] \cdot \sim M[x]$
——————————   ——————————
$\sim S(x) \vee P(x)$ $S[x] \cdot \sim P[x]$

As can be seen, none of these cancels out, in each case because the middle term fails to cancel out in its two occurrences.

To the contrary, in the following arguments the middle term cancels out (after using UN in the first case) but the resulting terms are the wrong ones:

Every M is P No M is P Every P is M
n is M Every S is M Some S is not M
——————   ——————   ——————————
n is not P Every S is P Some S is P

$\sim M(x) \vee P(x)$ $\sim M(x) \vee \sim P(x)$ $\sim P(x) \vee M(x)$
Mn $\sim S(x) \vee M(x)$ $S[x] \cdot \sim M[x]$
——————   ——————————   ——————————
$\sim Pn$ $\sim S(x) \vee P(x)$ $S[x] \cdot P[x]$

Since there are hundreds of invalid syllogisms, we can give only a few samples, but the general principle holds: After the application of UP or UN, an invalid syllogism either does not cancel or cancels to the wrong terms.

Table 6-1

The following ways of speaking are especially hard to translate:

FORM	Only A are B
EQUIVALENT TO	Every B is A
SYMBOLIC TRANSLATION	$\sim B(x) \vee A(x)$
EXAMPLE	Only Hobbits have hairy feet.
	i.e., Every hairy-footed person is a Hobbit.
FORM	All A is not B
EQUIVALENT TO	In some contexts means All A are non-B
	i.e., No A are B. But often equivalent to
	Some A is not B, especially if *all* is stressed.
SYMBOLIC TRANSLATION	$\sim A(x) \vee \sim B(x)$ *or else to* $A[x] \cdot \sim B[x]$
	depending on which meaning above is chosen.
EXAMPLES	(All) elves are not afraid of the ghosts of men.
	i.e., No elves are afraid of the ghosts of men.
	All Hobbits are not suspicious of elves.
	i.e., Some Hobbits are not suspicious of elves.
FORM	Nothing except A is B
EQUIVALENT TO	Every B is A
SYMBOLIC TRANSLATION	$\sim B(x) \vee A(x)$
EXAMPLE	Nothing except a Hobbit is hairy-footed.
	i.e., Every hairy-footed person is a Hobbit.
FORM	No A fails to be B
EQUIVALENT TO	Every A is B
SYMBOLIC TRANSLATION	$\sim A(x) \vee B(x)$
EXAMPLE	No Hobbit fails to be hairy-footed.
	i.e., Every Hobbit is hairy-footed.
FORM	Nothing is A unless it is B
EQUIVALENT TO	Every A is B
SYMBOLIC TRANSLATION	$\sim A(x) \vee B(x)$
EXAMPLE	Nothing is a Hobbit unless it is hairy-footed.
	i.e., Every Hobbit is hairy-footed.
FORM	Anything except A is B
EQUIVALENT TO	Every non-A is B
SYMBOLIC TRANSLATION	$\sim \sim A(x) \vee B(x)$ *or* $A(x) \vee B(x)$
EXAMPLE	Anything except the Ring would be safe in Gandalf's keeping.
	i.e., Everything that is not the Ring would be safe in Gandalf's keeping.

Exercise 6-1

Symbolize and check for validity the following syllogisms from Lewis Carroll's Symbolic Logic.

1. Some unauthorized reports are false;
   All authorized reports are trustworthy.
     Some false reports are not trustworthy.

2. Some pillows are soft;
   No pokers are soft.
     Some pokers are not pillows.

3. Improbable stories are not easily believed;
   None of his stories is probable.
     None of his stories is easily believed.

*4. No thieves are honest;
   Some dishonest people are found out.
     Some thieves are found out.

5. No muffins are wholesome;
   All puffy food is unwholesome.
     All muffins are puffy.

6. No birds, except peacocks, are proud of their tails;
   Some birds that are proud of their tails cannot sing.
     Some peacocks cannot sing.

7. Warmth relieves pain;
   Nothing that does not relieve pain is useful in toothache.
     Warmth is useful in toothache.

8. No bankrupts are rich;
   Some merchants are not bankrupts.
     Some merchants are rich.

9. Bores are dreaded;
   No bore is ever begged to prolong his visit.
     No one who is dreaded is ever begged to prolong his visit.

*10. All wise men walk on their feet;
   All unwise men walk on their hands.
     No man walks on both.

11. No wheelbarrows are comfortable;
   No uncomfortable vehicles are popular.
     No wheelbarrows are popular.

12. No frogs are poetical;
   Some ducks are unpoetical.
     Some ducks are not frogs.

13. No emperors are dentists;
    All dentists are dreaded by children.
       No emperors are dreaded by children.
14. Sugar is sweet;
    Salt is not sweet;
       Salt is not sugar.
15. Every eagle can fly;
    Some pigs cannot fly.
       Some pigs are not eagles.

Soriteses and Enthymemes

Another part of traditional syllogistic logic that is easily handled by our methods is the theory of *soriteses*, arguments involving chains of syllogisms. Consider the argument at the beginning of the chapter.

When I work a logic example without grumbling, you may be sure it is one that I can understand;

This sorites is not arranged in regular order like the examples I am used to;

No easy example ever makes my head ache;

I can't understand examples that are not arranged in regular order like those I am used to;

I never grumble at an example, unless it gives me a headache.

The argument can be reconstructed as a chain of syllogisms after some reshuffling of the premises, but without any reshuffling we can symbolize it in our system and "solve" this sorites to find what conclusion follows from it:

Let   *Gx* # *x* is a logic example I grumble at

     Ux # is a logic example I understand

     Rx # *x* is a logic example in regular order like the ones I am used to

     Ex # *x* is an easy logic example

     Hx # *x* is a logic example that makes my head ache

      t # this sorites

We can symbolize as follows:

1.	$\sim\sim G(x) \vee U(x)$	Every example I don't grumble at is an example I understand;
2.	$\sim Rt$	This sorites is not arranged in regular order like the ones I am used to;
3.	$\sim E(x) \vee \sim H(x)$	No easy example is an example that makes my head ache;
4.	$\sim\sim R(x) \vee \sim U(x)$	Every example not arranged in regular order like the ones I am used to is one I don't understand;
5.	$\sim G(x) \vee H(x)$	Every example I grumble at is an example that gives me a headache.

and complete the argument as follows:

6.	$U(x) \vee H(x)$	1, 5 CC
7.	$H(x) \vee \sim R(x)$	4, 6 CC
8.	$\sim\sim R(x) \vee \sim E(x)$	7, 3 CC
9.	$\sim\sim Rt \vee \sim Et$	8 UN
10.	$\sim Et$	2, 9 SC

"This sorites is not easy."

Sometimes soriteses are given with the conclusion supplied, and one merely has to prove the conclusion. But quite often soriteses are given as puzzles in reasoning, and the student is left to find as well as prove the conclusion (see the exercises at the end of this section). Cancellation methods are especially apt for this purpose, for whatever remains when all possible cancellations have been done is the conclusion of the sorites. Most logic books, including this one, borrow from a series of ingenious soriteses constructed by Lewis Carroll, author of *Alice in Wonderland*. The example above is one of Carroll's.

Another part of traditional syllogistic logic was the theory of enthymemes, syllogisms with either one premise or the conclusion left out.

If the conclusion is left out, it will be turned up by cancellation methods; whereas if a premise is left out, one has merely to see what combination of terms needs to be supplied to yield that conclusion. Thus if someone argues:

Every Hobbit is fond of comfort.
Therefore, someone fond of comfort is not a Wizard.

we can symbolize:

$\sim H(x) \vee F(x)$
$F[x] \cdot \sim W[x]$

and see that the missing premise is

$H[x] \cdot \sim W[x]$

"Some Hobbit is not a Wizard," for only that premise will cancel with the original premise to give the desired conclusion.

Of course some enthymemes and some soriteses are invalid and in that case we cannot complete the chain of cancellations or not supply a premise which will cancel to yield a conclusion.

In fact once the basic idea that syllogistic arguments work by the cancellation of middle terms is grasped there is nothing especially difficult about the solution of any syllogistic argument, whether syllogism, soritese, or enthymeme.

Exercise 6-2

Find the conclusion, if any, of these enthymemes from Lewis Carroll's Symbolic Logic. *Use the cancellation method.*

1. Audible music causes vibration in the air;
    Inaudible music is not worth paying for.
2. He gave me five pounds;
    I was delighted.
3. No old Dons are fat millers;
    All my friends are old millers.

*4. Flour is good for food;
  Oatmeal is a kind of flour.
5. Some dreams are terrible;
  No lambs are terrible.
6. No rich man begs in the street;
  All who are not rich should keep accounts.
7. No thieves are honest;
  Some dishonest people are found out.
8. All wasps are unfriendly;
  All puppies are friendly.
9. All improbable stories are doubted;
  None of these stories is probable.
10. "He told me you had gone away."
  "He never says one word of truth."

Exercise 6-3

Translate into symbols, and find and prove the conclusion of each of the following soriteses from Lewis Carroll's Symbolic Logic.

1. No books sold here have gilt edges, except what are in the front shop;
  All the authorized editions have red labels;
  All the books with red labels are priced at 5 shillings, and upwards.
  None but authorized editions is ever placed in the front shop.
2. Remedies for bleeding that fail to check it are a mockery;
  Tincture of Calendula is not to be despised;
  Remedies that will check the bleeding when you cut your finger are useful;
  All mock remedies for bleeding are despicable.
3. None of the unnoticed things met with at sea are mermaids;
  Things entered in the log, as met with at sea, are sure to be worth remembering;
  I have never met with anything worth remembering, when on a voyage;
  Things met with at sea that are noticed are sure to be recorded in the log;
*4. Animals that do not kick are always unexcitable;
  Donkeys have no horns;
  A buffalo can always toss one over a gate;

No animals that kick are easy to swallow;
No hornless animal can toss one over a gate;
All animals are excitable, except buffaloes.

5. No birds except ostriches are 9 feet high;
There are no birds in this aviary that belong to anyone but me;
No ostrich lives on mince pies;
I have no birds less than 9 feet high.

6. A plum pudding that is not really solid is mere porridge;
Every plum pudding served at my table has been boiled in a cloth;
A plum pudding that is mere porridge is indistinguishable from soup;
No plum puddings are really solid, except what are served at my table.

7. No interesting poems are unpopular among people of real taste;
No modern poetry is free from affectation;
All your poems are on the subject of soap bubbles;
No affected poetry is popular among people of real taste;
No ancient poem is on the subject of soap bubbles.

8. All the fruit at this show that fails to get a prize is the property of the committee;
None of my peaches have got prizes;
None of the fruit sold off in the evening is unripe;
None of the ripe fruit has been grown in a hot-house;
All fruit that belongs to the committee is sold off in the evening.

9. Promise breakers are untrustworthy;
Wine drinkers are very communicative;
A man who keeps his promises is honest;
No teetotalers are pawnbrokers;
One can always trust a very communicative person.

10. No kitten that loves fish is unteachable;
No kitten without a tail will play with a gorilla;
Kittens with whiskers always love fish;
No teachable kitten has green eyes;
No kittens have tails unless they have whiskers.

Problems with Syllogistic Logic

There are some differences between syllogistic logic as we do it and the traditional logic of syllogisms taught in schools from Aristotle up to the nineteenth century. Some of these differences are due to a difference in interpretation about certain relations said to hold between different standard form statements with the same subject and predicate. According to the traditional *square of opposition*, which we discuss below, an *every* and a *some . . . not* statement with the same subject and predicate were *contradictories*, (e.g., "Every Hobbit is fond of comfort" and "Some Hobbit is not fond of comfort") as were the corresponding *no* and *some* statements (e.g., "No Hobbit is fond of comfort" and "Some Hobbit is fond of comfort"). Contradictory statements are such that both cannot be true but one or the other must be true. Our way of writing these statements makes this fairly clear: $\sim S(x) \vee P(x)$ and $S[x] \cdot \sim P[x]$ are such that after the use of UP you could cancel either the $S[x]$'s or the $P[x]$'s to get $P[x]$ and $\sim P[x]$ or $S[x]$ and $\sim S[x]$, so if both were true we could derive a contradiction.

However, the traditional doctrine also held that a *some* statement followed from the *every* statement with the same subject and predicate, and a *some . . . not* statement followed from the corresponding *no* statement. Modern logicians reject this implication because it depends on the assumption, which is sometimes false, that there *are* things of the kind mentioned in the subject term. It might be true by definition, for example, that "Every unicorn has a single horn" but false that there were any unicorns, so we would not want to infer "Some unicorn has a single horn" from "Every unicorn has a single horn."

In terms of our symbolism the difficulty is that although $\sim S[x] \vee P[x]$ follows from $\sim S(x) \vee P(x)$, the *some* statement $S[x] \cdot P[x]$ does not. The traditional logicians seem to have simply assumed that something of the kind mentioned in the subject term existed. If this were always true, then the *some* statement would follow from the *every* statement:

1. $\sim S(x) \vee P(x)\}$ $S[x] \cdot P[x]$?
2. $S[x]$ Assumption of existence of S's
3. $\sim S[x] \vee P[x]$ 1 UP
4. $P[x]$ 1, 3 SC
5. $S[x] \cdot P[x]$ 2, 4 Conj.

Where the assumption is justified, the *some* statement *will* follow from the corresponding *every* statement, and the *some . . . not* statement from the corresponding *no* statement. When these implications hold, the *every* statement and the corresponding *no* statement become *contraries*—both can be false but both cannot be true—and the *some* and *some . . . not* are *subcontraries*—both can be true but both cannot be false. Putting this in tabular form gives us the traditional *square of opposition*.

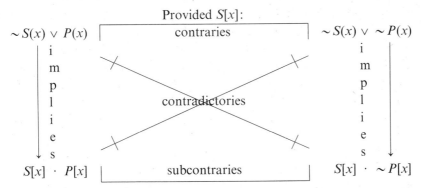

However, if $S[x]$ is false, both the *every* and the *no* statements can be true, and both the *some* and the *some . . . not* statements can be false, and the traditional square of opposition collapses. Because in many interesting cases we cannot be sure if $S[x]$ is true, the traditional square of opposition has only limited application.

The modern way of treating syllogistic logic has some problems of its own. Consider a case where we know that no things of a particular kind (unicorns, for example) exist. We could write this as $\sim U(x)$. But if we have the rule Addition, discussed in Chapters Three and Four, we can derive $\sim U(x) \lor A(x)$ from $\sim U(x)$, where Ax is any predicate. For example:

Let $Fx \quad \# \quad x$ is fierce

We can derive both "Every unicorn is fierce," $\sim U(x) \lor F(x)$, and "No unicorn is fierce," $\sim U(x) \lor \sim F(x)$, from $\sim U(x)$. Both of these universal statements are said to be *vacuously* true because the antecedent of the conditional "If anything is a unicorn, it is fierce/not fierce" is *vacuous*— that is, it refers to an "empty class," a group of nonexistent creatures.

It is not just Addition that is the problem here, however. If *every* and *some . . . not* statements are contradictories, and *no* and *some* statements are contradictories, then *some* and *some . . . not* statements about unicorns—$U[x] \cdot F[x]$, $U[x] \cdot \sim F[x]$—will both contain the false component $U[x]$ and therefore both be false, so it follows that both of their contradictories $\sim U(x) \lor F(x)$ and $\sim U(x) \lor \sim F(x)$ will be true. One can see why the traditional square of opposition breaks down on the modern interpretation of standard form statements.

One way of getting around this problem is to regard universal affirmative statements as *including* the existence of their subject classes: "Every unicorn is fierce" would be $(\sim U(x) \lor (F(x)) \cdot U[x]$ and "No unicorn is fierce" would be $(\sim U(x) \lor \sim F(x)) \cdot U[x]$. This makes the two statements contraries again since the *every* statement implies $F[x]$ and the *no* statement implies $\sim F[x]$. They cannot both be true, but if there are no unicorns, both will be false because the component $U[x]$ will be false. However, this does not mean that the *some* and *some . . . not* statements will be subcontraries; if $U[x]$ is false both will be false, and subcontraries cannot both be false.

But if the corresponding *some* and *some . . . not* statements are not subcontraries, and the corresponding *every* and *no* statements *are* contraries, then to avoid inconsistency we must say that the corresponding *every* and *some . . . not* are not contradictory, or that the corresponding *no* and *some* statements are not contradictories. If the *every* and *no* were both false, their contradictories would both be true; if one was false, one of the contradictories would be true; they cannot both be true, so *some* and *some . . . not* could not both be false and would be subcontraries.

However, it turns out that we need get rid of only *one* of the contradictory relationships. Lewis Carroll was well aware of this (not all recent logicians have been) and came down firmly on the side of rejecting the contradictory relation between *every* statements and the corresponding *some . . . not* statement. To do this, it turns out that we need to assert that *every* statements, *some* statements, and *some . . . not* statements all imply the existence of their subject terms, but that *no* statements do *not* imply the existence of their subject terms. This leads to the rather odd "Carrollian" square of opposition which has corresponding *no* and *every* statements as contraries, corresponding *no* and *some* statements as contradictories, but no subcontrary relations and no contradictory relations between an *every* statement and the corresponding *some . . . not* statement.

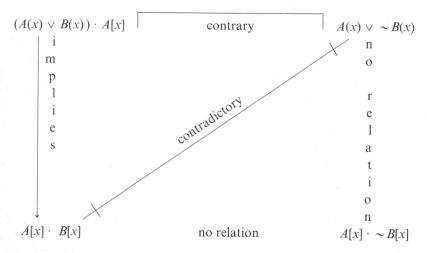

Since $A[x] \cdot B[x]$ and $A[x] \cdot \sim B[x]$ are not subcontraries, they can both be false; but since $A[x] \cdot \sim B[x]$ is not contradictory to $(\sim A(x) \vee B(x)) \cdot A[x]$, this does not mean that both contraries will be true. Both contraries cannot be true: If $A[x]$ is false, $(\sim A(x) \vee B(x)) \cdot A[x]$ will be false; and if $A[x]$ is true, then one of the two must be false, since $B[x]$ would follow from $\sim A(x) \vee B(x)$ and $\sim B[x]$ would follow from $\sim A(x) \vee \sim B(x)$—in both cases by UP and SC.

The relationship between $\sim A(x) \vee \sim B(x)$ and $A[x] \cdot B[x]$ is justified by the same arguments used earlier in this chapter, but the denial of $(\sim A(x) \vee B(x)) \cdot A[x]$ would be a complex statement that would not be contradictory to $A[x] \cdot \sim B[x]$. Carroll's system then is quite consistent and, although rather complex, would be a viable alternative to the accepted way of looking at the square of opposition and the proper way to write standard form statements.

The significant point is that there are plausible variant interpretations on matters of importance. No logical system is uniquely satisfactory and none *completely* fits *all* of our intuitions about the relationship of statements in ordinary language. The "vacuous truth" of universal statements with "vacuous" antecedent terms is an odd and counterintuitive feature of the modern interpretation, but older interpretations had their problems also. Carroll's interpretation is less simple and symmetrical than either the traditional Aristotelian interpretation or the "modern" interpretation that denies all of the square of opposition relations except contradiction between *every* and *some . . . not* and between *no* and *some*.

Nonsyllogistic Arguments

For all their very limited and artificial form, syllogistic arguments are surprisingly flexible and useful. But it is not difficult to extend the symbolic apparatus we already have to cover arguments more complex than those that can be handled by purely syllogistic methods. Consider, for example, the following argument:

Every Sauron-hating dwarf supports Gandalf.
Some Sauron-hating rangers support Gandalf.
Everyone who supports Gandalf has something in common with anyone who supports Gandalf.
There are some Sauron-hating dwarves.
Therefore, some rangers have something in common with some dwarves.

Let Sx # x hates Sauron

Dx # x is a dwarf

Rx # x is a ranger

g # Gandalf

Uxy # x supports y

Cxy # x has something in common with y

We can symbolize as follows:

1. $(S(x) \cdot D(x)) \supset U(x)g$
2. $(S[x] \cdot R[x]) \cdot U[x]g$
3. $(U(x)g \cdot U(y)g) \supset C(x)(y)$ $\Bigg\}$ $(R[x] \cdot D[x]) \cdot C[x][y]?$
4. $S[x] \cdot D[x]$

This argument is, in fact, a quite complex one, involving as it does one statement, 4, that contains *two* universal quasi-names. But given the methods of Chapter Five and our term-changing rules, we can prove the conclusion as follows:

1. $(S(x) \cdot D(x)) \supset U(x)g$
2. $(S[x] \cdot R[x]) \cdot U[x]g$
3. $(U(x)g \cdot U(y)g) \supset C(x)(y)$ $\Bigg\}$ $(R[x] \cdot D[y]) \cdot C[x][y]?$
4. $S[y] \cdot D[y]$
5. $(S[y] \cdot D[y]) \supset U[y]g$ 1 UU, UP
6. $U[y]g$ 4, 5 MP
7. $U[x]g$ 3 Simp.
8. $U[x]g \cdot U[y]g$ 6, 7 Conj.
9. $(U[x]g \cdot U[y]g) \supset C[x][y]$ 3 UP
10. $C[x][y]$ 8, 9 MP
11. $R[x]$ 2 Simp.
12. $D[y]$ 4 Simp.
13. $(R[x] \cdot D[y]) \cdot C[x][y]$ 10, 11, 12 Conj.

This argument, of course, is much too complex to be done by syllogistic methods. Of the four premises only the fourth could be regarded as a standard form statement, and none of the steps involved Cancel and Collect to eliminate a middle term. We could have used a less complex argument to begin with, but this one illustrates several points of interest. Because it had two premises involving existential quasi-names, we had to use two existential quasi-names (remember the restriction discussed when existential quasi-names were introduced). It was also our first argument using two quasi-names in one statement.

So long as we have two universal or two existential quasi-names in one statement, there is relatively little room for confusion, though even then some ambiguities are possible. But with mixed existential and universal quasi-names, there are many possible ambiguities. Consider, for example, the statements "Everyone admires someone" and "There is someone whom everyone admires." The first statement allows for different people each admiring their own choices. Frodo might admire Bilbo, Bilbo might admire Gandalf, and so on. But the second statement says that there is some single person who is admired by *everyone*, a far more improbable statement. Yet with quasi-names it would seem that both would have to be symbolized as

$$A(x)[y]$$

The problem raised here is that of one quasi-name that is "subordinate to" or "within the scope of" another. We will discuss this problem in the next chapter and extend our system to take care of it.

Refutation

Let us now look at the problem of refutation in the simple system. Standard treatments of syllogistic logic are somewhat broader than standard treatments of statement logic in that, besides proofs of given conclusions, the solution of soriteses and enthymemes sometimes involves finding an unstated conclusion. But refutation in the sense of ways to *disprove* a disputed conclusion receives not much more attention in standard treatments of syllogistic logic than it receives in standard treatments of statement logic.

There are some useful things to be said about refuting universal and particular statements. A universal statement, of the standard form "Every A is B," can be refuted by just one counterexample: one case of something that is A but not B. But to disprove a particular statement "Some A is B" we have to prove the truth of a universal negative "No A is B," which can often be very difficult. Similarly, to refute a statement of the form "No A is B" we need only show that some A *is* B, but to disprove "Some A is not B" we would need to prove the universal affirmative "Every A is B."

To refute the conclusion or one of the premises of a syllogistic argument we need, of course, another argument. Sometimes this is unrelated to the original argument, but in a number of interesting cases a proof and a refutation are the same except for one premise. For instance, the argument against the existence of God from the fact of evil can be stated as a syllogism:

No Universe in which unjustified evil exists is a Universe in which God exists.

The actual Universe is one in which unjustified evil exists.

The actual Universe is one in which God does not exist.

However, a believer in God can give the following argument:

No Universe in which unjustified evil exists is a Universe in which God exists.
Our Universe is one in which God exists.

Our Universe is one in which unjustified evil does not exist.

The first premise, which is the major premise, is something on which many atheists and the theists can agree. But by changing the minor premise they come to very different conclusions: The atheist's argument is a refutation of the minor premise of the theist's argument, and the theist's argument is a refutation of the minor premise of the atheist's argument.

Interestingly enough, it is not usually the case that simply changing one premise of a valid syllogism from positive to negative changes the conclusion from positive to negative. There are three cases where changing the major premise of a valid syllogism from *every* to *no* or from *no* to *every* leads to a reversal of the conclusion:

Every M is P	No M is P
n is M	n is M
n is P	n is not P
No M is P	No M is P
Every S is M	Every S is M
Every S is P	No S is P
Every M is P	No M is P
Some S is M	Some S is M
Some S is P	Some S is not P

But in other valid syllogisms no such simple relation exists; and even in these three pairs it must be the major premise that is reversed.

Any valid syllogism is such that the denial of the conclusion together with either one of the other premises implies the denial of the remaining premise. This is simply a consequence of the fact that valid syllogisms have only two premises and are valid proofs. *If* both premises are true, then the conclusion must be true; so if the conclusion is false, then one of the premises must be false. If we take one of them as a premise of a new argument, then the falsity of the other one will follow from that premise and the denial of the conclusion.

The atheist-theist argument above illustrates this general pattern, and a third argument is possible:

Our Universe is one in which God exists.

Our Universe is one in which unjustified evil exists.

Some Universe in which God exists is a Universe in which unjustified evil exists.

This is not a syllogistic argument by the traditional rules, but it can be shown to be valid by our rules:

Let o #   our Universe

           Gx # x is a universe in which God exists

           Ex # x is a universe in which unjustified evil exists

Then we can symbolize and argue as follows:

1. Go ⎫
2. Eo ⎭ $G[x] \cdot E[x]$

3. $Go \cdot Eo$ 1, 2 Conj.
4. $G[x] \cdot E[x]$ 3 NP

This conclusion, "Something is a Universe in which God exists and that something is a Universe in which unjustified evil exists," ($G[x] \cdot E[x]$), is, of course, the contradictory of "No universe in which unjustified evil exists is a universe in which God exists," ($\sim E(x) \lor \sim G(x)$), which was our original major premise.

In longer syllogistic arguments, such as soriteses, or in nonsyllogistic predicate logic arguments, we can say, in general, that if they are valid proofs, the denial of the conclusion together with all the remaining premises except one will imply the denial of that premise. If the argument is a valid refutation, the conclusion itself together with all the remaining premises except one will imply the denial of the remaining premise.

These principles hold true even if the remaining premise is a superfluous one that plays no part in the argument, provided we have a system
that includes Addition and therefore includes the rule Contradiction, since
in a valid proof the nonsuperfluous premises joined with the denial of the
conclusion would be a contradiction, and with the rule Contradiction
anything follows from a contradiction. (Similarly, in a valid refutation
the conclusion joined with all the nonsuperfluous premises would be a
contradiction.)

To illustrate this point consider the following argument:

Every *Hobbit* is *fond* of comfort.
Every *Took* is a Hobbit.
Pippin is a Took.
Merry is not a Took.
Therefore, *Pippin* is fond of comfort.

We could symbolize and prove the conclusion as follows:

1. $\sim H(x) \lor F(x)$
2. $\sim T(x) \lor H(x)$ $\Big\}$ Fp
3. Tp
4. $\sim Tm$
5. $\sim T(x) \lor F(x)$ 1, 2 CC
6. $\sim Tp \lor Fp$ 5 UN
7. Fp 3, 6 SC

and we can see that premise 4 is superfluous. Nevertheless, the denial of
the conclusion and premises 1–3 imply the denial of 4 by Contradiction:

1. $\sim H(x) \lor F(x)$
2. $\sim T(x) \lor H(x)$ $\Big\}$ Tm
3. Tp
4. $\sim Fp$
5. $\sim T(x) \lor F(x)$ 1, 2 CC
6. $\sim Tp \lor Fp$ 5 UN
7. Fp 3, 6 SC
8. $Fp \cdot \sim Fp$ 7, 4 Conj.
9. $\sim Tm$ 8 Contrad.

Of course, like all Reductio arguments, this one has the curious feature
that we could just as well have proved the opposite of the conclusion we

arrived at, or in fact any conclusion at all, since anything follows from a contradiction. Since we define an invalid argument as one that is neither a valid proof nor a valid refutation, we can make the rather strong statement that in an invalid argument it is never true that joining either the conclusion or the denial of the conclusion to all but one of the premises will enable us to prove the denial of the remaining premise (that is, to refute the remaining premise). Of course, any statement can be refuted by *some* argument: Even a logical truth can be validly refuted by contradictory premises and Contradiction. (This does not mean a logical truth can ever be condemned as false, since contradictory premises can never be *true*.)

Invalidity

In simple cases you can see by looking that a conclusion does not follow from a set of premises. Sometimes, of course, you can refute a proposed conclusion, show that the premises imply the denial of the supposed conclusion. But many complex arguments leave open their conclusions; it is possible neither to prove *nor* to refute a proposed conclusion. How can we be sure that this is the situation? Mere inability to give a proof or refutation is not conclusive; we may have missed some possible proof or refutation.

As it turns out, there is no completely general solution to this problem for predicate logic. But for the comparatively simple system of this chapter some reasonably reliable rules of thumb can be given:

1. First, rewrite the premises in the style of the simple system of Chapter Three, so that every line is either a disjunction of simple statements or a simple statement. For convenience we will allow some lines to be conjunctions of simple statements and add Cancel and Join to the machinery of Chapter Three.
2. Second, make use of UN, NP, UP, and UU to make all possible transformations of names or quasi-names *in the premises or conclusion* to other names or quasi-names *in the premises or conclusion*.
3. Third, perform all possible cancellations, including those involving use of Repetition to "double-cancel" with some lines.

If the conclusion is not among the remaining lines and the negation of the conclusion is not among the remaining lines, the premises leave the conclusion open.

From simple argument these rules of thumb are easy to apply. In the invalid syllogism

Every P is M
Some S is M
Some S is P

we symbolize:

1. $\sim P(x) \vee M(x)$⎫
2. $S[x] \cdot M[x]$ ⎬ $S[x] \cdot P[x]$
                              ⎭

The only possible use of UN, NP, UP, or UU is:

3. $P[x] \vee M[x]$ 1 UP

and there are *no* possible cancellations. However, in the more complex argument

Everyone from Bree is either a *Hobbit* or a *man*.
Nob is from Bree.
Sam is not from *Bree*.
No *Gamgee* is a *man*.
Sam is a Gamgee.
Nob is not a *man*.
Therefore, Nob is a Hobbit and Sam is a Hobbit and not a man.

we symbolize as follows:

1. $\sim B(x) \vee H(x) \vee M(x)$⎫
2. Bn ⎪
3. $\sim Bs$ ⎬
4. $\sim G(x) \vee \sim M(x)$ ⎬ $Hn \cdot Hs \cdot \sim Ms?$
5. Gs ⎪
6. $\sim Mn$ ⎭

We would have to use UN on 1 and 4 to both n and s:

7. $\sim Bn \vee Hn \vee Mn$ 1 UN
8. $\sim Bs \vee Hs \vee Ms$ 1 UN

9.	$\sim Gn \lor Mn$	4 UN
10.	$\sim Gs \lor Ms$	4 UN

Since there are no existential quasi-names, we would have no need to use UP. Since there are no other universal quasi-names, there is no use for UU or NP. The possible cancellations are:

11.	$Hn \lor Mn$	2, 7 SC
12.	Hn	6, 11 SC
13.	Ms	5, 10 SC

and the valid but irrelevant

14.	$\sim B(x) \lor H(x) \lor \sim G(x)$	1, 4 CC
15.	$\sim Bn \lor Hn \lor \sim Gn$	7, 9 CC
16.	$\sim Bs \lor Hs \lor \sim Gs$	8, 10 CC

No other cancellations yield new lines: Hs is not among the lines left, therefore the conclusion is false, by Special Rule of Proof for Conjunctions. (In a conjunctive conclusion *all* conjuncts must be true.) Therefore, the argument leaves open its conclusion as a whole, though it does establish the weaker conclusion $Hn \cdot Ms$.

I have called this method a set of rules of thumb. It is not totally mechanical, since as arguments get more complex you may miss some applications of UN, NP, or UP, or neglect some possible cancellations. But it is an effective method in practice because you only have to try out combinations of six rules—UN, NP, UP, UU, SC, and CC—and in practice many of these will not apply to a given argument. While cumbersome, the method is no more so than truth-table methods used in more standard treatments of logic and it is even slightly more foolproof.

Chapter Summary

In this chapter we introduced the subject-predicate way of writing statements with the conventions that predicates are symbolized as capital letters and proper names are symbolized as small letters written to the *right* of the predicate. We explained universal and existential quasi-names and gave a table of translations for common statements (Table 6-1). We discussed four new rules for "name changing" within subject-predicate statements:

Universal to Name (UN)

$$\frac{A(x)}{An}$$

---

where A is any predicate or string of predicates, (x) is any universal quasi-name, n is any proper name, and every occurrence of (x) is replaced by n.

Name to Particular (NP)

$$\frac{An}{A[x]}$$

Restriction on NP: $[x]$ is any existential quasi-name that has not been used earlier in the argument, and every occurrence of n must be replaced by $[x]$.

Universal to Particular (UP)

$$\frac{A(x)}{A[x]}$$

Restriction on UP: Every occurrence of (x) must be replaced by $[x]$.

Universal to Universal (UU)

$$\frac{A(x)}{A(y)}$$

Restriction on UU: (y) is any universal quasi-name other than (x), but every occurrence of (x) must be replaced by (y).

Using these rules and cancellation methods, we were able to demonstrate all the equivalences of standard form statements in syllogistic logic, and to give proofs of all those syllogistic arguments regarded as valid by modern logicians. With these rules and the complete system of statement logic, we were able to show the validity of a number of arguments more complex than could be dealt with by syllogistic logic. Refutations and proofs of invalidity were briefly discussed, and some rules of thumb given for showing that a conclusion is left open by given premises.

The major weakness of the system of predicate logic developed in this chapter is that it is unable to handle arguments that involve the subordination of one universal or existential quasi-name to another. In the system of the next chapter this defect will be remedied, and other extensions of the methods of predicate logic will be considered.

Practical Applications

Check your Argument File for arguments that you could not handle using statement logic or traditional syllogistic logic. See if you can now deal with those arguments. Keep an eye out for the use of words like *all*, *each*, *every*, *some*, and *most*. Not all of these will be parts of arguments, but some will be clues to arguments with which you can now deal. (Hint: Look for arguments that apply general principles to specific cases.)

Exercise 6-4

The following arguments can be handled by the methods of this chapter. If a conclusion is given, see if the argument is a valid proof or refutation of that conclusion. If no conclusion is given, find one if possible. If no conclusion follows from the premises, write NC.

1. Nothing that emits radio waves and ultraviolet radiation with far greater intensity than a typical star can be a star. Quasars emit radio waves and radiation with far greater intensity than a typical star. Therefore . . .

2. Quasars are receding from Earth at a higher speed than any visible galaxy. The greater the speed of recession, the greater the distance. Therefore, quasars are more distant than any visible galaxy.

3. Are quasars supergalaxies? If quasars are supergalaxies, then the diameter of a quasar must be much greater than the diameter of a galaxy. But the diameter of a quasar is much less than the diameter of a galaxy.

*4. If quasars are more distant than any visible galaxy, then they are incredibly luminous. Anything that luminous must be either a supergalaxy or not a complex of stars at all. Quasars are not supergalaxies. Therefore . . .

5. Either quasars are incredibly luminous and very distant or they are comparatively close and not incredibly luminous. If quasars are comparatively close, they must have been hurled from the exploding centers of galaxies. If quasars were hurled from the exploding centers of galaxies, then some quasars would be coming in the direction of Earth. No quasars are coming in the direction of Earth. So, we must conclude that quasars are incredibly luminous.

Exercise 6-5

Within the last hundred years archeological excavations on the island of Crete have revealed ruins of elaborate, many-storied palaces built and rebuilt between 3000 B.C. *and 1500* B.C. *A German geologist, Hans Georg Wunderlich, in his book* The Secret of Crete (*New York: Macmillan, 1974*), *argues that these palaces were not lived in but were, in fact, vast tombs for the dead. The first five arguments below are simplified versions of some arguments given by Wunderlich, the second five are counterarguments by his opponents. Symbolize the arguments and show whether the conclusions follow from the premises.*

1. Some of the stairways, thresholds, etc., of the palaces were made of gypsum, which would wear down easily, but which shows little sign of wear in some places where wear would be expected. If the palaces were intended as tombs, there would be little wear and stairways and thresholds

The Palace of Knossos, west side of Great Court (reconstruction).

could be made of soft stone. Therefore, the palaces were intended as tombs.

2. Some artifacts found in the palace are imitations in less expensive material of metal or stone objects or else seem too fragile for everyday use. If such artifacts are found in a place, there is a probability that the place is a burial site. Therefore, there is a probability that the palaces were burial sites.

3. Some doors in the palaces seem to be grooved to receive panels. If such panels were designed to move, they would slide up to the ceiling or down into floor. If they slide into the floor, they would be easily immobilized by dirt getting into the opening. If they slide up to the ceiling, they would not go up high enough to allow useful access to the rooms. If the panels were easily immobilized or did not allow useful access, they would be impractical. If the panels were designed to move, they would not be impractical. Therefore, they were not designed to move.

*4. If the panels were not designed to move, then if there were any panels they would be permanently closed. If the panels were permanently closed, it is very probable that the palace rooms were used for burials. So if the panels were not designed to move up or down, it is probable that the palace rooms were designed for burials.

5. Many rooms in the palaces that have been identified as living quarters are interior rooms with no windows. If ancient Cretans valued light and air, then these rooms are not living quarters. If they are not living quarters, they may have been used for burials. Therefore, if ancient Cretans valued light and air, these rooms might have been used for burials.

6. If gypsum is protected from the weather and receives light traffic, it will show little sign of wear. The gypsum stairs and thresholds were protected from the weather and received only sandaled or barefoot traffic. Such traffic is light traffic; therefore, the gypsum would show little sign of wear.

7. Wealthy and somewhat decadent cultures often produce fragile goods and make imitations of one material in another. If the Cretan palaces were the work of a wealthy and somewhat decadent culture, then such artifacts might be expected to be found in living areas and not just in burial sites. The Cretan culture was wealthy and somewhat decadent, therefore such artifacts might be expected to be found in living areas.

8. Folding doors are movable but do not move up and down. If Cretans used folding doors, then the panels that fit into the grooves could be movable even if they did not move up or down. Cretans did use folding doors, so the panels that fit into the grooves were movable.

9.   If the panels were movable, they were probably not permanently closed. If they were not used for burials, the palace rooms were not permanently closed. The panels were movable, so the palace rooms were not used for burials.

10.   Cretan weather is hot and muggy or cold and windy. If it is hot and muggy, interior rooms without windows are cool and comfortable. If it is cold and windy, interior rooms without windows are more easily heated if charcoal braziers are used for heat. Charcoal braziers were used for heat. If rooms are either cool and comfortable or easily heated, then they are suitable for living quarters. Therefore, in the Cretan climate interior rooms without windows are suitable for living quarters.

Exercise 6-6

Symbolize and prove using predicate logic the following arguments from Leibnitz's Abridgment of the Theodicy. *Give a dictionary.*

1.   Whoever does not choose the best is lacking in power or in knowledge or in goodness.

    God does not choose the best in creating this world.

    Therefore, God is lacking in power or in knowledge or in goodness.

2.   Whoever makes things in which there is evil, which could have been made without any evil, and the making of which could have been omitted, does not choose the best.

    God has made a world in which there is evil, a world that could have been made without any evil, and the making of which could have been omitted altogether.

    Therefore, God has not chosen the best.

3.   If there is more evil than good in intelligent creatures, then there is more evil than good in the work of God.

    There is more evil than good in intelligent creatures.

    Therefore, there is more evil than good in the work of God.

*4.   If it is always impossible not to sin, then it is always unjust to punish.

    Now it is always impossible not to sin, or in other words every sin is necessary.

    Therefore, it is always unjust to punish.

5.   All that is predetermined is necessary.

    Every event is predetermined.

    Sin is an event.

    Therefore, every event is necessary and consequently sin is necessary.

6. That which is future, that which is foreseen, that which follows from its causes, is predetermined.

Every event is such.

Therefore, every event is predetermined.

7. Whoever can prevent the sin of another and does not do so, but rather contributes to it, although he is well informed of it, is accessory to that sin.

God can prevent the sin of intelligent creatures, but he does not do so, and rather contributes to it by his concurrence and by the opportunities which he brings about, although he has a perfect knowledge of it.

Therefore, God is an accessory to sin.

8. Whoever produces all that is real in a thing, is its cause.

God produces all that is real in sin.

Therefore, God is the cause of sin.

9. Whoever punishes those who have done as well as it was in their power to do, is unjust.

God does so.

Therefore, God is unjust.

10. Whoever gives only to some, and not to all, the means that produces in them effectively a good will and saving faith, has not sufficient goodness.

God does this.

Therefore, God has not sufficient goodness.

CHAPTER SEVEN

Predicate Logic:
The Complete System

AQUINAS'S ARGUMENT

The following is a famous argument for the existence of God by St. Thomas Aquinas:

The existence of God can be proved from the nature of the efficient cause. In the world of sense we find there is an order of efficient causes. There is no case known (neither is it, indeed, possible) in which a thing is found to be the efficient cause of itself; for so it would be prior to itself, which is impossible. Now in efficient causes it is not possible to go on to infinity, because in all efficient causes following in order, the first is the cause of the interme-diate cause, and the intermediate is the cause of the ultimate cause, *whether the intermediate cause be several, or one only. Now to take away the cause is to take away the effect. Therefore, if there be no first cause among efficient causes, there will be no ultimate, nor any interme-diate cause. But if in efficient causes it is possible to go on to infinity, there will be no first efficient cause, neither will there be an ultimate effect, nor any intermediate efficient causes; all of which is plainly false. Therefore it is necessary to admit a first efficient cause, to which every-one gives the name of God.*

Is the argument valid? Can the conclusion be proved from these premises?

How can we extend the basic principles of predicate logic?

We will do this in several stages. First we will introduce the idea of a *relational predicate*, then the *quantifiers*, then *instantiation-generalization rules*, and finally *quasi-predicates* and *predicate quantification*. Let us begin with relational predicates. As we pointed out in Chapter Three, some simple statements state a relation between more than one person or thing. For example: "Bilbo admires Gandalf." We have avoided such predicates in our discussion of predicate logic because of the difficulty of dealing with them by the methods used so far, but now we are ready to take a look at them.

So long as we have only relational predicates with proper names or relational predicates with one quasi-name and one or more proper names, we can take care of them by the methods we have already used. If

Mxy	#	*x* admires *y*
Hx	#	*x* is a Hobbit
g	#	Gandalf
b	#	Bilbo Baggins

We can write:

Bilbo is a Hobbit: *Hb*
Gandalf is not a Hobbit: $\sim Hg$
Bilbo admires Gandalf: *Mbg*
Gandalf admires Bilbo: *Mgb*
If Bilbo admires Gandalf, then Gandalf admires Bilbo: $Mbg \supset Mgb$

But consider a general statement such as "Everyone admires some-one." This could mean that each person admires some person or other—different people admiring different people—or it could mean that everyone admires some one person—the same person being admired by everyone. But there is no way to distinguish the two meanings.

Quantifiers

To solve this and other problems of translation from English to symbols, we introduce a new device: the *quantifier*. Just as our quasi-names parallel many uses of *anyone, everyone, someone*, etc., in English (e.g., "If anyone is a Hobbit, then that person is fond of comfort"), so our new technique parallels some English constructions. Sometimes we say, "Take anyone at all—if that person is a Hobbit, then that person is fond of comfort," or "There is at least one person such that he is a Hobbit and fond of comfort." In these constructions we make it clear that we are talking about anyone or about someone and then go on to say something about anyone or someone, using pronouns that refer back to the *anyone* or *someone* of whom we are talking.

We could use this technique to clarify the two statements above: "For anyone at all there is at least one person such that the first person referred to admires the second person referred to" and "There is at least one person such that for anyone at all the second person referred to admires the first person referred to." This is somewhat awkward and, in practice, we might prefer other ways of expressing the idea. The awkwardness lies mostly in keeping the pronouns straight, although if there is a difference of sex or number such phrases are no less awkward; for example:

For every woman there is some man such that she admires him.
There is a man such that for every woman she admires him.
For every individual there is some group such that he or she admires them.
There is a group such that for every individual he or she admires them.

Our symbolic device has the advantages of the English construction we have been discussing, without its disadvantages. We use the letters x, y, z, etc., in parentheses before the expression to indicate *for every individual* or *for some individual*, using $(\forall x)$, $(\forall y)$, etc., for the *every* and $(\exists x)$, $(\exists y)$, etc., for the *some*, and use the same letter without parentheses in the name place of predicate expressions as English uses pronouns. To symbolize "Every Hobbit is fond of comfort" or "If anyone is a Hobbit, then that person is fond of comfort," we write, "For any individual if that individual is a Hobbit, then that individual is fond of comfort," or in symbols:

$$(\forall x)(Hx \supset Fx)$$

The parentheses around $Hx \supset Fx$ mark the "scope" of the quantifier $(\forall x)$, just as parentheses indicated the scope of $\sim$ in Chapter Four. The two x's, like pronouns, refer back to that initial *for any individual*.

Similarly, to symbolize "Somebody is a Hobbit and that person is hairy-footed," we write, "There is at least one individual such that that person is a Hobbit and that person is hairy-footed," or in symbols:

$$(\exists x)(Hx \cdot Fx)$$

So far we have not had any real advance over the techniques of Chapter Six. But now we can solve the problem of the two relational statements we started out with. "Everyone admires someone" becomes:

$$(\forall x)(\exists y)(Mxy)$$

This is equivalent to the English paraphrase, "For any individual there is at least one individual such that the first individual mentioned admires the second individual mentioned," but the letters, which make clear which "pronoun" refers back to which quantifier, make the symbolic form considerably less awkward than the English. In fact, logicians sometimes need expressions like $(\forall x)(\exists y)(Mxy)$ in a sort of jargon midway between English and the symbols: "For any x there is a y such that x admires y."

The second statement, "Somebody is admired by everybody," can now be written as:

$$(\exists y)(\forall x)(Mxy)$$

which is equivalent to the English paraphrase, "There is at least one individual such that for any individual the first individual referred to is admired by the second individual referred to." Or in logician's jargon, "There is a y such that for any x, x admires y."

Since the universal quantifiers refer to *any* individual, $(\exists y)(\forall x)(Mxy)$ has the consequence that the individual in question admires himself or herself. To avoid this consequence if we do not want it, we would have to have a new predicate:

Sxy # x is the same as y

and a more complex statement:

$(\exists y)(\forall x)(\sim Sxy \supset Mxy)$

"There is an individual, y, such that for any individual, y, if x is not the same as y, then x admires y."

Quantifiers and Quasi-Names

In Chapter Six we introduced the idea of quasi-names, symbols that played a role similar to that of certain words in English such as *everything* and *something*. We used quasi-names to express generality without quantification: A statement such as "Every Hobbit is fond of comfort" was written $H(x) \supset F(x)$, and a statement such as "Some Hobbit is fond of comfort" was written $H[x] \cdot F[x]$. The second occurrence of the quasi-name played a role like that of a pronoun referring back to the first occurrence: "If anyone is a Hobbit, then *that* person is fond of comfort," "Someone is a Hobbit and *that* person is fond of comfort." We had one-way rules for going from a universal quasi-name to the name of an individual, from the name of an individual to an existential quasi-name, and from a universal quasi-name to an existential quasi-name:

Universal to Name (UN)	Name to Particular (NP)	Universal to Particular (UP)
$\dfrac{Z(x)}{Zn}$	$\dfrac{Zn}{Z[x]}$	$\dfrac{Z(x)}{Z[x]}$

where Z stands for any predicate or sequence of predicates with the same name or quasi-name. There was also a convenient two-way rule which said that the letter used for a universal quasi-name could be changed, if convenient:

$$\frac{Z(x)}{Z(y)}$$ Provided that every occurrence of one letter is exchanged for an occurrence of the other letter.

Since our new techniques seem to be able to do anything the quasi-name techniques of the last chapter could do and can do more besides, one might wonder why we did not introduce these techniques immediately. The answer is that when we use "quantified" statements (i.e., statements with quantifiers) in arguments we either have to introduce a whole new set of complicated rules or introduce something like quasi-names at certain stages of the argument. We already have the quasi-name techniques, all we have to do is build a bridge between these techniques and quantifiers, which will be quite easy.

Consider, for example, an argument like:

1. $(\forall x)(Ax \supset Bx)$
2. $(\forall x)(Bx \supset Cx)$ } $(\exists x)(Cx)$
3. An

In quantified form we have no way of going from the premises to the conclusion. We can, of course, introduce a whole new set of rules for getting from statements like 1 and 2 to $(\forall x)(Ax \supset Cx)$, from this to $An \supset Cn$, and from Cn to $(\exists x)(Cx)$. These rules could involve applying our statement logic rules to quantified statements directly, or they could involve dropping quantifiers temporarily and restoring them, using statement logic on the nonquantified statements resulting from the dropped quantifiers.

The second technique has proved far more flexible and usable, and most systems of predicate logic contain "instantiation" rules—rules for dropping quantifiers—and "generalization" rules—rules for restoring quantifiers. But there is often a good deal of confusion as to what the statements resulting from dropping quantifiers actually are. Sometimes they are explained as containing variables—letters that do not stand for any individuals but which are merely placeholders, marking places where names of individuals can be inserted. But the techniques used with these "instantiated" statements are often inconsistent with the supposition that the letters that refer back to the dropped quantifiers are to be regarded as placeholders. A statement with placeholders is like a statement with blanks or a statement containing pronouns with no referent. For example:

Let Fx # x is frozen
        Dx # x will die

Then if $Fx \supset Dx$ means "If ——— is frozen, ——— will die" or "If it is frozen, it will die," both of these are forms of statements rather than statements. They are neither true nor false—we cannot decide which unless we know what is being referred to. If we are referring to a rabbit, they may be true; if we are referring to a frog, they may be false (frogs have survived freezing over several months).

This being so, if the letters in question were mere placeholders, it is hard to see how we could use truth-table shortcut, truth functional connectives, or statement logic rules, all of which presuppose that we are dealing with statements that are either true or false.

Instantiation and Generalization Rules

Actually, most reasonable sophisticated systems of predicate logic interpret the letters that refer back to a dropped quantifier as quasi-names, although the term may not be used and the distinction between placeholders and quasi-names may not be made explicit. The system introduced in this chapter makes it explicit that when we drop quantifiers we replace the letters that referred back to the dropped quantifiers with quasi-names. Of course, if we choose we can ignore the meaning of the quasi-names and simply treat (x) and $[x]$ in expressions like $H(x) \supset F(x)$ or $H[x] \cdot F[x]$ as convenient devices for dropping quantifiers and keeping track of which quantifiers have been dropped. The parentheses tell us that a universal quantifier has been dropped and can be restored, while the brackets tell us that an existential quantifier has been dropped and can be restored. Of course, when we have a universal quasi-name we can use UN or UP to get to proper names or to existential quasi-names, but since UN and UP are one-way rules, we will not be able to get back a universal quasi-name and therefore cannot get back a universal quantifier. If we have an expression containing a name, we can use NP to get an existential quasi-name and then an existential quantifier. But this is

again a one-way street: We cannot get back from an existentially quantified statement to a name. Making use of these one-way rules from
Chapter Six makes our rules for dropping and adding quantifiers essentially quite simple, though the rules have a number of restrictions attached
to them. We need two two-way rules, but they are subject to a number of
restrictions. Especially, unlike most two-way rules, they must be applied
to complete lines and not to parts of lines. Because of the restrictions,
we will write these rules flanked by asterisks as warning signs. The two
rules are:

Universal Instantiation $(\forall w)(Zw)$
and Generalization $*\overline{}*$
(UIG) $Z(w)$

Restrictions: The $(\forall w)$ must not be within the scope of a $\sim$ or another
quantifier; the scope of $(\forall w)$ must be the complete expression; and in
going from $Z(w)$ to $(\forall w)(Zw)$, there must be no existential quasi-names
in $Z(w)$ and no universal quasi-names or bound variables derived from
(w) by earlier steps using UU:

Existential Instantiation $(\exists w)(Zw)$
and Generalization $*\overline{}*$
(EIG) $Z[w]$

Restrictions: The $(\exists w)$ must not be within the scope of a $\sim$ or another
quantifier; the scope of the $(\exists w)$ must be the whole expression; and in
going from $(\exists w)(Zw)$ to $Z[w]$, $[w]$ must not occur in any previous line of
the argument in which this EIG is used. (In order to meet this last restriction we may sometimes have to use a new letter, e.g., going from $(\exists x)(Fx)$
to $F[y]$).

Restrictions on the Instantiation and Generalization Rules

Several things need to be made clear about the way these rules are stated.
The letter w, which we do not often have occasion to use for quantifiers,
is used as a stand-in for any letter x, y, z, etc., used in a quantifier and
the accompanying letters that refer back to the quantifier (these letters
are called *variables* from now on). The capital letter Z, which again we
seldom use ordinarily, is in these rules a stand-in for any predicate,

negated or not, or any series of predicates joined by connectives. The
predicate or sequence of predicates may have other proper names, quasi-
names, or variables referring to other quantifiers inside the one with
which we are dealing. Thus:

$(\forall x)(Fx)$

$(\forall x)(Gax)$

$(\forall y)(Fy \supset Gy)$

$(\forall z)(\exists x)(Hxw \supset Jxz)$

and so on, are all instances of $(\forall w)(Zw)$ in our first rule. There must always
be variables that refer back to the quantifiers. A "vacuous" quantifier,
one with no accompanying variables, is as nonsensical as a connective
without two statements to connect, so that, for example:

$A \lor$ $(\forall x)(Fa)$ $(\forall x)(\exists y)(Fy)$

are all nonsensical expressions.

It is not always nonsensical but it is very confusing to have the same
letter used in the same line with different quantifiers. Thus we will also
avoid such expressions as:

$(\forall x)(Fx) \supset (\exists x)(Gx)$ $(\forall y)(\forall y)(Gyy)$ $(\forall z)(\exists z)(Hzz)$

and so on. The first is merely awkward, but in the second we do not know
if the extra $(\forall y)$ has any function, and in the third we do not know which
variable goes with which quantifier.

As a result of these difficulties with vacuous quantifiers and with the
same letter used on the same line in two quantifiers, we will understand
the rules in such a way that they will never operate to get us from or to
such expressions. Another thing of which we must be sure in applying the
rules is that when we go from a quantified statement to one with quasi-
names, each variable that refers back to the quantifier we drop is changed
to the same quasi-name, and when we go from an expression with quasi-
names to one with a quantifier, each quasi-name is changed to a variable
that refers back to the same quantifier.

These general restrictions apply to all the rules, but each rule has one
specific restriction. The restriction on EIG prevents us from lumping

together existence statements that refer to different individuals. Thus if:

Bx # x is black

we may know that something is black, $(\exists x)(Bx)$, and that something else is not black, $(\exists x)(\sim Bx)$. Without the restriction we could argue as follows:

1.	$(\exists x)(Bx)$		
2.	$(\exists x)(\sim Bx)$	$\Bigg\}$ $(\exists x)(Bx \cdot \sim Bx)$?	
3.	$B[x]$	1 EIG	
4.	$\sim B[x]$	2 EIG (Forbidden)	
5.	$B[x] \cdot \sim B[x]$	3, 4 Conj.	
6.	$(\exists x)(Bx \cdot \sim Bx)$	5 EIG	

and from true premises get a contradictory conclusion. The restriction prevents this by making us use a new quasi-name at line 4.

The restriction on UIG prevents certain illegitimate quantifier switches. For instance, $(\exists y)(\forall x)(Dxy)$ is stronger and more restrictive than $(\forall x)(\exists y)(Dxy)$. We want to be able to go from $(\exists x)(\forall x)(Dxy)$ to $(\forall x)(\exists y)(Dxy)$, but not vice versa. If it were not for our restriction, we could proceed as follows:

1.	$(\forall x)(\exists y)(Dxy)$	
2.	$(\exists y)(D(x)y)$	1 UIG
3.	$D(x)[y]$	2 EIG
4.	$(\forall x)(Dx[y])$	3 UIG (Forbidden)
5.	$(\exists y)(\forall x)(Dxy)$	4 EIG

The restriction forbids the use of UIG of line 4 and prevents the invalid exchange. The second clause of the restriction presents the invalid argument:

*1.	$Z(w)$	ACP
*2.	$Z(y)$	1 UU
*3.	$(\forall y)(Zy)$	2 UIG
4.	$Z(w) \supset (\forall y)(Zy)$	1–3 RCP
5.	$(w)(Zw \supset (\forall y)(Zy))$	4 UIG (Forbidden)

Steps 1–4 do not break any rules, but when we get to step 5 we find that the bound variable y was obtained from (w), the quasi-name that we are trying to universally generalize. The restriction forbids this and bars the invalid argument.

Exchange and Distribution Rules

The rules, you will notice, forbid use of UIG or EIG to go from a quantifier to a quasi-name if the quantifier in question is in the scope of a $\sim$.
Does this mean we cannot instantiate at all in those cases? Not directly;
but we can use a new set of two-way rules to handle such cases. These
rules are collectively called:

Quantifier Exchange (QE)

$$\frac{(\forall w)(Fw)}{\sim(\exists w)\sim(Fw)} \qquad \frac{(\exists w)(Fw)}{\sim(\forall w)\sim(Fw)}$$

These rules together with Double Negation enable us to change a universal
quantifier *preceded* by a $\sim$ to an existential quantifier *followed* by a $\sim$,
and an existential quantifier *preceded* by a $\sim$ to a universal quantifier
followed by a $\sim$:

$$\frac{\sim(\forall w)(Fw)}{(\exists w)\sim(Fw)} \qquad \frac{\sim(\exists w)(Fw)}{(\forall x)\sim(Fw)}$$

We will also call these Quantifier Exchange. When we want to go from a
quantifier in the scope of a $\sim$ to a quasi-name we use QE to "move
through" the $\sim$ as above, and then we can use UIG or EIG on the new
quantifier.

    The rules also forbid using UIG or EIG to go from a quantifier to
a quasi-name, which is called *instantiating*, when the quantifier is in the
scope of another quantifier. To instantiate a quantifier inside another one,
we must first instantiate the outside one, and only then can we instantiate
the inner one. Going from quasi-names to quantifiers, which is called
generalizing, is not forbidden if there is a $\sim$ or another quantifier outside
the expression with quasi-names, but the quantifier added must go *outside*
the $\sim$ or the other quantifier.

    Another useful set of rules for manipulating quantified statements
are the *Quantifier Distribution* (QD) Rules:

$$\frac{(\forall w)(Fw \cdot Gw)}{(\forall w)(Fw) \cdot (\forall w)(Gw)} \qquad \frac{(\exists w)(Fw \vee Gw)}{(\exists w)(Fw) \vee (\exists w)(Gw)}$$

$$\frac{(\forall w)(Fw) \vee (\forall w)(Gw)}{(\forall w)(Fw \vee Gw)} \qquad \frac{(\exists w)(Fw \cdot Gw)}{(\exists w)(Fw) \cdot (\exists w)(Gw)}$$

These enable us to "distribute" a quantifier, somewhat as De Morgan's Rules enable us to distribute a ∼. There are no separate rules for ⊃ or ≡, but by using DMI and DME and the QD rules we can distribute quantifiers in expressions with ⊃ and ≡.

Notice that the second two distribution rules are one-way rules: You cannot go from (∀w)(Fw ∨ Gw) to (∀w)(Fw) ∨ (∀w)(Gw) or from (∃w)(Fw) · (∃w)(Gw) to (∃w)(Fw · Gw). From "Everything is circular or not circular," we cannot get to "Everything is circular or everything is not triangular." Similarly, we cannot go from "Something is triangular and something is circular" to "Something is both triangular *and* circular."

The distribution rules are convenient for dealing with some arguments where we cannot get the results we need by instantiation and generalization. For instance, suppose we know that either something is on fire or something is smoldering. We want to show that something is either on fire or smoldering:

$$(\exists x)(Fx) \lor (\exists x)(Sx)\} \qquad (\exists x)(Fx \lor Sx)$$

We cannot instantiate the premise, since neither quantifier has the whole line as its scope—and even if we could, we would have to use two existential quasi-names since we have two existential quantifiers. If we had two existential quasi-names, we could not generalize to one quantifier. But we can move from the premise directly to the conclusion without instantiation by QD.

A Sample Proof

We are now ready to do some proofs and refutations. Consider first the proof that was given as an example earlier:

1. $(\forall x)(Fx \supset Gx)$ ⎫
2. $(\forall x)(Gx \supset Hx)$ ⎬ $(\exists x)(Hx)?$
3. Fn ⎭

First we instantiate lines 1 and 2:

4. $F(x) \supset G(x)$ 1 UIG
5. $G(x) \supset H(x)$ 2 UIG

We can now use Hypothetical Syllogism:

6. $F(x) \supset H(x)$ 4, 5 HS

At this point we use UN to get:

7. $Fn \supset Hn$ 6 UN

and Modus Ponens to get:

8. Hn 7, 3 MP

Then NP to get:

9. $H[x]$

and finally EIG to get:

10. $(\exists x)(Hx)$

This is slightly longer than a proof might be if we had, for example, a rule for going directly from a universally quantified statement to an expression containing a proper name, or from an expression containing a proper name to an existentially quantified statement. But our rules have the advantage that, except when we are actually dropping or adding quantifiers (or using QE), all of our operations are done by rules we are already familiar with—either statement logic rules like HS or rules like UN and NP with which we had practice in the last chapter.

A Sample Refutation

Consider now a more complex argument:

1. $(\exists y)(Fy \cdot \sim Gy) \supset (\exists x)(Jx \cdot (Lx \cdot Hx))$
2. $(\forall x)(Jx \supset Lx)$ $(\exists y)(Fy \cdot \sim Gy)?$
3. $(\forall x)((Lx \cdot Hx) \supset Kx)$
4. $\sim(\exists x)(Lx \cdot Kx)$

Line 1 cannot be instantiated since the quantifiers have only part of the expression as their scope. Lines 2 and 3 can be instantiated with no trouble:

5. $J(x) \supset L(x)$ 2 UIG
6. $(L(x) \cdot H(x)) \supset K(x)$ 3 UIG

But before we can instantiate 4 we must use QE to "move the $\sim$ through":

7.	$(\forall x) \sim (Lx \cdot Kx)$	4 QE
8.	$\sim (L(x) \cdot K(x))$	7 UIG

Premise 8 is not useful in this form, so let us use De Morgan's Rules:

9. $\sim L(x) \vee \sim K(x)$

Looking at the possibilities of doing something with these premises we find that we can use Destructive Dilemma:

10. $\sim J(x) \vee \sim (L(x) \cdot H(x))$ 9, 6, 5 DD

Using De Morgan's Rules gives us:

11. $\sim (J(x) \cdot (L(x) \cdot H(x)))$ 10 De M

We can now restore the quantifier:

12. $(\forall x) \sim (Jx \cdot (Lx \cdot Hx))$ 11 UIG

Use QE again:

13. $\sim (\exists x)(Jx \cdot (Lx \cdot Hx))$ 12 QE

We now have the denial of the consequent of Premise 1, so we can use MT:

14. $\sim (\exists y)(Fy \cdot \sim Gy)$ 13, 1 MT

which means that we have a refutation of the proposed conclusion.
    We could also have done this refutation by a conditional proof using Reductio:

1.	$(\exists y)(Fy \cdot \sim Gy) \supset (\exists y)(Jx \cdot (Lx \cdot Hx))$
2.	$(\forall x)(Jx \supset Lx)$
3.	$(\forall x)((Lx \cdot Hx) \supset Kx)$
4.	$\sim (\exists x)(Lx \cdot Kx)$

Steps 5–8 will be the same:

5.	$J(x) \supset L(x)$	2 UIG
6.	$(L(x) \cdot H(x)) \supset K(x)$	3 UIG
7.	$(\forall x) \sim (Lx \cdot Kx)$	4 QE
8.	$\sim (L(x) \cdot K(x))$	7 UIG

To do a refutation we assume the conclusion we want to refute and try
to derive a contradiction:

*9.	$(\exists y)(Fy \cdot \sim Gy)$	ACP
*10.	$(\exists x)(Jx \cdot (Lx \cdot Hx))$	9, 1 MP
*11.	$J[x] \cdot (L[x] \cdot H[x])$	10 EIG
*12.	$J[x]$	11 Simp.
*13.	$L[x] \cdot H[x]$	11 Simp.
14.	$J[x] \supset L[x]$	5 UP
15.	$(L[x] \cdot H[x]) \supset K[x]$	6 UP
*16.	$L[x]$	12, 14 MP
*17.	$K[x]$	13, 15 MP
18.	$\sim L(x) \vee \sim K(x)$	8 De M
19.	$\sim L[x] \vee \sim K[x]$	18 UP
*20.	$\sim L[x]$	17, 19 SC
*21.	$L[x] \cdot \sim L[x]$	16, 20 Conj.
*22.	$\sim (\exists y)(Fy \cdot \sim Gy)$	21 Contrad.
23.	$(\exists y)(Fy \cdot \sim Gy) \supset \sim (\exists y)(Fy \cdot \sim Gy)$	9–22 RCP
24.	$\sim (\exists y)(Fy \cdot \sim Gy) \vee \sim (\exists y)(Fy \cdot \sim Gy)$	23 DMI
25.	$\sim (\exists y)(Fy \cdot \sim Gy)$	24 Rep.

You will notice that part of the complication of this reductio refutation results from the fact that first we had to use UIG to get universal
quasi-names, the UP to get existential quasi-names. So long as we are
clear about what we are doing, there is no objection to telescoping these
steps and going directly from a universally quantified statement to existential quasi-names, citing both rules; for example:

5.	$J[x] \supset L[x]$	2 UIG, UP

But in a complex argument we may not know what quasi-names we will
need until we reach the appropriate part of the argument. This is especially
true of a reductio argument, where we often just go on trying things until

we reach a contradiction. Many arguments can be tidied up and shortened once we see what the conclusion is and have seen a way of getting there, but when we are groping for a conclusion it is useful to just instantiate the premises and then see what we can do with them.

A technique useful in working out a proof in tentative form, and which can be used regularly if it does not cause confusion, is "lazy" instantiation. To do this we simply renumber the line, cross out the quantifier, and put the appropriate quasi-name parentheses around the variables. For example, we could go from Premise 2 in the last argument to:

5 2 $(\forall x)(J(x) \supset L(x))$ 2 UIG

or:

5 2 $(\forall x)(J[x] \supset L[x])$ 2 UIG, UP

There is no way of giving a set of rules or even very complete instructions for doing proofs and refutations in predicate logic. In addition to the rules of thumb for proofs given in Chapter Four, all we can say is that you should instantiate where possible, use QE where there is a $\sim$ in front of a quantifier, work toward the conclusion by statement logic means, and when you have the conclusion in quasi-name form use UIG or EIG to restore quantifiers, presuming that the desired conclusion is quantified.

Extensions of Predicate Logic

We will now take a brief look at an interesting but complex extension of predicate logic. So far we have kept predicates constant and used quasi-names and quantifiers with variables for subjects. But there is no technical reason why we should not use "quasi-predicates," predicate quantifiers and predicate variables. Consider, for example: "Bilbo Baggins has some property" or "Every property Bilbo Baggins has, the uncle of Frodo Baggins has." If

b #   Bilbo Baggins
u #   the uncle of Frodo Baggins

and we use (F), (G), (H), $[F]$, $[G]$, $[H]$, etc., as quasi-predicates, we can state these as:

$[F]b$

$(F)b \supset (F)u$

There is no reason to restrict quasi-predicates to one-place properties; we can use them with relational properties. If

$g \quad \# \quad$ Gandalf

we could write, for example:

$(F)bg \supset (F)ug$

"Any relation Bilbo Baggins has to Gandalf, the uncle of Frodo Baggins has to Gandalf."

We can use quasi-predicates and quasi-names together, for example:

$[F][x]g$

"Someone has some relation to Gandalf."

For the same reasons we introduced quantifiers for individuals, we need to introduce them for predicates. "For every relation a has to b there is some relation b has to a":

$(\forall F)(\exists G)(Fab \supset Gba)$

is different from "There is a relation such that for every relation a has to b, b has *that* relation to a":

$(\exists G)(\forall F)(Fab \supset Gba)$

In doing proofs with quasi-predicates and predicate quantifiers we will assume that we have essentially the same rules, with the same restrictions, as we had for quasi-names and individual quantifiers. Thus, for example, if Bilbo Baggins admires Gandalf, then Bilbo has some relation to Gandalf:

1.	Mbg	
2.	$[F]bg$	1 NP
3.	$(\exists F)(Fbg)$	2 EIG

And if every relation Bilbo Baggins has to Gandalf, the uncle of Frodo has to Gandalf, then if Bilbo Baggins admires Gandalf, the uncle of Frodo admires Gandalf:

1. $(\forall F)(Fbg \supset Fug)$
2. $(F)bg \supset (F)ug$ 1 UIG
3. $Mbg \supset Mug$ 2 UN

"Name" in UN or NP is, of course, not literally correct now that we are going from quantifiers to quasi-predicates, but I am trying to avoid giving a whole new set of titles for essentially the same rules.

Note that we do not give any special way of distinguishing relational quasi-predicates or quantifiers over relational predicate variables from the one-place cases, except by looking at how many individual names or quasi-names or variables are attached to that predicate. For the quantified cases we have to look at the body of the expression after the quantifier (this is called the *matrix* of the expression) to see whether we are talking about a one-place predicate or a relation. If this causes confusion, we could easily introduce some mark for how many places a predicate has, for example: $(\forall F)(Fx)$, $(\forall F_2)$, (Fab), $(\forall F_3)$ $(Fabc)$, etc. This might become important if we wanted to talk about all one-place predicates, all two-place predicates, and so on.

However, some logicians think that all many-placed predicates can be reduced to one-place predicates. For each relational predicate, for example, "x admires y," we can form one-place predicates "admiring y," "being admired by x," etc., with which we can say anything we can say with relational predicates. If we take this line, then if the uncle of Frodo has all the one-place predicates that Bilbo has, the uncle of Frodo also has the property "admiring Gandalf," etc.; so for any relation to any individual Bilbo has, the uncle of Frodo has it also.

Exercise 7-1

Symbolize each of the following statements. Give your own dictionary.

1. Every quasar emits more radio waves than any star.
2. No star emits as much ultraviolet radiation as any quasar.
3. No visible galaxy has as great a red shift as any quasar.
*4. If all quasars were hurled from exploding galaxies, then some quasars would be coming toward Earth.

5. If all quasars were supergalaxies, then no quasar would go through a complete cycle of variations in a week.
6. For every quasar there is some visible galaxy nearer to Earth than that quasar.
7. For every visible galaxy there is some quasar more distant from Earth than that galaxy.
8. Every supergalaxy is larger than any galaxy and every galaxy is larger than any quasar.
9. There is one quasar smaller than any other quasar and this quasar is larger than any star.
10. There is a smallest quasar and no star is larger than that quasar, but every galaxy is larger than it is.

Exercise 7-2

Give proofs or refutations of the proposed conclusions. If there is no conclusion indicated, draw the appropriate conclusion.

1. $(\forall x)(Ax \supset \sim(Bx \vee Dx))$
   $(\forall x)(Ax \supset (Ex \supset (Bx \vee Fx)))$ $\left.\right\}$ $(\forall x)(Ax \supset ((Ex \supset Fx) \supset$
   $(\forall x)(Ax \supset (Gx \supset (Dx \vee Hx)))$ $(Gx \supset Hx)))$?

2. $(\forall x)(Jx \supset (Kx \vee Lx))$
   $(\forall x)(Mx \supset Nx)$ $\left.\right\}$ $(\exists x)(Mx \cdot \sim Lx)$?
   $(\forall x)(Mx \supset \sim Kx)$

*3. $(\forall x)(Ox \equiv Px)$
   $(\forall x)(Qx \supset Px)$ $\left.\right\}$?

4. $(\forall x)((Rx \cdot Sx) \equiv ((Tx \cdot \sim Ux) \cdot \sim Vx))$
   $(\forall x)(Yx \supset ((Tx \cdot \sim Ux) \cdot \sim Vx))$ $\left.\right\}$?

5. $(\forall x)(\sim Cxx)$
   $\sim(\forall x)(Ex \supset (\exists y)(Cyx \cdot \sim Syx))$ $\left.\right\}$?
   $(\forall x)(Dx \supset (Cxx \vee (\exists y)(Cyx \cdot \sim Syx)))$

6. $(\forall x)((\exists F)(Fx) \supset (Sxx)$
   $\sim(\exists x)(F)(\sim Fx)$ $\left.\right\}$ $(\exists x)(Sxx)$?

7. $(\forall x)((\exists F)(Fx) \supset (x = x))$
   $(\forall x)((\forall F)(Fx) \supset \sim(x = x))$ $\left.\right\}$?

8. $(\forall x)((\forall F)(Fx) \supset ((x = x) \cdot \sim x = x))$ $(\forall F)(Fx)$?

9. $(\forall x)(\forall y)((\forall F)(Fx \equiv \sim Fy) \supset (G)(\sim Gxy))$ $(\forall x)(\forall y)(\forall F)(Fx \equiv$
   $\sim Fy) \supset \sim Cxy)$?

10. $(\forall x)(\forall y)(\sim(x = y) \supset (F)(Fx \equiv \sim Fy)$
     $(\forall x)(\forall y)(\forall F)(Fx \equiv \sim Fy) \supset \sim Cxy)$ $\Big\}$?

Identity

Cases where one individual has every property that another has are especially important, because this seems to be what is meant by identity. In fact, identity between individuals can be defined in this way. If, in general, $a = b$ is our way of writing "a is identical with b," then we can write a definition:

$a = b = \text{def. } (\forall F)(Fa \equiv Fb)$

or in terms of quasi-names:

$a = b = \text{def. } ((F)a \equiv (F)b)$

This definition is the basis for several rules having to do with identity. We will express these using a and b and c as stand-ins for any name or quasi-name, and Zx as a stand-in for any predicate or sequence of predicates (as in our statement of UIG and EIG). The rules are:

Commutation for Identity (Com Id)	$\dfrac{a = b}{b = a}$
Transitivity for Identity (Trans Id)	$\dfrac{\begin{array}{c} a = b \\ b = c \end{array}}{a = c}$
Identity (Id)	$\dfrac{\begin{array}{c} a = b \\ Za \end{array}}{Zb}$
Negation of Identity (Neg Id)	$\dfrac{\begin{array}{c} Za \\ \sim Zb \end{array}}{\sim(a = b)}$

All of these follow directly from the definition of identity above.

It is useful to have a separate symbol for identity, since given it we can say certain things quite clearly and concisely. For example, if I wish to talk about *the* person who is the uncle of Frodo, one way of interpreting this is to say that there is *at least* and *at most* one individual who is Frodo's uncle. Suppose I want to say that this individual is a Hobbit. I can say:

$$(\exists x)((Uxf \cdot Hx) \cdot (\forall y)(Uyf \supset (y = x)))$$

where Uxy # x is the uncle of y

           f #   Frodo

That is: There is at least one individual who is Frodo's uncle and is a Hobbit, and for any individual who is Frodo's uncle that individual is the same as the individual of whom we are speaking.

Definite descriptions seem to be just a simple and useful device for doing something in our symbolic system rather like what we do with *the* phrases in English. But some major problems can at least be clarified and perhaps even solved by using definite descriptions. For example, take statements about nonexistent things or persons, such as "the mountain made of pure gold" or "the present King of France." What are we to make of statements about such nonentities? Do we, just by talking about them, have to assume that they have some sort of existence? Writing statements about such nonentities in the form just suggested yields the result that such statements are definitely false. Thus, if someone says, "The present *K*ing of France is *b*ald," we can write this as:

$$(\exists x)((Kx \cdot By) \cdot (\forall y)(Ky \supset (y = x)))$$

This statement implies $(\exists x)(Kx)$, and since that is false the statement as a whole is false.

However, if I want to say, "The *f*irst man on the moon was an *A*merican," we can write it as:

$$(\exists x)((Fx \cdot Ax) \cdot (\forall y)(Fy \supset (y = x)))$$

which is true because there *is* at least and at most one person, Neil Armstrong, who was the first man on the moon and he is an American. Thus we can make true statements about existing things, but statements about nonentities turn out to be false. This seems to do away with the lurking feeling that by talking about a thing we somehow have to assume its existence. An interesting and historically important argument with which we can now deal is Aquinas's causal argument for the existence of God, given at the beginning of this chapter. The argument is as follows:

> *The existence of God can be proved from the nature of the efficient cause. In the world of sense we find there is an order of efficient causes. There is no case known (neither is it, indeed, possible) in which a thing is found to be the efficient cause of itself; for so it would be prior to itself, which is impossible. Now in efficient causes it is not possible to go on to infinity, because in all efficient causes following in order, the first is the cause of the intermediate cause, and the intermediate is the cause of the ultimate cause, whether the intermediate cause be several, or one only. Now to take away the cause is to take away the effect. Therefore, if there be no first cause among efficient causes, there will be no ultimate, nor any intermediate cause. But if in efficient causes it is possible to go on to infinity, there will be no first efficient cause, neither will there be an ultimate effect, nor any intermediate efficient causes; all of which is plainly false. Therefore it is necessary to admit a first efficient cause, to which everyone gives the name of God.*

The only dictionary we would actually need to deal with this argument is:

Cxy # x causes y

However, we will simplify the argument by using the additional predicates

Ex # x is a cause
Dx # x is caused

These two predicates can actually be defined in terms of our first two:

Ex = def. $(\exists y)(Cxy)$
Dx = def. $(\exists y)(Cyx)$

To simplify the argument, we will use Ex and Dx, even though they could be eliminated.

The first premise we will symbolize is "There is no case . . . in which a thing is found to be the efficient cause of itself . . ." (we will regard the rest of this sentence as a supporting argument which is outside of our present scope). This can be symbolized as:

$(\forall x)(\sim Cxx)$

Another premise we will need is "In efficient causes it is not possible to go on to infinity." We can approach the symbolization of this argument indirectly by asking what an infinite regress in causes would mean. Evidently, to assert an infinite regress in causes is to say that every cause is caused by something other than itself, or:

$(\forall x)(Ex \supset (\exists y)(Cyx \cdot \sim(x = y)))$

To get Aquinas's premise, we simply deny this, to get:

$\sim(\forall x)(Ex \supset (\exists y)(Cyx \cdot \sim(x = y)))$

We need also to add a premise that was too obvious to be stated in Aquinas's argument: "If something is caused, it is caused by itself or by something else," which is:

$(\forall x)(Dx \supset (Cxx \vee (\exists y)(Cyx \cdot \sim(x = y))))$

With these three premises we can prove Aquinas's conclusions that a "first," or uncaused, cause exists:

$(\exists x)(Ex \cdot \sim Dx)$

The proof is as follows:

1. $(\forall x)(\sim Cxx)$
2. $\sim(\forall x)(Ex \supset (\exists y)(Cyx \cdot \sim(y = x)))$ $\left.\right\}$ $(\exists x)(Ex \cdot \sim Dx)$
3. $(\forall x)(Dx \supset (Cxx \vee (\exists y)(Cyx \cdot \sim(y = x))))$
4. $(\exists x)\sim(Ex \supset (\exists y)(Cyx \cdot \sim(y = x)))$ 3 QE
5. $(\exists x)(Ex \cdot \sim(\exists y)(Cyx \cdot \sim(y = x)))$ 4 DMI, De M, DN
6. $E[x] \cdot \sim(\exists y)(Cy[x] \cdot \sim(y = [x]))$ 5 EIG
7. $D[x] \supset (C[x][x] \vee (\exists y)(Cy[x] \cdot \sim Sy[x]))$ 3 UIG, UP
8. $C[x][x]$ 1 UIG, UP
9. $\sim(\exists y)(Cy[x] \cdot \sim(y = [x]))$ 6 Simp.

10. $\sim C[x][x] \cdot \sim(\exists y)(Cy[x] \cdot \sim(y = [x]))$ 8, 9 Conj.
11. $\sim(C[x][x] \lor (\exists y)(Cy[x] \cdot \sim(y = [x])))$ 10 De M
12. $\sim D[x]$ 11, 7 MT
13. $E[x]$ 6 Simp.
14. $E[x] \cdot \sim D[x]$ 12, 13 Conj.
15. $(\exists x)(Ex \cdot \sim Dx)$ 14 EIG

   Notice several things about the argument. From the purely technical point of view it has several points of interest. It combines transformations by Quantifier Exchange with inferences and equivalences first met with in propositional logic. The relative simplicity of the proof is obtained by leaving two quantified statements uninstantiated; otherwise, further transformations and reshufflings would have been necessary. What we are doing in the proof is fairly clear, but it is not at all easy to reproduce each step of the proof in ordinary language.

   From the philosophical point of view, the proof makes it clear that anyone who wishes to deny Aquinas's conclusion must deny one of his premises. Premise 3 is hardly disputable—if a thing is caused at all, it must either be self-caused or caused by something else. Therefore, the objector has to deny Premise 1 or Premise 2 (or both) or else admit Aquinas's conclusion.

Iota and Lambda Expressions

This way of interpreting *the* expressions, which are also called *definite descriptions*, can be extended into a special notation, the *iota operator*. We write a *name* constructed out of a predicate with a quantifier-like expression consisting of a variable letter preceded by a Greek iota which looks like this ι. Then, for example:

$(\iota x)(Uxf)$

would be the *name* "the unique individual who is the uncle of Frodo," and we could write the *statement*

$H(\iota x)(Uxf)$

"the unique individual who is Frodo's uncle is a Hobbit."

This statement is by definition equivalent to the one we had earlier. In fact, we can give a rule Definition of Iota Operator (DIO):

$Z(\imath w)(Yx)$

$(\exists w)((Yw \cdot Zw) \cdot (\forall v)(Yu \supset (u = w)))$

(where Y and u supplement Z and w as stand-ins).

We can give a similar "namelike" expression for predicates using a Greek letter lambda (λ) written before an individual variable letter so that, for example:

$(\lambda x)(Hx)$

stands for "the property individuals have when they are Hobbits," and:

$(\lambda x)(Uxf)$

stands for "the property individuals have when they are the uncle of Frodo Baggins."

How could we use lambda expressions in *statements*? To do so we would have to introduce the notion of a *property of a property*. Being Red, for example, is a property of individuals, but being a color is a property of properties of individuals, such as red, yellow, blue, etc. If we write a property of properties with a superscript 2 (e.g., C^2) standing for "_____ is a color," we can write, for example:

$\sim C^2(\lambda x)(Hx)$

"The property of being a Hobbit is not a color property."

When we write properties of properties in a dictionary, properly speaking we should write them with lambda expressions, but for convenience we will just put a capital letter, usually F, G, H, etc., as a placeholder for names of predicates. That is, our dictionary entry will be:

C^2F # F is a color

rather than:

$C^2(\lambda x)(Fx)$ # $(\lambda x)(Fx)$ is a color

There is no technical reason not to have properties of properties of
properties and so on, but we will not go into the complications involved
in these.

I have several times said there is no *technical* reason not to have
certain techniques or notations. Some philosophers object to the extension
of predicate logic to quantification over predicates on philosophical
grounds, and, in fact, there are some interesting problems connected with
such extensions. But, in general, I would argue that it is better to have the
language, the technical apparatus, to make statements, even if we think
these statements philosophically questionable.

Chapter Summary

In this chapter we extended the basic principles of predicate logic by
introducing quantifiers and two two-way rules that control dropping and
adding quantifiers:

Universal Instantiation and Generalization $\qquad (\forall x)(Zw)$
(UIG) $\qquad\qquad\qquad\qquad\qquad\qquad\qquad * \overline{} *$
$\qquad\qquad\qquad\qquad\qquad\qquad\qquad\qquad\quad Z(w)$

Restrictions: The $(\forall w)$ must not be within the scope of a $\sim$ or another
quantifier; the scope of $(\forall w)$ must be the complete expression; and in
going from $Z(w)$ to $(\forall w)(Zw)$, there must be no existential quasi-names in
$Z(w)$ and no universal quasi-names or bound variables derived from (w)
by earlier steps using UU.

Exsitential Instantiation and Generalization $\qquad (\exists w)(Zw)$
(EIG) $\qquad\qquad\qquad\qquad\qquad\qquad\qquad * \overline{} *$
$\qquad\qquad\qquad\qquad\qquad\qquad\qquad\qquad\quad Z[w]$

Restrictions: The $(\exists w)$ must not be within the scope of a $\sim$ or another
quantifier; the scope of the $(\exists w)$ must be the whole expression; and in
going from $(\exists w)(Zw)$ to $Z[w]$, $[w]$ must not occur in any previous line
of the argument in which this EIG is used. (In order to meet this last
restriction we may sometimes have to use a new letter, e.g., going from
$(\exists x)(Fx)$ to $F[y]$).

After looking at some proofs involving these new rules, we briefly
examined some extensions of predicate logic; especially, we gave rules
for identity:

Commutation for Identity (Com Id)	$a = b$ $\overline{\overline{b = a}}$

Transitivity for Identity (Trans Id)	$a = b$ $b = c$ $\overline{a = c}$

Identity (Id)	$a = b$ Za $\overline{\overline{Zb}}$

Negation of Identity (Neg Id)	Za $\sim Zb$ $\overline{\sim (a = b)}$

We concluded with a brief discussion of some further extensions of predicate logic: iota expressions, lambda expressions, and properties of properties.

Practical Applications

Check your Argument File for arguments that you could not handle with earlier systems of logic. These are likely to involve statements with more than one *every* or *some*. (Hint: Even commercials are sometimes a source of interesting examples—for instance, the baked goods company slogan, "Everybody doesn't like something, but nobody doesn't like Bleep!")

Exercise 7-3

For the following proof:

1. $(\forall x)(Dx \supset (\forall F)(\forall G)(Fx \supset Gx))$ $\sim (\exists(x))(Dx)$?
2. $D(x) \supset (\forall F)(\forall G)(F(x) \supset G(x))$
3. $D(x) \supset (\forall G)(D(x) \supset G(x))$
4. $D(x) \supset (D(x) \supset \sim D(x))$
5. $(D(x) \cdot D(x)) \supset \sim D(x)$

6. $D(x) \supset \sim D(x)$
7. $\sim D(x) \lor \sim D(x)$
8. $\sim D(x)$
9. $(\forall x)(\sim Dx)$
10. $\sim (\exists x)(Dx)$

1. Justify each line.
2. Is the justification of any line questionable?
3. If $Dx \ \# \ x$ is divine (i.e., x is God), what does the premise say? What does the conclusion say?
*4. The premise is one attempt to capture the idea that in a divine being there would be no distinction of properties—that all properties of a divine being are in some sense the same. What other ways could this idea be captured in our symbolism?
5. Is there a way of saying that all the properties of a divine being are the same without allowing a proof of this kind?

Exercise 7-4

In the following arguments for and against evolutionary theory:

A. Symbolize the argument.
B. Show whether the odd-numbered arguments give valid proofs of their conclusions.
C. Show whether the even-numbered arguments are valid refutations of the conclusions of the previous even-numbered statements.
D. If an argument is invalid, see if you can supply a premise that will make it valid when added to the existing premises or substituted for an existing premise.
E. If an argument is valid, identify the most questionable or controversial premise.

1. If Hempel's theory of scientific explanation is correct, a theory explains phenomena if and only if it could have predicted them in advance. There are many phenomena that evolutionary theory claims to explain, but which it could not have predicted in advance. Thus either Hempel's theory is wrong or evolutionary theory claims to explain many phenomena that it cannot explain.

2. *On the contrary:* Evolutionary theory makes use of probabilistic laws. If a theory makes use of probabilistic laws, it predicts patterns of occurrence in repeated events rather than predicting individual phenomena. If all this is true, then evolutionary theory claims to explain phenomena if and only if they are patterns of occurrences in repeated events which evolutionary theory claims to predict but cannot predict. Hempel's theory is correct, and it allows for probabilistic laws.

3. Evolutionary theory cannot predict any patterns of occurrences in repeated events, for the following reasons: Many such predictions depend on predictions of geological or climatic changes. Evolutionary theory cannot predict geological or climatic changes. And if one thing depends on another and you cannot predict the event on which the other depends, you cannot predict the dependent event.

*4. *On the contrary:* If one science depends on another for part of its data, then if the science depended on for data can predict, so can the dependent science. Geology and meteorology can predict patterns of occurrences in repeated phenomena—therefore, so can evolutionary theory.

5. Either evolutionary theory can explain away all apparently teleological phenomena as the result of natural selection, or evolutionary theory has failed. Reproductive systems are an apparently teleological phenomenon. To explain a phenomenon as the result of natural selection assumes that a reproductive system exists. What is assumed by a theory cannot be explained by that theory. Therefore, evolutionary theory has failed.

Exercise 7-5

*Symbolize the following statements. Give your own dictionary and use =
and iota and lambda expressions where possible.*

1. Michael Ventris is the man who deciphered Linear B.

2. The person who helped Michael Ventris in the decipherment of Linear B is the author of a book about Michael Ventris.

3. The person who deciphered Linear B was a young architect who was not a professional archeologist.

*4. The person who helped Michael Ventris was a philologist and he teaches at Cambridge University.

5. The director of the Heraklion Museum and the person who helped Michael Ventris discovered the other half of a tablet deciphered by Ventris.

6. Being an archeologist is not a necessary condition for deciphering tablets dug up by archeologists.

7. Being a philologist is a useful qualification for deciphering tablets dug up by archeologists.

8. Having a good visual memory is an important qualification for deciphering unknown systems of writing.

9. Having a good visual memory is useful for being an architect as well as for deciphering unknown alphabets.

10. Being the person to decipher Linear B is as likely to lead to lasting fame as being the architect of a famous building.

Exercise 7-6

The following arguments are suggested by Thomas Aquinas's Summa Theologica, *Question 2, Article 2. Do the following:*

A.   Symbolize each argument.
B.   Check the argument to see if it is a valid proof or a valid refutation of the statement "God exists."
C.   If the argument is not valid, see if you can supply any plausible premise or premises to make it a valid proof or refutation.
D.   If the argument is valid, discuss whether it is sound.
E.   If you think the argument is sound, discuss how the premises might be established.

1.   Does God exist? It would seem not, for if God existed a perfectly good being would exist. But if a perfectly good being existed, no evil could exist. But evil does exist.
2.   Does God exist? It would seem not, for the Universe could be explained perfectly well even if God doesn't exist.
3.   Whatever comes into existence has a cause for its existence. Nothing causes itself. It cannot be the case that everything is caused by something else. Thus something exists that is a cause but is not caused. Something that is a cause but is not caused would be the same as God.
4.   Whatever changes is changed by something. Nothing changes itself. It cannot be true that everything that changes is changed by something else. Thus something exists that changes things but is not itself changed. Such a being would be the same as God.
5.   Whatever exists either exists at all times whether or not anything else exists, or else it either does not exist at all times and exists because something else exists. If everything did not exist at some time, then there would have been a time at which nothing existed. But if there was ever a time when nothing existed, nothing would exist now. Something exists now. Therefore, something exists that exists at all times and exists whether or not anything else exists. This something would be the same as God.
*6.   If there is a designer of the Universe, then God exists. If there were no designer of the Universe, unintelligent things would not behave in an orderly and understandable way. But unintelligent things do behave in an orderly and understandable way.

7. If there are real differences in goodness between things, then there must be a Supreme Good. A Supreme Good would be the same as God. But there are real differences in goodness between things.

8. If someone is perfectly good, then if permitting evil to exist brings about greater good, that person will permit evil to exist. Thus it is not true that a perfectly good person will not permit evil. If some perfectly good person will permit evil, then the greatest objection to God's existence is overcome and God exists.

9. If the Universe cannot be explained without God, then God exists. If causation, change, and existence cannot be explained without God then the Universe cannot be explained without God. But causation, change, and existence cannot be explained without God.

10. If the existence of God is the best explanation of causation, change, existence, goodness, and the order of the Universe, then God exists. There is no better explanation of these things than God.

CHAPTER EIGHT

Probability

THE ESP PROBLEM

The following test of extrasensory perception (ESP), or telepathy, is proposed. Three subjects—A, B, C—at widely separated locations will, on a given day at 6:00 P.M. Eastern Standard Time, select one card from a group of five cards. A will try to "broadcast" his choice telepathically to B and C; B will try to receive A's message and choose the same card A has chosen and "broadcast" his choice to C; and C will try to receive A's "broadcast" as well as B's and choose the same card as A and B. Suppose they all choose the same card. How likely is it that this event occurred by pure chance?

What are the basic principles of reasoning where we have probabilities rather than certainties?

So far we have given only a very rough and ready characterization of inductive arguments and the difference between induction and deduction. There are at least two possible ways of doing this and each has its difficulties. The first way is to characterize inductive arguments as arguments such that the conclusion is *probable*, or *highly probable*, if the premises are true. For example, if I argue:

Almost all the people who saw *Star Wars* enjoyed it.
Isaac Asimov saw *Star Wars*.
_____
Isaac Asimov enjoyed it.

the conclusion does not follow deductively from the premises, as it would if the first premise were "*All* the people who saw *Star Wars* enjoyed it." But, it might be argued, the premises do make the conclusion probable, or even highly probable.

The difficulty with this characterization of inductive arguments is that it is very hard to make it precise or give reasonable rules for distinguishing good and bad inductive arguments. For example, consider the argument:

Almost all the people who saw *Star Wars* enjoyed it.
The critic who wrote a nasty put-down of *Star Wars* saw *Star Wars*.
_____
The critic who wrote a nasty put-down of *Star Wars* enjoyed it.

It is much the same as the previous argument in structure, but because we know that the critic panned the film the conclusion does not seem even probable. In a deductive argument of similar structure we would have a premise about *all* who saw *Star Wars*, but in this argument we have a premise about only almost all who saw *Star Wars*. The difference is crucial even for a probabilistic conclusion, because we know that some members of the class in question may not have the characteristic in question and we may have some information that indicates that the individual concerned is in this subgroup.

There are other problems too. How great a percentage is "almost all"? How great a probability is represented by "highly probable"? When we clarify such points and try to restate the argument in such a way that it contains no information that weakens the probability of the conclusion, we come up with an argument something like this:

Eighty-seven percent of those who saw *Star Wars* enjoyed it.
Sam is a member of the audience selected at random.
_____
Sam probably enjoyed *Star Wars*.

Given the truth of the premises, we might want to say that the conclusion was "87 percent probable." If Sam is really selected at random, then surely we have 87 chances out of 100 of getting a person who enjoyed the movie. So if the premises are true, the percentage of people who enjoyed the film must be related to the chance that a member of the audience selected at random has enjoyed it.

Probability and Inductive Arguments

But when we have a precise numerical probability like this (if we do) we need some standard way of expressing it as a percentage, a fraction, or a decimal and some standard way of writing statements of probability.

We will use the convention of writing probabilities as fractions rather than as percentages or decimals, and where S is a statement we will write "the probability of S is m/n" as $Pr(S) = m/n$. Thus if S stands for "Sam has enjoyed *Star Wars*" and that probability is 87 out of 100, then we can write:

$$Pr(S) = \frac{87}{100}$$

We can now give a new characterization of inductive arguments: Inductive arguments, we might say, are arguments whose conclusion is a probability statement.

The difficulty with this way of characterizing inductive arguments is that there is a part of mathematics, the theory of probability, that gives us rules, which are essentially *deductive* rules, for manipulating probabilities. The rules of probability theory assume that we have some probability statements to start off with, for example, that the probability of statement *A* is *m/n* and the probability of *B* is *k/n*. Probability theory tells us how to start with such probabilities and get the probability of ∼ *A* or ∼ *B* or *A* ∨ *B* or *A* · *B*. We will shortly be having a brief look at probability theory, but first let us finish our discussion of how to characterize inductive arguments. Some, but not all, inductive arguments could be characterized as having statements that are not statements of probability as premises and a probability statement as conclusion. This will take care of the example we have been using and many other inductive arguments, but it would be too restrictive as a general characterization. Probably the best preliminary definition of an inductive argument we can give is that it is an argument that reasons from incomplete data—data that will not support a deductive conclusion—to a conclusion expressed in terms of probability or likelihood (we will see in due course what a likelihood is and how it differs from a probability).

Fundamentals of Probability

Before getting to inductive arguments proper we must understand at least the fundamentals of the mathematical theory of probability, in order to understand probabilities as they occur in inductive arguments. Thus the remainder of this chapter will be concerned with probability theory and Chapter Nine will deal with elementary inductive logic.

As we noted earlier, mathematical probability theory has to start with some probability statements. Probability theory itself is not concerned with how we get the probability of the elementary statements, any more than deductive logic is concerned with how we get the truth or falsity of elementary statements. Inductive logic may, as we will see, be concerned with how we get probabilities in the first place, but for the moment we want to consider only the manipulation of probabilities we already have.

Therefore, we will begin by using probabilities connected with gambling devices such as cards, dice, etc. Probability theory, in fact, began when a gambler approached a distinguished philosopher and mathematician, Blaise Pascal (1623–1662), with some problems connected with gambling. Cards, dice, and their manipulations, such as the shuffling of cards, the throwing of dice, etc., are deliberately designed to give a series of events that are not predictable in detail but that have definite

probabilities. When you throw a single die you have no way of knowing
which of the six sides will face upwards, but you know that each side of a
correctly made, unloaded die will turn up about one out of every six
times on the average. This means that the probability of each face is one
out of six, or 1/6.

We will use throws of a single die or a pair of dice as our examples
in our preliminary explanation of probability theory, then apply what
we have learned to more complex cases. We will begin by considering
how we get the probability of the denial of a statement when we know
the probability of the statement itself. In the case of a single throw of a
die it is fairly clear that if the probability of getting a particular side, say
the side with six dots, is 1/6, then the probability of *not* getting that side
must be 5/6. In general, a probability of 1 represents certainty that a
statement is true, a probability of 0 represents certainty that a statement
is false. The probability of the negation of a statement is 1 minus the
probability of the statement:

$$Pr(\sim A) = 1 - Pr(A)$$

We can see from this that the denial of a certainly true statement is
certainly false, and that the denial of a certainly false statement is certainly
true. If $Pr(A) = 1$:

$$Pr(\sim A) = 1 - 1 = 0$$

If $Pr\ A = 0$:

$$Pr(\sim A) = 1 - 0 = 1$$

In fact, our truth table for negation in Chapter Four

p	$\sim p$
T	F
F	T

can be rewritten with 1 for True and 0 for False:

p	$\sim p$
1	0
0	1

and we can see that our previous rule for negation was a special case of the probabilistic rule, or to put it another way, that our probabilistic rule for negation is a generalization of the rule in statement logic.

The Addition Rule

What about the probability of $A \vee B$ when we have the probabilities of A and B? In the case of the die we can see, for example, that the probability of getting a five or a six is $\frac{2}{6}$; we have two chances out of six of getting *either* a five *or* a six. In general:

$$Pr(A \vee B) = Pr(A) + Pr(B)$$

where A and B are statements that are mutually exclusive, that is, statements that cannot both be true. This condition is satisfied in the case of the die, since you can get only one face up at a time: You can't have *both* a five and a six.

We can see that when we are dealing with statements that are certainly true or certainly false, the probability of $A \vee \sim A$ will always be 1, since if A has probability 1, $\sim A$ will have probability 0, and vice versa, and $1 + 0 = 1$ and $0 + 1 = 1$. Of course A and $\sim A$ cannot both be true, so our condition is satisfied. But also, no matter what the probability of A is

$$Pr(A \vee \sim A) = 1$$

will always be true, since if $Pr(A)$ is m/n

$$Pr(A \vee \sim A) = m/n + 1 - m/n = 1$$

no matter what m and n are. We can now define what is meant by a tautology in probability theory—a statement form such that it has a probability of 1 for any probability assigned to its component statements. As we will see, all the tautologies of statement logic are also tautologies in this new sense.

What about the probability of $A \vee B$ where A and B are not mutually exclusive; could both be true? Consider the probability of getting either a six *or* an even number on one throw of a die. The probability of getting a six is $\frac{1}{6}$, the probability of getting an even number is $\frac{3}{6}$ since half the six numbers on a die are even. But if we add $\frac{1}{6}$ to $\frac{3}{6}$ to get $\frac{4}{6}$ we would be wrong, since we have counted six twice. The even numbers on a die are two, four, and six, so the probability in question is the probability of getting a six or a two or a four *or a six*. To get the right figure we must subtract the value of the six we counted the second time; in general, where A and B are not mutually exclusive:

$$Pr(A \lor B) = Pr(A) + Pr(B) - Pr(A \cdot B)$$

For our example the chance of getting *both* a six and an even number is $\frac{1}{6}$, just the probability of getting a six. So our figures are:

$$\frac{1}{6} + \frac{3}{6} - \frac{1}{6} = \frac{3}{6}$$

which is the correct probability for getting either a six or an even number.

The simpler rule we gave earlier is a special case of our more complex rule, since if A and B are mutually exclusive, $Pr(A \cdot B) = 0$ and thus we add $Pr(A)$ to $Pr(B)$ and subtract 0 if we use the complex rule, and ignore $Pr(A \cdot B)$ if we use the simpler rule, which comes to the same thing. We will refer to these two rules as the Simple Addition Rule and the Complete Addition Rule respectively. Statement logic again provides us with a special case of the Complete Addition Rule. Our truth table for $\lor$ was:

p q	$p \lor q$
T T	T
T F	T
F T	T
F F	F

Rewritten with 1 and 0 it is:

p q	$p \lor q$
1 1	1
1 0	1
0 1	1
0 0	0

and we can see that if two statements A and B are both true we get:

$1 + 1 - 1 = 1$

if the first is true and the second false we get:

$1 + 0 - 0 = 1$

if the first is false and the second true we get:

$0 + 1 - 0 = 1$

and if both are false we get:

$0 + 0 - 0 = 0$

by applying the Complete Addition Rule, and this is just what the truth table definition of $\vee$ gives us.

The Multiplication Rule

In the case we considered it was obvious what value we should give to $Pr(A \cdot B)$, but in many cases we will need to calculate this value. Again we have a simple rule, the Simple Multiplication Rule:

$$Pr(A \cdot B) = Pr(A) \times Pr(B)$$

which holds when A and B describe events that are independent, that is, when the occurrence of the event described by A has no effect on the occurrence of the event described by B, and vice versa.

A good example of independent events would be two throws of a single die or one throw of two dice. Dice have no memory, so the fact that a die has come up a certain number on the last throw does not affect the probabilities of its coming up that number (or any other) on the next throw. And dice do not consult, cooperate, or connect in any way, so that one die coming up a certain number does not affect the probability of another die coming up that number or any other. It does not matter which example we use, but since in many standard dice games two dice are thrown together, we will use that as an example.

Consider then the probability of getting two sixes, or two of any given number, or in general any two specified numbers, on one throw of two dice. The events are independent, so our figures are:

$$\frac{1}{6} \times \frac{1}{6} = \frac{1}{36}$$

However, most dice games are played in such a way that it is the *sum* of the numbers on the two dice that matters. There is only one way of getting a two (one and one) and only one way of getting a twelve (six and six). But there are two ways of getting a three: you may have a two on the first die and a one on the second, or vice versa. Thus we must make a more complex calculation. Let us write the probability of getting a three as $Pr(H)$, the probability of getting a two as $Pr(W)$, the probability of getting two and one as $Pr(W \cdot N)$, and so on. Then:

$$Pr(H) = Pr((W \cdot N) \vee (N \cdot W))$$
$$= \frac{1}{36} + \frac{1}{36} = \frac{2}{36}$$

The number seven is important in many dice games because there are more ways of getting a sum of seven on one throw of two dice than of any other sum. We can get a sum of seven in any of the following ways:

First die	Second die
6	1
5	2
4	3
3	4
2	5
1	6

Since there are six ways of getting a seven, the probability of getting a seven is $\frac{6}{36}$ or $\frac{1}{6}$.

There is a more complex version of the multiplication rule, for cases where the events in question are not independent. Consider a game where one die is thrown twice and you win if the second throw gives a number *higher* than the first throw. The chance of any given pair of numbers is still $\frac{1}{36}$, but only some pairs will be winning ones, and the probability of whether you win or lose depends on the number thrown on the first die. For example, if you throw a six, you lose, since you cannot throw a higher number. If you throw a one, you have five chances out of six of throwing a higher number, and so on.

Suppose we want to know the probability of throwing a four and then winning. The probability of throwing a four is $\frac{1}{6}$, the probability of winning given that you have thrown a four is $\frac{2}{6}$, since having thrown a four you can win with either a five or a six. So the probability of throwing a four *and* winning is $\frac{1}{6} \times \frac{2}{6} = \frac{2}{36}$.

The general rule involved here is the Complete Multiplication Rule:

$$Pr(A \cdot B) = Pr(A) \times Pr(B/A)$$

where $Pr(B/A)$ is not $Pr(B$ divided by $A)$, which would not make sense, but rather the conditional probability of B supposing that A were true, as in the case we have just considered.

Again there is a parallel with statement logic, but all we need is the Simple Multiplication Rule. The truth table for · is:

p q	$p \cdot q$
T T	T
T F	F
F T	F
F F	F

Rewritten with 1 and 0 it is:

p q	$p \cdot q$
1 1	1
1 0	0
0 1	0
0 0	0

Using the multiplication rule we find that if both statements are true, we have $1 \times 1 = 1$, whereas if either or both statements are false, we have $1 \times 0 = 0$ or $0 \times 1 = 0$ or $0 \times 0 = 0$. If a statement is true, it is true whether or not some other statement is true, and if it is false, it is false whether or not another statement is false. Thus we can ignore the conditional probability in the Complete Multiplication Rule in such cases.

Incidentally, we can now define independence without talking about events; A and B are independent statements if and only if

$$Pr(B) = Pr(B/A)$$

and

$$Pr(A) = Pr(A/B)$$

In the ESP problem at the beginning of this chapter we can calculate the probabilities as follows: If A, B, and C choose the same card by pure chance, then the probabilities will be independent. A has one chance in five of picking the first of the five cards, so has B, and so has C. So the chance that they all pick the first card is $\frac{1}{5} \times \frac{1}{5} \times \frac{1}{5}$ or $\frac{1}{125}$. But for them all to pick the *same* card, all could pick the first card *or* all could pick the second card *or* all could pick the third card *or* all could pick the fourth card *or* all could pick the fifth card. So the probability that all pick the same card is:

$$\frac{1}{125} + \frac{1}{125} + \frac{1}{125} + \frac{1}{125} + \frac{1}{125}$$

which is $\frac{5}{125}$ or $\frac{1}{25}$. (Since the outcomes are independent and mutually exclusive, we can use the simpler forms of both the multiplication and the addition rule.) So the result that all pick the same card, although impressive, may not be as impressive as it seems: It would occur by pure chance once out of 25 times.

Cards used to test ESP.

Exercise 8-1

The Greeks and Romans played a dicelike game with the knucklebones of sheep, which have two rounded ends on which they cannot stand, two narrow sides, one concave and one convex, and two wider sides, one concave and one convex. If the narrow convex side came up, it counted 1. The broad convex side counted 3. The broad concave side counted 4, and the narrow concave side counted 6. Since the knucklebones were irregular, there were probably no dependendable probabilities, but suppose that the probabilities of getting a given side on one throw are given by the following table:

Side	Score	Probability
Narrow Convex	1	4/10
Broad Convex	3	3/10
Broad Concave	4	2/10
Narrow Concave	6	1/10

The simplest form of dice game played with these bones was as follows: Any number of players in turn threw two knucklebones. The values of the two knucklebones were totaled. The highest number won; in a tie the first player to throw the number won. Answer the following questions in terms of this information.

1. The highest possible throw, called the "Venus throw," was two sixes (12). What would be the probability of this throw?
2. The lowest possible throw, called "the dog," was two ones (2). What would be the probability of this throw?
3. Intermediate numbers (between 2 and 12) could be made by more than one combination of dice. For example, a throw of ten could be gotten by throwing a six and a four or a four and a six. What is the probability of getting a ten?
*4. What is the probability of getting a five?
5. What is the probability of getting a six?
6. What is the probability of getting a seven?
7. What is the probability of getting an eight?
8. What is the probability of getting a nine?
9. What is the probability of getting an eleven?
10. What is the probability of getting a four?

11. What number seems to play the same role that seven plays in ordinary dice games?

12. You are playing with one other player. You have thrown a ten and it is the other player's turn. What is the probability that you will win?

*13. In view of the physical makeup of the knucklebones, explain the values given to each side.

14. What is the relation of values to probabilities in our table?

15. Suppose you can make an additional bet after your own throw. When would you be inclined to do so?

Conditional Probability

The conditional probability we use in the Complete Multiplication Rule can itself be defined. In general:

$$Pr(A/B) = \frac{Pr(A \cdot B)}{Pr(B)}$$

To see how this works in our imaginary dice game (the same in which you win if your second throw is higher than your first), we have to know the probability of winning in general. The winning combinations are:

1,2	2,3	3,4	4,5	5,6
1,3	2,4	3,5	4,6	
1,4	2,5	3,6		
1,5	2,6			
1,6				

That is, these 15 out of the 36 possible throws will result in a win. So the probability of a win in general is 15/36. The conditional probability of winning given that you have first thrown a four will be:

$$Pr(W/F) = \frac{Pr(W \cdot F)}{Pr(F)}$$

You might think that this was:

$$\frac{\frac{15}{36} \times \frac{1}{6}}{\frac{1}{6}} = \frac{15}{36}$$

but that would give us the wrong figure. The problem is that winning and getting a four are not independent; given that you have won, there are two chances out of fifteen that you won with a combination starting with a four. So the correct figures are:

$$\frac{\frac{15}{36} \times \frac{2}{15}}{\frac{1}{6}} = \frac{\frac{30}{540}}{\frac{1}{6}} = \frac{180}{540} = \frac{2}{6}$$

which is the same number we arrived at before.

As we can see from this example, the use of the Conditional Probability Rule may involve us in further conditional probabilities, and, in general, each of the rules leads into the others. It is thus impossible to eliminate any of the rules or define any of the probabilities independently of the others. The situation is inherent in probability theory, which is a device for manipulating given probabilities.

Bayes' Theorem

An extremely important rule for dealing with probabilistic arguments can be derived by combining the multiplication rule:

$$Pr(A \cdot B) = Pr(A) \times Pr(B/A)$$

with the conditional probability rule:

$$Pr(A/B) = \frac{Pr(A \cdot B)}{Pr(B)}$$

Since the top part of the right-hand expression is $Pr(A \cdot B)$, we simply replace this by what $Pr(A \cdot B)$ is equal to—that is, by $Pr(A) \times Pr(B/A)$ to get:

$$Pr(A/B) = \frac{Pr(A) \times Pr(B/A)}{Pr(B)}$$

This apparently simple manipulation of two basic rules seems obvious now, but it was not noticed until some time after the beginnings of probability theory. The first man to derive this theorem was Thomas Bayes, an Anglican clergyman who lived around the time of our Revolutionary War. His discussion of it was published after Bayes' death by his friend Richard Price, another Anglican clergyman and an important moral philosopher. As we will see in the next chapter, the Reverand Bayes not only discovered the theorem but was also the first to argue that it gives the basic pattern for inductive reasoning. Many philosophers and mathematicians have agreed with Bayes, and the possible applications of this innocent-seeming theorem still arouse lively controversy among statisticians and logicians.

Exercise 8-2

A simple form of fortunetelling with cards can be set up as follows: Only the court cards of hearts and clubs are used. Black jacks are said to foretell injury, red jacks to foretell travel. Black queens supposedly foretell failure in love, red queens success in love. Black kings are supposed to represent failure in business or career, red kings success. The court cards are shuffled and four cards are dealt face down, then turned up one at a time. Two cards that have an opposing significance are interpreted as meaning neither event will occur. Assuming travel and success are good luck, what is the probability of the following "fortunes"?

1. A fortune predicting only good luck.
2. A fortune predicting travel, injury, success in love, and failure in business.
3. A fortune predicting all bad luck.
*4. A fortune predicting travel, failure in love, or success in business.
5. A fortune predicting injury or travel, and success in either love or business.

Assume that a statistical survey has been made and for a certain group the actual probabilities of travel, injury, success, etc., are as follows:

Travel	$\frac{1}{4}$
Injury	$\frac{1}{4}$
Success in love	$\frac{1}{2}$
Failure in love	$\frac{1}{2}$
Success in business	$\frac{1}{2}$
Failure in business	$\frac{1}{2}$

(Assume the probabilities of travel, injury, and success or failure at love or business are independent of each other.)

6. If a fortune predicts travel and failure in business for one of the group in question, what is the chance that both of these predictions will be fulfilled?

7. What is the probability that one of the predictions will be fulfilled?

8. What is the probability that neither of the predictions will be fulfilled?

9. Compare the probabilities in 6 to 8 with that of the fortune.

10. How would you design an experiment to check the reliability of predictions made by this method of fortunetelling?

Conditional Statements and Probability

Of the statement connectives given in Chapter Four we have so far shown that we can get similar results from probability theory and truth tables for $\sim$, $\vee$ and $\cdot$. What about $\supset$? Somewhat surprisingly, we have two alternatives. We can write $A \supset B$ as $Pr(\sim A \vee B)$, or we can write it as $Pr(B/A)$. For the values 1 and 0, these come to the same thing. For if A is true, $\sim A$ will be false, that is, have a value of 0. Thus if A is true and B is true, we get:

$$0 + 1 - 0 = 1$$

If A is false and B true, we get:

$$1 + 1 - 1 = 1$$

If A is false and B false, we get:

$$1 + 0 - 0 = 1$$

And only if A is true and B false do we get:

$$0 + 0 - 0 = 0$$

This gives us the familiar table:

p q	p ⊃ q		p q	p ⊃ q
T T	T		1 1	1
T F	F		1 0	0
F T	T		0 1	1
F F	T		1 1	1

But also, if the $A \supset B$ is written as $Pr(B/A)$, we get the same result. Remember with 1 and 0 we can use the simpler form of the multiplication rule:

$$Pr(B/A) = \frac{Pr(A \cdot B)}{Pr(A)}$$

If A and B are both true, we get:

$$\frac{1 \times 1}{1} = 1$$

If A is true and B false, we get:

$$\frac{1 \times 0}{1} = 0$$

If A is false and B true, we get:

$$\frac{1 \times 0}{0} = 1$$

And if A is false and B false, we get:

$$\frac{0 \times 0}{0} = 1$$

(You will remember from mathematics classes that $n/n = 1$. The special case of $\frac{0}{0}$ can be treated as an example of this.) So we have the same truth table as before. The equivalent result of $Pr(B/A)$ holds only for the 1, 0 case; in general, a conditional probability cannot be rewritten this way. Thus we cannot rewrite:

$$Pr(W/F) \quad \text{as} \quad Pr(\sim F \vee W)$$

The second expression would give us:

$$\frac{5}{6} + \frac{15}{36} - \frac{13}{36} = \frac{32}{36}$$

which, of course, is not the right figure. (The $\frac{13}{36}$ which we subtract is the probability of not getting a four *and* winning: the 13 out of 15 winning combinations that do not have an initial four.)

Granted that there is a difference for cases involving probabilities, which of the two analogues of *if . . . then* in probability theory is preferable? It depends to some extend on what we want to say. Suppose while playing our dice game we are told by someone, "If you get a four on the first throw, you will win." Interpreting this in the usual way for material implication, we can take this statement as "Either you will not get a four on the first throw or you will win." As we saw:

$$Pr(\sim F \vee W) = \frac{32}{36}$$

and the statement is therefore very probable. But it gains this probability because it is quite probable ($\frac{5}{6}$ or $\frac{30}{36}$) that you will *not* get a four on the first throw. The remaining $\frac{2}{36}$ represent those two of the 36 possible pairs of throws that are winning throws and have four as their first component. So if you do throw a four on your first throw, the high probability of $\sim F \vee W$ does not entitle you to infer with high probability that you will win. In fact, there is no general rule that enables you to reason:

$$Pr(\sim A \vee B) = n/m$$
$$\underline{Pr(A) = 1}$$
$$Pr(B) = k/m$$

However, the conditional probability $Pr(W/F)$ represents another interpretation of what someone might mean by, "If you get a four, you will win." On this interpretation the statement means, "Suppose that you get a four; in that case you will win." As we saw:

$$Pr(W/F) = \frac{2}{6}$$

because once you have a four, either a five or a six will give you a win.

Exercise 8-3

Gamblers sometimes bet on the cut of cards. Each one picks up part of the deck and shows the card at the bottom of the part of the deck he has lifted.

The highest card wins. If equal cards are drawn, both cut again. Suppose you are playing this game against one opponent and that you are using only the K, Q, 3, 2, A of hearts. Suppose also that you always go first. First using Pr(If A then B) = Pr(∼A ∨ B), and then using Pr(If A then B) = Pr(B/A), find a numerical probability for each of the following statements.

1. If you get a court card, you will win.
2. If you get an ace, two, or three, you will not win.*
3. If your opponent gets a court card, you will lose.
*4. If your opponent gets an ace, you will win.
5. If you get a king, you will not lose.

Logical Rules and Probabilistic Analogues

For conditional probabilities we have an argument rather like *modus ponens*:

$$Pr(A/B) = m/n$$
$$Pr(A) = 1$$
$$\overline{Pr(B) = m/n}$$

That is, in our dice game case the fact that

$$Pr(W/F) = \frac{2}{6}$$

tells you that if you do throw a four, your probability of winning is $\frac{2}{6}$. In general, all of our familiar patterns of argument from statement logic can be restated as probability arguments. For example, Simple Cancellation and Cancel and Collect come out as:

$$Pr(A \vee B) = 1$$
$$Pr(\sim A) = 1$$
$$\overline{Pr(B) = 1}$$

$$Pr(A \vee B) = 1$$
$$Pr(\sim B \vee C) = 1$$
$$\overline{Pr(A \vee C) = 1}$$

You can see in SC that if $Pr(\sim A) = 1$, then $Pr(A) = 0$, and so $Pr(B) = 1$ must be true if $Pr(A \vee B) = 1$ is true. Similarly, in CC if $Pr(B) = 1$, then $Pr(\sim B) = 0$, and $Pr(C) = 1$ must be true if $Pr(\sim B \vee C) = 1$ is true.

---

* Aces are "low," that is, they count as equal to one, and so are the lowest in value.

If $Pr(B) = 0$, then $Pr(A) = 1$ must be true if $Pr(A \lor B) = 1$ is true. But if either $Pr(A) = 1$ or $Pr(C) = 1$, or both, then obviously $Pr(A \lor C) = 1$.

The probabilistic analogues to these arguments are more complex. For example, the analogue of SC is:

$$Pr(A \lor B) = m/n$$
$$Pr(\sim A) = k/n$$
$$\overline{Pr(B) - Pr(A \cdot B) = m/n - (1 - k/n)}$$

That is, if we know, for example, that $Pr(A \lor B) = \frac{1}{2}$ and $Pr(\sim A) = \frac{3}{4}$, then we know that $Pr(A) = 1 - \frac{3}{4} = \frac{1}{4}$. We can then see that since $Pr(A \lor B) = Pr(A) + Pr(B) - Pr(A \cdot B)$, then $Pr(B) - Pr(A \cdot B)$ must be the value of the whole expression—$\frac{1}{2}$ in this case minus the value of $Pr(A)$, $\frac{1}{4}$ in this case—so here the probability of the conclusion is $\frac{1}{4}$. (If we knew that A and B were mutually exclusive, the value of $Pr(B)$ would be $\frac{1}{4}$.)

There is a probabilistic analogue of Cancel and Collect, but it is so complex and so weak as to be not worth stating. The probability of any of our rules written as a statement is always one; for example:

$$Pr(\sim((A \lor B) \cdot (\sim B \lor C)) \lor (A \lor C)) = 1$$

But what we have been doing is giving rules analogous to our statement logic rules which enable us to state something about the probability of a conclusion given the probability of premises. We can do this for SC, but not, or not usefully, for CC.

We have emphasized before that joining Addition to the cancellation rules gives an expansion of simple statement logic, so it is interesting to see how Addition fares in the probabilistic system. For 1 and 0 Addition holds true without qualification:

$$Pr(A) = 1$$
$$\overline{Pr(A \lor B) = 1}$$

Since if $Pr(A) = 1$ and $Pr(B) = 0$, then $Pr(A \lor B) = Pr(A) + Pr(B) - Pr(A \cdot B) = 1 + 0 - 0 = 1$, and if $Pr(B) = 1$, then $Pr(A \lor B) = Pr(A) + Pr(B) - Pr(A \cdot B) = 1 + 1 - 1 = 1$. The probabilistic analogue of Addition is, as we might expect, more complex:

$$Pr(A) = m/n$$
$$\overline{Pr(A \lor B) \geq m/n}$$

(where $k \geq j$ means that k is greater than or equal to j). The reasoning is as follows: If $Pr(B)$ is zero, we add nothing to $Pr(A)$ and $Pr(A \vee B) = Pr(A)$. But if $Pr(B)$ is greater than zero, we do add something to $Pr(A)$ since, even if A and B are not mutually exclusive, $Pr(A \cdot B)$ must always be less than either $Pr(A)$ or $Pr(B)$—because $Pr(A \cdot B)$ results from multiplying $Pr(A)$ and $Pr(B)$ or $Pr(A)$ and $Pr(B/A)$. So if $Pr(B)$ is greater than zero, $Pr(A \vee B)$ is greater than $Pr(A)$. Some of our two-way rules will have analogues that follow from simple mathematical considerations; for example:

$$Pr(A) + Pr(B) = Pr(B) + Pr(A)$$
$$Pr(A) \times Pr(B) = Pr(B) \times Pr(A) \qquad \text{etc.}$$

Other two-way rules will follow from statement logic:

$$Pr(A \vee B) = Pr(B \vee A)$$
$$Pr(A \cdot B) = Pr(B \cdot A)$$
$$Pr(A) = Pr(\sim \sim A) \qquad \text{etc.}$$

In general, logically equivalent statements will always have the same probability, a point that will become important in a later chapter.

The Meaning of Probability

Let us now turn to the problem of what is meant by probability. So far we have been treating cases involving gambling devices where, as we will see, all the major theories coincide. But as soon as we get away from such artificially simple cases, we find a divergence of interpretations of what is meant by a probability statement. Consider a simple case of some interest. Take an ordinary thumbtack. It has a broad head and a narrow, pointed pin or tack portion; in profile it is like the letter T. If we throw this thumbtack against a wall or similar surface so it comes to rest on a floor or other flat horizontal surface, it will either land point uppermost like an upside-down T ($\perp$) or leaning on its point and the edge of its "head," like a leaning T ($\nearrow$). Occasionally, it might stick in the surface it lands on and be fully upright like an ordinary T. If we call the first possibility "point" and the other possibilities "head," then we have two possible positions in which the thumbtack can land.

In fact, we could imagine other possibilities, such as landing precisely on the edge of the head and balancing. Though for practical purposes we can ignore these, if we want to include all logical possibilities, we could call any position where the point was up and the head flat on the surface on which it lands "point" and *any* other position "head."

Now what is the probability that a given thumbtack will land point, and the corresponding possibility that it will land head? The following are some possible answers to this question, with some objections to each answer.

Four Interpretations of Probability

1. The logical possibility interpretation: All logical possibilities are equally probable. Depending on how you count logical possibilities, this would give $Pr(\text{point}) = \frac{1}{2}$ and $Pr(\text{head}) = \frac{1}{2}$, or else give equal probabilities to all distinguishable possible final positions of the tack, for example, $\frac{1}{4}$ each to ⊥, T, ↗, and ⊢.

Objections: First, this is unworkable because there is no clear way of distinguishing all logical possibilities, and different ways give different probabilities. For instance, point has probability $\frac{1}{2}$ if we divide the first way, probability $\frac{1}{4}$ if we divide the second way, and probability $\frac{1}{180}$ if we divide the positions from ⊥ to T into 180 degrees and give each degree an equal probability. Second, this suggestion is unrealistic, for a little experimentation with most standard thumbtacks shows that ↗ is the most frequent position, ⊥ much less frequent, and ⊢ and T never or almost never occur.

2. The subjective or personal probability interpretation: Probabilities represent degrees of belief or confidence or are related to the odds we would give on a bet. Thus if we believe that, for example, ↗ is twice as likely as ⊥ or would give odds of two to one on ↗ occurring, the probability of ↗ is $\frac{2}{3}$ and that of ⊥ $\frac{1}{3}$.

Objections: If these probabilities are assigned on the basis of mere guess or whim, they are worthless; if they are based on objective factors in the situation in question, we should go directly to those instead of considering our beliefs or the odds we might give.

3. The frequency interpretation: If we perform a series of tests, for example, a series of throws of a standard thumbtack, the probability of heads is the ratio of heads in our series of tests to all trials. For example, if we try 100 throws and 76 heads come up, the probability of a head will be $\frac{76}{100}$ or roughly $\frac{3}{4}$.

Objections: There are technical problems with this, including problems about very short series of tests (e.g., two throws) and very long (especially infinite) series of tests. More seriously, a frequency theory would give us no way of assigning probabilities to statements about events that are not part of a series of tests. For example, I might have a wineglass in my hand and wonder about the probabilities of its landing upright, upside down, or on its side if I threw it gently onto a fairly soft surface. Before I make any trials, someone drops a plate on it and smashes it. Should I say that *no* probability can be assigned to the various possibilities I have considered? Or suppose I consider the probability that some public official will be reelected. An election is a unique event, not part of a sequence of tests made under the same conditions. Am I to say that I cannot apply the notion of probability here?

4. The propensity interpretation: This view says that given the laws of nature and the factual situations that obtain, we can distinguish certain outcomes as being more likely than others and, if we know enough, assign an exact probability. For example, a physicist or engineer might look at a thumbtack and, using his or her knowledge of the laws of gravity, momentum, etc., calculate that some outcomes were likelier than others. Given exact information about dimensions, weight, force of throw, etc., the physicist or engineer might even be able to calculate an exact probability.

Objections: It is not clear what the relevant laws, etc., would be in some cases, for example, the election of Jimmy Carter. Furthermore, a normal way of testing propensities, tendencies, and the like, would be by a series of tests, which brings us back to the frequency theory. Defenders of the propensity theory can argue that their theory includes the strong points of other theories. They claim to want not all the *logical* possibilities to calculate probability, but all the *physical* possibilities—all the outcomes consistent with the laws of nature. Often the obvious logical possibilities (e.g., heads and tails when a coin is thrown) are the same as the physical possibilities. The nonobvious logical possibilities, such as a coin's spinning forever and never descending, are ones they do not want to consider, and these are ruled out by natural laws. Furthermore, the propensity theorist can grant that if our subjective possibilities are based on experience and knowledge, they will quite often coincide at least roughly with those given on a propensity interpretation, and that, where feasible, a series of tests is an excellent way to discover a propensity or tendency. But, the propensity theorists argue, their view lacks the unworkability and unrealistic aspects of the logical possibility view, the possible arbitrariness of the subjective view, and the restrictiveness of a straight frequency view. Propensity theorists disagree about how to handle cases involving human decisions: Some believe those can be included under psychological laws analogous to the laws of physics, whereas other propensity theorists broaden the notion of propensity or tendency to cover cases of free decisions which cannot be brought under laws.

There is something to be said for all of the views we have considered, and the debate is far from over. But any view, to be considered plausible at all, must meet the objections that have been posed and must, in some way, include the strong points of the other theories. At the moment, the propensity theory seems to have done the best job of meeting these requirements, though still not a completely satisfactory job.

Chapter Summary

In this chapter we saw the basic rules for manipulating probabilities. The Negation Rule:

$$Pr(\sim A) = 1 - Pr(A)$$

The Simple Addition Rule for mutually exclusive cases:

$$Pr(A \vee B) = Pr(A) + Pr(B)$$

and the Complete Addition Rule:

$$Pr(A \vee B) = Pr(A) + Pr(B) - Pr(A \cdot B)$$

The Simple Multiplication Rule for independent cases:

$$Pr(A \cdot B) = Pr(A) \times Pr(B)$$

and the Complete Multiplication Rule:

$$Pr(A \cdot B) = Pr(A) \times Pr(B/A)$$

We examined the Conditional Probability Rule:

$$Pr(A/B) = \frac{Pr(A \cdot B)}{Pr(A)}$$

We also showed that ordinary statement logic is a special case of probability theory where the only values considered are one and zero, and we examined some probabilistic analogues of statement logic rules.

Finally, we considered some leading interpretations of probability statements and briefly considered their pros and cons. The exercises that accompany this chapter will give you some drill in applying the principles of probability theory and introduce you to some interesting philosophical applications of probability.

Practical Applications

Check your Argument File for arguments involving probability. Keep an eye out for uses of probabilistic terms and statements. Not all statements of probability involve arguments, but many do. See if you can check statements of probability and arguments about probability with what you have learned in this chapter. (Hint: If you are at all interested in gambling, try checking the odds on some game with which you are familiar, to see if they are fair. Many common gambling devices and games give a decided advantage to the dealer or to the "house.")

Exercise 8-4

1. Many characteristics of organisms can be explained in terms of inheritance, with each characteristic being determined by one or more *genes* which come in pairs. Organisms that reproduce sexually receive one gene of each pair from the mother, one from the father. The characteristics of the organism are determined by a gene *pair*; thus in a flowering plant, genes RR would make the flower red, RW or WR would make it pink, and WW would make it white. If the parent organisms have both R and W genes and the probability of getting either gene from either parent is $\frac{1}{2}$, what is the probability that the progeny will be red? That they will be white? That they will be pink? (Hint: *All* combinations are equally likely, as with heads and tails in coin tossing.)*

2. How do the probabilities change if one parent has only R genes? If one parent has only W genes? If both parents have only R genes? If both parents have only W genes?

* The examples in this exercise were suggested by J. L. Hodges and E. L. Lehman, *Elements of Probability* (San Francisco: Holden-Day, 1965), chap. 4, sec. 5.

3. Assume that human beings have genes *H* and *G* such that combinations *HH* and *HG* result in normal blood, but combination *GG* gives rise to a blood disease that is always fatal before the person reaches puberty. A person with gene combination *HG* is thus a "carrier": normal himself or herself but capable of having offspring with the fatal *GG* combination if he or she mates with another carrier. Suppose Jane, an adult, had a brother who died of the disease, which proves her parents were both carriers. What is the probability that Jane is a carrier?

*4. Suppose that instead of Jane's brother it was her *mother's* brother who died of the disease. What does this prove about the mother? Assuming Jane's father is not a carrier, what is the probability that Jane is a carrier?

5. Figure the probabilities if instead of brother or uncle it was Jane's first cousin who had the disease. Do the same if it was her great-aunt.

6. Jane is a carrier and plans to marry Mark. It is not known whether Mark is a carrier, but the proportion of carriers in the general population is $\frac{1}{100}$. What is the chance that children of Jane and Mark will get the disease?

7. Jane and Mark have had one healthy child. How does this affect the probability that Mark is a carrier? (Hint: Use Bayes' theorem.)

8. Jane and Mark have a second healthy child. What is the probability now that Mark is a carrier?

9. Suppose that Jane does not know whether she is a carrier but had an uncle with the blood disease. Using the same figure ($\frac{1}{100}$) for Mark, what is now the probability that their first child will be healthy?

10. Using the same data for Jane and Mark as in Number 9, figure the probability that both are carriers if they have one healthy child.

Exercise 8-5

David Hume (1711–1776) was one of the first philosophers to consider philosophical problems connected with probability. The following quotations from Book I, Sections XI and XIII of Hume's Treatise on Human Nature *contain some of his remarks on probability. For each quotation discuss the following questions: A. What theory about probability does Hume seem to be using? (He may seem to be using different theories in different quotations.) B. Is what Hume says open to any objections or criticisms? (If so, state the criticisms.)*

1. Chance is nothing real in itself, and, properly speaking, is merely the negation of a cause. Its influence on the mind is contrary to that of causation; and it is essential to it, to leave the imagination perfectly indifferent, either to consider the existence or non-existence of that object, which is regarded as contingent. A cause traces the way to our thought, and in a manner forces us to survey such certain objects, in such certain relations. Chance can only destroy this determination of the thought, and leave the mind in its native situation of indifference; in which, upon the absence of a cause, it is instantly re-instated.

2.   Since an entire indifference is essential to chance, no one chance can possibly be superior to another, otherwise than as it is composed of a superior number of equal chances. For if we affirm that one chance can, after any other manner, be superior to another, we must at the same time affirm, that there is something, which gives it the superiority, and determines the event rather to that side than the other: That is, in other words, we must allow of a cause, and destroy the supposition of chance; which we had before established. A perfect and total indifference can never in itself be either superior or inferior to another.

3.   Where nothing limits the chances, every notion, that the most extravagant fancy can form, is upon a footing of equality; nor can there be any circumstance to give one the advantage above another. Thus unless we allow that there are some causes to make the dice fall, and preserve their form in their fall, and lie upon some one of their sides, we can form no calculation concerning the laws of hazard. But supposing these causes to operate, and supposing likewise all the rest to be indifferent and to be determined by chance, it is easy to arrive at a notion of a superior combination of chances. A die, that has four sides marked with a certain number of spots, and only two with another, affords us an obvious and easy instance of this superiority. The mind is here limited by the causes to such a precise number and quality of the events; and at the same time is undetermined in its choice of any particular event.

*4.   It is indeed evident, that we can never by the comparison of mere ideas make any discovery, which can be of consequence in this affair, and that it is impossible to prove with certainty, that any event must fall on that side where there is a superior number of chances. To suppose in this case any certainty, were to overthrow what we have established concerning the opposition of chances, and their perfect equality and indifference.

It should be said, that though in an opposition of chances it is impossible to determine with *certainty*, on which side the event will fall, yet we can pronounce with certainty, that it is more likely and probable, it will be on that side where there is a superior number of chances, than where there is an inferior.

5. The likelihood and probability of chances is a superior number of equal chances; and consequently when we say it is likely the event will fall on the side, which is superior, rather than on the inferior, we do no more than affirm, that where there is a superior number of chances there is actually a superior, and where there is an inferior there is an inferior; which are identical propositions, and of no consequence.

6. We shall suppose a person to take a die, formed after such a manner as that four of its sides are marked with one figure, or one number of spots, and two with another; and to put this die into the box with an intention of throwing it: This is plain, he must conclude the one figure to be more probable than the other, and give the preference to that which is inscribed on the greatest number of sides. He in a manner believes, that this will lie uppermost; though still with hesitation and doubt, in proportion to the number of chances, which are contrary: And according as these contrary chances diminish, and the superiority increases on the other side, his belief acquires new degrees of stability and assurance.

7. This die formed as above, contains three circumstances worthy of our attention. *First*, certain causes, such as gravity, solidity, a cubical figure, etc., which determine it to fall, to preserve its form in its fall, and to turn up one of its sides. *Secondly*, a certain number of sides, which are supposed indifferent. *Thirdly*, a certain figure, inscribed on each side. These three particulars form the whole nature of the die, so far as relates to our present purpose; and consequently are the only circumstances regarded by the mind in its forming a judgment concerning the result of such a throw.

8. There is no point of ancient history, of which we can have any assurance, but by passing through many millions of causes and effects, and through a chain of arguments of almost an immeasurable length. Before the knowledge of the fact could come to the first historian, it must be conveyed through many mouths; and after it is committed to writing, each new copy is a new object, of which the connection with the foregoing is known only by experience and observation. Perhaps, therefore, it may be concluded from the preceding reasoning, that the evidence of all ancient history must now be lost; or at least, will be lost in time, as the chain of causes increases, and runs on to a greater length. But as it seems contrary to common sense to think, that if the republic of letters, and the art of printing continue on the same footing as at present, our posterity, even after a thousand ages, can ever doubt if there has been such a man as Julius Caesar; this may be considered as an objection to the present system.

9.   And indeed it must be confessed, that in this manner of considering the subject, (which however is not a true one) there is no history or tradition, but what must in the end lose all its force and evidence. Every new probability diminishes the original conviction; and however great that conviction may be supposed, it is impossible it can subsist under such reiterated diminutions. This is true in general; though we shall find afterwards, that there is one very memorable exception, which is of vast consequence in the present subject of the understanding.

10.   If all the long chain of causes and effects, which connect any past event with any volume of history, were composed of parts different from each other, and which it were necessary for the mind distinctly to conceive, it is impossible we should preserve to the end any belief or evidence. But as most of these proofs are perfectly alike, the mind runs easily along them, jumps from one part to another with facility, and forms but a confused and general notion of each link. By this means a long chain of argument, has as little effect in diminishing the original vivacity, as a much shorter would have, if composed of parts, which were different from each other, and of which each required a distinct consideration.

CHAPTER NINE

Inductive Logic

A PROBLEM IN INDUCTION

The following diagram is a plan of the Bronze Age palace of Knossos in Crete. (Solid black lines represent walls standing at the time the palace was destroyed about 1400 B.C. Close-set rows of single lines are stairs; small squares are pillar bases.)

1. What problems are suggested to you by various features of this plan?
2. Does the fact that this was the first story of a multi-storied palace solve any of these problems? How?
3. Suggest hypotheses to explain the problems you have raised in your answer to Number 1 above.
4. The room numbered 2 seems to have been a throne room. Do its size and placement raise any problems? How might these be solved?
5. What was probably the main entrance to the palace? Why? Why did you eliminate other possibilities?

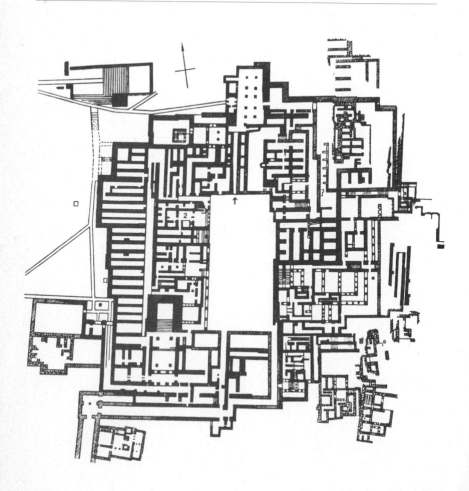

What are the basic principles of reasoning when our information is uncertain or incomplete?

In the course of life, we are often faced with the necessity of making the best decision possible on the basis of information that is incomplete, in one way or another. Sometimes there is simply no way of obtaining complete information; if any decision at all is to be made, it must be made on the basis of the partial information that it is possible to obtain. In this sort of situation deductive logic is not usually a great deal of use. Either no deductive conclusions can be drawn from the information available, or such conclusions as can be drawn are not what is needed—they do not provide a solution to the problem at hand. However, we are not discussing situations where the information available provides no sound basis for decision, or situations where the information does not favor one alternative over another and the decision is purely a matter of taste. The sorts of cases we shall consider here are those in which a reasonable decision can be made regarding, as we say, the "logical thing to do," but in which the reason, the logic, is not deductive.

What are some examples of this sort of case? One very common situation would be one in which we know that a large majority, though not all, of some group or class have a certain characteristic, and we are wondering if a member of that group or class has that characteristic. For example, we know that most Moslems would be highly offended if offered pork, although a small minority would not. It would certainly be "reasonable" and "logical" to eliminate pork from the menu, even though we can draw no *deductive* conclusion from the premises "Most Moslems do not eat pork" and "X is a Moslem." Another commonplace sort of case is this: We are considering buying a barrel of apples. Reaching into the barrel we draw out half a dozen apples (from various parts of the barrel) and find that four out of the six are rotten. Now from the information that four apples are rotten, nothing follows deductively as to the hundred-odd left in the barrel; but we would be regarded as very foolish, indeed, if we bought the barrel (at least, for the price of a barrel of good apples and without further investigation). A final example might be the ordinary sort of situation where we base our estimate of what will happen in the future on what has happened in the past. Perhaps Y, an old school friend, is known to us as having been frequently dishonest and unreliable in the past; he now requests the temporary loan of a large sum of money. Now unless we had very strong and convincing evidence that he had mended his ways and that they would stay mended, it would be rather foolish to lend him the money and expect ever to see it again. This does not mean that we might not be moved by sentiment or generosity to help him, but it would be wise to regard the assistance as a gift rather than a loan.

It is a common element of conclusions drawn from evidence such as this that they are expressed in terms of probability. "*Probably* Mr. X will be offended if you offer him pork''; ''it is *very likely that* many of the apples in the barrel are rotten''; ''it is *improbable* that you will ever see your money again if you loan it to Y.'' When it is necessary, as it often is, to make a ''yes'' or ''no'' decision on the basis of a judgment expressed in terms of probability, we sometimes find we have made a wrong decision. You do not offer Mr. X pork, and later find he is one of the minority who ignore this prohibition of Islam, at least when eating with non-Moslems. You do not buy the barrel of apples, and a friend who does finds almost all of them good. You trust Y with the money against your better judgment, never expecting to see it again, and he repays you promptly. Such are the pitfalls of probable judgment, but they should not (although they sometimes do) cause us to distrust this process of judgment itself. Making judgments on probable evidence is a sort of gamble, but one we all must constantly take. We should be, and usually are, satisfied with our methods of judgment if we come out reasonably well in the long run.

The Logic of Inductive Reasoning

It would be theoretically interesting, and perhaps practically helpful as well, to understand a little better the processes by which such judgments are reached. How much can we conclude from information that most members of a class possess a characteristic? How unlikely is it that four out of six apples drawn from a barrel of mostly good apples should be rotten? How much can past experience tell us about the future? A complete answer to such questions would take the form of a formal logic of *inductive* reasoning. But no such logic exists today.

Why not? We all make inductive judgments, recognize them when we encounter them, are able to tell good ones from bad ones. Furthermore, all of the sciences in some of their parts, and some of the sciences in all of their parts, use inductive reasoning, either formal quantitative inductive reasoning in the form of statistical inference, or informal non-quantitative reasoning in the form of probable arguments from incomplete data. Furthermore, statistics, which is the science of making inductive inferences from data resulting from counting and measuring, has undergone tremendous development within the last 50 years; in almost all the social sciences and in many parts of the physical sciences, a knowledge of statistics is an essential part of the scientist's equipment. From the most esoteric parts of the quantum theory to the ordinary ''public opinion poll'' we find inferences from incomplete data to probable conclusions. But no adequate logical description of this kind of inference is available.

One possible explanation of this surprising fact is that there are no comprehensive accounts of induction for the same reason that there are no comprehensive accounts of walking and running. The ordinary sorts of inductive argument, like the ordinary sorts of walking and running, are learned in childhood, and these are sufficient for ordinary purposes. If we become research scientists, we need training in special statistical techniques, just as, if we become long-distance runners or sprinters, we need training in special athletic techniques. But ordinarily, most of us need not bother our heads about how to walk or how we reason; we merely do it.

This is plausible enough and may even be true, but there are still some very good reasons for carrying on our inquiry into inductive inference and hoping to construct eventually a comprehensive inductive logic. First, the most familiar things are the most fascinating and the greatest challenge to our understanding, which is why philosophy is perpetually interesting. Second, I suspect that there is a good deal of lazy, inefficient inductive reasoning done in all walks of life (and a great deal of lazy, inefficient walking for that matter) which could perhaps be remedied if the process were better understood. Lastly, inductive reasoning is increasingly important to science; and an understanding of science in all its aspects is increasingly important to all of us.

Induction and Statistical Inference

There are a good many points from which we might begin an inquiry into inductive inference, but there are some obvious advantages to beginning with a form of inductive reasoning that is highly successful in its own sphere and highly formalized—the science of statistics. Certainly, a good deal of the subject matter of statistics will be inapplicable to non-quantitative inductive inference, and perhaps not every valid form of inductive inference will be represented in statistical practice. But just *because* the logically distinct methods of statistics are few and its structure is formal, we will be able to see in statistical methods the logical skeleton of at least some valid inductive methods of inference.

We will begin with a form of inductive inference that appeared very early in the history of the mathematical theory of probability and statistics—before, in fact, there was any science of statistics, and probability theory was a branch of speculative mathematics suggested by gambling problems. This is the famous Bayes' Theorem or Bayes' Rule. Thomas Bayes, an English clergyman of great mathematical ability, was a member of the Royal Society and published several mathematical papers during his lifetime. After his death in 1767, his friend Richard Price, also a clergyman (and an able moral philosopher) went through his papers and sent to the Royal Society a paper containing the theorem and a mathematical proof of it. It was published in 1773 with a preface by Price, in which he declares that the theorem is "by no means merely a curious speculation in the doctrine of chances, but . . . a sure foundation for all our reasonings concerning past facts and what is likely to be hereafter." For a time "Bayes' Rule" was accepted as giving mathematical expression to the process of learning from experience. After some overenthusiastic and unrealistic applications of it by supporters and some damaging criticism, it fell out of favor with both philosophers and mathematicians. Recently it has come back into favor among some statisticians.

The second form of statistical inference we will examine is the "testing of statistical hypotheses," a familiar but much misunderstood form of statistical inference. Finally, we will consider a family of methods that includes the method of maximum likelihood and some other common statistical methods.

Throughout, we will try to relate the logical principles embodied in these statistical methods to common-sense inferences in daily life, and to nonstatistical inductive inferences in the sciences. The examples used will be largely from the social sciences because such examples can be followed without extensive background in the science concerned. We will begin with examples of extreme simplicity, so that the principles may be more easily grasped, and proceed by degrees to more lifelike cases.

Factors in Judging Hypotheses

Probable inferences from incomplete data can be more or less satisfactory. Typically, we begin with some evidence or observations and put forward a *hypothesis*, a statement which if true would account for or explain the facts. Because the evidence or observations are accounted for by the hypothesis, because they are what we would expect to be true if the hypothesis is true, we regard the evidence as supporting the hypothesis, making it more likely that it is true. Thus there is a two-way relation between facts and the hypothesis: the hypothesis explains the facts and the facts support the hypothesis. When a hypothesis H is allegedly supported by evidence E, there are three factors we would like very much to know. The first factor is the amount of plausibility possessed by H

before E came under observation. If H is a statement that is extremely surprising, which runs very much counter to our expectations in such matters, we will require a great deal of evidential support before we agree to it. Another thing we would like to know is the expectedness of E itself. If E is very commonplace and could be plausibly explained in a number of ways, very little can be built on it. The third factor we would normally be curious about is how well H *explains* E. If we assume H to be true, is E what we would expect to occur? It will be useful to symbolize these three factors using the familiar symbols of probability theory. $Pr(H)$ (read: probability of H) will be the probability, or degree of plausibility of H, our hypothesis, at the beginning of a given problem. $Pr(E)$ (read: probability of E) will be the corresponding probability, or degree of expectedness, of the evidence E. $Pr(E/H)$ (read: probability of E *given* H) is the expectedness of E if H is assumed to be true. As always in probability theory, $Pr(H) = 0$ will indicate that a hypothesis has no probability, $Pr(H) = 1$ will indicate that it is certain, and $Pr(H) = \frac{1}{2}$ will indicate that our opinion is evenly balanced with regard to H: It may, or equally probably may not, be true. All probabilities fall between 0 and 1 (all this applies, of course, to $Pr(E)$ and any other probabilities).

It is obvious that some of these factors are interdependent. If $Pr(E)$ is very low—that is, if E is extremely surprising—we will be much more inclined to accept a very improbable hypothesis to explain it. A very improbable hypothesis, however, is given very little support by evidence that can be plausibly explained in a number of ways. If E is quite surprising and we are able to explain it by a very plausible and acceptable hypothesis, we are sometimes willing to accept a certain amount of implausibility in the explanation if this is not too great. One could try to work out systematically the relations of these factors in this a posteriori way: reasoning from statements about probabilities that are intuitively satisfactory to a theory of the relations between these factors. There is no need to do this, however, for Thomas Bayes, in the essay mentioned earlier, presented an equation that offers an intuitively satisfying and widely accepted account of the relation between these factors. Bayes' Theorem, expressed in the symbolism which we have just given, is:

$$Pr(H/E) = \frac{Pr(H) \times Pr(E/H)}{Pr(E)}$$

That is: The probability of a hypothesis H, given evidence E, is equal to the initial probability of H times the probability of E given H, all this divided by the initial probability of E.

A careful examination of this equation will show that it satisfies the intuitive requirements mentioned above. For example, the smaller $Pr(E)$ the larger the value of the right-hand term; if a hypothesis has some initial plausibility and gives a fairly good explanation of a body of evidence, then the more unexpected the evidence the greater the probability of the hypothesis on that evidence. If the values of $Pr(H)$ and $Pr(E)$ are moderately closed (e.g., if both are very surprising), they will tend to cancel out, and the ruling factor will be $Pr(E/H)$, that is, how well H explains E. It is probably possible to make the strong claim that most intuitively satisfying relations among these three factors are satisfied by the Bayesian equation, and that no counterintuitive results can be derived from it.

An Illustration of Bayes' Theorem

Bayes' Theorem can be proved mathematically: As we saw in Chapter Eight on the theory of probability, it can be derived in a very few steps from some very fundamental definitions in the mathematical theory. Neither this nor its intuitively satisfying aspects, however, give guarantee that it will be of use in understanding and formalizing inductive inference; but we can begin to see if this is the case by examining a simple example. After we have a better grasp of *how* Bayesian inference works, we will be in a better position to debate *why* it works.

Imagine the following situation: We have six envelopes, one containing five black marbles, another four black and one white, another three black and two white, another two black and three white, another one black and four white, and the last five white. A "picture" may help:

B B B B B
W B B B B
W W B B B
W W W B B
W W W W B
W W W W W

We shuffle the envelopes (they are indistinguishable when sealed), tear a corner off one, and draw marbles out one at a time. Suppose we draw out one black marble: What probability does this "evidence" give to, for example, the hypothesis that we have the envelope that contains all black marbles? Bayes' Theorem gives particularly neat and satisfying results in this simple case.

We have to solve the equation

$$Pr(H/E) = \frac{Pr(H)Pr(E/H)}{Pr(E)}$$

for this situation. What is $Pr(H)$? Since there are six envelopes, and we must have one of them, but do not know which one, $Pr(H)$ is evidently $\frac{1}{6}$: The envelope we have is just as likely to be the one with all black marbles as it is to be any other. $Pr(E/H)$ is evidently 1, or certainty: If we do have the envelope with all black marbles, we could *only* draw a black marble from it. $Pr(E)$ is more complex: In order to arrive at it we have to take into account the other possible hypotheses, and the likelihood of a draw of one black marble if *they* are true. Let us number our hypotheses:

H_1 (We have the envelope with all black.)   B B B B B
H_2 (We have the envelope with 1W, 4B.)   W B B B B
H_3 (We have the envelope with 2W, 3B.)   W W B B B
H_4 (We have the envelope with 3W, 2B.)   W W W B B
H_5 (We have the envelope with 4W, 1B.)   W W W W B
H_6 (We have the envelope with all white.)   W W W W W

We can see easily that if H_2 were true, there would be four chances out of five of drawing one black marble; if H_3 were true, three chances out of five, etc. To get $Pr(E)$ we must multiply each of these "chances of getting a black ball if H is true" by the probability of H in each case, and add these six results:

$$\frac{1}{6} \times 1 \;+\; \frac{1}{6} \times \frac{4}{5} \;+\; \frac{1}{6} \times \frac{2}{5} \;+\; \frac{1}{6} \times \frac{1}{5} \;+\; \frac{1}{6} \times 0 \;=\; \frac{1}{2}$$

This is the chance of getting a black ball on all the hypotheses together. It is the expectedness of a draw of one black in our little "universe" of marbles.

So we have numerical values for all our factors, and solving

$$P(H/E) = \frac{\frac{1}{6} \times 1}{\frac{1}{2}}$$

we get $P(H/E) = \dfrac{1}{3}$

Before we discuss this figure, we will give a table of the numerical value of $P(H/E)$ for each of the three events:

E_1 = a draw of one black ball

E_2 = a draw of two black balls

E_3 = a draw of one black ball and one white ball

	H_1	H_2	H_3	H_4	H_5	H_6
E_1	$\frac{5}{15}$	$\frac{4}{15}$	$\frac{3}{15}$	$\frac{2}{15}$	$\frac{1}{15}$	0
E_2	$\frac{10}{20}$	$\frac{6}{20}$	$\frac{3}{20}$	$\frac{1}{20}$	0	0
E_3	0	$\frac{4}{20}$	$\frac{6}{20}$	$\frac{6}{20}$	$\frac{4}{20}$	0

There are several things we might note on this table. For example, as soon as we draw one black ball, we are sure that we do not have the envelope with all white balls; so $Pr(H/E)$ is *at least* $\frac{1}{5}$ (rather than $\frac{1}{6}$ as $Pr(H)$ was before any draws). But also, there is the fact that the *first* ball we drew was black; this would be fairly unlikely if we had the envelope with only one black ball, or even if we had the one with only two. (Not impossible, but unlikely.) So that in giving a probability of $\frac{1}{3}$ or $\frac{5}{15}$ for H_1 on E_1, Bayes' Theorem is completely in accord with common sense. But note that H_2 has a probability very close to that of H_1, and even H_5 down at the end has the small but by no means negligible probability of $\frac{1}{15}$.

Now if *two* black balls are drawn in a row, we see that it is about an even chance that we have the envelope with all black balls. H_2 is not so close in probability to H_1, and the least likely hypothesis is now quite improbable. But what if the next ball drawn is a white one instead? Of course, we have to give up the idea that we have the envelope with all black balls. All we can say now is that it seems about equally probable that H_3 or H_4 is true—that is, that we have one of the three and two envelopes. But neither is *very* probable, and we might just as well have one of the four and one envelopes; it is all very uncertain.

The more one goes over this simple example, the more one is convinced that Bayes' Theorem gives a very good rule indeed for one sort of inductive reasoning.

If all inductive inference would fit neatly into a Bayesian pattern, inductive logic would be extremely simple. But it does not—any more than all deductive inference fits neatly into a syllogistic pattern. The pattern between Bayes' Theorem and the syllogism, by the way, is worth drawing; both are intuitively satisfactory but make somewhat unrealistic demands as to what must be known before inferences can be drawn. (With syllogistic inference you must have at least one universal statement, for example.) Both have been accepted for a time as *the* pattern of inference in their respective spheres. When this was proved untrue, both suffered somewhat unjustly; their validity was questioned even in cases where they were applicable.

Objections to Bayes' Theorem

What are the main objections to Bayes' Theorem? Chiefly, a theoretical one, which is surmountable, and a practical one, which is not. The theoretical objection can be stated in various ways; perhaps the fairest and yet most damaging is as follows: Consider $Pr(H)$ in any Bayesian inference. Now either the value of $Pr(H)$ is known from previous experience, or it is not. If it is not known from previous experience, whence do we derive it? If it is known from previous experience, how was it known before that experience? If the answer is again "previous experience," we keep asking the question until we arrive at the point where there was no previous experience relative to H. Our original difficulty then arises again: If $Pr(H)$ is not known from previous experience, how is it known?

The answer to this question is simple in principle. It is that every tautologous statement may be given an a priori probability of 1, every self-contradiction may be given an a priori probability of 0, and all non-tautologous, noncontradictory statements, including all empirical statements, may be given an a priori "logical" probability somewhere between 0 and 1. Working this out in detail is a tremendous task, and the only philosopher who has come even close to success is Rudolf Carnap.* The idea behind Carnap's nearly successful attempt is simple enough. For the universe of discourse in which we are interested, we list all the individuals and give each a unique designation. Then we list all of our predicates. We then proceed to write all the possible sentences that affirm or deny each predicate of each individual in turn. These are called "state descriptions"; each defines a "possible world"—a logically possible state of our universe. Any two state descriptions having the same structure

* See Rudolf Carnap, *The Logical Foundations of Probability* (University of Chicago Press, 1950).

(that is, one can be obtained from the other by substituting some designations of individuals for others) are regarded as equiprobable. Also, any two structures are regarded as equally probable; the total probability given the state descriptions of one structure must equal the total probability given to the state descriptions of any other structure. We can then define the a priori possibility of any statement about our universe as the sum of the a priori probabilities of all those state descriptions that imply it: the sum of the probabilities of all "possible worlds" in which this statement comes out true.

Our marble "universe" of black and white marbles, discussed earlier, could easily be handled in these terms. The six hypotheses would have to be regarded as "structures," since we did not bother with proper names, but one can easily see how a statement, for example, "At least one marble in this envelope is white," could be implied by some hypotheses and not others, and would have a probability equal to the sum of the probabilities of those hypotheses. (In this case the statement St would be true if H_2, H_3, H_4, H_5, or H_6 was true, therefore $Pr(St) = \frac{5}{6}$.) One could easily number the marbles and make this an entirely Carnapian scheme.

Now one can see that this solves *in principle* the difficulty that was raised. Since it is theoretically possible to follow this procedure for a universe of any size, it is always true to say that any noncontradictory statement has, theoretically, a calculable a priori probability, which will increase or decrease as empirical evidence becomes available. For very simple universes we can even calculate this probability. Thus the *theoretical* objection to Bayesian inference is answered.

However, a practical difficulty remains and is in many cases insurmountable. It is simply that most of the time we are unable to calculate the a priori probability of a hypothesis and have no information that will enable us to give it an a posteriori probability. As anyone knows, scientists and detectives are rarely in a position to say that the probability of a hypothesis on which they are working is equal to any definite figure; at most, they can say a given hypothesis is "probable" or "improbable," or perhaps "very probable" or "very improbable." Distinctions any finer than this are usually a matter of guesswork.

Furthermore, the same difficulties afflict $Pr(E)$. The ideal method of determining $Pr(E)$, you will remember, was to add the product of its probability for one possible hypothesis and the probability of that hypothesis to the same product for each of the other possible hypotheses. Obviously, if $Pr(H)$ is usually unattainable, this goes down the drain, even if one is able to enumerate all possible hypotheses in a given situation. But even if we could determine $Pr(E)$ by other means, it does not seem to be the case that we could give it any more precision than $Pr(H)$. It seems that the best we can do is to know that $Pr(H)$ and $Pr(E)$ *exist*, and to have some idea of their comparative magnitude in favorable cases.

This leaves us with the factor $Pr(E/H)$, and we have two alternatives: either to use arbitrary values for $Pr(H)$ and $Pr(E)$, or to ignore them altogether. Some philosophers have achieved very interesting results using the first method. But it is not very defensible, and in practice arbitrary $Pr(H)$ and $Pr(E)$ and no $Pr(H)$ or $Pr(E)$ come to about the same thing. Modern statisticians have followed the course of ignoring $Pr(H)$ and $Pr(E)$ and employing only $Pr(E/H)$. This is the probability of E if H is true, but it can also be read "backwards," as it were, to tell you something about H if E is true. Used in this way, it is technically called a *likelihood*. Modern statistics uses *likelihood inference* rather than Bayesian inference. We will next examine this new pattern of inductive inference.

Bayesian inference has a strong appeal to intuition, and in some cases, where all its requirements are met, is an entirely satisfactory form of inductive inference. But the attempt to make Bayesian inference account for all inductive inferences could only end in failure; lacking realistic values for $Pr(H)$ and $Pr(E)$, users of Bayesian methods were forced to use arbitrary values derived from such questionable principles as "the principle of indifference," or "the principle of equal distribution of ignorance." And these arbitrary assumptions eventually landed them, in many cases, in self-contradictions. This sort of thing quite soon gave Bayes' Theorem a bad name, and until after the second World War, most mathematicians and statisticians, along with most philosophers of science who had considered the matter, had a critical attitude towards Bayesian inference. This attitude was strengthened by the fact that there had been gradually developed on the part of the philosophers a new theory of nondeductive inference and on the part of the statisticians new methods of inductive inference, which seemed satisfactory in themselves and appeared to have no relation to the Bayesian type of inference—indeed, seemed drastically opposed to it.

Popper's Theory

The philosophical theory was in large part the work of Karl Popper.* Its main tenets were: (1) there is, in fact, no such thing as inductive inference; (2) the method of science is the hypothetico-deductive method;

---

* See Karl Popper, *The Logic of Scientific Discovery* (London: Hutchinson and Co., 1959).

and (3) the concept of probability cannot meaningfully be applied to statements such as scientific hypotheses. The chief way the philosophers attempted to support (1) and (3) was by attempting to prove (2). Their claim was not so much that they had strong negative arguments against inductive inference or the assigning of probabilities to hypotheses as that the hypothetico-deductive method made these methods useless. Everything that was supposed to be done by "induction," they said, could be done better by the hypothetico-deductive method, which was the method actually used by science.

Their account of the hypothetico-deductive method was this: One began with a theory or hypothesis which, although it might be suggested by past observations or experiments, was essentially the result of a creative process for which no rules could be given. One then deduced by (strictly deductive) logical or mathematical arguments as many observations or consequences as possible from the theory or hypothesis, and proceeded to test these by observation or experiment. If any observational consequences of the theory proved false, then, of course, the theory was false. As long as one kept on testing consequences of hypotheses without any of them proving false, those hypotheses continued to be provisionally accepted. But though confidence in a hypothesis might increase as it survived repeated tests one after another, the hypothesis would never acquire even probability, much less certainty. It would always be accepted only provisionally, subject to instant dismissal if it proved unsatisfactory. To use an academic metaphor, a hypothesis could never acquire tenure.

In some ways this appears to fit in very well with the actual situation in some sciences, especially in the science of physics, where theories and hypotheses are highly mathematical, observational consequences are mathematically deduced and compared with exact experiments, and such major changes have taken place that many important theories are regarded as little more than "hypotheses that hold the field." Scientists in many areas would probably agree that an important part of "scientific method" is the testing of hypotheses by comparing their consequences with observation.

However, there are certainly some highly unrealistic elements in this picture. It might be granted that the creation of a scientific hypothesis, like the discovery of a mathematical proof, is a process for which no rules can be given. But most of the rest of the account is open to question. For example, it seems to be assumed that the result of one's deductions from the hypothesis can be straightforwardly compared with experience and an equivocal result obtained; if the theory predicts N as the value of a variable, measurement should give a value of N for that variable, and if it does not, the theory must be rejected. But any acquaintance with experimental science leads one to realize that if this were true, the slaughter of theories would be immense; hardly any theory now held would survive. Typically, if the theory predicts a value of N for a variable, the experimenter finds that the results of his or her measurements are a number of values scattered around N with a dispersion of Q. The experimenter then has to analyze these data to discover whether the dispersion is within the limits of experimental error, or could normally have occurred by chance.

Not only is this the case, but also quite often the theory is not obliging enough to predict N simply, but rather predicts N with probability A, and M with probability B. Examples could be multiplied but, in general, the idea of "comparing a prediction from theory with observation" conceals a multitude of difficulties, many of which lead us back in the direction of probabilities.

Also, while certainly scientists are not given to assigning numerical probabilities to their theories or hypotheses, it is undeniable that they normally hold them with varying degrees of conviction. Some theories are regarded as established beyond doubt, others as so firmly established that only very striking results could undermine them, and so forth. Certainly, all are theoretically dispensable and disprovable, but there is no serious expectation that any of the more established theories will be disproved. At most, a theory will be modified or seen as a special case in a more general theory. A situation where a science is in transition and old theories are tottering is an exceptional one, and it is only in such a situation that theories are usually regarded as completely provisional and subject to instant change or rejection on new data. The idea that science is a sort of mechanical process by which a hypothesis is fed into the machine and its consequences are mechanically deduced and then tested until one fails to agree with reality, whereupon the hypothesis is mechanically rejected, seems to be founded on what some philosophers think science should be like, rather than on actual observation of science.

Actually, what does seem to happen in many scientific investigations is the test of two or more hypotheses against each other. Frequently, one is a hypothesis that has held the field for some time but has not been completely successful in explaining a certain range of phenomena. The second hypothesis is frequently a new competing hypothesis which, if successful, will replace the older hypothesis. In some cases it is possible to find an experimental test that will enable us to test the older hypothesis in a decisive way: The older hypothesis makes a definite prediction such that if the prediction is falsified by experience, the older hypothesis must be false. But far more often, we reject a hypothesis because something occurs that is very improbable if the hypothesis is true. This reason for rejection is not decisive: Very improbable events do sometimes occur. But, especially if we have a new alternate hypothesis that explains the same range of phenomena as the old hypothesis but gives a high probability to the occurrence to which the old theory gives a low probability, we often reject a hypothesis on the basis of a simple disjunction—*either* the hypothesis is false *or* a very improbable event has occurred. This may be called a *low* likelihood method. Its major virtue is that it often gives us very good grounds for rejecting a hypothesis, especially when the likelihood is very low, while its major defect is that it is essentially negative. It does not enable us to say anything very positive about the surviving hypotheses, and if one has a likelihood of 0.01 on our evidence while the other has a likelihood of 0.1, we would probably reject the first hypothesis and not reject the second. But this would not establish the second (unless we also knew that these were the only two possible hypotheses and one must be true).

Exercise 9-1

For each of the following phenomena suggest two incompatible hypotheses each of which would give a high probability to the phenomenon in question. Suggest a way of deciding between the two hypotheses by experiment or further observation.

1. Increased sexual permissiveness.
2. Increased interest in gourmet cooking.
3. Decreasing membership in many main-line religious denominations.
4. Increasing membership in many new religious cults or groups.
5. Increasing distrust of science and scientists.
6. The decline of the Republican Party.
7. The rise of Women's Liberation.
*8. Declining interest in space exploration.
9. Increasing interest in nature.
10. Decline in the use of drugs and increase in the use of alcohol among younger people.
11. Violence in big-city high schools.
12. Unemployment.

13. Inflation.
14. Movement of population from large cities.
15. Movement of population to "sun belt" states in the South and West.

Exercise 9-2

*Father Brown and Flambeau are investigating the mysterious circumstances
following the (natural) death of the Earl of Glengyle, last of the rapacious
Ogilvie clan of whom it was said:*

> *As green sap to the summer trees
> Is red gold to the Ogilvies.*

*The last of the clan, however, is reputed to have been a fanatic about honesty
and had as his only servant a companion, Israel Gow, who had attracted
his attention in the following way: On bringing a telegram to the castle,
Gow had been overtipped with a valuable gold coin by mistake for a small
copper coin. On discovering the mistake, the honest but literal-minded Gow
had brought back the exact difference between the value of the coin he had
been given and that which he had been told he was being given. Gow has
been in charge of the castle since Glengyle's death. On their arrival at the
castle, the detectives find the following puzzling items:*

1. *Precious stones without their settings.*
2. *Heaps of loose snuff without any horn, pouch, or snuffbox.*
3. *Little heaps of small metal springs and wheels.*
4. *Candles without any candleholders of any kind.*

*Challenged to connect these items in any reasonable way, Father Brown
produces the following three hypotheses:*

A. *Glengyle was fanatically opposed to the French Revolution. He was
an enthusiast for the* ancien régime, *and was trying to reenact literally the
family life of the last Bourbons. He had snuff because it was the eighteenth-
century luxury, wax candles because they were eighteenth-century lighting.
The mechanical bits of iron represent the locksmith hobby of Louis XVI;
the diamonds are for the Diamond Necklace of Marie Antoinette.*
B. *The late Earl of Glengyle was a thief. He lived a second and darker
life as a desperate housebreaker. He did not have any candlesticks because
he only used these candles cut short in the lantern he carried. The snuff he*

employed as the fiercest French criminals have used pepper: to fling it
suddenly in dense masses in the face of a captor or pursuer. But the final
proof is in the curious coincidence of the diamonds and the small steel
wheels. Surely that makes everything plain to you? Diamonds and small
steel wheels are the only two instruments with which you can cut out a
pane of glass.

C. Glengyle had found, or thought he had found, precious stones on his
estate. Somebody had bamboozled him with those loose brilliants, saying
they were found in the castle caverns. The little wheels are some diamond-
cutting affair. He had to do the things very roughly and in a small way,
with the help of a few shepherds or rude fellows on these hills. Snuff is the
one great luxury of such Scotch shepherds; it's the one thing with which
you can bribe them. They didn't have candlesticks because they didn't
want them; they held the candles in their hands when they explored the
caves.*

Answer the following questions.

1. For the first hypothesis discuss how well the hypothesis explains
the evidence, noting any items not explained.
2. Do the same for the second hypothesis.
*3. Do the same for the third hypothesis.
4. Which hypothesis seems best supported by the evidence?
5. Devise a hypothesis of your own that will adequately explain all the
data plus the following additional items: (a) lead for mechanical pencils,
but no pencils; (b) a walking stick with the top missing; (c) some illumi-
nated manuscripts with the halos and the name of God cut away. In
addition, it becomes known that (d) Israel Gow has removed the head
from Glengyle's corpse, but intends to return it; and (e) Gow has been
named in Lord Glengyle's will to inherit one thing. What is it and how
does it account for the other puzzling items?

Exercise 9-3

The following are summaries of plot elements of some of Chesterton's
other Father Brown stories. In each case suggest a hypothesis that will
account for all of the data. Suggest how the hypothesis might be tested.

1. Called to the house of Arnold Aylmer, who is afraid of being killed
by a man named Strake, Father Brown is admitted by a man in a dressing

* G. K. Chesterton, "The Honor of Israel Gow" in The Innocence of Father Brown (New
York: Dodd Mead and Company, 1911).

gown who claims to be Aylmer but seems curiously unfamiliar with the
house. The man tells a dramatic tale of a threat to kill him by Strake,
whom he describes as a sort of flying wizard who kills by supernatural
means. He shows Father Brown a gun loaded with a silver bullet with
which he will defend himself. The man goes out of the room to get some
evidence and Father Brown hears a shot and a cry. The man in the dressing
gown comes in, claiming to have shot Strake as he swooped out of the air.
Rushing out, Father Brown finds a man in a black cloak and hat in the
middle of a snow-covered lawn with no footprints. The cloak is too long
for him, supporting the idea that he flew rather than walked, but Father
Brown remembers seeing a similar cloak and hat hanging near the door
he has just come out of. What has happened?

2. A writer is found stabbed, with a note in his own handwriting which
reads, "I died by my own hand." A curious feature of the note is that it
is written near the top of a sheet of paper and the right-hand corner of
the sheet has been clipped off. One of the suspects declares that this is a
fad of the writer; that all of his paper is cut in this odd way. Sure enough,
on checking they find a stack of paper with the corners cut in the same
way. On looking around, Father Brown finds the corners that were cut
off the sheets, but one fewer corner than there are sheets (counting the
sheet on which the note is written). Also, the manuscript on which the
writer is currently working seems to have been destroyed. What has
happened?

3. A man sitting in a latticework summerhouse wearing a light-colored
coat has been stabbed. The door was under observation and no one has
gone in the summerhouse. The back of the summerhouse is hidden by
bushes, but there is no entrance in back. About the time the body is
discovered, one of the suspects is throwing sticks in the ocean for the
murdered man's dog to retrieve. The dog does not retrieve the last stick
thrown, which is the suspect's cane, but comes back to shore whimpering
and acting strangely. Reconstruct the crime.

*4. A murder is committed in an apartment building with only one
entrance. The entrance has been under observation by several impartial
witnesses who swear that no one entered or left the building during the
crucial time. The murderer turns out to be the mailman who delivers
mail to that building. Why did the witnesses report that no one entered
or left the building at the time in question?

5. A man has been threatened by enemies. Working alone in his office
in a small old-fashioned office building, he hears shouts and a shot
outside. People in the outer office hear him rush to the window and fling

it open. Then there are bumping sounds and those in the next office rush in to find the man gone. (The only door leads through the outer office.) The body is not underneath the window: it is later found caught high in a tree on the other side of the office building, with the neck broken. The man who fired the shot is found but his gun contains only blanks. How was the murder committed?

Examples of Inductive Reasoning

Despite their limitations, low-likelihood methods are an important pattern of inductive reasoning. Some examples may help us see this.

1. A friend bets us that he can flip a coin seven times and have it come up heads each time. We examine the coin, which appears normal, and make the bet. He wins. What is the likelihood that the coin is a normal one? Well, normal coins are approximately fair; that is $Pr(\text{Heads}) = Pr(\text{Tails}) = \frac{1}{2}$. So the probability of throwing heads seven times in a row if the coin is normal is roughly $\frac{1}{2} \times \frac{1}{2} \times \frac{1}{2} \times \frac{1}{2} \times \frac{1}{2} \times \frac{1}{2} \times \frac{1}{2} = \frac{1}{128}$. Now such a sequence of heads could, and sometimes does (roughly once in 128 times), happen on seven throws of a fair coin. But we would have very grave doubts as to the hypothesis that this coin was fair, even on this evidence alone. If we also discover that this man has won money on the same bet from all our friends, that in hundreds of tosses the coin has always come up heads, we would be quite certain that the coin was *not* a normal one. But this would still not tell us *how* the coin was loaded, for example; it would give us no positive data.

2. In 1958 an anthropologist, Frank Lynch, was investigating the social structure of a small town in the Philippine Islands. He had a strong reason to believe that there were, in fact, two social classes in this town, and he hypothesized that the inhabitants were aware of this two-class structure. He was driven to reject this hypothesis by the following evidence: A. Past experience showed that where there was a conscious class structure in a society, there were names for at least one of the classes in the language, and usually a variety of slang and formal names (e.g., nineteenth-century England's "upper class," "toffs," "lower class," "working class," etc.). No such names could be found in the language of the townspeople. B. A randomly selected group of townspeople were asked to place their fellow townspeople in social classes. Their replies showed the following characteristics: (1) There was no agreement among these "raters" as to the number or membership of the classes into which they classified people; (2) In many cases people were placed *between*, rather than in, classes by the raters; and (3) The social classes used by the raters in their classification were so loose that frequently the rater changed his mind as to the number of classes in the course of the interview! On the basis of this evidence, Lynch rejected the hypothesis that there was a conscious and agreed-upon class system in the town.

Obviously, it is *possible* that there may be social classes in a society of which people are aware but for which they have no names. Also, it is *possible* that the raters were aware of a two-class system, but because of lack of communication, deceitfulness, religious taboo, etc., did not give the interviewing anthropologist any indication that they were conscious of it. But the improbability of these conjectures is so great that there is obviously very good reason for rejecting the hypothesis. We have, then, this very interesting situation: that likelihoods derived from experimental data that are nonquantitative figure in the rejection of a scientific hypothesis. This example provides, it is hoped, something of a bridge between the somewhat artificial quantitative example of the black and white balls, and such common-sense inferences as those given in the last set of exercises. (Many anthropologists and other social scientists hope to make their arguments and conclusions more objective and conclusive by moving in the direction of greater "quantification"—that is, more quantitatively expressed premises and arguments—and, no doubt, where this is possible it is highly desirable. But it is not always possible, at least at present.)

Levels of Significance

Before we leave low-likelihood inference, there is a difficulty that must be met. It is the problem of "where to draw the line" in low-likelihood inference—how much improbability we will put up with before rejecting a hypothesis. Some philosophers have argued that this is a purely valuational or "ethical" decision, and they receive support from the widely popular theory of hypothesis testing in statistics.

This theory may be informally stated as follows. Suppose that before an experiment we agree to reject the hypothesis being tested if its likelihood is under 0.05. If we continued to make this sort of experiment, and most of our rejections were based on likelihoods under, but very close to, 0.05, this would mean that about once in 20+ times we would be misled by chance occurrences into accepting a hypothesis that was, in fact, false. This acceptance of a false hypothesis is called an "error of the first kind."

However, if, in order to minimize this risk, we reject only hypotheses with a *very* low likelihood, we run the risk of committing an "error of the second kind," rejecting a true hypothesis. By making our requirements too stringent, we make unreasonable demands on the evidence: If we choose a very low breaking point, for example, 0.001, we will miss significant results.

Some statisticians argue that our choice of a breaking point (technically called a level of significance) must be influenced by how much we wish to avoid errors of each of these kinds. Since this is usually a valuational decision, some philosophers have claimed that inductive inference contains a necessary reference to ethical considerations. Though many people are unhappy at this "intrusion of ethics into logic," the influence of the philosophers and the statisticians has gained it fairly wide acceptance.

Other statisticians have pointed out that such valuational elements are entirely foreign to tests of scientific hypotheses, however great a part they may play in, for example, industrial uses of statistics. And indeed, the whole argument seems to rest on several confusions, the most important one being a confusion between *results* and *reactions*. The *result* of a test of a scientific hypothesis is a probability or likelihood statement, giving a probability or likelihood relation between the evidence and the hypothesis. The *action* the experimenter decides to take on this result may be rejection, further investigation, rechecking of data, etc., but is logically distinct from the result itself. No doubt there are all sorts of reactions to a hurricane warning, or an ordinary weather report, but this does not mean that meteorology is a branch of Ethics. The decision to reject a hypothesis at a certain "level of confidence," whether made before or after the result is known, is a decision distinct from that result.

There are other flaws in the account given above. Primarily they are: 1. that prior decisions based on utility as to what kinds of error we wish to minimize are the very antithesis of a scientific method, which ideally strives to attain truth at no matter what cost, not to minimize costly errors; 2. that the assumption that repeated experiments will be made in exactly the same circumstances of exactly the same sort of hypothesis is an unjustified idealization (as is the assumption that all results will be near the breaking point), and it is only by such an idealization that one can talk about "1 out of 20 cases resulting in errors of the first kind"; and 3. that "acceptance" and "rejection" are left far too vague— either acceptance or rejection is always provisional, and an experimenter may pursue a "rejected" hypothesis in which he or she believes, or ignore an "accepted" hypothesis that is just barely within the limits of acceptance but appears to have no practical significance.

In fact, the whole effort to make statistical tests a mechanical "accept or reject" procedure is highly questionable. It is far more common for the results of an experiment to yield a very definite probability or likelihood statement that the experimenter has no idea of how to interpret, or what to do with!

We have been considering inferences in which $Pr(H)$ and $Pr(E)$ cannot be known, but in which $Pr(E/H)$ is known and is low, causing us to doubt the truth of H. However, there is another form of inference used in statistics and daily life, where $Pr(H)$ and $Pr(E)$ are unknown, but in which $Pr(E/H)$ is known and is *high*. If one hypothesis were being considered in isolation, a high likelihood would very often incline us to believe the truth of that hypothesis—if we had no reason to think that $Pr(H)$ was abnormally low in relation to $Pr(E)$. The situation that has received far more attention in statistics, however, is the case where we have two or more rival hypotheses, and have reason to believe that one of them must be true. In this case it appears reasonable to choose the hypothesis with the maximum likelihood on the evidence, even when this is not especially high.

Examples of Maximum-Likelihood Reasoning

Obviously, the principle of maximum likelihood is a widely useful pattern of inductive inference. Let us consider some examples:

1. Three coins have been selected at random from a bag. We know that the bag contains some two-headed coins and some normal coins. We flip each coin and record whether it comes up heads or tails. If H_0 is the hypothesis that none of the coins is two-headed, H_1 that one is, H_2 that two are, H_3 that all are, and E_0 the observation that none comes up heads, E_1 that one comes up heads, E_2 that two come up heads, and E_3 that all come up heads, then we can make this table:

	H_0	H_1	H_2	H_3	E_1
E_0	$\frac{1}{8}$	0	0	0	$\frac{1}{8}$
E_1	$\frac{3}{8}$	$\frac{1}{4}$	0	0	$\frac{5}{8}$
E_2	$\frac{3}{8}$	$\frac{2}{4}$	$\frac{1}{2}$	0	$1\frac{3}{8}$
E_3	$\frac{1}{8}$	$\frac{1}{4}$	$\frac{1}{2}$	1	$1\frac{7}{8}$
Sum	1	1	1	1	

If we read *down* the column headed H_0, H_1, etc., on this table we have the *probability* of each observation on each hypothesis. Since we have all the possibilities the probabilities add up, of course, to 1 (since if, e.g., E_1 is true, *either E_0 or E_1 or E_2 or E_3* must happen, and therefore, $E_0 \vee E_1 \vee E_2 \vee E_3$ is the "universal" or certain event).

If we read *across* the rows beginning E_0, E_1, etc., we have the *likelihood* of each hypothesis on each observation. They do *not* sum to 1, not being probabilities, and in some cases (E_2) their sum is greater than 1. This is a striking reminder that likelihoods are *not* probabilities, and that, for example, a likelihood of 0.1 does *not* mean that given this evidence, this hypothesis will be true one time out of ten. As long as we remember that likelihoods are not probabilities, we will have no trouble with them.

This is especially striking in this instance, because if E_3 were observed, the hypothesis with maximum likelihood would be H_3, that all the coins were double-headed. The likelihood is 1; and it is tempting to say, "Oh, this means that if all the coins come up heads, it is certain that they are all double-headed." But, of course, it means nothing of the kind. While this event would occur *all* the time if all three coins were double-headed, it would occur half the time with one normal and two double-headed coins, one time in four with two normal and one double-headed, and one time in eight with all normal coins. This being so, we would treat this particular maximum-likelihood solution with a good deal of reserve. If we were forced to make a guess right now as to which hypothesis was true, H_3 would be our best bet if E_3 had been observed. But we would rather not bet at all on such scanty evidence. Most people who dislike or distrust maximum-likelihood estimates seem to do so because they expect too much of them, which is rather unreasonable. All that maximum-likelihood methods can do is to tell us which way the evidence points; they cannot supply deficiencies in the evidence itself.

2.   In the course of an attempted robbery at a fur warehouse, a watchman is shot. Police discover an irregularly shaped piece of cloth clutched in his hand. Half an hour later, on the outskirts of the city, police pick up a man speeding out of the city. He has a torn-out place in the lining of his coat which exactly matches in fabric and shape the piece of cloth clutched in the watchman's hand. A test shows he has recently fired a gun. He has a record of armed robbery, including some fur thefts. The man is put on trial for murder. This is a case of "circumstantial evidence," and a fairly strong one. But it would seem that only the hypothesis that he was the killer of the watchman could explain these facts *and* the match of the cloth with his torn overcoat lining. The hypothesis that he is the killer seems to have maximum likelihood on the evidence.

Very probably most juries would convict on this evidence, but would not recommend the death penalty. This reflects both the fact that the evidence is very strong, and the fact that there is usually a lurking doubt about circumstantial evidence, no matter how strong. And this is a reflection in human terms of the mathematical reminder at the end of our last example: No matter how high the likelihood, how well a hypothesis explains the evidence, it may always be the case that some other hypothesis is true.

3. For our final example, let us return to Lynch, the anthropologist, and his Philippine town. Despite his rejection of the hypothesis that there was a *conscious* two-class system in the town, the anthropologist eventually concluded that there were, in fact, two classes in the community under study. The basis of his conclusions was the following evidence:

A. Although there was no rater agreement as to number of classes, and *names* were not given to classes, raters tended to refer to one group in the community with a certain set of locutions and to another group with another set. For example: Some people were referred to as "well off" (literally, "not suffering") and as "big people"; others were referred to as "badly off" (literally, "suffering") and as "little people." There tended to be good rater agreement as to the main content of these two groups, even though they were not thought of as "social classes," or referred to when the anthropologist asked for a class description of the community.

B. These two groups agreed very well with the group that had, and the group that did not have, economic security.

C. People in the town showed by their behavior that they recognized an "upper class" that *gave* favors, had certain religious and political functions, and was invited to certain sorts of affairs (roughly a "private dinner party" type of affair), and a "lower class" that *sought* favors from the upper class, had few or no religious and political functions, and was invited only to certain other types of social affairs (roughly a "grand celebration on local feast day" type of affair). For example: "Big" people were the officers of voluntary associations, entertained visitors to the town, were sought as sponsors at baptisms and marriages of "little" people, etc.

D. In pre-Hispanic times there was a "noble-commoner" society of this type in the Philippines. The Hispanic conquest imposed a "conqueror-subject" society for a long period. Thus there was a two-class pattern of long standing.

E. Interpreted in the light of the two-class hypothesis, the ratings made previously followed an intelligible pattern. For example: Lower class raters tended to see a multiplicity of classes, and to be uncertain of placement.

Lynch concluded that on the basis of this evidence one was compelled to conclude that a two-class system was operating regardless of how widely raters differed regarding community stratification. (Of course, the merest sketch of the actual evidence has been presented here.)

This is a fairly clear case of a maximum-likelihood inference in nonquantitative terms, made in the course of a scientific investigation. It exhibits the usual characteristic of maximum-likelihood inferences, that although other hypotheses are possible which might be somewhat likely on the evidence, the one chosen gives the greatest probability to the observed evidence. Its high likelihood is due largely to the fact that if it is assumed to be true, the observed evidence is about what might be expected. Not everything is perfectly explained (why did the raters disagree?), but there appears to be no other explanation that will do more justice to the facts.

Essentially, then, like all probable inference, a maximum-likelihood inference says, "This is the best estimate available on the evidence we have." It does not, cannot, and need not, say, as deductive inference does, "The facts being thus and so, this follows necessarily."

Objections to Maximum Likelihood

There are some objections to maximum likelihood, but they seem to have their source in rather unreasonable expectations as to how much the method should do. Sometimes the method is expected to work miracles and remedy defects in the evidence. Another difficulty is that maximum-likelihood methods enable us to derive contradictory estimates of the truth of hypotheses. In the celebrated story of the blind men and the elephant, each, from the evidence at hand, derived a "maximum likelihood" hypothesis as to what the elephant was like. The man who grasped the tail thought elephants resembled snakes, while the man who felt a leg thought them rather like trees.

These objections are alike in that they derive paradoxical results from maximum-likelihood methods by ignoring part of the whole picture. Obviously, what we need is some sort of rule of maximum evidence and minimum hypothesis—a rule that requires us to take into account all the available evidence before deciding for or against the hypothesis, and to explain it by a hypothesis as simple as possible. One *could* do this by simply making it a requirement or postulate of one's theory of inductive inference. But there are grave difficulties both in the concept of "total evidence" and of "simplest hypothesis."

Fortunately, we need no such outside rule if we return, when this sort of difficulty threatens, to our starting point, that is, to Bayes' Theorem.

The first requirement, that of maximum evidence, is "built in" to Bayes' Theorem in the following way. If we are endeavoring to prove a hypothesis H on evidence E, then it is evidently to our advantage to gather as many bits of evidence as possible. For if this evidence is empirical, it will not be tautologous and will have a probability less than 1. Since we will be considering $Pr(H)$ given E_1 *and* E_2 *and* E_3, etc., we will, by the rules of probability, multiply these decimals or fractions by each other. Thus the more evidence the smaller $Pr(E)$ and, by the form of Bayes' Theorem, the greater the factor by which the likelihood will be multiplied. Thus if the likelihood can be increased, it will be by gathering more evidence, which leads to the desired rule: "To maximize likelihood, gather as much evidence as possible." (Of course, if H does *not*, in fact, explain all the evidence, the likelihood will fall as evidence accumulates. But it can only be decided whether the likelihood is great or small by actually gathering all available evidence.)

Thus many occasions on which likelihood inference seems to lead to paradox are actually cases where information is *available* as to $Pr(H)$ or $Pr(E)$—but this information has not been taken into account. And any inference that ignores relevant evidence will be unsound. Likelihood inference comes into its own, however, when we do *not* have this additional information. Using likelihood inference when a Bayesian inference could be made instead is rather like trying to use a flashlight at noon. But this does not mean that a flashlight is not highly useful at midnight.

There are some who will be discontent with the relatively modest claims and competence of induction as it actually is. They may hanker for some more dazzling and perfect method; but like all of us they will continue to conduct their lives on the basis of the sort of common-sense inductive reasoning that has been described.

Chapter Summary

In this chapter we began by exploring the idea of inductive arguments as ways to make the best decision possible on the basis of incomplete information. We saw that the conclusions of inductive arguments are usually expressed as probability statements. We examined the role of Bayes' Theorem in inductive reasoning, first in simple and artificial cases, then in more realistic cases. We then looked at some difficulties in the practical application of Bayes' Theorem, and discussed Karl Popper's Theory of Induction and a maximum-likelihood approach for cases where we have no realistic prior probabilities. We concluded that real-life inductive arguments can often be understood as Bayesian or maximum-likelihood arguments, and that at least some criticism of inductive reasoning arises from asking more of induction than it can provide.

Practical Applications

Check your Argument File for inductive arguments. Keep an eye out for scientific arguments that you may encounter in everyday life. See if you can state the hypotheses involved and put the argument as a Bayesian or maximum-likelihood argument. (Hint: The science sections of news magazines are a good source of information about contemporary scientific developments. Even better are such magazines as *Scientific American* and *Psychology Today*.)

Exercise 9-4

Eleusis (*pronounced ee-*loo-*sis*) *is a game for three or more players. It makes use of the standard deck of playing cards. Players take turns at being the "dealer," who has no part in the actual play except to serve as a kind of umpire. The dealer deals to the other players until one card remains. This is placed face up in the center of the table as the first card of the "starter pile."*

After the cards are dealt and the "starter card" is in place, the dealer makes up a secret rule that determines what cards can be played on the starter pile. It is this rule that corresponds to a law of science; the players may think of the dealer as Nature or, if they prefer, as God. The dealer writes his or her rule on a piece of paper, which is then folded and put aside.

This is for later checking to make sure that the dealer does not upset Nature's uniformity by changing the rule. For each player the object of the game is to get rid of as many cards as possible. This can be done rapidly by any player who correctly guesses the secret rule.

An example of a very simple rule is: "If the top card of the starter pile is red, play a black card. If the top card is black, play a red card."

After the rule is written, the game begins. The first player takes any card from his hand and places it face up on the starter card. If the card conforms to the secret rule, the dealer says "Right" and the card remains on the starter pile. If it violates the rule, the dealer says "Wrong." The player then takes back the card, places it face up in front of him, and the turn passes to the next player on the left. Each player must play one card from his hand at each turn. His "mistake cards" are left face up in front of him and spread slightly so that they can be clearly identified. The correctly played cards that form the starter pile are also fanned along the table so that all the cards can be seen.

Each player tries to analyze the cards in the starter pile to discover the rule governing their sequence. The player then forms a hypothesis that can be tested by playing what he or she thinks is a correct card, or by playing a card he or she suspects will be rejected.

Details of scoring, etc., need not concern us, but we will use this game as an example of the invention and testing of hypotheses. The following are examples of accepted and rejected cards in games played with different secret rules. Try to devise a hypothesis about the secret rule that accounts for all the accepted and rejected cards. (Keep in mind that the last card accepted is the top card of the starter pile, which often plays a part in the rules; see, e.g., the rule given above.) Distinctions about which player played the card are ignored; standard abbreviations for cards and suits are used; "Yes" means accepted and "No" means rejected.

Game 1.   Starter Card 6C. 2D No, 8C No, JD Yes, 3S No, 5H No, 2S Yes, 6D No, QH No, 10H No, 3D Yes, AS No, 9D No, 10D Yes, 7H No, 2C Yes, KH Yes, 4D Yes, QC Yes, 4S No, AD No, KS No, 9S No, 6H Yes.

Game 2.   Starter Card 9D. 5D Yes, 8D Yes, 4C No, 9C No, 10S No, KC No, 2H No, 7S No, JH No, JC No, AC No, 10H No, 4S No, 7C No, 7D No, 5C No, 3H No, 8S Yes, QD No, 8H Yes, 4H Yes, AH Yes, 6S No, QS No.

*Game 3.   Starter Card QH. 6D No, 5H No, 3C No, 3S No, 8C No, 2D No, 6H No, 5S No, 4D No, KS Yes, 10H Yes, 4S No, 7C No, 7D No, 6S No, QS Yes, 9D Yes, 5D No, 8D No, 8S No, JS Yes, JD Yes, 10D No, 2C No, AC No.

Game 4. Starter Card 10C. KH No, 7H Yes, JC Yes, JH No, 3H Yes, 5C No, 7S No, 2H Yes, KD No, KC Yes, 10S Yes, 9C No, 4C No, AH Yes, 4H Yes, 8H Yes, QD No, 3D Yes, 2S No, 6C No, 9S No, AD Yes, QC Yes, 9H Yes, AS No.

Game 5. Starter Card 5C. AD No, AS Yes, 10C Yes, 7H Yes, JC No, 3H Yes, 2H Yes, KC No, 10S No, AH Yes, 4H Yes, 8H Yes, 3D Yes, 9H Yes, KH Yes, JH Yes, 6S No, 5D Yes, 8D Yes, 8S No, 10D Yes, 2C No, AC No, QH Yes, KS No.

Exercise 9-5

The following facts about the destruction of the Bronze Age Minoan culture in Crete have been discovered by archeologists in recent years:

A.   The palace of Knossos and many other Minoan palaces in Crete were all destroyed about 1450 B.C.

B.   The island of Thera, about 30 miles from Crete, was destroyed by a volcanic explosion somewhere around 1500 B.C., causing great waves (tsunamis) and earthquakes on Crete and other nearby islands.

C.   The palace of Knossos, but no other palace, was restored after the destruction of 1450 B.C. and had a period of new vigor accompanied by a new style in pottery and ornaments.

D.   The themes of war and hunting, which had previously been absent from Cretan art, began to be emphasized at this time, along with more traditional Cretan themes.

E.   The records kept of harvests, storage, etc., at Knossos during this period were in the same general kind of writing as older records, but were in Greek, not in the language of Crete.

Do the following:

1.   Invent a hypothesis that accounts for A, but not for B, C, D, or E. How could it be confirmed?

2.   Invent a hypothesis that relates A and B, but not C, D, or E. How could it be confirmed?

3.   Invent a hypothesis that accounts for C in light of A and B, but does not account for D or E. How could it be confirmed?

*4.   Invent a hypothesis that relates A, B, C, and D, but not E. How could it be confirmed?

5.   Invent a hypothesis that relates A, B, C, D, and E. How could it be confirmed?

The Palace of Knossos, west side of Great Court (reconstruction).

Exercise 9-6

The palace of Knossos in Crete was a center of the Bronze Age Minoan culture. It was destroyed and rebuilt several times, but finally destroyed about 1400 B.C., mainly by fire. Archeological evidence (fire-blackening on masonry near wooden beams) shows that a strong southerly wind was blowing at the time the palace burned. The following table gives the probability of a strong (force 6 or higher on the Beaufort scale) southerly wind in this area for each month.

January	February	March	April	May	June
$\frac{24}{1000}$	$\frac{44}{1000}$	$\frac{35}{1000}$	$\frac{35}{1000}$	$\frac{10}{1000}$	$\frac{5}{1000}$

July	August	September	October	November	December
$\frac{0}{1000}$	$\frac{1}{1000}$	$\frac{1}{1000}$	$\frac{6}{1000}$	$\frac{15}{1000}$	$\frac{36}{1000}$

Given this information and the assumption that the prior probability that Knossos was destroyed in any given month is $\frac{1}{12}$, we are going to calculate the probability that Knossos was destroyed in various months, given the evidence of the strong southerly wind. We will call this evidence E_1, the hypothesis that Knossos was destroyed in January H_1, that it was destroyed in February H_2, and so on.

1. First calculate $Pr(E)$ given that $Pr(E) = Pr(H_1) \times Pr(E_1/H_1) + Pr(H_2) \times Pr(E_1/H_2) + Pr(H_3) \times Pr(E_1/H_3) \cdots + Pr(H_{12}) \times Pr(E_1/H_{12})$. (For $Pr(E_1/H_1)$, etc., use the figures for the appropriate month from the table above.)

2. Calculate $Pr(H_1/E_1)$, $Pr(H_2/E_1)$, and $Pr(H_3/E_1)$.

3. Calculate $Pr(H_4/E_1)$, $Pr(H_5/E_1)$, and $Pr(H_6/E_1)$.

4. Calculate $Pr(H_7/E_1)$, $Pr(H_8/E_1)$, and $Pr(H_9/E_1)$.

5. Calculate $Pr(H_{10}/E_1)$, $Pr(H_{11}/E_1)$, and $Pr(H_{12}/E_1)$.

Justify the following statements using the calculations above:

6. The chances that the palace was destroyed between July and September are negligible.

7. It is possible but not very probable that it was destroyed in May, June, October, or November.

*8. The most likely months, on the evidence of the wind, are between December and April.

Further evidence from agricultural records found on clay tablets in the palace shows that sheep belonging to the palace had been sheared and wool distributed to textile workers; this could not have happened before May. The grain harvest had begun but, unless the records are incomplete, was not finished. This harvest would begin in May and be finished by June. There is no record of the grape harvest, which would be completed by October. In light of this information:

9. Give an argument for the most probable month or months for the destruction of the palace of Knossos.

10. Under what conditions might the destruction have occurred in October or November? What evidence might be discovered that would make these months more probable?

Source of information: John Chadwick, *The Mycenaean World* (Cambridge: Cambridge University Press, 1976).

CHAPTER TEN

Frontiers of Logic

THE LAZY ARGUMENT

An argument for determinism, called in ancient times the "Lazy Argument," goes as follows:

Take any event in the future, say your death. It is necessarily true that either you will die tomorrow or that you won't. Thus it is necessarily true that you will die tomorrow or necessarily true that you won't die tomorrow. The same argument applies to each day in the future. You can't change what is necessarily true, so the time of your death is already fixed and unalterable. Thus you might as well adopt a fatalistic attitude about your death. Since the same argument can be applied to every event in the future, you should be a fatalist about everything.

What is wrong with this argument?

What new systems are logicians developing, and what are their uses?

Logicians are working in a number of interesting areas, including the logical structure of questions and of commands—logical systems that differ from standard logic in that standard logic deals only with statements. Other variations from accepted logical techniques now being investigated are "free" predicate logics where the use of a quantifier does not indicate that what is being quantified over actually exists, and multi-valued logics which differ from standard logic in considering values other than truth and falsity. In the area of inductive logic, confirmation theory may eventually become an independent subdivision of logic.

The logical systems we will consider in this chapter, however, are a related group of systems that have interesting and important philosophical applications: modal logic, which is the logic of necessity and possibility; epistemic and doxastic logic, which is the logic of knowledge and belief; deontic logic, which is the logic of obligation and permissibility; and tense logic, which is the logic of time. Modal logic is the oldest and best developed of these systems and the others resemble modal logic to a greater or lesser extent, as we will see.

Modal Logic: Operators and Connectives

We will begin with the simplest and least controversial form of modal logic—model statement logic. We begin the development of this system by adding to the complete system of statement logic two new operators and two new connectives. Any three of the four new additions can be defined in terms of the fourth one, so in one way it does not matter where we start. Let us consider first the notion of logical necessity. A true statement is logically necessary if it is true no matter what happens—true in every conceivable state of affairs. Thus, "This book is printed on white paper" is true but not necessarily true; the publisher could have printed it on yellow or light blue or gray paper. But a tautology like "A book is printed on white paper or it is not printed on white paper" is not only true but necessarily true; one of the disjuncts is satisfied no matter what happens. Similarly, a false statement is necessarily false if it is false no matter what happens, false in any conceivable circumstances. "This book is printed on pink paper" is false but not necessarily false; it *could* have been true given certain decisions by the publisher. But the contradiction "This book is printed on white paper and it is not printed on white paper" is false in every conceivable circumstance.

When we wish to say that a statement A is necessarily true, we will write a box $\Box$ in front of the statement, so $\Box A$ means "A is necessarily true." If we wish to say that A is necessarily false, we will write $\Box \sim A$. We can now introduce our other new operator and our new connectives. To say that some statement is possibly true is to say that it is not necessarily false, so "It is possible that A," which we will write as $\Diamond A$, can be defined as follows:

$$\Diamond A = \text{def. } \sim \Box \sim A$$

(where = def. means "is equivalent to by definition").

The two connectives we will need are *Strict Implication* and *Strict Equivalance*. Two statements, A and B, are strictly equivalent if it is logically true that they are materially equivalent, and a statement A strictly implies another statement B if it is logically true that A materially implies B. Using $\rightarrow$ for strict implication and $\equiv$ for strict equivalence, we can write their definitions as follows:

$$(A \rightarrow B) = \text{def. } \Box(A \supset B)$$
$$(A \equiv B) = \text{def. } \Box(A \equiv B)$$

To make good the claim that any three of these additions to statement logic can be defined in terms of the fourth, we can define $\Box$ in terms of each of the others. We could then use $\Box$ to define the remaining ones:

$$\Box A = \text{def. } \sim \Diamond \sim A$$
$$\Box A = \text{def. } (A \equiv (A \lor \sim A))$$
$$\Box A = \text{def. } (\sim A \rightarrow A)$$

The last sounds a bit odd until we remember that in our complete system of statement logic we learned that the denial of a tautology is a contradiction, and that from a contradiction any statement follows.

We could also use the principle that if two expressions are equivalent by definition they can be written with a strict equivalence between them and can be substituted for each other in any statement. So we could go from

$$\Box A \equiv (\sim A \to A)$$

to

$$\Box A \equiv \Box(\sim A \supset A)$$

by the definition of strict implication just given, then to

$$\Box A \equiv \Box(A \lor A)$$

by Definition of Material Implication and Double Negation, and to

$$\Box A \equiv \Box A$$

by Repetition.

Presently we will see some exceptions to the principle that expressions equivalent by definition can be substituted in *any* statement, but since equivalence by definition is one kind of logical equivalence, and strict equivalence is logical equivalence, we can use the principle that logically equivalent expressions can be substituted for each other within the scope of the modal operators $\Box$ and $\Diamond$. This is a principle that has no exceptions.

Modal Logic Rules

Any system of modal logic will contain two principles which we will express as strict implications. The first, which we will call *Necesse ad Esse* (NE), says that what is logically true is true:

$$\Box A \to A$$

The second, which we will call *Esse ad Posse* (EP), says that what is true is logically possible:

$$A \to \Diamond A$$

The definitional interconnections between $\Box$ and $\Diamond$ noted above can be expressed as strict equivalences:

$\Box A \equiv\; \sim \Diamond \sim A$

$\Diamond A \equiv\; \sim \Box \sim A$

By substituting $\sim A$ for A and using double negation we get further strict equivalences:

$A \equiv\; \sim \Diamond A$

$A \equiv\; \sim \Box A$

These four equivalences will be referred to collectively as Modal Operator Exchange (MOE). Together with NE and EP they form the core of any system of modal logic.

We will regard all the tautologous implication of Chapter Four as strict implication and all the tautologous equivalences of Chapter Four as strict equivalences, and thus in a sense all the rules of our complete system of statement logic become modal principles. In fact, ordinary statement logic becomes a logical consequence of modal logic; we have such modal principles as, for example:

$(A \cdot B) \rightarrow A$

$\sim (A \cdot B) \equiv (\sim A \lor \sim B)$

and these imply the more familiar forms

$(A \cdot B) \supset A$

$\sim (A \cdot B) \equiv (\sim A \lor \sim B)$

by the definitions of strict implication and strict equivalence and the rule NE.

It will be useful to add explicitly the definitions of the two connectives to our system. Definition of Strict Implication (DSI):

$(A \rightarrow B) \equiv \Box (A \supset B)$

and Definition of Strict Equivalence (DSE):

$(A \equiv B) \equiv \Box (A \equiv B)$

The rules given so far—NE, EP, MOE, DSI, DSE—and the modal version of our statement logic rules provide us with an adequate (in fact, more than adequate) basis for a basic system of modal logic, which we will call S1. In S1 the following useful rules can be derived from the basic set of rules above:

Strict Consequentia Mirabilis (SCM) $\Box A \equiv (\sim A \to A)$
Strict Negative Consequentia Mirabilis (SNCM) $\Box \sim A \equiv (A \to \sim A)$
(Another) Definition of Strict Implication (DSI)
    $(A \to B) \equiv \sim \Diamond (A \cdot \sim B)$
Negation of Strict Implication (NSI) $\sim (A \to B) \equiv \Diamond (A \cdot \sim B)$
Strict Transposition (STransp.) $(A \to B) \equiv (\sim B \to \sim A)$
Strict Commutation (SCom.) $(A \equiv B) \equiv (B \equiv A)$
Strict Complementarity (SComp.) $(A \equiv B) \equiv (\sim A \equiv \sim B)$
Negation of Strict Equivalence (NSE) $\sim (A \equiv B) \equiv \Diamond (\sim A \equiv B)$
(Another) Definition of Strict Equivalence (DSE)
    $(A \equiv B) \equiv ((A \to B) \cdot (B \to A))$
And many others.

Modal logic was studied by the Classical Greek logicians and by the Medievals, but the modern development of modal statement logic was almost entirely due to the great American logician C. I. Lewis, from whom we have borrowed most of our symbols and the idea of developing modal logic as a basic system to which additional rules may be added to strengthen the basic system. Lewis developed five systems, which he labeled S1, S2, S3, S4, and S5, and we will follow his development.

Some rules that *cannot* be proved from any of the rules given so far are the rules for Modal Operator Distribution (MOD):

$\Box (A \cdot B) \equiv (\Box A \cdot \Box B)$

$\Diamond (A \vee B) \equiv (\Diamond A \vee \Diamond B)$

$(\Box A \vee \Box B) \to \Box (A \vee B)$

$\Diamond (A \cdot B) \to (\Diamond A \cdot \Diamond B)$

Note that the converses of the two strict implications are *not* rules.

The Lazy Argument given at the beginning of this chapter commits the fallacy of going from $\Box (A \vee \sim A)$ to $\Box A \vee \Box \sim A$, which is an instance of the converse of the third distribution rule. To see that this converse should *not* be a rule we can give the following argument: If we had $\Box (A \vee B) \to (\Box A \vee \Box B)$ as a rule, there would be no distinction between factual truth and necessary truth. Take a factual truth, that my name starts with P. This is true but might be false: If

$M \quad \# \quad$ my name starts with P

we would symbolize this as $M \cdot \diamond \sim M$. But $M \vee \sim M$ is a necessary truth. So $\square(M \vee \sim M)$ is true. If we had the supposed rule, we could argue as follows:

1.	M	$\left.\vphantom{\begin{matrix}1\\2\end{matrix}}\right\}$ $\square M$	
2.	$\square(M \vee \sim M)$		
3.	$\square M \vee \square \sim M$		2 supposed rule
4.	$\diamond M$		1 EP
5.	$\sim \square \sim M$		4 MOE
6.	$\square M$		3, 5 SC

Since the same argument applies to any factual truth, adopting the supposed rule would abolish the distinction between factual truth and necessary truth. The determinist might want to do this, but if he "argues" for determinism by using a rule that presupposes that there is no distinction between factual and necessary truth, he begs the question.

Adding the MOD rules to S1 gives us S2. The rules seem reasonable, but in some extensions of modal logic they can give rise to surprising consequences, as we will see.

Another set of rules, which we will call Strict Implication of Operators (SIO), is as follows:

$(A \rightarrow B) \rightarrow (\square A \rightarrow \square B)$

$(A \rightarrow B) \rightarrow (\diamond A \rightarrow \diamond B)$

$(A \rightarrow B) \rightarrow (\square \sim B \rightarrow \square \sim A)$

$(A \rightarrow B) \rightarrow (\diamond \sim B \rightarrow \diamond \sim A)$

These rules cannot be proved from any of the previous rules of S1 and S2, and they form the basis of the third system, S3. Many modal logicians feel that S3 is a satisfactory system of modal logic that does justice to all of our intuitions about the interconnections of necessity, possibility, and truth.

The remaining two systems are more controversial. The rules which, added to S3 give us S4, are called the Weak Reduction Principles (WRP):

$\square A \equiv \square \square A$

$\diamond A \equiv \diamond \diamond A$

They are "reduction principles" because, if they are accepted as rules, any number of repetitions of $\square$ or $\diamond$ can be reduced to one occurrence, somewhat as in basic statement logic any odd number of $\sim$'s can be reduced to one, and any even number of $\sim$'s to none, by Double Negation.

If we add to the S4 rules the Strong Reduction Principles (SRP):

$$\square A \equiv \diamond \square A$$

$$\diamond A \equiv \square \diamond A$$

we get S5, the strongest of Lewis's five systems. (Stronger systems have been devised, but they are mainly of technical interest.) Many modal logicians find the Strong Reduction Principles extremely implausible. If we accept them, however, we have the technically useful result that any number of mixed modal operators can be reduced to a single operator. For instance:

$$\square \diamond \diamond \diamond \square \diamond \square \square \square \diamond A$$

reduces to $\diamond A$.

Modal logic can be studied simply as a fascinating logical puzzle. Hundreds of interesting and sometimes surprising derived rules can be proved from the basic rules of any of the five systems; intermediate systems (e.g., stronger than S2 but weaker than S3) can be devised; different rules can be used as starting points. There is a truth-table-like method of disproof, though not of proof, for modal logic, but modal logic can also be used as a tool in attacking many philosophical problems, bringing clarity and precision to many puzzling arguments.

The Nature of Necessity

To make use of modal logic in this way we may have to extend the meaning of terms like "necessary" and "possible." So far we have spoken as if we were concerned with logical necessity in a rather narrow sense; a statement is necessarily true if it is true "no matter what happens," "true in every conceivable state of affairs." The narrowest way of interpreting this is to say that we mean that the denial of a logical necessary statement is self-contradictory, in the sense that from the denial of a necessary statement we can derive a formal self-contradiction of the form $A \cdot \sim A$ simply by the rules of basic logic and the definition of terms.

But there may be a wider sense even of logical necessity. Some state-ments may be necessary in the sense that we cannot imagine or conceive a state of affairs that would make them false, but these statements may be such that we cannot derive a contradiction from their denial simply by the rules of basic logic and the definition of terms. Thus, "All bachelors are unmarried" is logically true in the narrow sense of "bachelor" defined as "unmarried male," and the statement can be rewritten as "All un-married males are unmarried." To deny this would be to say that some unmarried males are not unmarried, an obvious contradiction.

However, consider another classical example: "Nothing is red all over its surface and green all over its surface at the same time." It seems inconceivable that the denial of this could be true, but there seems no way of deriving a contradiction from the denial simply by substituting defini-tions and using basic logic.

There are other situations such that we can imagine, in the sense of forming a mental picture of, their occurrence, but feel somehow that they "can't happen." We can form a mental picture of the whole universe suddenly popping into existence from nothing at some time in the past, for no reason whatsoever. But we reject this possibility not just as very improbable, but as in some sense out of the question. Most people would say that "Something can't just pop into existence from nothing, for no reason" is a necessary truth, though perhaps not a *logically* necessary truth. We might call this "ontological" necessity.

Again, we tend to think of some things as "scientifically impossible" or "against the laws of nature" and think of the laws of nature as being in some sense necessary or unbreakable. We can call this "nomological" necessity (from Greek *nomos* law). Finally, a very weak sense of necessary is given by the idea that something is necessarily true if it is true at all times. Thus it might happen to be true at all times that no one named Snicklefritz was married to anyone named Buzzfuz. This would be like a necessary truth in some ways, but we would hesitate to say that it was necessary in any strong sense. We might call this "chronological" necessity.

It would seem that any statement that was necessary in any of the stronger senses of necessity would be necessary in all the weaker senses. Thus logical necessity would imply ontological necessity, ontological necessity would imply nomological necessity, and nomological necessity would imply chronological necessity. If a statement was necessarily true in any of these senses, of course, it would be true. However, the corre-sponding forms of possibility would go in reverse order. Logical possi-bility, the mere absence of contradiction, would be the weakest form of possibility. Ontological possibility, merely not being totally out of the question, would be next weakest. Nomological possibility, bare consistency with the laws of nature, would be next. Finally, chronological possibility, which amounts to being true at *some* time, would be the strongest form of possibility. If A is true, it would, of course, be possible in all these senses.

The result of these reflections is a "modal line." If we use $\Box^o$ to symbolize ontological necessity, $\Box^n$ for nomological necessity, $\Box^c$ for chronological necessity, and $\Diamond^o$, $\Diamond^n$, $\Diamond^c$ for the corresponding senses of possibility, we can write the relations between the forms of necessity and possibility as follows:

$$\Box A \to \Box^o A \to \Box^n A \to \Box^c A \to A \to \Diamond^c A \to \Diamond^n A \to \Diamond^o A \to \Diamond A$$

where the unadorned box and diamond are logical necessity and possibility, and the arrows indicate implication relations.

It seems safe to assume that all the rules of S1, S2, and S3 hold for all forms of necessity and possibility. But the controversial S4 and S5 principles might hold for some varieties and not others. Thus chronological necessity seems to obey both the weak and strong reduction principles: If A is true at all times, it is true at all times that A is true at all times, and vice versa. And if it is true even at some time that it is true at all times that A, it would seem that it is true at all times that A (and vice versa).

But logical necessity may obey neither S4 nor S5 rules. If it is contradictory to deny A, does it follow that it is contradictory to deny that it is contradictory to deny A? And if it is consistent to affirm that it is contradictory to deny A, does this mean that it is contradictory to deny A?

Applications of Modal Logic

These seemingly technical problems have their importance in philosophically interesting applications of modal logic. One famous argument for the existence of God is St. Anselm's ontological argument which tries to argue for the existence of God from the definition of God and the conceivability of God's existence. A modern version of the argument due to Charles Hartshorne* can be stated as follows:

Let G # God exists

* *The Logic of Perfection*, (La Salle, Illinois: Open Court Publishing Co., 1962), Chap. 2.

Now God by definition is a being such that if He exists it must be necessary that he exists:

1. $G \rightarrow \Box G$

But it is possible that God exists:

2. $\Diamond G$

Now if we have an S5 system, we can argue as follows:

3.	$\Diamond G \rightarrow \Diamond \Box G$	1 SIO
4.	$\Diamond \Box G$	3, 2 MP
5.	$\Box G$	4 SRP
6.	G	5 NE

Thus we have proved by a valid argument from plausible premises that God exists!

The argument has been criticized from a philosophical point of view as follows: If the necessity involved is logical necessity, Premise 1 is too strong, for arguably the kind of necessity "God exists" would have if it were true would not be logical necessity; even if God in some sense must exist, it could not be shown by definition of terms and basic logic that the denial of "God exists" implies a contradiction. If the possibility involved in Premise 2 is ontological possibility, Premise 2 is too strong, for arguably we do not know how to establish the *ontological* possibility of God's existence. If the sense of necessity in Premise 1 is ontological necessity, and the sense of possibility involved in Premise 2 is merely logical possibility, the argument becomes invalid because of this ambiguity. So, in any case, the argument fails.*

There have been a number of interesting defenses of and further criticisms of this modal version of the ontological argument. It is an interesting case of a classical philosophical problem clarified by logical techniques. There is still plenty of room for philosophical argument, but those who wish to defend the argument can see which premises need defense, and those who wish to attack it can see which premises are vulnerable. Even if both *premises* could be given an acceptable form, a good deal might turn on whether ontological modalities obey the S5 rule, the Strong Reduction Principle.

* See R. L. Purtill, "Hartshorne's Modal Proof," *Journal of Philosophy*, Vol. LXIII, No. 14, July 1966.

Another traditional argument that can be clarified by modal logic is the Master Argument for determinism. It can be stated as follows: The past cannot be changed. But for any event, say a sea battle, which might take place tomorrow, it was either true yesterday that the event would take place, or false yesterday that it would take place. But if it was true yesterday that the sea battle would take place, it must take place, and if it was false yesterday that it would take place, it cannot take place. So it is already decided whether the sea battle will take place. And since the same argument applies to any statement, the whole future is fixed and decided, so it is no use worrying or planning about the future.

To do justice to this argument we need a simple system of dating statements. Suppose the argument is given on the second day of some month, "yesterday" will then be the first and "tomorrow" will be the third.

Let S # (the untensed statement) a sea battle takes place
S^3 will express "It is true on the third (tomorrow) that a sea battle takes place" and
$(S^3)^1$ will express "It is true on the first (yesterday) that it is true on the third (tomorrow) that a sea battle takes place."

Since the past cannot be changed our first premise is:

1. $\Box(S^3)^1 \lor \Box(\sim S^3)^1$

That something being true yesterday means it must be true tomorrow can be expressed as:

2. $(S^3)^1 \to S^3$
3. $(\sim S^3)^1 \to \sim S^3$

We can then argue as follows:

4.	$\Box(S^3)^1 \to \Box S^3$	2 SIO
5.	$\Box(\sim S^3)^1 \to \Box \sim S^3$	3 SIO
6.	$\Box S^3 \lor \Box \sim S^3$	1, 4, 5 CD

This gives us the desired conclusion: that either the sea battle necessarily will occur or it necessarily will not occur.

Some philosophers have attempted to evade the conclusion by arguing that you cannot speak of statements being true *at a time*. But either this creates new problems about how statement can be true without being true at any time *or*, if it is claimed that any statements if true at all are true at all times, we can construct an even stronger version of the Master Argument.

The sense of necessity used in the premises is certainly not logical necessity. There is some plausibility in claiming that it is ontological necessity: It is just as much out of the question to change the past as it is to find something coming from nothing. But even if we say that it is some new sense of necessity—"unchangeability" perhaps—the argument still seems plausible.

The most radical, but in some ways the most satisfactory, solution was hinted at by Aristotle, who was one of the first to discuss the problem. This solution undercuts Premise 1 by denying that it *was* true or false yesterday that a sea battle would take place tomorrow. Some statements about future contingent events are radically indeterminate on this view; they may have a probability but they do not have *either* the value "true" *or* the value "false." This solution rejects what has been called the "principle of bivalence"—that any intelligible statement is either true or false. But a radical indeterminist may be unhappy with that principle anyway, since if every statement, including any statement about the future, has a truth value, one can get a Master Argument type of argument going and reach the conclusion that the future is fixed. There has been much discussion pro and con about this problem.

Epistemic Logic

Now that we have some familiarity with modal logic, it will be simpler to understand the systems that are similar to modal logic. Indeed, the first of these systems, epistemic logic—the logic of knowledge—is an exact parallel to modal logic, what we will call a *paramodal* logic. All of the rules of modal logic can be reinterpreted with knowledge in place of necessity. Unlike necessity, however, knowledge always involves a person who has the knowledge. For many purposes it will not matter who the person is, so long as it remains the same person throughout a given argument. We will use the lower case n as a dummy name therefore, so that KnA stands for "n knows A" and, for example, $KnA \to \sim Kn \sim A$ would symbolize "If n knows A, then n does not know $\sim A$." This holds whether we substitute my name or yours, or that of any person at all, for n; thus n functions as a sort of universal quasi-name.

There is no single word in English that represents the idea that it is not true that someone does not know something. So we will use the phrase "for all n knows," which is defined as:

$$FnA = \text{def. } \sim Kn \sim A$$

Thus all the Epistemic Operator Exchange (EOE) rules become true by definition:

$$KnA \equiv \; \sim Fn \sim A$$
$$FnA \equiv \; \sim Kn \sim A$$
$$\sim KnA \equiv Fn \sim A$$
$$\sim FnA \equiv Kn \sim A$$

The rules corresponding to NE and EP also hold true:

Knowledge to Truth (KT) $KnA \rightarrow A$
Truth to Epistemic Possibility (TEP) $A \rightarrow FnA$

These rules say that if anyone knows something, that thing is true, and if something is true, it cannot be known to be false. The first rule can be misunderstood as being stronger than it is. It does not mean that we can find out the truth of something merely by consulting our state of mind; rather it says that we do not call a state of mind knowledge unless it is awareness of something actually true. The transposition of KT brings this out:

$$\sim A \rightarrow \; \sim KnA$$

That is to say, if something is false, no one can know it. This is the way we use the concept of knowledge; knowing a false statement is a contradiction in terms. As in other cases, of course, we sometimes use a contradiction for rhetorical effect: "His shortcut saved so much time, he was two hours late," "She knew it, but she was wrong." In the first sentence we are saying he saved no time at all, in the second that she did not know it after all.

We can also define two connectives, Epistemic Implication and Epistemic Equivalence. "A epistemically implies B for n" will be symbolized and defined as:

Definition of Epistemic Implication (DEI) $A \overset{e}{\underset{n}{\rightarrow}} B \equiv Kn(A \supset B)$

and "*A* is epistemically equivalent to *B* for *n*" will be:

Definition of Epistemic Equivalence (DEE) $A \overset{e}{\underset{n}{\leftrightarrow}} B \equiv Kn(A \equiv B)$

Both of these are relative to individuals; *A* may epistemically imply *B* for me but not for you, because I know that if *A* is true then *B* is, but you do not.

Just as with modal logic, we can get progressively stronger systems of epistemic logic by adding rules. The rules Epistemic Operator Distribution (EOD)

$$Kn(A \cdot B) \equiv (KnA \cdot KnB)$$
$$Fn(A \vee B) \equiv (FnA \vee FnB)$$
$$(KnA \vee KnB) \rightarrow Kn(A \vee B)$$
$$Fn(A \cdot B) \rightarrow (FnA \cdot FnB)$$

give us a system similar to S2. The parallels to SIO are *not* the rules

$$(A \rightarrow B) \rightarrow (KnA \rightarrow KnB), \text{ etc.}$$

for we often fail to know the logical consequences of what we know. Rather the rules Implication of Epistemic Operators (IEO) use epistemic implication:

$$A \overset{n}{\underset{e}{\rightarrow}} B \rightarrow \quad KnA \overset{n}{\underset{e}{\rightarrow}} KnB$$
$$A \overset{n}{\underset{e}{\rightarrow}} B \rightarrow \quad FnA \overset{n}{\underset{e}{\rightarrow}} FnB$$
$$A \overset{n}{\underset{e}{\rightarrow}} B \rightarrow \sim KnB \overset{n}{\underset{e}{\rightarrow}} \sim KnA$$
$$A \overset{n}{\underset{e}{\rightarrow}} B \rightarrow \sim FnB \overset{n}{\underset{e}{\rightarrow}} \sim FnA$$

The first rule says, in effect, that if you know that if *A* is true then *B* is, then you know that if you know *A* you will know *B*. This seems intuitively satisfactory to some logician, but not to others. The stronger rules

Weak Epistemic Reduction (WER) $KnA \equiv KnKnA$
$\qquad\qquad\qquad\qquad\qquad\qquad FnA \equiv FnFnA$

Strong Epistemic Reduction (SER) $KnA \equiv FnKnA$
$\qquad\qquad\qquad\qquad\qquad\qquad FnA \equiv KnFnA$

are even more controversial. Do we always know that we know when we know? If for all we know we know something, do we know it? Both principles are least dubious.

The applications in which epistemic logic has so far proved useful mostly have to do with skeptical arguments against the possibility of knowledge. For instance, skeptics have argued: "If you know, you can't be wrong. It is always possible that we are wrong, so we never really know." If we symbolize "If you know, you can't be wrong" as $Knp \rightarrow p$, this is harmless enough, but the argument becomes:

1. $Knp \rightarrow A$ ⎱
2. $\Diamond \sim A$ ⎰ $\sim KnA$

and the argument is invalid; the conclusion does not follow. If, however, we strengthen the first premise to $Knp \rightarrow \Box A$, the argument is valid:

1. $KnA \rightarrow \Box A$ ⎱
2. $\Diamond \sim A$ ⎰ $\sim KnA$
3. $\sim \Box A$ 2 MOE
4. $\sim KnA$ 1, 3 MT

However, $KnA \rightarrow \Box A$ is implausibly strong; merely because we know something does not make it necessarily true, in any sense of "necessarily true." Other arguments for skepticism have similar faults; either the premises are too strong or the argument is invalid.

Doxastic Logic

The logic of belief, doxastic logic, is not a para-modal logic. We can let BnA stand for "n believes A" and introduce a weak operator "n doesn't disbelieve A" defined as:

$DnA = \text{def. } \sim Bn \sim A$

giving us a full set of Belief Operator Exchange (BOE) rules:

$BnA \equiv \sim Dn \sim A$

$DnA \equiv \sim Bn \sim A$

$\sim BnA \equiv Dn \sim A$

$\sim DnA \equiv Bn \sim A$

We can also define Doxastic Implication and Doxastic Equivalence:

Definition of Belief Implication (DBI) $A \xrightarrow[b]{n} B \equiv Bn(A \supset B)$

Definition of Belief Equivalence (DBE) $A \xrightarrow[b]{n} B \equiv Bn(A \equiv B)$

However, we do not have rules parallel to NE and EP; neither $BnA \to A$ nor $A \to DnA$ is a rule of logic. That we believe something does not make it true, and that something is true does not mean we believe it. Thus doxastic logic is a *quasi-modal* logic: like modal logic in some respects, but unlike it in others.

The Belief Operator Distribution (BOD) rules seem reasonable to many logicians, but they are still controversial:

$Bn(A \cdot B) \equiv (BnA \cdot BnB)$

$Dn(A \vee B) \equiv (DnA \vee DnB)$

$(BnA \vee BnB) \to Bn(A \vee B)$

$Dn(A \cdot B) \to (DnA \cdot DnB)$

So also are the Implication of Belief Operator (IBO) rules

$A \xrightarrow[n]{b} B \to BnA \xrightarrow[n]{b} BnB$

$A \xrightarrow[n]{b} B \to DnA \xrightarrow[n]{b} DnB$, etc.

Even more controversial is the rule

$BnA \to DnA$

which is equivalent to

$\sim \Diamond (BnA \to \sim Bn \sim A)$

This rule says, in effect, that a person cannot have inconsistent beliefs. This is connected with the question of whether someone can believe the impossible, whether

$\sim \Diamond A \to \sim BnA$

should be a rule of logic. There have been some interesting controversies about these points.*

* See R. L. Purtill, "Believing the Impossible," AJATUS XXXII, 1970, and J. Hintikka, *The Intentions of Intentionality and Other New Modals for Modalities* (Boston: D. Reidel Publishing Co. 1975) Chapter Nine.

Deontic Logic

Another quasi-modal logic is deontic logic, the logic of obligation and permissibility. We usually speak of *actions* as being obligatory, permissible, etc., but to make deontic logic parallel with other kinds of logic we usually use *OnA* for "*n* is obliged to make it true that *A*," where *A* describes some action. Thus if I want to say, "Jones is obliged to support his children" we might let

j # Jones

S # Jones supports his children

and write

OjS

The advantage of the rather awkward "make it true that" terminology is that we can use *On* as an operator on statements. Most logicians are agreed that permissibility is related to obligation in just the same way as possibility is related to necessity, so that the Deontic Operator Exchange (DOE) holds true. Letting *PnA* stand for "*n* is permitted to make it true that *A*," the rules of deontic logic will be:

Deontic Operator Exchange (DOE)

$$OnA \equiv \ \sim Pn \sim A$$
$$PnA \equiv \ \sim On \sim A$$
$$\sim OnA \equiv Pn \sim A$$
$$\sim PnA \equiv On \sim A$$

Definition of Deontic Implication (DDI) $A \overset{d}{\underset{n}{\to}} B \equiv On(A \supset B)$

Definition of Deontic Equivalence (DDE) $A \overset{d}{\underset{n}{\leftrightarrow}} B \equiv On(A \equiv B)$

Deontic Operator Distribution (DOD)

$$On(A \cdot B) \equiv (OnA \cdot OnB)$$
$$Pn(A \lor B) \equiv (PnA \lor PnB)$$
$$(OnA \lor OnB) \to On(A \lor B)$$
$$Pn(A \cdot B) \to (PnA \cdot PnB)$$

Implication of Deontic Operators (IDO)

$$A \overset{d}{\underset{n}{\to}} B \to OnA \overset{d}{\underset{n}{\to}} OnB$$
$$A \overset{d}{\underset{n}{\to}} B \to PnA \overset{d}{\underset{n}{\to}} PnB$$

As before, the "reduction principles"

$OnA \equiv OnOnA$ and $OnA \equiv PnOnA$

are controversial. So also is the principle

$OnA \rightarrow PnA$

which is equivalent to

$\sim \Diamond (OnA \cdot On \sim A)$

and connected with the "ought implies can" principle

$OnA \rightarrow \Diamond A$

Some deontic logicians have claimed that there are two kinds of obligation with corresponding senses of permissibility. *Prima facie* obligation is defined in such a way that if there is a moral rule which says that we should do a thing, we have a *prima facie* obligation to do it. But since moral rules can conflict in a given case, it is possible to be obliged to do incompatible things. Thus $\sim \Diamond (OnA \cdot On \sim A)$ does not hold for *prima facie* obligation.

However, our *strict obligation* is our strongest *prima facie* obligation: what we should do all things considered. (This assumes we have a way of settling conflicts of moral rules.) Strict obligations cannot conflict, and if we use $O'nA$ to stand for "*n* is strictly obliged to make it true that A," and $P'nA$ to stand for "*n* is strictly permitted to make it true that A" then

$O'nA \rightarrow P'nA$
$\sim \Diamond (O'nA \cdot O'n \sim A)$

and

$O'nA \rightarrow \Diamond A$

will all be rules of logic.

Combining doxastic and deontic logic will enable us to distinguish between objective and subjective obligations. If *n* is actually obliged to bring it about that A is true, we will write OnA or $O'nA$, but if a person merely believes that he or she has an obligation, we would write $BnOnA$ or $BnO'nA$. It may very well be the case that praise and blame—our moral evaluation of the *person*—are based on subjective obligations, what a person sincerely believes he or she is obliged to do. But if, as we usually think, people can be mistaken about their obligations, then our evaluation of the *action* will depend on what the person was actually obliged to do. However, if someone wants to explore a completely subjective ethics, we could "collapse" objective obligation into subjective obligation by having the rules

$OnA \equiv BnOnA$

$PnA \equiv BnPnA$

What has been given so far is what might be called the "standard" system of deontic logic. It does not, of course, contain the rules

$OnA \rightarrow A$ or $A \rightarrow PnA$

since we often do not do things we are obliged to, and do things we are not permitted to. But even the rules it does contain may be too strong. Several paradoxical consequences can be derived from the standard system. If someone tells us that we are permitted to mail a certain letter, it certainly seems odd to be able to reach the conclusion that we are permitted to mail it or burn it.

L # n mails the letter, and

B # n burns the letter

we can argue as follows:

1. PnL Premise
2. $PnL \lor PnB$ 1 Addition
3. $Pn(L \lor B)$ 2 DOD

This is known as Ross's Paradox (from Alf Ross, a Scandinavian economist and philosopher who first discovered it).

One way of avoiding Ross's Paradox and other odd consequences of the standard system is to weaken the DOD rules* to

$(OnA \cdot OnB) \rightarrow On(A \cdot B)$

$Pn(A \lor B) \rightarrow (PnA \lor PnB)$

* See R. L. Purtill, "Paradox Free Deontic Logics," *Notre Dame Journal of Formal Logic* Volume XVI, No. 4, October 1975.

However, some philosophers do not agree with this way of avoiding Ross's Paradox or do not agree that the "paradox" is truly paradoxical*. As in most areas we discuss in this chapter, controversy continues and there is no consensus as to a solution.

Exercise 10-1

Prove the following statements using as premises any of the rules of S1, S2, and S3 systems of modal statement logic.

1. $((A \rightarrow B) \cdot \Diamond(A \cdot C)) \rightarrow (\Diamond B \cdot \Diamond C)$
2. $((A \rightarrow B) \cdot \sim\Diamond(B \cdot C)) \rightarrow \sim\Diamond(A \cdot C)$
3. $((A \rightarrow C) \cdot (B \rightarrow D) \cdot \Diamond(A \cdot B)) \rightarrow (\Diamond C \cdot \Diamond D)$
*4. $((A \rightarrow C) \cdot (B \rightarrow D) \cdot \sim\Diamond(C \cdot D)) \rightarrow \sim\Diamond(A \cdot B)$
5. $\Box A \equiv ((B \rightarrow A) \cdot (\sim B \rightarrow A))$
6. $\sim\Diamond A \rightarrow (A \rightarrow B)$
7. $\sim(A \rightarrow B) \rightarrow \Diamond A$
8. $\sim(B \rightarrow A) \rightarrow \Diamond \sim A$
9. $(\sim\Diamond A \cdot \sim\Diamond B) \rightarrow \sim\Diamond(A \vee B)$
10. $(\sim\Diamond A \cdot \sim\Diamond B) \rightarrow (A \equiv B)$

Exercise 10-2

*1.	$\Diamond A \rightarrow \Diamond KnA$	ACP
*2.	$\Diamond(A \cdot \sim KnA) \rightarrow \Diamond Kn(A \cdot \sim KnA)$	1, Subst. $(A \cdot \sim KnA)/A$
**3.	$Kn(A \cdot \sim KnA)$	ACP
**4.	$KnA \cdot Kn \sim KnA$	3
**5.	KnA	4 Simp.
**6.	$Kn \sim KnA$	4 Simp.
**7.	$\sim KnA$	6
**8.	$KnA \cdot \sim KnA$	5, 7 Conj.
*9.	$\sim\Diamond Kn(A \cdot \sim KnA)$	3–8
*10.	$\sim\Diamond(A \cdot \sim KnA)$	2, 9
*11.	$A \rightarrow KnA$	10
12.	$(\Diamond A \rightarrow \Diamond KnA) \rightarrow (A \rightarrow KnA)$	1–11

1.   Justify each line of the proof that is not justified. Supply missing steps if necessary.

---

* See the articles in *Deontic Logic*, edited by Risto Hilpinin (Boston: D. Reidel Publishing Company, 1973).

2. Does a parallel proof hold with *Bnp* or *Onp* replacing *Knp?* Why or why not?

3. Does a parallel proof hold with *Onp* replacing *KnP?* Why or why not?

*4. Translate the premise into English and comment on what it says.

5. Translate the conclusion into English and comment on what it shows.

Exercise 10-3

The following groups of statements are epistemic, doxastic, and deontic parallels to theorems of modal logic. For each statement:

A. If it can be proved in the relevant system, give a proof.

B. If you think it cannot be proved, say why you think so.

C. State whether or not the statement seems plausible when applied to examples in English.

1. $(Kn(A \supset B) \cdot Kn(A \cdot C)) \rightarrow Kn(B \cdot C)$

2. $((Kn(A \supset B) \cdot Kn(C \supset D)) \cdot Fn(A \cdot C)) \rightarrow Fn(B \cdot D)$

3. $KnA \equiv (Kn(B \supset A) \cdot Kn(\sim B \supset A))$

*4. $(Kn \sim A \cdot Kn \sim B) \rightarrow Kn \sim (A \vee B)$

5. $(Kn \sim A \cdot Kn \sim B) \rightarrow Kn(A \equiv B)$

6. $(Bn(A \supset B) \cdot Bn(A \cdot C)) \rightarrow Bn(B \cdot C)$

7. $((Bn(A \supset B) \cdot Bn(C \supset D)) \cdot Dn(A \cdot C)) \rightarrow Dn(B \cdot D)$

8. $BnA \equiv (Bn(B \supset A) \cdot Bn(\sim B \supset A))$

9. $(Bn \sim A \cdot Bn \sim B) \rightarrow Bn \sim (A \vee B)$

10. $(Bn \sim A \cdot Bn \sim B) \rightarrow Bn(A \equiv B)$

11. $(On(A \supset B) \cdot On(A \cdot C)) \rightarrow On(B \cdot C)$

12. $((On(A \supset B \cdot On(C \supset D)) \cdot Pn(A \cdot C)) \rightarrow Pn(B \cdot D)$

13. $OnA \equiv (On(B \supset A) \cdot On(\sim B \supset A))$

14. $(On \sim A \cdot On \sim B) \rightarrow On \sim (A \vee B)$

15. $(On \sim A \cdot On \sim B) \rightarrow On(A \equiv B)$

Tense Logic

Yet another system with some links to modal logic is tense logic, the logic of time. As we saw earlier, one weak interpretation of necessity is truth at all times, and in some problems about determinism a question arises as to whether some statements about the future do or do not at present have a truth value. We now need to explore this problem in more depth. Some philosophers have claimed that to talk of a statement being true at a time is a confusion between sentences and statements. A *sentence* such as "The President of the United States is from Georgia" can be used to make a true statement in 1978, but could not have been used to make a true statement in 1968. But the *statement* "The President of the United States is from Georgia" as actually uttered in 1978, is equivalent to the dated statement "The President of the United States in 1978 is a Georgian." Such statements properly spelled out do not change their truth value.

This view often goes along with the view that statements if they are true at all are always true. On this view, if someone in 1968 had said, "The President of the United States in 1978 will be a Georgian," this statement would have *been* true then, even though perhaps it could not have been *known* to be true.

However, some philosophers disagree with both views just given. They argue that a statement such as "The President of the United States on July 4, 1978, is a Georgian" *becomes* true on July 4, 1978, and before that was not true. If someone had said in 1968 that the President of the United States in 1978 would be a Georgian, his prediction would have "*come* true," as we say—that is, *become* true at the appropriate time. But it would not have *been* true when uttered in 1968, and neither would its denial have been true. In many ways, this view, which when spelled out involves a probabilistic, many-valued logic, is more interesting for logical purposes than the view that statements if true at all are always true.

There are several different systems of tense logic; some approaches are very close to modal logic, while others are quite different. We will consider a simple system with considerable similarity to modal logic. In this system, being true at some time in the past will play a role somewhat similar to necessity, and being true in the future will play a role somewhat similar to possibility. Being true now will play the role that in earlier systems was played by just being true. We will also want to indicate a number of time units in the past or future at which the statement in question is true. So our basic expressions will be:

PkA # A was true k time units ago

FkA # A will be true in k time units

Using the lower-case o as a zero, we will express "A is true now" as PoA. We will sometimes want to use universal or existential quantifiers over time units; in fact, we define a sense of possibility and necessity in this way. Chronological necessity can be defined as:

$$\Box^c A = \text{def. } (k)(PkA \cdot FkA)$$

and chronological possibility as:

$$\Diamond^c A = \text{def. } (\exists k)(PkA \lor FkA)$$

Of course, the usual rules for possibility and necessity will hold for $\Box^c A$ and $\Diamond^c A$, but also some parallels will hold for Pkp and Fkp. Thus it will hold true that

$$PkA \to PoA$$

That is, if something was true in the past, it is true now. Also, it will be true that

$$PoA \to FkA$$

That is, if something is true now, it will be true in the future. These statements do not mean, of course, that, for example, "George Washington *is* President" is true now, or that "Jimmy Carter *is* President" will be true in 1999. But the dated statement "George Washington was President in 1778" is true at all times since 1778 and so is true now, and the dated statement "Jimmy Carter is President in 1978" is true now and so will be true at all future times.

The parallels to the Modal Operator Exchange rules

$$PkA \equiv \sim Fk \sim A$$

and

$$FkA \equiv \sim Pk \sim A$$

do not, of course, hold, although

$$PkA \to \sim Fk \sim A$$

is a rule because if something is true in the past it will be true, and so not false, in the future:

$$PkA \rightarrow FkA$$

follows from our first two rules.

Again, parallels to the Modal Operator Exchange rules will hold:

$$Pk(A \cdot B) \equiv (PkA \cdot PkB)$$
$$Fk(A \vee B) \equiv (FkA \vee FkB)$$
$$(PkA \vee PkB) \rightarrow Pk(A \vee B)$$
$$Fk(A \cdot B) \rightarrow (Fka \cdot FkB)$$

But there seems no reason why the last two rules should not be equivalences rather than implications:

$$(PkA \vee PkB) \equiv Pk(A \vee B)$$
$$Fk(A \cdot B) \equiv (FkA \cdot FkB)$$

For if, for example, it was true 200 years ago that George Washington was President in 1778, or it was true 200 years ago that Sam Adams was President in 1778, this seems equivalent to "It was true 200 years ago that either George Washington or Sam Adams was President."

Some parallels to Strict Implication of Operators will hold; certainly

$$Pk(A \supset B) \rightarrow Pk(PkA \supset PkB)$$

and

$$Pk(A \supset B) \rightarrow Pk(\sim PkB \supset \sim PkA)$$

The two other parallels

$$Pk(A \supset B) \rightarrow Pk(FkA \supset FkB)$$

and

$$Pk(A \supset B) \rightarrow Pk(\sim FkB \supset \sim FkA)$$

will hold if $A \supset B$ is the kind of statement such that if it was true in the past, it will continue to be true in the future. Even if we assert that many statements true in the future were not true in the past (e.g., "Jimmy Carter will die in Plains, Georgia" may be neither true nor false now or in 1778), still *some* statements about the future were true in the past—at least, logical truths, ontological truths, etc.

The parallels to the Strong Reduction Principles

$$PkA \equiv Fk \; PkA$$
$$FkA \equiv Pk \; FkA$$

would create a problem. We may want to deny the second one especially, since it seems to say that if something is true in the future, it was true in the past that it would be true in the future; we have seen the difficulties this creates.

Thus the parallels to modal logic with *PnA* and *FnA* give us an S4-like quasi-modal system—*quasi*-modal because the exchange rules do not hold. We also need some additional rules that have no modal parallels, such as a rule for adding temporal units:

$$FkFjA \equiv F(k+j)A$$
$$PkPjA \equiv P(k+j)A$$

For example, if it will be true in 5 years that it will be true in 10 more years that A, then it will be true in 15 years that A, and vice versa (and similarly with past times).

Another quite "unmodal" rule is:

$$Fk \sim A \rightarrow \; \sim FkA$$

That is to say, A will be false in k time units implies that it is not true that A will be true in k time units. However, if some statements are now neither true *nor* false, $\sim FkA \rightarrow Fk \sim A$ will *not* be a rule: $\sim FkA$ may mean that A will be neither true or false in k time units. Of course, in modal logic $\sim \Diamond A \equiv \Diamond \sim A$ is *not* a rule.

Another nonmodal rule is:

$$Fk(A \supset B) \rightarrow (FkA \supset FkB)$$

That is, if it will be true in n time units that if A is true, B is then true if A is true in k time units, B will also be true in k time units. The modal parallel

$\Diamond (A \supset B) \rightarrow (\Diamond A \supset \Diamond B)$ is *not* a rule of modal logic.

Modal Predicate Logic

So far we have been considering only statement logic versions of most of our logical systems. When we mix quantifiers with some of the operators we have considered, the results can be interesting but they are complex and controversial. To give some idea of the complexities, let us consider modal predicate logic. Statements such as:

$\Box (x)(Fx)$
$\Box (\exists x)(Fx)$
$\Diamond (x)(Fx)$
$\Diamond (\exists x)(Fx)$

create no special problems; they are just special cases of

$\Box A$

and

$\Diamond A$

But when modal operators are *inside* the scope of quantifiers, as in, for example:

$(x)\Box (Fx \supset Gx)$
$(x)(Fx \supset \Diamond Gx)$
$(\exists x)\Box (Fx)$
$(\exists x)(Fx \cdot \Diamond Gx)$ etc.

we have both new problems and new possibilities.

The possibilities include expressing and clarifying statements and also analyzing arguments. For example, the statement "Any being with free will may possibly choose evil," where

Fx # x is a being with free will
Ex # x chooses evil

seems to be best expressed as:

$(x)(Fx \supset \Diamond Ex)$

This is not equivalent to:

$\Diamond(x)(Fx \supset Ex)$

or to any expression with the possibility operator outside the quantifier. But it is a statement we may very well want to use in a philosophical argument.

The distinction between statements with modal operators that are outside the scope of a quantifier may correspond partly to a distinction between what are called *de dicto* modality and *de re* modalities. A *de dicto* modality is a "possibly" or "necessarily" which applies to a *statement*, as "It is possible that we will run out of energy" or "It is necessarily true that nine is greater than seven." But *de re* modalities, it is said, apply to *things* rather than statements (in Latin *de re* means roughly "of a thing" and *de dicto* means roughly "of something said"). The idea of a necessity or possibility that applies to a thing rather than a statement is a puzzling one, and some have denied that it is an intelligible idea. However, it does seem to make sense to talk of properties I *do* have (e.g., having a beard), properties I *might* have had (e.g., being cleanshaven), and properties I *must* have if I am to exist at all (e.g., being human). Agreeably, if *I* exist it must be as a human being—a dog or a log could not be *me*.

When we come to write statements such as "*P*urtill is possibly *c*leanshaven" or "*P*urtill is necessarily *h*uman," there seems at first no distinction between *de re* and *de dicto*. We could treat

$\Diamond Cp$ and $\Box Hp$

as *de dicto* modalities, but if we have statements such as

$Hp \cdot \Diamond Cp$ or $\sim Cp \cdot \Box Hp$

and existentially generalize these statements, we arrive at statements such as

$(\exists y)(Hx \cdot \Diamond Cx)$ or $(\exists y)(\sim Cx \cdot \Box Hx)$

where the modal operators are inside the scope of the quantifiers. So one possible view is that the *de dicto*/*de re* distinction is one which only comes into play when quantifiers are used, and is adequately represented by the distinction of statements in which modal operators do not occur within the scope of quantifiers and statements in which they do.

Another possible view, however, would make the distinction between *de re* and *de dicto* a distinction between whether the modality is attached to the statement or to the predicate. We have no standard notation for attaching a modality to a predicate, but we might introduce the convention:

$$Hx \quad \# \quad x \text{ is human} \qquad H^{\square}x \quad \# \quad \text{is necessarily human}$$

Given this notation we could distinguish between $\square Hp$ which would be *de dicto* on this view and $H^{\square}p$ which would be *de re*. This would partly correspond with our previous distinction: In quantified statements the "modalized" predicates would be within the scope of quantifiers.

Critics of this second view would ask what a statement like $H^{\square}p$ would mean if it did not mean $\square Hp$, and challenge supporters of this view to produce alleged *de re* statements that could not be paraphrased into *de dicto* statements. If we stick to the first way of distinguishing *de re* from *de dicto*, we can show that some *de re* statements—i.e., statements with the modal operators inside the scope of quantifiers—cannot be reduced to any *de dicto* statement—i.e., any statement with modal operators only outside the scope of quantifiers. (This assumes we have rules like those given above; but the reasonableness of this rule can be argued independently of the *de re/de dicto* controversy.)

Modal syllogisms, which were first discussed by Aristotle, are one example of arguments that can be clarified by quantified modal logic. Suppose I have premises of the form

$$\square (x)(Fx \supset Gx)$$
$$\square (x)(Gx \supset Hx)$$

Am I entitled to conclude

$$\square (x)(Fx \supset Hx)?$$

Or if I have

$$\square (x)(Fx \supset Gx) \qquad \Diamond (x)(Fx \supset Gx)$$

or

$$(x)(Gx \supset Hx) \qquad \Diamond (x)(Gx \supset Gx)$$

what am I entitled to conclude? Aristotle did his best with such problems, but most of the solutions to the problems given by Aristotle and his three immediate successors are confused and inconsistent.

However, if we add some modal operator-quantifier exchange rules to predicate logic, we can give satisfactory solutions to the problems raised by Aristotle and show what confusions can or cannot be drawn from syllogistic premises involving modal operators. The rules we need are:

Quantifier Modal Exchange (QME)1 $(\forall x)\Box(Fx) \equiv \Box(\forall x)(Fx)$
Quantifier Modal Exchange (QME)2 $\Diamond(\exists x)(Fx) \equiv (\exists x)\Diamond(Fx)$
Quantifier Modal Exchange (QME)3 $\Diamond(\forall x)(Fx) \to (\forall x)\Diamond(Fx)$
Quantifier Modal Exchange (QME)4 $(\exists x)\Box(Fx) \to \Box(\exists x)(Fx)$

These rules have been the subject of much controversy but, together with the rules of propositional modal logic, they enable us to solve Aristotle's problems.

We will leave most of the filling in of this statement for one of the exercises at the end of this chapter, but we will give one example of how these techniques can be applied. Aristotle held that a statement of the form "Necessarily No F is G" is equivalent to its converse "Necessarily No G is F." This is fine if we interpret "Necessarily No F is G" as

$$\Box(x)(Fx \supset \sim Gx)$$

and "Necessarily No G is F" as

$$\Box(x)(Gx \supset \sim Fx)$$

because the expressions inside the modal operator are logically equivalent, and we can replace logical equivalents with each other inside a modal operator.

But Aristotle also thought that a syllogism of the form

Necessarily No G is H
Every F is G
_____
Necessarily No F is H

was valid. If we symbolize it as

$$\Box(x)(Gx \supset \sim Hx)$$
$$(x)(Fx \supset Gx)$$
_____
$$\Box(x)(Fx \supset \sim Hx)$$

then Aristotle is wrong; the argument is invalid. If we symbolize it as

$$(x)(Gx \supset \square \sim Hx)$$
$$(x)(Fx \supset Gx)$$
$$\overline{(x)(Fx \supset \square \sim Hx)}$$

the argument can be shown to be valid, but this formulation of the *No* statement is inconsistent with what Aristotle says about conversion of statements of the form "Necessarily No *F* is *G*," for

$$(x)(Gx \supset \square \sim Hx)$$

is not equivalent to

$$(x)(Hx \supset \square \sim Gx)$$

So Aristotle must be wrong in one of the two views he holds—either his view about conversion or his view about syllogisms with one necessary premise.

Difficulties in Quantified Modal Logic

Some of the difficulties in quantified modal logic involve instantiation within the scope of modal operators. For example:

Let Tx # x is equal to 12

$\qquad Gx$ # x is less than 13

$\qquad a$ # the number of Apostles

If there were no restrictions or instantiating in the scope of modal operators, we could argue as follows:

1. $(x)(Tx \supset \square Gx)$ $\Big\}$ $\square Ga$?
2. Ta
3. $Ta \supset \square Ga$ 1 UI
4. $\square Ga$ 3, 2 MP

The premises seem plausible, but the conclusion seems implausible; surely Christ could have selected 14 Apostle if he chose.

To solve problems of this kind we need restrictions on instantiation to proper names in the scope of a necessity operator. No examples have so far been invented to show that we need restrictions on instantiation in the scope of possibility operators or restrictions on instantiation to quasi-names, but it might turn out that we do need such restrictions.

All of the known problem cases can be solved by two restrictions. One on UI forbids going from $\Box(x)(Fx)$ to $\Box Fa$ unless we know independently that $\Box Fa \lor \Box \sim Fa$. The other restriction involves identity: If $\Box Fa$ and $a = b$, we cannot use identity to get $\Box Fb$ unless we know that $\Box(a = b)$. A full discussion of these problems and possible solutions to them is outside the scope of this book, but it is worth noting that some very competent logicians have serious reservations about quantified modal logic.

All of the systems we have considered have some philosophical interest in themselves, and both modal logic and epistemic logic have proved useful in helping to solve some philosophical problems. The other systems we have looked at briefly may very well prove to have important philosophical applications, but so far most of the interest has been focused on building workable systems, and few important applications of doxastic logic, deontic logic, or tense logic have been found to date. But we can learn a great deal from the attempt, even the unsuccessful attempt, to make a logical system using such concepts as belief, obligation, and time.

Chapter Summary

We began by looking at *propositional modal logic:* We found any modal logic is characterized by having the following rules:

Modal Operator Exchange (MOE)
$\Box A \equiv \sim \Diamond \sim A$
$\Diamond A \equiv \sim \Box \sim A$

Necesse ad Esse (NE)
$\Box A \to A$

Esse ad Posse (EP)
$A \to \Diamond A$

Stronger systems are characterized by having further rules.

Modal Operator Distribution (MOD):

$$\Box(A \cdot B) \equiv (\Box A \cdot \Box B)$$
$$\Diamond(A \lor B) \equiv (\Diamond A \lor \Diamond B)$$
$$(\Box A \lor \Box B) \rightarrow \Box(A \lor B)$$
$$\Diamond(A \cdot B) \rightarrow (\Diamond A \cdot \Diamond B)$$

gives us S2. Strict Implication of Operators (SIO):

$$(A \rightarrow B) \rightarrow (\Box A \rightarrow \Box B)$$
$$(A \rightarrow B) \rightarrow (\Diamond A \rightarrow \Diamond B)$$

etc., gives us S3. The Weak Reduction Principles (WRP):

$$\Box A \equiv \Box\Box A$$
$$\Diamond A \equiv \Diamond\Diamond A$$

give us S4. And the Strong Reduction Principles (SRP):

$$\Box A \equiv \Diamond\Box A$$
$$\Diamond A \equiv \Box\Diamond A$$

give us S5.

We then looked at a *para-modal logic*, *epistemic logic*, which has exact parallels to modal logic rules with *KnA* substituted for $\Box A$, etc. For example:

$$KnA \rightarrow A$$
$$Kn(A \cdot B) \rightarrow (KnA \cdot KnB) \quad \text{etc.}$$

We then considered some *quasi-modal logics*, such as doxastic logic, deontic logic, and tense logic, which are similar to modal logic in some ways but lack parallels to some modal logic rules.

In considering these logical systems we looked at a number of philosophical arguments, such as the Ontological Argument and the Master Argument, which can be clarified by means of the logical systems we have been discussing. We noted that some of the more recently developed logical systems have no outstanding philosophical applications to date, but that the very formulation of these systems increases our understanding of certain problem areas.

Practical Applications

Look in your Argument File for arguments involving modality, knowledge, belief, obligation, or time. Keep an eye out for uses of key terms such as "possibly," "necessarily," "obligatory," "permissible," etc. See if you can state and check any arguments you find by using the techniques of this chapter. (Hint: Many discussions of such topics as Time, Free Will, God, etc., will contain interesting arguments that you now may be able to handle.)

Exercise 10-4

Each of the following passages involves in some way a principle of logic discussed in this chapter. Identify the principle and comment on the argument in light of the principle.

1.   Alice knew that her first name began with an "L."*

2.   "I know what you're thinking about," said Tweedledum, "but it isn't so, nohow."

"Contrariwise," continued Tweedledee, "if it was so it might be; and if it were so, it would be; but as it isn't, it ain't. That's logic"*

3.   "I can't believe *that!*" said Alice. "Can't you?" the Queen said in a pitying tone. "Try again: draw a long breath, and shut your eyes."

Alice laughed. "There's no use trying," she said, "one *can't* believe impossible things."

"I daresay you haven't had much practice," said the Queen. "When I was your age, I always did it for half an hour a day. Why sometimes I've believed as many as six impossible things before breakfast."*

*4.   "Seithenyn," said Taliesin, "has slept twenty years under the waters of the western sea, as King Gwythno's Lamentations have made known to all Britain."

"They have not made it known to me," said Seithenyn, "for the best of all reasons that one can only know the truth; for, if that which we think we know is not truth, it is something which we do not know. A man cannot know his own death; for, while he knows anything, he is alive;

* Lewis Carroll, *Alice in Wonderland.*

at least, I never heard of a dead man who knew anything, or pretended to know anything: if he had so pretended, I should have told him to his face he was no dead man."*

5. "Your mode of reasoning," said Taliesin, "unquestionably corresponds with what I have heard of Seithenyn's: but how is it possible Seithenyn can be living?"

"Every thing that is, is possible, says Catog the Wise," answered Seithenyn, with a look of great sapience. "I will give you proof that I am not a dead man; for, they say, dead men tell no tales: now I will tell you a tale, and a very interesting one it is."*

Exercise 10-5

The following statements have all been claimed to be true by some logicians. A. Translate them into our symbolism. B. Discuss whether they are provable in the systems discussed in this chapter. C. Discuss how plausible the statement is in terms of examples.

1. If A is factually true, it is possible that it is factually false.
2. If A logically implies B, then if you know A, you know B.
3. If A is logically necessary, it is obligatory.
*4. If A is permissible, it is logically possible.
5. If n believes he or she is obliged to do A, then n *is* obliged to do A.
6. If A is ever true, then it is always true.
7. "It is true that either A or not-A" is the same as "Either A is true or A is not true", so since "Either A or not-A" is always true, it is always true that A or always true that not-A.
8. "There is something that may be on fire" is not the same as "It may be that there is something on fire."
9. What neither is true nor will be true is impossible.
10. Something that neither is true nor will be true is still possible.

Exercise 10-6

Aristotle makes the following claims about modal syllogisms.

In a valid categorical syllogism:
If both premises are necessary, the conclusion is necessary.
If both premises are possible, the conclusion is possible.

* Thomas Love Peacock, *Adventures of Elphin.*

If the major premise is necessary, the conclusion is necessary (if the minor premise is factual).

If the major premise is possible, the conclusion is possible (if the minor premise is factual).

Some of these claims are true, some false.

1. For the true claims, give a proof that they are true.
2. For the false claims, show in some way that they are false.
3. Theophrastus modified Aristotle's view and said that the conclusion must be as weak as the weakest premise. Is this correct? Show that it is or is not for the case Necessary Premise—Factual Premise.
*4. Do the same for the case Factual Premise—Possible Premise.
5. Do the same for the case Necessary Premise—Possible Premise.

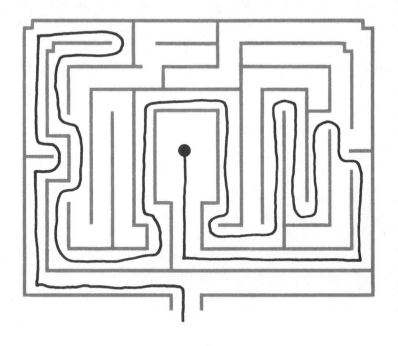

APPENDIX A

Answers to
Selected Exercises

Chapter One

Exercise 1-1

NUMBER 2:

The premises are, "If eating the cake makes Alice grow larger she can reach the key, and if eating the cake makes Alice grow smaller she can creep under the door. If she can reach the key or crawl under the door she will get into the garden."

The conclusion is, "Alice will get into the garden." The conclusion does not follow from the premises unless we add the premise, "Eating the cake will make Alice grow larger or eating the cake will make Alice grow smaller." But this premise is questionable.

NUMBER 8:

There are several arguments here. One is (Premises) "If Rule Forty-two were the oldest rule in the book, it would be Number One. It is not Number One." (Conclusion) "It is not the oldest rule in the book." This argument is valid, but might not be sound: If Rules One to Forty-one were old rules that had been removed from the book, Rule Forty-two might be the oldest rule *left* in the book. This argument is a reply to part of a larger argument: (Premises) "If there is a rule in effect that all people more than a mile high must leave the court, then if Alice is more than a mile high she must leave the court. Alice is more than a mile high." (Conclusion) "Alice must leave the court." Alice attacks both premises of the argument: She denies that she is a mile high and questions whether Rule Forty-two is a legitimate rule (by the argument we just discussed).

Exercise 1-2

NUMBER 4:

The stated purposes of the passage can be found in the first paragraph: to welcome new students and to introduce them to the school. An unstated purpose seems to be to urge students to behave in certain ways. Whether these purposes were adequately served by the passage would involve some knowledge of the students to whom it was addressed. You might ask yourself if you would regard it as an adequate welcome and introduction, and whether you would be inclined to act as recommended.

Exercise 1-3

NUMBER 2:

Primary use: command.
Secondary use: inform.

Exercise 1-4

NUMBER 3 (partial answer):

Most of these arguments seem to be inductive because at best they would give a high probability to their conclusion. For each argument you might try to show that even if the premises were true, the conclusion might be either true or false. You could do this by giving a conclusion different from that given which could be true or false even if the premises were true.

Exercise 1-5

NUMBER 5:

If the barber is a male who is clean-shaven then the claim could not be true, since if the barber shaved himself it would falsify his claim not to shave anyone who shaved himself, and if anyone else shaved him it would falsify his claim to shave everyone who didn't shave himself. But the barber could be female, a bearded male, etc. If the puzzle rules out these possibilities it becomes a paradox—in fact, a version of one of the paradoxes discussed in the section on Logical Paradoxes.

Exercise 1-6

NUMBER 3:

It depends on whether the agreement takes precedence or the court decision takes precedence. Presuming the court has jurisdiction over such a private agreement, it seems reasonable to say that the decision of the court takes precedence over the previous agreement, since Protagoras has sued Euathlus and Euathlus does not dispute the jurisdiction of the court. So, whatever the court decides should be done, without regard to the previous agreement. However, this does not tell the court how to decide. If you were judge, what would your decision be. Why?

Exercise 1-7

NUMBER 2:

(Premises) "Past experience has shown that creation of a pathogenic bacterium requires a large number of factors not present in laboratory strains (namely, ability to survive, cause disease, be transmittable). It is unlikely that adding a small piece of foreign DNA will add these factors." (Understood Premises) "The research will involve adding a small piece of foreign DNA. The proposed laboratory is safe and should be built if creation of a pathogenic bacterium is unlikely." (Conclusion from first three premises) "Creation of a pathogenic bacterium is unlikely." (Conclusion from all premises) "The proposed laboratory is safe and should be built." Comments: The argument is fairly convincing, supposing that the premises are true.

The argument from the first three premises to the first conclusion is inductive and has the general form, "B will not happen unless A does: A is unlikely to happen so B is unlikely to happen." If the second understood premise is true, the second conclusion would follow deductively from it and the first conclusion.

NUMBER 8:

(Premises) "People who believe that something is not dangerous are not to be trusted to protect others from it. The committee in question would be composed of people who do not believe that this research is dangerous." (Conclusion) "The committee in question is not be trusted to protect others from the dangers of this research." Comments: The argument is valid but the premises are arguable. Proponents of the research would claim that their belief in the safety of the research is founded on evidence and does not disqualify them as protectors, since the belief would change if evidence of danger came to light. The real argument is probably over the question of whether their belief in the safety of the research is reasonable and well founded. This critic's argument seems to assume that it is not.

Exercise 1-8

NUMBER 3 (partial answer):

The passage as a whole is an argument for the conclusion that a wise person will study logic. It contains a number of subarguments: Depending on how these are broken down, you could find as many as six or as few as two or three. For instance, the second, third, and fourth paragraphs all have to do with the consequences of premises or hypotheses we have granted for the sake of argument. We could distinguish several separate arguments or regard them all as part of one argument. Giving a number is not what is important in this answer: What is needed is to point out premises and conclusions.

Chapter Two

Exercise 2-1

NUMBER 2:

Fallacy of Assumed Premise. Assumes you want a *Bleep* car or truck, or at least want some characteristics in a car or truck which *Bleep* cars or trucks have.

NUMBER 10:

Fallacy of Association. The advertiser hopes that you have a favorable attitude toward luxury (and perhaps to the "naturalness" of leather) and that this will carry over into a favorable attitude toward *Bleep* airline.

Exercise 2-2

NUMBER 4:

Which products are most advertised will depend to some extent on the magazine and on other factors such as the season. In magazines like *Time* and *Newsweek*, you will probably find that cigarettes, liquor, and new automobiles are the most frequently advertised items. These products are alike in being luxuries (we can survive very well without smoking, drinking liquor, or having the latest model car). They are also alike in being products in which there is a great deal of competition but not a great deal of real difference among the most popular brands.

Exercise 2-4

NUMBER 2:

The writer of the article seems to think that Darwin's theory is based mainly on the observation of many similarities between human beings and animals. The writer offers an alternate explanation of these similarities in terms of Shaftsbury's theory, but no reason is given for preferring Shaftsbury's theory to Darwin's. This is a version of the kind of weak argument discussed under Ad Hoc Hypotheses. If you have studied Darwin's theory, you will be able to give a better answer to this question; but even if you know very little of either Darwin's theory or Shaftsbury's, you can see that all the author is doing is proposing an alternate hypothesis without giving reasons to prefer that hypothesis.

Exercise 2-5

NUMBER 2:

This actually involves an invalid deductive argument: The speaker seems to be giving the invalid argument himself, but may be accusing his opponents of giving it. From "If such facilities are built, the research is dangerous" it does not follow that "If such facilities are not built, the research is not dangerous," any more than from "If my pet is a dog, it eats meat" it follows that "If my pet is not a dog, it does not eat meat" (my pet could be a cat, which eats meat).

NUMBER 10:

The argument is explicitly identified as an analogy argument: whether it is a good one depends on how similar the cases are in relevant respects. There is probably some danger of a Beyond the Point fallacy here, assuming rather than arguing that the DNA research *is* dangerous. (The mixed metaphor "pulling the fog over the eyes" is what the speaker really said.)

Exercise 2-6

NUMBER 4:

This statement involves an argument from authority: We could ask the usual questions about "Mr. Hume's" identity and qualifications. Hume's argument seems to involve a fallacy of circumstances: Because lower class whites could rise socially did not mean that a black person of comparable talents could do so in the face of racial prejudice. In fact, as Kant and Hume should have known, some black persons who were given opportunities did show "superior gifts" and earned respect from those not hopelessly prejudiced. A good contemporary example was Dr. Samuel Johnson's black friend and servant, Frank Barber.

Chapter Three

Exercise 3-1

NUMBER 2:

1. $B \lor \sim F$ ⎫
2. F ⎬ B?
3. B 1, 2 SC

NUMBER 8:

1. $\sim P \lor J$ ⎫
2. $\sim J \lor G$ ⎭ $\sim \sim G \lor \sim P$?
3. $\sim P \lor G$ 1, 2 CC
4. $G \lor \sim P$ 3 Com.
5. $\sim \sim G \lor \sim P$ 4 DN

Exercise 3-2

NUMBER 2:

1. $K \lor C$ ⎫
2. $\sim C \lor S$ ⎬ $\sim S$
3. $\sim K$ ⎭
4. C 1, 2 SC
5. S 2, 4 SC
The conclusion is refuted.

Exercise 3-3

NUMBER 2:

1. $\sim L \lor G$	L #	Alice grows larger
2. $\sim S \lor G$?	S #	Alice grows smaller
3. $\sim E \lor L \lor S$	G #	Alice gets into the garden

4. $\sim E \vee L \vee G$ 2, 3 CC
5. $\sim E \vee G \vee G$ 4, 1 CC
6. $\sim E \vee G$ 5 Rep.

E # Alice eats the cake

NUMBER 8:

$\left. \begin{array}{l} \sim R \vee \sim M \vee L \\ \sim R \vee N \end{array} \right\} \sim L$

R # Rule 42 is the oldest
M # Alice is a mile high
L # Alice must leave the court
N # Rule 42 would be Number One

Does not cancel to conclusion.

Exercise 3-4

NUMBER 2:

1. $\left. \begin{array}{l} \sim E \vee \sim M \vee S \\ \end{array} \right.$
2. $\left. \sim \sim M \vee I \quad \right\} I?$
3. $\sim V \vee \sim M$

E # The Universe is expanding
M # There is more matter than M
S # The expansion will stop
I # The Universe will expand infinitely
V # The matter in the Universe is all visible

Does not cancel to conclusion.

Exercise 3-5

NUMBER 2:

$\left. \begin{array}{l} \sim W \vee \sim P \vee R \\ \sim E \vee R \end{array} \right\} \sim E \vee P$

W # Words are written in a vowels and syllables
P # They are pure vowels
R # They occur rarely inside words but often at beginnings
E # They are 8, 38, or 61.

Does not cancel to conclusion.

Exercise 3-6

NUMBER 2:

1. $\left. \begin{array}{l} \sim B \vee V \\ \end{array} \right.$
2. $\left. B \qquad \right\} ?$
3. V 1, 2 SC

B # We define *bee* by saying what bees have in common
V # We define *virtue* by saying what virtues have in common

NUMBER 7:

<table>
<tr><td>1.</td><td>$\sim W \vee A$</td><td rowspan="4">} ?</td><td></td></tr>
<tr><td>2.</td><td>$\sim N \vee \sim A$</td><td></td></tr>
<tr><td>3.</td><td>$\sim N$</td><td></td></tr>
<tr><td>4.</td><td>$\sim N \vee \sim W$</td><td>1, 2 CC</td></tr>
</table>

W	#	Virtue is wisdom
A	#	Virtue must be acquired
N	#	Virtue comes by nature

Chapter Four

Exercise 4-1

NUMBER 4:

$$(((E \supset S) \cdot (L \supset D)) \cdot L) \supset S$$

$p\ q\ r$	$(((p \supset q) \cdot (r \supset p)) \cdot r) \supset q$			
T T T	T T T T T T T T T T			
T T F	T T T T F T T F F T T			
T F T	T F F F T T T F T T F			
T F F	T F F F F T T F F T F			
F T T	F T T F T F F F T T T			
F T F	F T T T F T F T F T T			
F F T	F T F F T F F T T T F			
F F F	F T F T F T F F F T F			

VALID

NUMBER 7:

$$((M \equiv E) \cdot \sim M) \supset \sim E$$

$p\ q$	$((p \equiv q) \cdot \sim p) \supset \sim q$		
T T	T T T F F T T F T		
T F	T F F F F T T T F		
F T	F F T F T F T F T		
F F	F T F T T F T T F		

VALID

Exercise 4-2

NUMBER 4:

$V \supset (O \supset \sim A)$

NUMBER 7:

$$((F \supset O) \cdot (\sim F \supset O)) \supset ((H \supset (V \supset \sim A)) \cdot (\sim H \supset (V \supset \sim A)))$$

or

$O \supset (V \supset \sim A)$ (see Table 4-1)

Exercise 4-3

NUMBER 1:

Statement 7 does follow from 4, by the following argument.

1. $V \supset (O \supset \sim A)$} $O \supset (V \supset \sim A)$
2. $(V \cdot O) \supset A$ 1 Exp.
3. $(O \cdot V) \supset \sim A$ 2 Com.
4. $O \supset (V \supset \sim A)$

Exercise 4-4

NUMBER 2:

   F T F
1. $A \equiv B$

   T FFF
2. $\sim(B \cdot C)$ F

   F T T FFF A?
3. $C \supset \sim(B \cdot A)$

   TF T F
4. $\sim A \vee C$ Invalid as proof; try a refutation.

NUMBER 8:

1. B } $A \supset B$?
2. $B \vee \sim A$ 1 Add.
3. $\sim A \vee B$ 2 Com.
4. $A \supset B$ 3 DMI

Exercise 4-5

NUMBER 2:

1. $(A \cdot B) \supset C$} $A \supset C$?
2. B
*3. A ACP
*4. $A \cdot B$ 3, 2 Conj.
*5. C 4, 1 MP
6. $A \supset C$ 3–5 RCP

NUMBER 8:

1. $F \supset (M \cdot \sim U)$
2. $C \supset (P \supset F)$ } $P \cdot \sim M$?
3. C

   4. $P \supset F$ 3, 2 MP
  *5. $P \cdot \sim M$ ACP
  *6. P 5 Simp.
  *7. F 6, 4 MP
  *8. $M \cdot \sim U$ 7, 1 MP
  *9. M 8 Simp.
 *10. $\sim M$ 5 Simp.
 *11. $M \cdot \sim M$ 9, 10 Conj.
 *12. $\sim(P \cdot \sim M)$ 11 Contr.
  13. $(P \cdot \sim M) \supset \sim(P \cdot \sim M)$ 5–12 RCP
  14. $\sim(P \cdot \sim M) \vee \sim(P \cdot \sim M)$ 13 DMI
  15. $\sim(P \cdot \sim M)$ 14 Rep.

Exercise 4-6

NUMBER 2:

1. $E \supset \sim R$ ⎫ E # Your arguments are effective
2. $\sim E \supset \sim A$ ⎬ $R \supset \sim A$ R # You rely on accepted rules
3. $\sim\sim R \supset \sim E$ 1 Transp. A # I need to answer your arguments
4. $R \supset \sim E$ 3 DN
5. $R \supset \sim A$ 4, 2 HS

NUMBER 8:

1. $E \supset \sim W$ ⎫ E # God exists
2. $(W \supset \sim E) \supset \sim A$ ⎬ ? W # Evil is what we would expect
3. $\sim\sim W \supset \sim E$ 1 Transp. A # There can be an argument from
4. $W \supset \sim E$ 3 DN   the world to God
5. $\sim A$ 4, 2 MP

Chapter Five

Exercise 5-1

NUMBER 4:

A. Some judge is a person who loses his or her temper.
B. Some person who loses his or her temper is a judge.
C. Some judge is not a person who does not lose his or her temper.
D. I.
E. No terms distributed.

Exercise 5-2

NUMBER 5:

A. Invalid. Breaks Rule 3: negative premise and positive conclusion.

B.

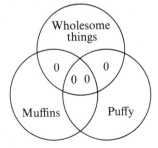

Invalid. Diagraming premises does not diagram conclusion.

Exercise 5-3

NUMBER 4:

A.   NC
B.   NP

NUMBER 8:

A.   NC
B.   Every good violinist is studious.

Exercise 5-4

NUMBER 4:

No boy under 12 is admitted as a boarder.
Every idle boy is under 12.
_____
No idle boy is admitted as a boarder.
Everyone who learns Greek is admitted as a boarder
_____
No idle boy is one who learns Greek.
Every red-haired boy is idle.
_____
No red-haired boy is one who learns Greek.

Exercise 5-5

NUMBER 4:

Every being with infinite power is infinite.
The First Being is a being with infinite power.
_____
The First Being is infinite.

Chapter Six

Exercise 6-1

NUMBER 4:

$\sim T(x) \lor \sim H(x)$ Invalid. Does not cancel to any conclusion.
$\sim H[x] \cdot F[x]$
_____
$T[x] \cdot F[x]$

NUMBER 10:

$\sim W(x) \lor F(x)$ Does not cancel to this conclusion,
$\sim \sim W(x) \lor H(x)$ but does cancel to $F(x) \lor H(x)$.
———————
$\sim F(x) \lor \sim H(x)$

Exercise 6-2

NUMBER 4:

$\sim F(x) \lor G(x)$ Cancels to "Oatmeal is good for food."
$\sim O(x) \lor F(x)$
———————
$\sim O(x) \lor G(x)$

Exercise 6-3

NUMBER 4:

1. $\sim \sim K(x) \lor \sim E(x)$
2. $\sim D(x) \lor \sim H(x)$
3. $\sim B(x) \lor T(x)$
4. $\sim K(x) \lor \sim S(x)$
5. $\sim \sim H(x) \lor \sim T(x)$
6. $\sim \sim B(x) \lor E(x)$
7. $\sim \sim K(x) \lor \sim \sim B(x)$ 1, 6 CC
8. $\sim \sim K(x) \lor T(x)$ 7, 3 CC
9. $T(x) \lor S(x)$ 9, 5 CC
10. $\sim \sim H(x) \lor \sim S(x)$ 8, 4 CC
11. $\sim D(x) \lor \sim S(x)$ 10, 2 CC
"No donkey is easy to swallow."

Exercise 6-4

NUMBER 4:

1. $\sim Q(x) \lor \sim D(x) \lor I(x)$ | Qx # x is a quasar
2. $\sim I(x) \lor S(x) \lor \sim C(x)$ | Dx # x is more distant than
3. $\sim Q(x) \lor \sim S(x)$ | any visible galaxy
4. $\sim Q(x) \lor \sim I(x) \lor \sim Cx$ 2, 3 CC | Ix # x is incredibly luminous
5. $\sim Q(x) \lor \sim Q(x) \lor$ 4, 1 CC | Sx # x is a supergalaxy
     $\sim D(x) \lor \sim C(x)$ | Cx # x is a complex of stars
6. $\sim Q(x) \lor \sim D(x) \lor \sim C(x)$ 5 Rep.
"If quasars are more distant than any
visible galaxy, then they are not complexes
of stars."

Exercise 6-5

NUMBER 4:

Px # x is a panel
Mx # x is designed to move
Cx # x is permanently closed
Rx # x is a palace room
Bx # x is used for burials
Ux # x is designed to move up and down
$\sim \sim M(x) \vee \sim P(x) \vee C(x)$
$\sim P(x) \vee \sim C(x) \vee \sim R(x) \vee B(x)$ $\}$ $\sim P(x) \vee \sim \sim U(x) \vee \sim R(x) \vee B(x)$

Does not cancel to indicate conclusion but does cancel to $\sim P(x) \vee \sim \sim M(x) \vee \sim R(x) \vee B(x)$. Would cancel to indicated conclusion only if $U(x)$ were the same as $M(x)$ or at least if $\sim M(x) \vee U(x)$ were true.

Exercise 6-6

NUMBER 4:

Sx # it is possible for x to sin
Jx # it is just to punish x
1. $\sim \sim S(x) \vee \sim J(x)$ $\}$ $\sim J(x)$
2. $\sim S(x)$
3. $\sim J(x)$ 1, 2 SC

Chapter 7

Exercise 7-1

NUMBER 4:

$(\forall x)(Qx \supset H(x)) \supset (\exists y)(Qy \cdot Cye)$
Qx # x is a quasar
Hx # x is hurled from an exploding galaxy
Cxy # x is coming toward y
e # Earth

Exercise 7-2

NUMBER 3:

1. $(\forall x)(Ox \equiv Px)$ $\}$?
2. $(\forall x)(Qx \supset Px)$
3. $O(x) \equiv P(x)$ 1 UIG
4. $Q(x) \supset P(x)$ 2 UIG

5. $(O(x) \supset P(x)) \cdot (P(x) \supset O(x))$ 3 DME
6. $P(x) \supset O(x)$ 5 Simp.
7. $Q(x) \supset O(x)$ 4, 6 HS
8. $(\forall x)(Qx \supset Ox)$ 7 UIG

Exercise 7-3

NUMBER 4:

One attempt might be $(\forall x)(\forall F)(\forall G)(((Dx \cdot (Fx \cdot G)) \supset (\forall y)(Fy \equiv Gy))$, which says that for any divine being and any two properties, if the divine being has both properties, then anything that had one would have the other. This sounds plausible for omnipotence and omniscience, for example. Another attempt might use the second order predicate $S^2 FG \# F$ is the same property as G:

$$(\forall x)(\forall F)(\forall G)(((Dx \cdot (Fx \cdot Gx))S^2(\exists y)(Fx(\exists z)(Gz)),$$

which says if a divine being has two properties, then they are the same z property. Even for omnipotence and omniscience, this is less plausible.

Exercise 7-4

NUMBER 4:

Sx # x is a science
Dxy # x depends on y
Px # x can predict
Gx # x is geology
Mx # x is meteorology
Ex # x is evolutionary theory

Two added premises are needed:
"Evolutionary theory depends on geology and meteorology" and "Evolutionary theory is a science."

1. $(\forall x)(\forall y)(((Sx \cdot Sy) \cdot Dxy) \supset (Py \supset Px))$
2. $(\exists(y)(Gy \cdot (Sy \cdot Py))$
3. $(\exists(y)(My \cdot (Sy \cdot Py))$ $(x)(Ex \supset Px)$
4. $(\forall x)(\forall y)(Ex \supset ((Gy \vee My)) \supset Dxy)\}$ [Added Premises]
5. $(\forall x)(Ex \supset Sx)$
6. $((S(x) \cdot S[y]) \cdot D(x)) \supset (P[y] \supset P[x]$ 1 UIG, UP
7. $G[y] \cdot (S[y] \cdot P[y])$ 2 UIG
8. $M[z] \cdot (S[z] \cdot P[z])$ 3 UIG
9. $(E(x) \supset (G[y] \vee M[y])) \supset D(x)[y]$ 4 UIG
*10. $E(x)$ ACP
*11. $(G[y] \vee M[y]) \supset D[x][y]$ 9, 10 MP

12.	$G[y]$	6 Simp.
13.	$G[y] \lor M[y]$	12 Add.
***14.**	$D[x][y]$	13, 11 MP
15.	$S[y] \cdot P[y]$	6 Simp.
16.	$E(x) \supset S(x)$	5 UI
***17.**	$S(x)$	10, 16 MP
***18.**	$(S(x) \cdot S[y]) \cdot D(x)[y]$	16, 17 Conj.
***19.**	$P[y] \supset P(x)$	18, 6 MP
20.	$P[y]$	15 Simp.
***21.**	$P(x)$	19, 20 MP
22.	$E(x) \supset P(x)$	10–21 RCP
23.	$(\forall x)(Ex \supset Px)$	22 UIG

Example 7-5

NUMBER 4:

$P(\iota x)(Hxm)\ T(\iota x)(Hxm)c$

Px	#	x is a philologist
Hxy	#	x helped y decipher Linear B
Txy	#	x teaches at y
m	#	Michael Ventris
c	#	Cambridge University

Example 7-6

NUMBER 6:

1.	$(\exists x)(Dxu) \supset (\exists y)(y = g)$	
2.	$\sim(\exists x)(Dxu) \supset \sim(\exists z)(Uz \cdot Bz)$	$(\exists y)(y = g)$
3.	$(\exists z)(Uz \cdot Bz)$	
4.	$\sim\sim(\exists x)(Dxu) \lor (\exists z)(Uz \cdot Bz)$	2 DMI
5.	$(\exists x)(Dxu)$	3, 4 SC, DN
6.	$(\exists y)(y = g)$	5, 1 MP

Chapter Eight

Exercise 8-1

NUMBER 4:

There is only one way to get a 5—by throwing a four and a one. The probability is $\frac{2}{10} \times \frac{4}{10} = \frac{8}{100}$.

NUMBER 13:

The highest values were presumably given to the most improbable events. Thus it seems that if shaken or thrown, the bones were unlikely to come to rest on the convex sides with the concave sides up. The narrower sides are presumably less stable than the broader sides. The values were thus probably roughly in inverse order to the probability of getting a side. However, the probabilities given are not intended to be realistic; they are intended to make it fairly easy to calculate the answers to the problem given.

Exercise 8-2

NUMBER 4:

The probability of getting a red jack (travel) is $\frac{1}{6}$. That leaves 5 cards and the chance of drawing a black queen (failure in love) is now $\frac{1}{5}$. The chance of getting a red king (success in business) is $\frac{1}{5}$, so the chance of getting *either* is $\frac{2}{5}$. The same applies for any order in which the cards are dealt (e.g., red king, red jack, black queen, red jack, red jack, red king, etc.), so the probability is $(\frac{1}{6} \times \frac{2}{5}) + \frac{1}{6} \times \frac{2}{5} = \frac{4}{30} = \frac{2}{15}$.

Exercise 8-3

NUMBER 4:

We must consider *ordered pairs* of cards: Since you always go first, any pair in which the first number is higher is a win for you. There are $5 \times 5 = 25$ ordered pairs of draws (A,1; A,2; A,3; A,Q; A,K; 2,1; 2,2; 2,3; 2,Q; 2,K; 3,1; 3,2; 3,3; 3,Q; 3,K; etc.). Five of these are ties. Of the remaining 20, 10 are wins for you, 10 are wins for your opponent. For $Pr(\text{If } A \text{ then } W) = Pr(\sim A \vee W)$ you need the formula

$$Pr(\sim A \vee W) = Pr(\sim A) + Pr(W) - Pr(\sim A \cdot W)$$

$Pr(\sim A)$ is $\frac{20}{25}$: Your opponent has 4 chances out of 5 of *not* getting an ace. $Pr(W)$ is $\frac{10}{25}$ or $\frac{2}{5}$, $Pr(\sim A \cdot W)$ is represented by the 6 out of 25 ordered pairs where your opponent had some card other than an ace. Thus the figures are:

$$\frac{20}{25} + \frac{2}{5} - \frac{6}{25}$$

The common denominator is 25.

$$\frac{20}{25} + \frac{10}{25} - \frac{6}{25} = \frac{24}{25}$$

Thus in 24 out of the 25 possibilities that do not result in a draw, *either* your opponent does not get an ace *or* you win. Calculating using $Pr(\text{If } A \text{ then } W) = Pr(W/A)$, we employ the formula

$$Pr(B/A) = \frac{Pr(A \cdot W)}{Pr(A)}$$

$Pr(A \cdot W)$ represents the cases where your opponent gets an ace and you win 5 out of 25 cases or $\frac{1}{5}$. He gets an ace in 5 out of the 25 possible cases or $\frac{1}{5}$. Thus the figures are:

$$\frac{\frac{4}{25}}{\frac{5}{25}} = \frac{4}{5}$$

This represents the fact that if your opponent draws an ace, any 4 of the 5 cards you draw will you a win (the other will lead to a draw and a replay).

Exercise 8-4

NUMBER 4:

The fact that Jane's mother's brother had the disease shows that Jane's mother's parents were both carriers. Thus Jane's mother had a 50 percent chance of being a carrier. If Jane's father is not a carrier, she cannot get the disease, but there is still a 50 percent chance that she is a carrier. She is sure to get an H gene from her father, but has a 50 percent chance of getting her mother's G gene.

Exercise 8-5

NUMBER 4:

A. Hume seems to be assuming that all logical possibilities are equally probable (the Logical Possibility Interpretation).
B. Hume seems to take two somewhat inconsistent positions: (1) That a mere consideration of probabilities can tell us nothing of importance. (2) That a consideration of probabilities, though it cannot tell us what *will* occur, *can* tell us what is likely to occur. If what is likely to occur is sometimes of importance, we could derive the contradictions: A consideration of probabilities can tell us nothing of importance, but it can tell us something of importance (i.e., what is likely to occur).

Chapter Nine

Exercise 9-1

NUMBER 8:

Hypothesis A: Decline of interest in space exploration is due to the end of manned missions and the increasing use of mechanical space probes.
Hypothesis B: Decline of interest in space exploration is due to disappointment that no evidence of life has been found on other planets.
Decision procedure: If Hypothesis A is true, interest in space exploration should increase with the next phase of space exploration, which will include many manned space station missions. If Hypothesis B is true, there should be no increase in interest with the next phase of space exploration, since space station research will offer no hope of finding evidence of life on other planets.

Exercise 9-2

NUMBER 3:

The third hypothesis would explain the diamonds, the wheels, and the snuff, but not why the diamonds were cut or why the snuff was not in any kind of container. "Some diamond-cutting affair" is much too vague as an explanation of the wheels.

Exercise 9-3

NUMBER 4:

The explanation offered in the story is that a person in uniform going about a routine job is "morally invisible"; people don't notice or remember the person, or if they do, don't think of mentioning that person in reply to a question like, "Did anyone go into the building?" For instance, someone might say, "I came home on the late bus and for the last few stops I was the only person on the bus." Since there must have been a driver, they were the only *passenger* but not the only *person* on the bus.

Exercise 9-4

NUMBER 3 (Game 3):

The rule is: "If the top card on the starter pile is red, accept any card higher in value than the top card. If the top card is black, accept any card lower or equal in value to the top card." Note that after a long run of rejections, the king of spades is accepted; but after that, the ten of hearts is accepted, leading to several rejections until the queen of spades is accepted, and so on.

Exercise 9-5

NUMBER 4:

Hypothesis: After the palaces were destroyed and Minoan civilization weakened by the side effects of the Thera eruption, Crete was invaded by descendants of the Hittite civilization on the Asian mainland. Since the Hittites were interested in war and hunting, D is explained. Invaders would probably hold one strong point, so C is explained. B explains why the powerful Minoan culture was weakened enough to be invaded, and B explains C.

However, E is not explained, since Asian invaders would not use Greek.

Exercise 9-6

NUMBER 8:

Your calculations in 1–5 will verify this, but you can see just by looking at the table that the highest probabilities for the southerly wind come in the months from December through April.

Chapter Ten

Exercise 10-1

NUMBER 4:

1. $A \rightarrow C$
2. $B \rightarrow D$ ⎫
3. $\sim \diamond (C \cdot D)$ ⎬ $\sim \diamond (A \cdot B)$
⎭
4. $\Box \sim (C \cdot D)$ 3 MOE
5. $\Box (\sim C \vee \sim D)$ 4 De M
6. $\Box (C \supset \sim D)$ 5 DMI
7. $C \rightarrow \sim D$ 6 DSI
8. $A \rightarrow \sim D$ 1, 7 HS
9. $\sim D \rightarrow \sim B$ 2 Transp.
10. $A \rightarrow \sim B$ 8, 9 HS
11. $\Box (A \supset \sim B)$ 10 DSI
12. $\Box (\sim A \vee \sim B)$ 11 DMI
13. $\Box \sim (A \cdot B)$ 12 De M
14. $\sim \diamond (A \cdot B)$ 13 MOE

Exercise 10-2

NUMBER 4:

The premise says that if a statement is logically possible, it is possible to know it. This sounds plausible, but as the next step shows, if this applies to any statement, it applies to $A \cdot \sim KnA$. So if the premise is true, it follows that if it is possible that A is true but n doesn't know it, then it follows that it is possible that n *knows* that A is true *and* that he or she doesn't know A. This already sounds paradoxical.

Exercise 10-3

NUMBER 4:

A. This can be proved as follows:
1. $Kn \sim A \cdot Kn \sim B$⎬ $Kn \sim (A \vee B)$
2. $Kn(\sim A \cdot \sim B)$ 1 MOD
3. $Kn \sim (A \vee B)$ 2 De M
B. Not applicable.
C. It seems plausible: If you know separately that each of two statements is false, you should know that neither one is true.

Exercise 10-4

NUMBER 4:

The principle of logic involved is $Knp \rightarrow p$ or its transposition $\sim p \rightarrow \sim Knp$. As Seithenyn says, "We can only know the truth, for if that which we think we know is not truth, it is something we do not know." Seithenyn also makes the more disputable claim that to know anything we must be alive. But if there is any kind of life after death, a dead person might know that he or she was dead, and might even communicate this knowledge, for example, by ghostly visitation.

Exercise 10-5

NUMBER 4:

A. $Pnp \to \Diamond p$
B. Not provable, see below.
C. This principle sounds plausible at first glance, but it transposes to $\sim \Diamond p \to \sim Pnp$, which is equivalent to $\Box \sim p \to On \sim p$. If this was a rule of logic, we could substitute $\sim p$ for p to get $\Box \sim \sim p \to On \sim \sim p$, which is equivalent to $\Box p \to Onp$. This has the odd effect of making it obligatory to bring about every necessary truth. This seems absurd, and is not provable in the system of Chapter Ten.

Exercise 10-6

NUMBER 4:

Consider a syllogism such as:

Every M is P	$(x)(Mx \supset Px)$
Every S is M	$(x)(Sx \supset Mx)$
Every S is P	$(x)(Sx \supset Px)$

which is valid in categorical form. Is it valid in this form?

$$\Diamond(x)(Mx \supset Px)$$
$$(x)(Sx \supset Mx)$$
$$\overline{(x)(Sx \supset Mx)}$$

We can argue as follows: It cannot be a rule of logic that

$$((p \cdot q) \to r) \to (\Diamond p \cdot q) \to \Diamond r$$

since if it were, we could derive the instance

$$((p \cdot \sim p) \to (q \cdot \sim q)) \to ((\Diamond p \cdot \sim p) \to \Diamond(q \cdot \sim q))$$

But this is wrong: The antecedent is a rule of logic (any contradiction implies any other contradiction), but if p is factually false, the antecedent of the strict implication in the consequent is true, but the consequent is false (since $\Diamond(q \cdot \sim q)$ is always false).

The principle in question might still hold if there was something about the syllogistic patterns that made the rule hold for syllogisms. But if you will investigate the various possibilities, you will not find any way of getting from the premises to the conclusion, whether by modal statement logic or by the rules involving quantifiers and modal operators.

APPENDIX B

Mazes

The history of mazes begins with legend, the legend of Minotaur, a bull-headed man-monster who lurked in the Labyrinth, a mazelike structure in Crete, devouring youths and maidens, and who was finally killed by the Athenian hero, Theseus. Archaeologists now believe that the legend of the Minotaur and the Labyrinth was based on memories of the Bronze Age civilization in Crete: the bull-headed monster being a confused memory of bull-leaping games played in the palaces of Crete, and the Labyrinth being based on memories of the complex structure of the palace of Knossos (see the ground plan at the beginning of Chapter Nine). Interestingly enough, one of the earliest known maze designs was found as a decoration on a minor staircase in the ruins of the palace of Knossos. (A slightly modified version of the design is used at the beginning of Chapter One.) However, almost all of the representations of the Labyrinth in classical times and in the Middle Ages were not mazes in the sense of being puzzles that offer a variety of possible paths, which need to be solved by reasoning or by trial and error. They were simply intricately winding designs that were *unicursal:* offering only one path with no alternate paths. One such maze is used at the beginning of Chapter Two.

A number of mazes has been constructed as paths divided by walls or hedges. Some early mazes of this type had religious or magical significance, but most of those constructed in the last few centuries have been made for amusement or decoration. One of the most famous of these is the hedge-maze in the garden of Hampton Court Palace in England, used at the beginning of Chapter Three. However, most modern mazes have never been constructed, but are patterns on paper offering challenges to ingenuity. The most usual kind of puzzle is to find your way to the center of the maze and back out again with the least amount of retracing your path. The mazes used in Chapters Four through Nine are increasingly intricate examples of this kind of maze. The maze for Chapter Seven was designed by the artist Michael Ayerton for a novel about the Labyrinth, and the maze for Chapter Eight is used as a sign for a London subway station. Devotees of puzzles and games have created increasingly intricate problems of a maze type, involving tracing a number of alternate paths to the center, going through specified points in a certain order, and so on. The maze for Chapter Ten has several alternate paths to the center.

Even for the type of maze-puzzle that consists only of finding the shortest path to the center, there is no mechanical solution. If all the "walls" of the maze are connected to each other, if there are no "islands" in the maze, then the path to and from the center can always be found. In a physical maze of this type, you need only put your hand on a wall and keep contact with the wall until you reach the center. The same process will bring you out to the entrance again. A similar process, hugging the "wall" of the maze in a maze on paper, will get you to the center of any maze without "islands" and back again to the entrance. But the paths to and from the center achieved by this method are almost never the shortest.

Surprisingly, one device for solving a maze is mentioned in the legend with which we began. In the legend, Ariadne, the daughter of Minos, the Cretan king, gave Theseus a reel of cord or strong thread to keep him from getting lost in the Labyrinth. After killing the Minotaur, Theseus followed the thread back through the maze: it had been fastened near the entrance. It is not clear in the legend whether Theseus had to find the center to find the Minotaur or whether he simply wandered until he encountered the monster.

In a physical maze, however, one can find the center of the maze by following the "hand-on-the-wall" rule, unreeling a cord or rope behind you. You can then stand still and reel in the cord. All of the loops formed by your wanderings through the maze will be straightened out, and the rope will indicate a direct path from the entrance, where it is tied, to the center. The equivalent on paper is finding the center by any workable method—"wall hugging" or trial and error—and then erasing all the loops formed by going into blind alleys or taking extra paths, and joining the resulting line into a direct path.

This applies to mazes without islands. In a physical maze where all of the walls are not connected, a rope or cord will reveal the situation: when your path leads you in a circle around the island you will encounter your own rope. You can then cross the corridor and use the hand-on-the-wall rule on the opposite wall to get to the center or the next interior island. (If you want the shortest path back you must first retrace your path to where the ropes crossed; otherwise, pulling at the center will just loop the rope harder around the island.)

There are other devices for finding direct paths, involving marking turns in some way as you take them, but they are much more complex than the rope method. If there are alternative paths to the center, the direct path gained by the rope method may not be *the* shortest path to the center, but no other method will guarantee the shortest path either. So strangely enough one of the most efficient ways of solving most mazes comes in the very legend with which the history of mazes begins.

Mazes are like logical proofs in several ways: (1) There is no mechanical way of finding a proof or of finding the shortest path to the center of a maze; (2) Once a proof has been given or the shortest path found there is no doubt that the solution is correct; (3) The solution of a maze, like the solution of a logical problem, requires ingenuity, creativity, and clear thinking. This is why the maze has been chosen as a design motif for this book.

APPENDIX C

Suggested Further Readings

Introductory Books with a Different Approach

Kahane, Howard, *Logic and Philosophy*, 3d ed., Belmont, Calif., Wadsworth, 1978.
Munson, Ronald, *The Way of Words*, Boston, Houghton Mifflin, 1976.
Purtill, Richard L., *Logic for Philosophers*, New York, Harper & Row, 1971.
Purtill, Richard L., *Logical Thinking*, New York, Harper & Row, 1972.
Salmon, Wesley, *Logic*, 2d ed., Englewood Cliffs, N.J., Prentice-Hall, 1973.

Books on Special Topics in Logic

Bartley, W. W., *Lewis Carroll's Symbolic Logic*, New York, Clarkson N. Potter, Inc., 1977 (syllogistic logic).
Carroll, Lewis, *Symbolic Logic and the Game of Logic*, New York, Dover, 1958 (syllogistic logic).
Hilpinen, Risto (ed.), *Deontic Logic*, Dordrecht, Holland, D. Reidel Publishing Co., 1971 (deontic logic).
Hughes, G. E., and M. J. Cresswell, *Introduction to Modal Logic*, London, Metheun and Company, 1968 (Modal Logic).
Lucas, J. R., *A Treatise on Time and Space*, London, Methuen and Co., 1973 (time and logic).
Skyrms, Brian, *Choice and Chance: An Introduction to Inductive Logic*, 2d ed., Belmont, Calif., Dickinson Publishing Co., 1975 (inductive logic).

INDEX

Rules for Propositional Logic

Simple System

Key Symbols	One-Way Rules			Two-Way Rules			
∨ ~	$A \lor B$ $\sim A$ ───── B Simple Cancellation (SC)	$A \lor B$ $\sim B \lor C$ ───── $A \lor C$ Cancel and Collect (CC)		$A \lor B$ ═════ $B \lor C$ Commutation (Com)	A ═════ $A \lor A$ Repetition (Rep)	A ═══ A A	A ═════ $\sim\sim A$ Double Negation (DN)
· ∨ ~	$\sim A \lor B$ $A \cdot C$ ───── $B \cdot C$ Cancel and Join (CJ)	A B ───── $A \cdot B$ Conjunction (Conj)	$A \cdot B$ ─── A B Simplification (Simp)	$A \cdot B$ ═════ $B \cdot A$ Commutation (Com)	A ═════ $A \cdot A$ Repetition (Rep)		
⊃ ~ ∨	$A \supset B$ A ───── B Modus Ponens (MP)	$A \supset B$ $\sim B$ ───── $\sim A$ Modus Tollens (MT)	$A \supset B$ $B \supset C$ ───── $A \supset C$ Hypothetical Syllogism (HS)	$A \supset B$ ═════ $\sim B \supset \sim A$ Transposition (Transp)	$A \supset B$ ═════ $\sim A \lor B$ Definition of Material Implication (DMI)		
⊃ · ∨ ~ ≡	$A \lor B$ $A \supset C$ $B \supset D$ ───── $C \lor D$ Constructive Dilemma (CD)	$\sim A \lor \sim B$ $C \supset A$ $D \supset B$ ───── $\sim C \lor \sim D$ Destructive Dilemma (DD)		$A \equiv B$ ═════ $(A \supset B) \cdot (B \supset A)$ Definition of Material Equivalence (DME)	$(A \lor B) \lor C$ ═════ $A \lor (B \lor C)$ Association (Assoc)	$(A \cdot B) \cdot C$ ═════ $A \cdot (B \cdot C)$	
· ∨ ~	A ─── $A \lor B$ Addition (Add)	$A \cdot \sim A$ ─── B Contradiction (Contrad)		$\sim(A \lor B)$ ═════ $\sim A \cdot \sim B$ 	$\sim(A \cdot B)$ ═════ $\sim A \lor \sim B$ De Morgan's Rules (De M)	$A \supset (B \supset C)$ ═════ $(A \cdot B) \supset C$ Exportation (Exp)	
⊃ · ∨				$A \supset B$ ═════ $A \supset (A \cdot B)$ Absorbtion (Absorb)	$A \cdot (B \lor C)$ ═════ $(A \cdot B) \lor (A \cdot C)$ Distribution (Dist)	$A \lor (B \cdot C)$ ═════ $(A \lor B) \cdot (A \lor C)$	